For Helen Flower Moore
From Penelope Johnson Allen

On the occasion of her graduation
from High School, Memphis, Tenn.
May 22, 1963

HORNETS' NEST

HORNETS NEST

The Signers Monument

This marker stands before the main entrance of the Mecklenburg County
Court House to honor the men who signed the Mecklenburg
Declaration of Independence of May 20, 1775.

Hornets' Nest

*The Story of Charlotte
and
Mecklenburg County*

LeGette Blythe
and
Charles Raven Brockmann

Published for
Public Library of Charlotte and Mecklenburg County
by
McNally of Charlotte
1961

Printed in the United States of America
Heritage Printers, Inc.
Charlotte, N. C.

Dedicated to
Irwin Belk and C. W. "Pat" Gilchrist

Foreword

INFORMAL in approach, this history of Charlotte and Mecklenburg County, North Carolina, is sponsored by the Chamber of Commerce and written under direction of the Public Library of Charlotte and Mecklenburg County.

The book is planned to serve two purposes. The first is to provide an interesting narrative history of city and county. The other is to serve as a reference book for answering the questions most frequently asked about the locality and its citizens.

Toward this end the authors have kept constantly in mind that people are more important than mere facts, events, or dates. This, then, is a history of people, people who have lived, wrought, planned, and dreamed.

Genealogical information will not be found herein. Hundreds of people are named and the achievements of many are noted, but any mention of their ancestry or descendants is purely coincidental.

Twentieth century organizations and people are treated rather fully here since earlier periods have been explored and accurately recorded by others. Among these are: D. A. Tompkins, *History of Mecklenburg County and the City of Charlotte* (2 vols.) (1903); Dr. John Brevard Alexander, *History of Mecklenburg County* (1902) and *Reminiscences of the Past Sixty Years* (1908); Julia M. Alexander, *Charlotte in Picture and Prose* (1906); Harriet Morrison Irwin, *History of Charlotte* (1882); and James M. Stenhouse, *Exploring Old Mecklenburg* (1952).

The historical perspective is 1960. Patriotic citizens are preparing to celebrate the bicentennial of the founding of Mecklenburg

County. Ample justification for such a jubilant occasion will be found in the lives and deeds of those who have brought the community to its present position of leadership in the Carolinas.

Credit for producing this long-needed history belongs to successive History Committees of the Charlotte Chamber of Commerce. The idea originated in 1954 when C. W. Gilchrist, president of the Chamber, appointed a twelve man committee under the chairmanship of Paul Whitlock, to devise ways and means for providing an up-to-date history of Charlotte and Mecklenburg County.

While this and subsequent committees accumulated considerable data from those who had published local histories elsewhere, nothing very definite was accomplished until the spring of 1958. At that time a new History Committee was appointed, headed by Irwin Belk as chairman and C. W. Gilchrist as vice chairman. Under the leadership of these men and with a generous donation arranged by the chairman of the committee, civic-minded firms and individuals volunteered to underwrite the venture. From many informal discussions concerning details connected with the writing and publishing of the history came the suggestion that, if possible, the whole enterprise be made a project of the Public Library.

This suggestion met with the approval of the History Committee and the director of the Library automatically became, for lack of a better term, managing editor of the history project. The resources of the Library were thus made available, as were the services of trained librarians who, more than any other group, know the questions asked and information sought most frequently by the public.

When the legislature of North Carolina made its spectacular one-day trip to Charlotte on March 4, 1959, a bill was introduced and passed unanimously by both branches amending the charter of the Public Library to permit the publication and sale of a history.

Thereupon, the trustees of the Public Library officially accepted the offer of the History Committee of the Chamber of Commerce. The result will, we hope, prove to be of lasting usefulness to present and future generations of Charlotte and Mecklenburg people.

HOYT R. GALVIN
Director, Public Library
of Charlotte and Mecklenburg County

Acknowledgments

THE writing of history more than any other literary enterprise puts writers in debt to other people. Historians, if left to their own devices, would never find much of the important data that gives color and life to their work. One of the wonders of civilized life is that there should be so many people willing to go to a great deal of trouble for a handful of infinitely less agreeable individuals who regard it as their mission to write books.

The first debt of the authors of this work is to those two hundred authorities who answered letters and innumerable telephone calls asking for information in their particular fields of knowledge. Of these, Mrs. Lillian Hoffman, City Clerk of Charlotte, deserves special mention for giving to our many requests her gracious and painstaking care. Mr. F. Wm. E. Cullingford gave freely of his tremendous fund of information about Masonry in Charlotte. Mrs. Lily Robertson McMahan shared her vast knowledge of Charlotte's educational activities.

We are grateful to all who responded to requests for pictures. Technical difficulties prevented using a few; space limitations forced rejection of many interesting people and views. Many of our pictures came in answer to appeals made by Julian Scheer, columnist for the *Charlotte News*. All pictures sent to Mr. Scheer and many others were processed by A. C. (Bill) Summerville without charge. This public service places the entire community in debt to these gentlemen. Collections of rare photographs were loaned by Judge Francis Clarkson and Mr. and Mrs. William Lewis Callum, III.

The tedious task of reading proof and verifying facts, spelling, and other details, was capably handled by Miss Mae Tucker and Miss Mary Louise Phillips of the Public Library staff. Authors would be helpless without such as these.

LeGette Blythe
Charles Raven Brockmann

Charlotte, North Carolina
September 1, 1961

CONTENTS

BOOK TWO

Cities are what men make them on land that is given of God.

AUTHOR UNKNOWN

HORNETS' NEST

BOOK ONE

THE STORY OF CHARLOTTE
and
MECKLENBURG COUNTY

A Narrative by

LeGette Blythe

PROLOGUE

A ND NOW the rolling gentle hills of northeastern Mecklenburg, the warm red clay of his native county. Home again, and good to be home.

All the way the flight had been pleasant. The shrimp cocktail had been appetizing, the filet mignon tender and juicy—broiled just enough, not too done, not too rare. The baked potato au gratin, the tossed salad, the tiny green limas, the hot rolls, the coffee, the ice cream, the champagne, everything had been prepared and served perfectly. Down through Virginia, his dinner finished and his stomach pleasurably filled, his whole frame comfortably relaxed, he had leaned back to enjoy the swift, smooth passage southward. And then they were over North Carolina and beneath them in fast procession had sped the green fields, the villages and small towns bunched so closely together that he was never out of sight of several at once, and the cities.

But now with sharpened interest he leaned forward and pushed his forehead against the pane to search out in the deepening twilight sights that surely in the not so long ago would have been to him easily recognizable. Yes, that would be Davidson and Cornelius, to the right and a little behind, stretched along the railroad. Peering, he picked out the dome of the college's Chambers Building and, high above the oaks and the elms of the campus, a church spire new to him. And ahead, coming to them from under the right wing, so that in a moment they would cross above it, that would be Huntersville, and just the other side of the village, the Mecklenburg Sanatorium.

5

He lifted his eyes to search westward to the snaking line of the Catawba River. Soon, he had read in a *Charlotte Observer* forwarded to him on the Continent months ago, a tremendous lake in this area would impound water for what would be the largest of all Duke's power plants. He narrowed his eyes to pick out, a mile or two east of the river, a white farmhouse on a green knoll; the farm after 200 years continued in his family's possession. Two full centuries of change. But there had been more change in his own lifetime, he told himself, than there had been in all the years of his Mecklenburg forebears. Since his birth, within the twentieth century, Mecklenburg's population had multiplied five times—some day he would look up the figures—and Charlotte's must have increased ten times over. In other developments the changes would be even more evident, and amazing. This airplane, for example. His thoughts flashed backward from the great *Golden Falcon* Electra on which he was flying three hundred miles an hour to that old World War I Jenny that had lifted him, with Meb Long at the controls, from a broomstraw field on Queens Road West for his first venture into the air. Yes, and the radio. He remembered when WBT, the third station to be licensed in the United States, was but a tiny amateur broadcasting station in Fred Laxton's basement. And television. Why, many promoters of modern Charlotte had not lived to see *Gunsmoke*.

But up front the light was flashing and the stewardess was announcing their approach to Charlotte. Fasten seat belts, crush out cigarettes. He glanced at his watch. Two hours and five minutes non-stop from Newark airport. In another four minutes, right on the schedule's nose, they should be on the ground. Two hours and nine minutes. George Washington came down to Charlotte, too, but from Philadelphia to Charlotte and on to Georgia and back to Philadelphia had required months—he would look up the facts on that journey.

He turned his head to look downward. Lights flicking on now in the thickening gloom, ribbons of lights lining what must be roads and streets, clusters of lights dotting the fields and woods. Charlotte already? He leaned against the window. No, not yet, for there are no tall buildings, no narrow lighted canyons that would be Tryon and Trade Streets. But over there, beyond the wing on his side, beyond the left wing, too—he raised his head and turned to look out in that direction—a flame was growing and lifting, and suddenly below him and all around were lights coming on as the day gave way to the night, lights everywhere, myriads of flashing, glowing lights. Charlotte now, and what a city it had become in the years since his leaving. Then straight ahead over his wing he saw a huge red sign:

CHARLOTTE

And in another moment they were down, and the great plane was taxiing toward the gate at which he would disembark.

His thoughts sped back to the day he had left Charlotte, and the long days before that momentous one. The Douglas Municipal Airport was Morris Field then, a sprawling wooden-barracks Air Corps training base, with what they called "the line," a string of frame structures skirting one side of a vast asphalt apron, as head-quarters and operational buildings, and scores of fast Army planes parked on that apron. Fast planes. Fast then, yes. He thought of today's planes that do two and three times the speed of sound. And only some sixteen years ago, wasn't it?

His mind began to recall long-gone days. Once when he was a youth—it was the summer when he had finished his first year at Chapel Hill—he had spent a week with a friend on a farm down here in the country. It was the country then, a long way down in Steele Creek, six miles from downtown Charlotte, four miles from where the Charlotte buildings started. Reece's home had sat right here, right at the end of the runway on which the *Golden Falcon* had sped to a stop. Now Reece is a doctor, dean of a great medical school.

But it was years after that summer before air transportation in Charlotte got its wings. He was on the newspaper then. He well remembered the old airport over on the Tuckaseegee road, and Johnny Crowell and the other old-timers who were Charlotte's first flyers. He shuddered when he recalled the old flimsy crates in which he had flown with those hardy pilots. Quickly he listed nationally famous flyers who had exhibited their skills before mar-veling thousands at the old airport: Post and Gatty; Ruth Nichols; the Hunter brothers, refueling aloft champions; Amelia Earhart;

Frank Hawks and his famous little white speedster *No. 13,* which would do three hundred miles an hour, an unbelievable speed in that day; the Navy's Captain Al Williams, whose only crackup was at the old Charlotte airport when he pancaked his plane into the side of a hill rather than endanger a crowd watching his stunting. And Tex Rankin, the incomparable stunter, and his outside loops.

And now—he was telling the smiling stewardess good-by and preparing to descend the steps—only the asphalt apron remains, unless some of those structures over there are parts of the old Morris Field facility, and this tremendous new airport building must testify to a phenomenal expansion of air travel into and out of Charlotte. When he got settled, he told himself, he would call the Chamber of Commerce and get the figures.

His friend was waiting at the gate. When they had greeted one another, they walked along the north concourse into the terminal lobby. As the glass panel closed behind them, he paused, looked about, exclaimed. The friend laughed. "We've grown up a bit since the old Morris Field days, eh? Actually, this section here has been added within the last year. And already they are talking of a second airport for Charlotte." He pointed to the marble stairs at the other end of the lobby. "Have you eaten? If you haven't, we can go up to the Dogwood Room on the mezzanine." He said he had had his dinner on the plane. "How about a cup of coffee? We can drop in the coffee shop over there while they're unloading the bags." But he didn't want any coffee either, he said, and they walked on past the Eastern Air Lines counters along the length of the right wall and around the corner and down the corridor to the baggage claim area.

"It's amazing," he said, as he handed the porter his check. "I haven't been away so long, and look at this!" He turned to confront his host, eyes narrowing. "What sort of traffic do you have out here anyway, John?"

"I don't know the exact figures," John replied, "but it's more than 700 movements each twenty-four hours. Eastern Air Lines alone has seventy-two flights, and Piedmont, Delta, United, and Southern maintain daily schedules. And then there are companies doing charter flights, and the Air National Guard is based here.

And there's considerable private flying. It's a busy place out here."
He paused, nodded his head toward the people still claiming baggage. "It's the same old story it was before you left Charlotte, except it's multiplied—now they're using the airplanes more and more. Business people coming into Charlotte and heading out, traveling men, salesmen, you name 'em. Charlotte's business, retail and wholesale, is expanding fast. We're growing. Went over 200,000 in the last census. Or did you know that?"

"Yes," he said, "I saw it in the papers. But it's hard to believe this is the place I left back in World War II days."

"Wait until we start for town," John said. "It's built up almost solid from here in. And it's like that almost all over the county. Mecklenburg is definitely urban now. And, in another decade, everybody is saying, the town's going to double in size—be 400,000. In fact—" his grin widened—"there was a story going the rounds some time back—they said it came from Lloyd's of London—that by the year 2000 Charlotte will have eight million population and be one of the largest cities in the world! But"—he gestured, palms up—"I don't take too much stock in that." He hesitated. "I will tell you one thing, though, that maybe you don't know. Since you left here we've started two colleges in Charlotte and already they're booming. Charlotte College and Carver College, both coeducational. Already Charlotte College, which right now is a junior college but before long will be a full four-year institution, they say, is almost as big as Davidson. In another ten years it'll be one of the biggest in the state."

"John"—gently he nudged his friend—"by any chance are you working for the Chamber of Commerce now? I know Clarence Kuester would be proud of you."

"No; not paid, anyway." His expression sobered. "You knew Clarence was dead?"

"Yes. Been dead ten or twelve years, hasn't he?"

"He died two or three months after he retired. Yes, about '48, I think." John shook his head slowly. "I wonder what Clarence would have thought of Charlotte today. He'd have been mighty proud. He was the greatest booster we ever had, and that's a fact."

"I agree. All the time I knew him—and that was a long time—he was Mr. Charlotte."

They walked out through the main entrance doorway to the car parked among scores on the broad paved aprons to the right and left. "The ultimate in modernity," he said, shrugging. "Parking meters at the airport—in Charlotte. We used to park right beside the hangar at the old airport, free, and for a week if we wanted to."

"Sure," John answered, "one of the indisputable signs of progress. Park half a mile from where you're going, park in a restricted zone, and get your car towed off by the cops. And when you go to the police station looking for it, nobody knows you; you pay off, that's all. Progress, man!"

"I'll find it different, I know. I used to walk up Tryon Street and know one out of every three or four people I passed——"

"Today you could walk from Morehead to the Barringer Hotel and be lucky to know three or four," John interrupted. "I haven't been away like you, but I'd be a stranger right on the Square. Charlotte's a city now."

"But it must have the same old spirit, John. They say Mecklenburgers never change."

"Maybe not. But there are so many new people; they've come in from everywhere. Charlotte's got to be a cosmopolitan place." John shrugged. "You know, nowadays Charlotte even goes Republican on the slightest provocation."

"So I've been hearing. But we did back in '28, you remember."

"Sure. But they used prohibition as an excuse for voting against Al Smith. Now they just step up and vote Republican, even proudly. There's been a big change in politics. They have a joke going around—and there's a lot of truth in it—that when a poor Baptist Democrat comes to town and begins to feel himself moving up in the world, he joins the country club, the Episcopal Church, and the Republican party; he figures that gives him status." John laughed. "But most of these new Republicans still hang on to the Democratic label—call themselves Democrats-for-Eisenhower, Democrats-for-Nixon, for Jonas. Some even vote the state and county Republican tickets and call themselves Democrats. In that way, of course, they can vote in the Democratic primaries. But, actually, Mecklenburg is fast becoming a two-party county."

"Then you think that the traditional spirit of Mecklenburg is lost, that all these new people coming in have so diluted the thinking of the natives that we have a different *genus Mecklenburgus* nowadays?"

"Oh, I wouldn't say that. I'd say that more probably the original Mecklenburgers, the old-family citizens, are changing the newcomers to their way of thinking and acting. I suppose the Republicans could put up a good argument in support of the contention that the county's swinging toward the GOP is but another evidence of Mecklenburg's independence-mindedness."

They were turning now into Wilkinson Boulevard. "The old road's changed little except it's more beaten up, I suppose you'll notice," John said. "But they've promised us a new one, and they are about ready to extend the new Interstate 85 that will take a great deal of the through traffic from this one. And you'll find a lot of new highways in and around Charlotte when you start looking the town over. You'll discover that many of the old landmarks have been torn down for new roads and streets, beautiful old homes for motels and parking lots. That, too, I suppose"—he shrugged—"is progress."

Past unbroken clusters of industrial plants, roadside chinaware displays, eating places, stores, groceries, Little Pittsburgh's steel plant, through a growing clutter of traffic, they approached and turned onto West Morehead. When they had driven along it a little way, his friend pointed to a building ablaze with lights high on the bluff to the right. "WBT," he said. "Moved here from the Wilder Building since you were home. They've got one of the finest radio and TV facilities in the whole country."

He nodded. And only a few years ago it had been in the basement of Fred Laxton's home. Charlotte is surely growing up fast, or time is indeed flying. Maybe both.

Now they were starting down the hill at Bryant Park, and a soft yellow glow, pin-pricked by a thousand-windowed checkerboard of bright lights and darkened offices, told him with a sudden nostalgic tightening in his throat that in moments now they would be in downtown Charlotte.

Once more the friend pointed. "There," he said, "over to the left of those others—that's the new Wachovia Building. See? The white one with the narrow tower-like structure at the side. It's on West Trade, across from the Selwyn. It's going to do a lot for that street.

Already a block down, two blocks, at the corner of Mint across the street from the post office, they're starting a fancy new motel. And say, you should see the one recently opened up on North Tryon, the Manger. And on South Tryon——" he pointed again. "It's a little dark but you can make out the steel frame going up, over there. That'll be the new American Trust Company building —only now it's the North Carolina National Bank, and a few months ago it was the American Commercial. The new building will cover the site of the old American Trust and the Commercial National. And, just across the street on Tryon, a fourteen-story office building is going up. But, say, you haven't seen the Union National Bank's new home—except now it's the First Union National—on the corner of South Tryon and East Third, where the old Mecklenburg court house used to sit. It's another pretentious structure for Tryon."

"John, the Chamber of Commerce should hire you. You've got the sales pitch."

"And I haven't even mentioned the Coliseum. But tomorrow you must ride out and see it. Oh, it's in town, but it's a long way from the Square. The biggest dome in the world; more than three hundred feet in diameter. Say, did you know you could put the Wilder building's eight stories inside the Coliseum and it would just reach to the dome? Why, they come here from all over the world, literally, to see the Coliseum, to get ideas for buildings they are planning for other cities, you know." He had reached Tryon and Morehead, and he turned left. "And another thing—" he tapped his friend on the shoulder with his right hand, temporarily removed from the steering wheel—"the Ovens Auditorium—named for Dave —is said to be the finest auditorium in the world."

They were passing the Observer Building. "You recognize that place, eh?"

"I'll say," he answered. "But little change there since Curtis Johnson's days."

"On the inside, yes, almost completely. The Knight chain bought *The Observer* and, more recently, *The News*. Now they're both in that building."

Up through the South Tryon Street canyon between the tall

buildings they rode in a blaze of light to Independence Square and across the bronze plaque commemorating the signing on that spot of the Mecklenburg declaration of independence. "North Tryon has changed considerably in the years you've been away," John began again. "Many of the handsome old homes have been torn down. The big Sears store stands where the William Phifer house used to be, the one, you know, in which they held the last meeting of the Confederate cabinet; and the Presbyterian College behind it is gone, too. And out beyond the Seaboard underpass WSOC has its new home—it's a TV station, too, now—and for miles along that street, out past Sugaw Creek Church, it's almost a solid mass of business places. But say, *there's* one building I want you to notice, and I hope tomorrow you'll get a chance to look it over." John pointed right. "The new library. Now, it really is something to boast about. Here's one place where they tore down a building— you remember the old Carnegie Library with the high steps up from the street—and put up a far better one on the same site. This library building, they say, is one of the best designed and most serviceable libraries in the whole country, really."

He laughed. "I'm not arguing. I agree; it certainly looks like it might be. But tell me, are they reading books in Charlotte?"

"Reading? Man, since this new countywide system got going, they've been putting out the books. After they began expanding the facilities, the circulation of books increased several times over. They also have new branches in Charlotte, three or four, maybe more, and new ones, too, in Davidson, Cornelius, Huntersville, Pineville, and Matthews—all well-designed, handsome buildings. Mecklenburg"—his grin was broad—"is going in for culture along with bank clearings and carloadings."

They were turning right at Eleventh Street when John ventured a glance toward the returning Mecklenburger. "Say, I've been giving you such a guided tour I haven't even asked you what you're planning to do and where you'll be living. Made any plans?"

"Well, John, for a few weeks I think I'll just take things easy— get around and look up some people. Then I may buy a few acres somewhere out from town and build myself a little house, maybe up there where they'll have that big lake. I've been thinking I might write a book or two." He paused, smiling. "You know, every newspaperman figures some day he'll write a book, but few ever get around to doing it."

John was thoughtful a moment. "But say, after you've done that, had your book published, and all—— Yes, by George, you're the very fellow to do it." They were crossing above the Southern Railway tracks now. "The very fellow!"

"To do what, John?"

"You're a native Mecklenburger; your roots go back to the county's earliest colonial days, even before it was a county. You've lived most of your life here; you know Mecklenburg—the people, history, traditions. But you have been away, too, just long enough to get a new, fresh look at us, to—to—well, analyze us, weigh the present, fast-growing, industrial, urban county against the two centuries of Mecklenburg's past." Now John was turning right on North Brevard on a course that eventually would see them in Myers Park. "By George, you're just the fellow to write a history of Mecklenburg County. We haven't had one in some fifty years, you know." His elbow nudged lightly. "How about it?"

"Well, this is pretty sudden. I've never given it a thought." He shrugged, for a moment was silent. "The story of Mecklenburg." He said the words slowly. "You know," he declared, suddenly warming, "Mecklenburg does have a great story, a unique, exciting, terrific story. Somebody ought to tell it. You're right, John. And I just may try to do it!"

1

THE BEGINNINGS

MECKLENBURGERS insist that few counties in America have as intriguing a story to tell as their own. They are convinced that Mecklenburg is unique; they declare that they can trace through their region's history from the earliest days a pattern of attitude and action demonstrably different from that of even the closest neighbors.

Many persons not of Mecklenburg birth or ancestry will agree. Scratch beneath the epidermis of a modern Mecklenburger whose forebears came to this section two centuries ago, those who are familiar with the county's history and tradition will suggest, and presently one will come upon old Squire John McKnitt Alexander himself. Nor is the statement entirely fanciful. The secretary of the convention that adopted Mecklenburg's declaration of independence had an elder son whose fourteen children were also prolific.

That Mecklenburg is recognized as being somewhat different is shown in references to this county, frequently and rather invidiously made in the legislative halls in Raleigh, as "the State of Mecklenburg." Nor has the designation always been given because of the fact that the county is North Carolina's most populous and affluent. It is a recognition rather of Mecklenburg's individuality.

One characteristic that seems to have been preserved intact through two centuries of seven or eight generations is an exuberance of determination not to be shoved or driven. Mecklenburgers, like most Americans, have been amenable to tactful leading, but inevitably they have balked at the first sensing of any effort to drive

15

them toward an action or an attitude. They have been that way since the county's beginning.

"One needs no further proof of the authenticity of the Mecklenburg declaration of independence than to live a few years in this county," an outsider-moved-in commented. "My next-door neighbor's great-great-great-grandfather signed that document of May 20, 1775. Doubt it? Not I! I'm quite certain that old colonial gentleman signed that paper. My neighbor is a living, breathing, walking document supporting that claim. *He* would have signed such a paper. *He* would sign one now."

Mecklenburg does have a dramatic story. And through the years the county has had the good fortune to have had her story recorded in published volumes. Even more fortunately, numerous documents contemporary with the making of its history have survived to authenticate the accounts related by the historians.

Within a century of the first settlers' coming, in fact, books recording the county's exciting and significant early years were being published. These earliest books have the authenticity and the freshness of the contemporary view, because in collecting material for these works their authors were able to talk with men and women whose fathers and mothers, and in some instances the persons themselves, had been actual participants in the stirring events of those pioneer times. Consequently, although history and tradition inevitably after a while begin inextricably to blend one with the other, Mecklenburgers can maintain logically that this county's actual history must have been little different from traditional accounts of it. Certainly any variance provable would not be found substantial enough to affect materially the Mecklenburg story as long recorded.

On what day the first white settler came into the region of the present Mecklenburg and exactly where he settled, for example, are facts that likely will never be definitely ascertained. Tradition long has held that Thomas Spratt in coming with his family southward from Pennsylvania was the first man to venture on wheels into the lush lands between the Yadkin and the Catawba. Tradition adds, charmingly and with documentary support, that a young fellow named Thomas Polk, enamored with the Spratts' daughter Susannah, or Susan, as she was called, followed them, and when they halted their wagon and settled a few miles south of what soon would be little Charlottetown, settled with them and before long married Susannah.

In the middle of this century it is of little importance to any one, except perhaps the professional historian or the genealogist digging among musty records, to be able to say on what day or month or even year the Spratts and Thomas Polk arrived in Mecklenburg. But it is immensely important that they came. Tom Polk in a few years after his coming would be one of Mecklenburg's leaders, the colonel of its militia, a man in the forefront of the early movement for independence, a determined and able fighter in the Revolution. And, more importantly, there would be many like him.

A great number of them would come southward from the Maryland and Pennsylvania border country; it was from this region that the Spratts and Tom Polk had set out toward the Carolina backwoods. Some in this venturing migration would stop before they reached Mecklenburg, but only for a few years; later they would cross the Yadkin and push to the Catawba's eastern bank, as did John Davidson, another sturdy figure in Mecklenburg's developing history.

In the main these people were descendants of Scots and Englishmen who, a century and a half earlier, had immigrated to Ireland. Differing in background and religion from the majority of the Irish, there had been very little intermingling of the races through the generations. The Irish called these people Ulstermen after the name of the province in which they settled. In America they are called the Scotch-Irish. The Scotch-Irish of early Mecklenburg were strongly Presbyterian in their determination to have both freedom of religion and government, along with freedom of the one from the other.

But some, too, would be coming into this new country from other directions. Northwestward from South Carolina's low country, through the port of Charleston, past swamps and flatlands into a rolling region of great forests and open waving-grass prairies, a country more to their upbringing and liking, would come other Scots, and Germans, Huguenots from France, even Swiss from their towering mountains. Another tide would roll down from

Virginia, principally Englishmen, as Samuel Wilson, seeking new opportunity; some would continue westward, but others would be content to venture no farther.

Though these people were the first settlers, they were not the first white men to come into the western back country. A tradition strongly supported says that the Spaniard Hernando de Soto, crossing up from Florida in his vain search for gold, passed not far southwest of Mecklenburg; that was two centuries before our first settlers came, and De Soto entered the country of the Cherokees, it is thought, through Hickory Nut Gap. Others followed De Soto. John Lederer, an Englishman, was said to have pushed westward over an Indian trail that many years later along a mile or two widened into Tryon Street.

But the stories of these explorers and first traders are all but lost in the gathered mist of many years. Happily, however, we do possess a fairly clear picture of the movements and the peoples converging upon our wilderness region after 1740 to establish their homes and become the progenitors of our citizenship and our civilization.

"Steadily, in lengthening and thickening streams they came—southward, northward, westward—some on horseback, some afoot, some riding in their tough two-wheeled carts and wagons, many of them bearing few possessions beyond stout hearts and great courage and simple abiding strong faith," the narrator in *Voice in the Wilderness* would proclaim 200 years later in 1955 to a great audience in cosmopolitan Charlotte. "So they came to Mecklenburg in the middle years of the eighteenth century, and they raised their sturdy log houses of peeled and hewn pine or oak or hickory or ash, and burned over the wild grasslands and chopped out clearings, and planted crops and reaped harvests, and reared families. They were hardy souls, those invaders of the wilderness who came seeking a better chance for themselves and their children in an undisturbed free land, a land in which they could dream and work to build their dreams, where they could live their own lives. For always in the forefront of their dreaming, always uppermost in their striving, was their determination to live and work and love and worship in freedom."

The story of Mecklenburg's four decades from the early seventeen-forties to the ending of the Revolution, then, is the lively narrative of the people's determination to be free and of their struggle to win and establish that freedom. And significantly, though not strangely, the definitely traceable beginnings of that determination go back to the first years of the eighteenth century and particularly to a youngster in the province of Ulster, in Ireland, who years later as a Presbyterian preacher in Mecklenburg would become the flaming evangel of freedom, the passionate exhorter to independence.

Two decades before American independence was achieved, this man was preaching in stentorian tones that men should not live under tyranny. In that early day no voice in all the colonies was raised more eloquently to bestir Americans to the asserting of their rights.

His name was Alexander Craighead. No name stands higher in the 200-year span of Mecklenburg's recorded story.

Craighead came as a seven-year-old boy with his parents and neighbors to Boston in 1714 from Ireland's County Donegal. After nine years in Massachusetts, the Craigheads moved to New Jersey and then into Delaware. In 1733 they went over into Pennsylvania, in whose Lancaster County that same year a baby was born to the James Alexanders and named John McKnitt. A year later young Craighead was licensed to preach.

But Craighead was an independent-minded minister and soon he was in trouble with his church courts. So he pushed on southward into the Valley of Virginia, from where in late January of 1758 he journeyed to Mecklenburg and visited the recently organized Rocky River Presbyterian Church. In April that congregation called him to be its pastor and in November he was duly installed as pastor of both Rocky River and the nearby Sugaw Creek Church. Quickly, as the colonists' difficulties with the King's agents increased, Pastor Craighead became the impassioned voice of Mecklenburg's protesting. But eight years later, a decade before the adoption at Philadelphia of the national Declaration of Independence, he was dead.

In the short years of his southern ministry Alexander Craighead had helped stir into motion a current that soon, like a mighty tide rolling across the colonies, would sweep away the tyrannical power of the British Empire's uncomprehending and uncompromising government. Under the influence of his still powerfully inspiring fiery spirit, Mecklenburg patriots would be among the first in America to challenge that government.

Until within little more than a decade before Pastor Craighead's arrival in what is now Mecklenburg, few permanent homes had been established in the region. Some six years before Craighead came, another Presbyterian minister, the Reverend John Thomson, whose Synod of Philadelphia had instructed him to make a missionary journey into the back country of North Carolina, visited his daughter, the wife of Samuel Baker, who lived near what is now the Mecklenburg-Iredell boundary line above Davidson. The minister's wife had died, and he established his residence at his daughter's; the son-in-law built for him a cabin in the yard of their home, and from it John Thomson went out to preach in the communities along the Catawba. The first sermons heard in Mecklenburg, tradition says, were those of the Reverend Mr. Thomson. One of these, there is evidence to indicate, was preached beneath a great tree that until a few years ago stood at the southern edge of Davidson. A recorded preaching site that has been marked was in the yard of Richard Barry's home about a mile north of where a few years later Hopewell Church would be built. Other places to which this early evangel brought the gospel included Cathey's Meeting House in Rowan—that would become Thyatira Church—and Sugaw Creek, and perhaps Rocky River, Poplar Tent, and a grove of great trees that one day would be the grounds of Charlotte's First Presbyterian Church.

But this minister's work in Mecklenburg soon was finished. Some two years after he came, even before the arrival of Craighead, he was dead. Tradition relates that he was buried beneath the floor of his little cabin, and adds that the strange resting place of John Thomson became Baker's graveyard, one of the oldest burying grounds in this area, perhaps the oldest. Soon this ancient graveyard will be lost within the vast area covered by Duke Power Company's Lake Norman.

After John Thomson went to his long rest in the red soil of Mecklenburg, another evangelist rode southward under instructions to make a missionary tour of the province of North Carolina's western regions. This man was Hugh McAden, born, like so many Mecklenburgers, in Pennsylvania of Scotch parents. Like others who would venture southward from the Pennsylvania-Maryland border country, McAden had been educated at Princeton. In his diary under date of October 12, 1755, when he reached Rocky River, he made the notation that here he preached to "some pretty judicious people—may the Lord grant His blessing." A week later, he further records, he was preaching at Sugaw Creek.

So, under the occasional ministering of a visiting man of God and, after Craighead's coming, his impassioned preaching, the settlements in Mecklenburg expanded, and as other settlers moved in, communities began to grow out from the centers at Hopewell and Sugaw Creek, down in Steele Creek and Providence, up at Centre in what is now southern Iredell, and over at Poplar Tent across the line in present Cabarrus.

The year before Craighead died, just a decade after Hugh McAden had ridden in, a man named Henry Eustace McCulloh as agent for Augustus Lord Selwyn donated a tract of 360 acres for the purpose of establishing a town upon it. In granting a huge tract to Lord Selwyn, the King had stipulated that the owner would be required to settle on it an average of one person for every 200 acres. The development of a town within the borders of his grant, Lord Selwyn saw, would raise materially and quickly his population average and thereby fortify his claim.

Already Mecklenburg was an established county. Three years before, on December 11, 1762, the Provincial Assembly had drawn a western boundary for Anson and proclaimed the territory west of it as Mecklenburg. The Selwyn contribution of 360 acres had been made to three commissioners empowered to hold it in trust for the new county, which should raise on it a court house, prison, and stocks.

But quickly the residents of the Rocky River community eastward began to protest that the courts should be held nearer them. The next year, 1766, the year of Preacher Craighead's death, Martin Phifer of Rocky River introduced in the Assembly a bill permitting the commissioners to lay off streets and lots in this tract given by Lord Selwyn and build a court house, prison, and stocks. But Phifer's bill did not provide that the new town would be the county seat at which the courts would sit. So Thomas Polk, who with Phifer represented Mecklenburg, caused the bill to be defeated.

That same year, because of the continuing fast growth of settlements west of the Catawba, a proposal was made that a new county be formed by drawing a western boundary of Mecklenburg at the Catawba and giving to the new county the territory west of the river. Should this be done, Polk and other residents of the area embraced by the lines of the present Mecklenburg realized at once, the town they were proposing to be the county seat would be considerably west of the center of the county, which in those days extended eastward to embrace the later counties of Cabarrus and Union. Clever strategy was required, canny Tom Polk and his neighbors realized, if the Rocky River citizens were to be outwitted. So they pooled forces in what would be perhaps Charlotte's first civic effort—a century and a half before the formation of the Chamber of Commerce—and built in the intersection of the roads a log court house and prison and stocks.

This little court house was soon succeeded, about 1774, it is believed, by another that would become the most storied structure in the county's history; a frame building, it sat on eight pillars ten feet high, of brick likely kilned nearby, high enough to permit a marketplace underneath, with rock walls three and a half feet high between the pillars. No authentic likeness of either building has survived, though partial sketches have been left by persons who had seen them and fanciful sketches have been drawn from these descriptions.

When Mecklenburg's legislators returned for the 1768 session of the Assembly, agitation for the establishment of the new county was renewed and grew more determined. At the same time Tom Polk was pressing for the incorporation of his town, called Charlotte for England's queen. Charlotte, they thought, was a pretty name and euphonious. But, more importantly, naming the new town Charlotte would be a smart move politically. Mecklenburgers even then understood quite well the meaning of the word expediency.

Polk won. On November 7, 1768, Charlotte was incorporated and commissioners were empowered and instructed to lay off a hundred acres in one-half-acre lots on which houses should be erected. Already some eighty lots had been taken and on them several houses had been built.

But 200 years later to a Mecklenburger interested in obtaining a behind-the-scenes appraisal of those legislative activities of 1768 there must be readily apparent a definite parallel between the doings of legislators then and today. Tom Polk's victory must have resulted from his willingness to engage in political horse-trading, because a month later—on December 5, 1768—an act was passed providing that on or after "April 10, 1769, the county of Mecklenburg shall be divided into two separate and distinct counties and parishes by a line beginning at Earl Granville's where it crosses the Catawba River; and the said river to the line of the South Carolina line; and that all that part of the said county which lies to the eastward of the said dividing line shall be a distinct county and parish, and shall remain and be called Mecklenburg County and St. Martin's Parish, and all that county lying to the westward of the said dividing line shall be one other distinct county and parish and called Tryon County and St. Thomas' Parish." The act further provided that courts for the new county should be held on the fourth Tuesdays of April, July, October, and January.

But what of the courts for the territory that remained Mecklenburg County?

Here, the researcher into colonial history must strongly suspect, the clever Polk collected Mecklenburg's political payoff. Even Governor Tryon may have given his wink toward its accomplishment. In August the Governor had visited Charlotte and in honor of that visit and ostensibly to commemorate it, but more likely to curry His Excellency's favor, the citizens of the village had named the principal street Tryon. The new county west of the Catawba likewise had been named Tryon, at Polk's suggestion, it might be surmised, surely with his approval.

But at any rate and however Polk accomplished it, the Assembly decreed that for the next seven years the courts of Mecklenburg should hold their sessions in the newly built court house in Charlotte. It was not until 1774, when the seven-year period had almost expired, that the still determined Tom Polk managed to obtain passage of his bill designating Charlotte as Mecklenburg's county seat. But, practically speaking, "auld Tam," early Mecklenburg's master politician, had won his battle that day in 1768 when he eased his seven-year provision through the legislative mill.

There were politicians, too, in those days.

2

COLONIAL PERIOD

S OCIAL historians studying the more than two-century story of
Mecklenburg might well agree that this community's character
has its roots in the independent-mindedness of her early citizenship.
Theirs was a continuing struggle to achieve and maintain a new
way of life.

In the beginning the fight was against the wilderness itself. With
the exception of the Indians, the first settlers were the most self-
sufficient residents Mecklenburg ever had; they were the original
exemplars of live-at-home. None had less with which to begin
building, none in this region's history would achieve more.

At their coming into the back country they had found no accou-
terments of civilization. All about them was land, millions of acres
of virgin great forests and open prairies waist-deep in luxuriant
grasses, and streams flowing with clear water, for the eroding plow
had not yet disturbed the rich red soil. On all sides magnificent distance rolled; westward it swept toward the unknown country of
the Cherokees. Over the land was a golden silence their children of
two centuries later would never experience, a solitude disturbed
but now and then by the sharp bark of a fox or the bellow of an
enraged buffalo or even sometimes the eerie howl of a wolf. And
above this vast quietude by day was the inverted immense blue
bowl of the heavens and by night the myriad stars. They had come
into a good and lonesome land.

No roads cut through the forests and grasslands; only animal
paths and Indian trails disclosed movement. There were no cleared
fields. Trees had to be cut or grass burned off before the settlers

could prepare land for planting crops. There were no houses, no blacksmith shops, no mills to grind the grain that would be raised, no schools, no churches, only the land and the streams and the blue sky above, and solitude and freedom and peace.

But there was a living to be won.

Those settlers had great courage, a stamina that would not yield, and much faith. They were willing and eager to work and create and build. They began to wrest a civilization from this wide wilderness, and houses and mills and churches and schools were soon pushing back the frontiers. And under the preaching of Parson Craighead and the leadership of such stalwarts as the Alexanders, the Davidsons, the Brevards, and young Hezekiah Balch of Poplar Tent, they rose up to challenge the authority of England.

One of the first troubles to arise in the back country was over land and taxes. At the time Mecklenburg County was established in 1762 by being sliced off the western portion of Anson, the southern boundary line of North Carolina had not been run definitely; the survey westward had ended south of Salisbury where the line between the Carolinas touched the road leading from Salisbury to Charleston. So, during the next several years when efforts were made to collect the taxes, some Mecklenburgers living in the vicinity of where this line if projected westward would run were a source of much trouble to the tax collectors. If North Carolina sheriffs sought to collect their taxes, those persons insisted that they were in South Carolina; if the collectors were South Carolina officers, they maintained with equal insistence that their homes were north of the line.

In the eastern counties and the middle regions of the province, Tryon's officers were being charged with corruption and extortion, the citizenship was rebelling against these officials, and the situation had so deteriorated that in Orange, Anson, and Rowan the citizens were banding together in an attempt to regulate their affairs. Soon they had come to be known as Regulators.

By early 1771 the Governor and the Regulators had reached an impasse. Tryon was determined to crush the regulation movement; the Regulators were equally adamant in refusing to submit to what they insisted was corrupt and oppressive government. The Governor sent General Hugh Waddell through Rowan and Mecklenburg to enlist troops, but few volunteered and these were never able to join Tryon. At the Yadkin near Salisbury they were turned back by a large force of Regulators who had assembled there to air their grievances and demand that the corrupt practices of the Tryon government be ended.

But it was to the dramatic exploit of nine young Rocky River men, rather than to this incident in the growing turmoil between the Royalist officials and the Regulators, that history and tradition have paid considerable attention. It was this reckless escapade that history would record as one of the first overt acts against royal authority in all the colonies.

On the night of May 2, 1771, not far from present Concord, wagoners bringing gunpowder and bullets from Charleston to General Waddell had camped on Phifer's Hill. These men had eaten their suppers and were asleep when the nine youths, with their faces blackened and otherwise disguised, slipped up to the ammunition wagons, laid powder trails out from them, and set fire to the powder. A moment later in the commotion of the exploding ammunition the nine "Mecklenburg Black Boys," or "Cabarrus Black Boys," as later they would be called, made their escape.

Two weeks after the burning of Tryon's powder—on May 16 over on Alamance Creek near present-day Burlington—Tryon and the Regulators clashed. Tryon, victorious over the poorly equipped and unorganized Regulators, ordered the hanging of a slow-witted boy named James Few, and several days later, after exhibiting them about the country manacled, hanged six others. Tradition says that among these fighting Regulators at Alamance Creek were several Mecklenburg men who brought back an account of the Governor's harsh treatment of the captives. At any rate, Tryon's administration of his office, culminating in his attack on the Regulators and his conduct afterwards, further inflamed the back country against him.

Resentment against Tryon and his royalist government had been building in Mecklenburg despite the fact that within two years after Charlotte's incorporation he had recommended to the Assembly that it establish "a public seminary in some part of the back country of this Colony for the education of youth" and that the institution be established in Charlotte. The school was chartered on January 15, 1771, as Queens College, the first such institution to be established south of Virginia. Edmund Fanning was its first president. To support it a tax was levied of "six pence per gallon on all rum brought into and disposed of in Mecklenburg County for ten years following the passage of this act," and tickets for a building lottery were sold throughout the province.

Queens College had hardly been started when Josiah Martin, the royalist governor who had succeeded Tryon, announced that King George had refused to approve its chartering. The manifest reason, it was insisted by Mecklenburgers, was the fact that Queens College was a Presbyterian institution whose operation would give encouragement to dissenters from the Church of England and would provide a fertile bed in which to germinate seeds of rebellion against the royalist government.

When the charter was refused for Queens College, one was sought for it after certain changes had been made in the provisions, one of which was a change to the name Queens Museum. But a charter was still refused, and for a time the school was operated without a charter. And when independence was declared, the name was changed again, this time to Liberty Hall Academy; under this name the institution was operated until the British under Cornwallis invaded Charlotte in September 1780.

The school had been established for the training of young men; in that day few girls sought an education on the level of study of the classics. It was built two blocks down Tryon Street from the little court house; it covered a part of the site on the southeastern corner of Tryon and Third Streets now occupied by the Jefferson Standard Building. After the invasion by Cornwallis, it was commandeered by the British general as a hospital for his sick and wounded Redcoats, as it had been previously by the Americans. Many Redcoats would be buried on its grounds. Long years later the bones of some of them would be uncovered by workmen excavating in preparation for beginning construction on the old school's site.

Liberty Hall Academy would not long survive the Revolution. In 1784 it would be rechartered and moved to Salisbury, where soon it would fail and be closed. But in its short years it served a high purpose. Many youths who would become important in the life of the young nation studied there, among them a strong-willed redhead named Andrew Jackson. It demonstrated in the few years of its operation, too, that the royalists had been right in thinking that it would become a seedbed of revolution against the royalists' way, for it was within the walls of this little classical school that Mecklenburg leaders would meet frequently in the challenging early years of the seventeen-seventies to discuss the darkening situation of the colonies and what the response should be in the Carolinas' back country.

Among these stalwarts of that time of crisis—and there would be many crises and many strong leaders to face them in the two centuries that would follow in Mecklenburg—were such men as Colonel Thomas Polk of Charlotte, John McKnitt Alexander of Hopewell and his brother Hezekiah from Sugaw Creek, John Davidson from Hopewell, young pastor Balch, and Ephraim Brevard, a one-eyed Princeton-taught doctor of the school's board of trustees and of its faculty. Out of the meetings in Liberty Hall Academy and at Alexandriana, nine miles north of Charlotte and more accessible to Balch's Poplar Tent neighborhood, would evolve the Mecklenburg declaration of independence. From a half-century after its writing and adoption, however, it would be both maligned and defended by one generation after another.

But, although the declaration has been called a fabrication of senile minds and a myth, the events leading up to the convention that did or did not promulgate this much debated document and the manner of its being called are substantially agreed upon by those who have studied the period.

In the eight years following Pastor Craighead's death, conditions in the colonies generally had grown worse and everywhere men were chafing under the harsh treatment of the British government. The people of Mecklenburg, though somewhat removed from the more settled eastern and middle regions of the province where injustices and ill treatment had grown more flagrant, were angered at the treatment being accorded their fellow colonists.

So, early in the spring of 1775, it was decided that should conditions become alarming enough to warrant the holding of a county-wide meeting, then Colonel Polk as commander of the county militia would be empowered to call such a convention. Conditions in the colonies and in the back country did not improve. Governor Martin's difficulties with the Provincial Assembly were increasing as he sought to dictate the course of provincial legislation. In Mecklenburg Colonel Polk acted by sending out notices instructing the citizens to elect two men from each militia district; the delegates were asked to assemble on May 19 at the court house in Charlotte.

This they did with enthusiasm. On the day of the meeting little Charlottetown was crowded with back countrymen. Such was their interest and concern that not only the delegates but virtually all the men of the region within a day's riding of Charlotte had crowded into the tiny village.

The delegates on assembling elected Abraham Alexander as chairman and John McKnitt Alexander as secretary. A committee was named to draw up a document for the convention's consideration; the members were Ephraim Brevard as clerk, Reverend Mr. Balch, and William Kennon, the latter a Salisbury lawyer. Brevard and Balch, and possibly Kennon, with other leaders in the back country, had been meeting at Queens Museum and out at Alexandriana in the months before, and in all probability, came to the meeting with a tentative draft of the document they expected to present for the delegates' consideration should such a convention be called.

More than half a century later John Davidson's certificate would declare that when the delegates "were perfectly organized for business, a motion was made to declare ourselves independent of the Crown of Great Britain, which was carried by a large majority. Dr. Ephraim Brevard was then appointed to give us a sketch of the Declaration of Independence, which he did." This indicates that independence was declared before the declaration text was offered. At any rate, however the order of procedure, during the day a courier rode into the village with startling, shocking news. Exactly a month before, he reported, British troops had fired on Americans at Lexington in Massachusetts colony.

The Mecklenburgers were incensed. Evidently they abandoned all caution, and the delegates began angrily to declare they were ready to challenge British authority. Several, however, remembered that after the defeat of the Regulators they had taken oaths to support the Crown. If they should now rebel, how could they then salve their consciences?

"But this oath was to be binding only so long as the King provided protection," someone hastened to suggest. "It was a two-party contract, binding only so long as both parties upheld it. Now that the King has withdrawn his protection, the oath no longer is binding." He pointed outside to a tree. "It is as though you had sworn loyalty to the King as long as the leaves were on that tree. That oath would be binding until in the winter the leaves fell off; then you would be free of the obligation. In the same way you swore allegiance to the King so long as he should give you his protection. But now that he has withdrawn that protection and has even fired on our brothers in Massachusetts, your oath no longer binds you. You are free."

His reasoning satisfied the conscientious delegates; they felt themselves free to join their brothers in concerted action. So they either declared their independence then and sent out a committee headed by Dr. Brevard to "give us a sketch of the Declaration," as Major Davidson recalled, and upon the committee's return with the draft of the document approved it; or they declared their independence in ratifying the document brought in, perhaps after a general consideration of its provisions was had. It is likely that nothing will ever be found that will reveal in detail the procedure on that first day of the convention's sitting. The delegates may have convened late in the afternoon shortly before the arrival of the rider bringing the news from Lexington, and were so provoked by the message he brought that they almost immediately voted to free themselves from the mother country. If this were the order followed, it may well explain the fact that the delegates sat early into the morning of May 20 before they formally adopted the declaration brought out by Brevard and his committee members.

This document consisted of six resolutions. The third of these "Resolved, that we do hereby declare ourselves a free and independent people, that we are and of right ought to be a sovereign and self-governing people under the power of God and the general Congress; to the maintenance of which independence we do solemnly pledge to each other our mutual co-operation, our lives, our fortunes, and our most sacred honor." It would become widely known as the Mecklenburg Declaration of Independence of May 20, 1775.

This paper, duly promulgated by the delegates, was read by Colonel Polk from the steps of the court house at noon to a wildly enthusiastic throng. Some of the men and boys were so excited that they threw their hats high into the air; one or two of the hats, witnesses recalled, lodged on the court house roof. The fact that they did was of little concern to anyone except the hats' owners, but it was an incident of considerable significance in the later efforts to prove that a declaration of independence was read publicly on that date.

With the precipitate throwing off of the royalist yoke, Mecklenburg on May 20 had no legitimate government, the delegates realized. What should be done to establish a new government, one that would supersede the rule of King George?

It was Saturday, and many of the delegates were a long way from home. And the establishment of a system of government to succeed the British rule should not be done in haste; it should be accomplished after study and deliberation. So it was agreed that an adjourned meeting be held, and the date was set for May 31.

Some early historians argue, however, that there was no May 31 meeting, that the Resolves were actually passed on May 20 within a short time after the adoption of the declaration. They reason that the May 31 date was placed on the copy of the Resolves as it was being sent off to certain newspapers for publication. There is, however, no controversy concerning the authenticity of these resolves that go together to establish a government for the county of Mecklenburg and proceed to set forth a plan for its operation.

But what of that declaration? Was such a document adopted on May 20, 1775, some fourteen months before the adoption of the national declaration on July 4 at Philadelphia? Or is the whole story, as some through the years have contended, but a fantastic myth?

3

THE REVOLUTIONARIES

Millions of words, often impassioned and frequently more resonant than reasoned, have been spoken and countless tens of thousands have been written in letters, books, historical journals, magazines, and newspapers on the subject of the Mecklenburg declaration of independence. It has been one of the nation's liveliest historical controversies, a continuing debate that has engaged the interest of historians from time to time in many sections of the nation. A vast preponderance of these spoken and written words has supported the claim that citizens of Mecklenburg County on May 20, 1775, assembled in convention in tiny Charlottetown, did in fact adopt and promulgate a declaration of independence from Great Britain. But for almost a century and a half there have been persons who honestly doubted the authenticity of the purported declaration, some who quite militantly sought to disprove it, and even a few who though palpably uninformed and refusing stubbornly to examine all evidence available, have claimed professional omniscience and, looking down their smug noses, continue solemnly to pronounce it the Mecklenburg myth.

What then are the facts? On what basis do those who scoff at the declaration deny its authenticity? And what evidence can its defenders offer in support of their contention that the declaration actually was adopted, as Mecklenburgers have long held? How does the controversy stand on the eve of the two-hundredth anniversary of this county's formation in 1762?

In any one-volume recital of this county's two-century history, an adequate discussion of the Mecklenburg declaration controversy manifestly would be impossible. Such a treatment would

require many pages; in fact, a large volume embracing newly discovered evidence could be done—and demands to be done—in
elaboration of this intriguing subject. As the May 1775 convention
recedes farther and farther into the mists of history and tradition,
fewer persons know and are concerned with the facts of this important story and the issues upon which the controversy about it
have been kept alive. Many of the most enthusiastic and vocal supporters of the declaration actually have little information upon
which to base that support. In the main, these persons contend that
a Mecklenburg declaration was promulgated on May 20, 1775, for
little more reason than that as loyal Mecklenburgers they wish to
defend their county's honor against those they consider its detrac-
tors. In the same way, on the other hand, few of those who deny
the authenticity of the declaration can offer valid reason for their
position; they seem to feel that skepticism and the challenging of
traditionally accepted viewpoints and positions are evidences of
intellectual freedom. Few who deny the authenticity of the May
20 document offer positive evidence in support of their negative
stand.

The preponderance of the evidence, if one looks carefully, intel-
ligently, and objectively into the subject, supports overwhelmingly
the contention that the delegates meeting in Charlottetown—it was
variously called Charlottetown, Charlotte, and Charlottesburg—on
Friday, May 19, 1775, actually framed a clearcut declaration of
independence which in the early morning hours of the next day
was enacted as the first such document to be promulgated in the
colonies. Significantly, not until forty-four years *after* these Mecklenburg patriots had convened in the little court house had anyone
challenged the authenticity of the May 20 declaration. Until then
not a voice is recorded as having been raised or a word having been
written in denial of the declaration story. And then the challenge
did not come from anyone in the vicinity of Mecklenburg or any
of the participants in the lively events of May 1775, but from
far-off Monticello in Virginia. Thomas Jefferson in a letter written
July 9, 1819, to John Adams expressed the opinion that "the paper
from Mecklenburg County, of North Carolina" was spurious.

But why was the author of the national declaration of July 4,
1776, at this late date attacking the Mecklenburg document? Had

he never heard of it before? Jefferson was replying to a letter from Adams, who had read in the June 5, 1819 issue of the *Essex Register* of Salem, Massachusetts, an article reprinted from the Raleigh (N. C.) *Register* of April 30, 1819. This article, prepared from material provided by Dr. Joseph McKnitt Alexander, son of John McKnitt Alexander, secretary of the Mecklenburg convention of May 19-20, 1775, dealt with that convention and the declaration adopted by it.

But why, critics might reasonably ask, had these Mecklenburgers waited forty-four years to publish the declaration? They insist that, as far as has been ascertained, the document was not published before that date. The reason seems plain. The action of the Mecklenburg patriots was considered premature and was not publicized in 1775 in accordance with the counsel of the North Carolina delegates to the Continental Congress. The colonists were still seeking conciliation with England and announcement that a county in North Carolina had revolted would have so inflamed the already precarious situation, the delegates feared, that further efforts at conciliation would have been futile.

Certain early historians of the declaration controversy argue that the declaration was published, however, contemporaneously with its promulgation. Reverend Francis L. Hawks, writing in 1837, and George W. Graham, M.D., in his *The Mecklenburg Declaration of Independence, May 20, 1775, and the Lives of Its Signers,* try to show that Governor Josiah Martin in a letter to the Earl of Dartmouth, written June 30, 1775, in which he said he had seen in a newspaper which he was sending him a document surpassing "all the horrid and treasonable publications that the inflammatory spirits of this Continent have yet produced," was referring to the Mecklenburg declaration. In a contemporary proclamation the Governor declared he had seen "a most infamous publication in the *Cape Fear Mercury,* importing to be Resolves of a set of people styling themselves a committee for the county of Mecklenburg, most traitorously declaring the entire dissolution of the laws, government, and constitution of this country."

But intermittent searching through a century and a quarter since the Reverend Mr. Hawks offered this argument has failed to produce any issue of the *Cape Fear Mercury* hidden away in government archives in London with a copy of the declaration in it, and historians generally believe that Governor Martin was referring to the May 31 Resolves and *not* to the declaration. Today's strongest supporters of the declaration's authenticity believe that publication of the paper in 1775 was purposely withheld.

This was the view of one of the staunchest defenders of the declaration whose exhaustive study of the controversy antedated publication of Reverend Mr. Hawks' argument. This student of the early history of North Carolina was Governor David L. Swain. It was he who wrote the preface to the State Pamphlet of 1831, issued by the General Assembly of North Carolina, titled *The Declaration of Independence by the Citizens of Mecklenburg County, on the Twentieth of May, 1775, with Accompanying Documents, Published by the Governor, under the Authority and Direction of the General Assembly of the State of North Carolina.* It was Governor Swain's conclusion that "there was *no* contemporaneous publication of the proceedings of the 19th and 20th of May."

That this *Cape Fear Mercury* did *not* contain the declaration text, as Governor Swain believed, supports the theory that promulgation of the declaration purposely was not publicized in those early days of the fight for independence. But why?

"We were premature," wrote John McKnitt Alexander in rough notes left among his papers. Mecklenburgers, having declared themselves free of the mother country, were standing alone in all America in defiance of King George's government. And even North Carolina's leaders, to repeat for emphasis, were counseling caution, moderation, and patience in the hope that reconciliation might be achieved. Publication of such a bold document would be highly inflammatory, they reasoned. In Philadelphia, where the Congress was sitting, the preponderant effort was exerted on the side of reconciliation with Great Britain, and very naturally attempts would be made to prevent publication of all articles that might further agitate the already grave situation. Supporting this contention is the fact that Philadelphia newspapers of that day, as far as diligent search has been able to reveal, did not publish even the May 31 Resolves, even though they were not the positive and challenging paper that the declaration was.

And certainly the Resolves were published in newspapers beyond the Carolinas, copied perhaps from the *Cape Fear Mercury* of Wilmington or the New Bern *North Carolina Gazette*, the two newspapers of the province, or the Charleston *South Carolina Gazette and Country Journal*. In fact, it was the discovery by Peter Force, able American historian, in 1838 in the *Massachusetts Spy or American Oracle of Liberty* of July 12, 1775, of an incomplete series of these resolves, and later the finding of a complete set, that gave those who deny the declaration a strong basis for their contention that the May 31 Resolves were the "true declaration" and that the traditionally accepted May 20 declaration was only imagined, that John McKnitt Alexander and those others who had testified to the genuineness of the May 20 document had been confused and in reality were thinking of the May 31 paper.

It is this theory that present day challengers of the May 20 document's authenticity support, though since the publication in 1907 of William Henry Hoyt's volume attacking the declaration, little has been published in attempts to gain adherents for that view. Critics now seem content to say they will not believe the May 20 paper authentic until adequate—to their satisfaction—contemporaneous supporting documentation is produced. And these disbelievers are unreasonable in their demands, declare supporters of the declaration, for while they accept many far less proved contentions of history as factual, they refuse to accept this, or even to weigh the mass of evidence, some of it startling and recently discovered, supporting it.

The controversy hardly will be settled, both supporters and attackers perhaps will agree, until one side or the other produces what both sides will consider incontrovertible evidence of a contemporaneous nature showing that the May 20 declaration was promulgated or that there was no such document. Will some long lost paper some day come to light to settle the argument?

But if the text of the declaration was not published contemporaneously with its adoption, why then, it might reasonably be asked, was it published in the *Raleigh Register* forty-four years after the May 1775 convention? The reason in this case, too, is clear.

In 1817 William Wirt, in his *Life of Patrick Henry*, asserted that Henry "gave the first impulse to the ball of the Revolution."

North Carolinians, noticing this claim, were unwilling to let it go unchallenged. Mecklenburg County, they had understood, actually had proclaimed itself independent of Great Britain some fourteen months before the colonial convention in Philadelphia had promulgated the July 4, 1776 declaration. In Washington Representative William Davidson of the Congressional district embracing Mecklenburg and his colleague in the Senate, Nathaniel Macon, set about obtaining evidence to support the Mecklenburg claim. Who could better provide such material than Mecklenburgers themselves, a number of whom, still living, had been participants in the May 1775 proceedings?

One of the results of their efforts was to procure certain important documentary material from Dr. Alexander, whose father had died the same year the Wirt book was published. This material supplied the information from which the Raleigh paper's article was prepared, and this article was reprinted in the *Essex Register* some five weeks later, where it was seen by Mr. Adams.

The retired second President thereupon wrote Mr. Jefferson that, in his opinion, in this quoted Mecklenburg document "The genuine sense of America at that moment was never expressed so well before, or since," and he sent along with his letter the copy of the Massachusetts paper. This praise of the Mecklenburg paper, particularly Mr. Adams' addition of "or since," might well have piqued the author of the national declaration, which had been promulgated not as the colonies' first declaration, but more than a year *after* Mecklenburg's, if there really had been a Mecklenburg declaration.

But even then, critics of Mr. Jefferson in his attack on the Mecklenburg paper point out in fairness to the Virginian, he did not deny the authenticity of the paper; he merely expressed a very strong doubt of its authenticity. "But what has attracted my peculiar notice," Mr. Jefferson wrote, after having thanked Mr. Adams for three recent letters from him, "is the paper from Mecklenburg County, of North Carolina, published in the *Essex Register*, which you were so kind as to enclose in your last, of June the 22nd. And you seem to think it genuine. I believe it spurious." He then goes on to question whether Dr. Alexander was a real man or "as fictitious as the paper itself about which the article had been written," and sharply to castigate North Carolina's delegates to the Continental Congress. "Now, you remember as well as I do, that we had not a greater Tory in Congress than Hooper; that Hewes was very wavering, sometimes firm, sometimes feeble, according as the day was clear or cloudy; that Caswell, indeed, was a good Whig and kept these gentlemen to the notch, while he was present; but he left us soon and their line of conduct became then uncertain until Penn came, who fixed Hewes and the vote of the State." But, Jefferson went on, in milder tone, "I must not be understood as suggesting any doubtfulness in the State of North Carolina. No State was more fixed or forward. Nor do I affirm positively that this paper is a fabrication, because the proof of a negative can only be presumptive. But I shall believe it such until positive and solemn proof of its authenticity shall be produced. And if the name of McKnitt be real, and not a part of the fabrication, it needs a vindication by the production of such proof . . ." Dr. Alexander customarily signed his name "J. McKnitt" and this is the way he had signed the article in the newspapers. Of course, despite Jefferson's suggestions, the name McKnitt was no fabrication.

The author of the national declaration doubtless would have been provoked to stronger words had he seen the letter written six days later, on July 15, 1819, to Reverend William Bentley of Salem, Massachusetts, in which Adams hinted—in fact, virtually charged—that Mr. Jefferson had used the Mecklenburg document in writing his own national declaration. He "was struck with so much astonishment on reading this document," Mr. Adams declared in his letter to the minister, "that I could not help inclosing it immediately to Mr. Jefferson, who must have seen it, in the time of it, for he has copied the spirit, the sense, and the expressions of it, verbatim, into his declaration of the 4th of July, 1776."

But after his letter to Reverend Mr. Bentley was dispatched, Mr. Adams received Thomas Jefferson's reply, for on July 21, eleven days after the third President had written to express the opinion that the Mecklenburg paper was spurious, Mr. Adams wrote that the letter from his Virginia contemporary "has entirely convinced me that the Mecklenburg resolutions are a fiction," and he wondered "Who can be the Demon to invent such a machine after five and forty years, and what could be his motive—was it to bring a

Charge of Plagiarism against the Congress of '76, or against you, the undoubted acknowledged draughtsman of the Declaration of Independence?"

Mr. Adams' words, of course, are as reckless as Mr. Jefferson's. Dr. Joseph McKnitt Alexander was no more a "Demon to invent such a machine after five and forty years" than he was a fictitious character and "a part of the fabrication." No other challenger of the Mecklenburg document's authenticity seriously has contended that any "Demon" or anyone else invented "such a machine," but some do contend that John McKnitt Alexander, innocently but because of advancing senility, in preparing years afterward "from memory" a copy of the declaration and a report of other May 1775 actions for his friend General William R. Davie, had confused the declaration with the subsequently enacted set of resolves. This contention, bolstered by the fact that supporters of the declaration have been unable to produce the original copy of the document or one that the critics will admit is contemporaneous with it, appears to be the principal basis of the argument that no declaration ever was promulgated.

This charge of senility was made against Mr. Alexander despite the fact that in 1800, when he made the Davie copy, he was but sixty-seven years old; he would live, still in good mind to the end of his life, seventeen years longer. And other participants in that stirring convention who left their testimony to the authenticity of the declaration were younger than he.

There have been some who have professed to agree with John Adams in his observation to Reverend Mr. Bentley that Mr. Jefferson "must have seen it, in the time of it." To support their contention, they point to the fact that Captain James Jack of Charlottetown, whose father Patrick Jack operated Jack's Tavern of Revolutionary fame, some time after the May convention, likely in early June and by the convention's appointment, carried certain Mecklenburg papers, presumably both the declaration and the May 31 Resolves, to the Continental Congress then in session at Philadelphia. These papers, Jack reported, were presented to North Carolina's delegates. Did Thomas Jefferson likewise see them, and did he use them in writing his national declaration?

Serious students of the controversy give little credence to the theory that Jefferson used the Mecklenburg paper, and then forty-four years later sought to cover his tracks by calling it a fabrication. But they likewise declare with vehemence that neither John McKnitt Alexander nor his son, Dr. Alexander, invented the declaration. The Alexanders were men of the highest character and reputation. And so were others of the period who either had taken part in the deliberations of the convention or were present as witnesses, or who on numerous occasions had heard from their elders accounts of those lively days in little Charlottetown.

Actually, neither Jefferson nor the Mecklenburgers were plagiarizing or inventing. Both the framers of the Mecklenburg document, themselves Princeton graduates and on a par culturally and intellectually with members of the Continental Congress, and of the national declaration, were merely writing into the two documents phrases, for instance, such as "are, and of right ought to be," that were current methods of expression. Such language was contained in the first resolution offered the Congress by Virginia's Richard Henry Lee: "Resolved, That these United Colonies are, and of right ought to be, free and independent States, that they are absolved from all allegiance to the British Crown, and that all political connection between them and the State of Great Britain is, and ought to be, totally dissolved." Certainly no one charges that Lee used phrases from the Mecklenburg paper.

Captain Jack in reporting on his return home from Philadelphia that he had presented the papers, as he had been instructed to do, to the North Carolina delegates did not mention Jefferson or any other except the North Carolinians. In a certificate signed December 7, 1819, however, in Elbert County, Georgia, where he was then living, Captain Jack declared that "I then proceeded on to Philadelphia, and delivered the Mecklenburg Declaration of Independence of May, 1775, to Richard Caswell and William Hooper, the Delegates to Congress from the State of North Carolina."

Captain Jack on returning home had reported also that in Philadelphia he had found the members of the Continental Congress still hopeful of reconciliation with Great Britain. Though the North Carolina delegates had appreciated the bold action of the Mecklenburg patriots, they had cautioned against publication of such a document as the declaration since that would further inflame the tense situation. Very probably the North Carolinians showed the Mecklenburg papers to certain of their colleagues in Philadelphia, but the documents were not given consideration by the Congress. Certainly Hooper and Hewes in the summer of 1775, judging by Jefferson's own description of them in his letter to John Adams, were among the more conservative delegates. It was only natural then that they should advise Mecklenburg to say little about this revolutionary step its citizens had taken.

Though no contemporary publication of the declaration text has been discovered, very strong evidence supports the contention that the material for a book published shortly after Jefferson's attack was being collected long before 1819. This was Francis Xavier Martin's history of North Carolina, which strongly supports the Mecklenburg declaration. Although the book did not come out until 1819, it was written *in the form in which it was published* some twenty years before, certainly not later than 1809, ten years before Jefferson had questioned the authenticity of the document. Martin, according to convincing supporting evidence, was assembling his material and working on his history from 1791 to 1809.

Another volume, published a year before Martin's history and written without collaboration in any way with Martin, also supports the declaration. It is Alexander Garden's *Anecdotes of the American Revolution.* Major Garden, a Charlestonian, served during the Revolutionary War with a number of soldiers from Mecklenburg. Both he and Martin were contemporaries of the early movement for independence and drew heavily upon their association with these men in preparing their books. Major Garden, for example, had been an aide to General Greene and an associate of Colonel Thomas Polk on the general's staff. He was also a friend of Dr. William Read of Charleston, who in 1781 was appointed hospital physician for the South with headquarters in Charlotte. In Charlotte he was frequently associated with Dr. Ephraim Brevard, John McKnitt Alexander, and others who had taken leading roles in the May 1775 convention. Is it not entirely probable, supporters of the declaration ask, that Major Garden learned from these men the stirring story of the convention and the declaration it promulgated?

The evidence in support of the declaration is extensive, therefore, and it goes back to the early years of Mecklenburg's independence.

But there are also certain natural supports of contemporary dating. One of the strongest of these was Major John Davidson's dubbing his son Benjamin Wilson Davidson "my independence boy" and the boy's being called "Independence Ben." Major Davidson was one of the signers.

Why such a nickname?

The reason becomes quite evident when it is revealed that he was born on May 20 in the year 1787. (He was not born on May 31, the day skeptics contend the only revolutionary action was taken—the passage of the May 31 Resolves.)

Benjamin Wilson Davidson's headstone in old Hopewell Church graveyard records his birth on May 20, 1787. Would John Davidson, a member of the convention, a signer of the declaration, only twelve years after the convention have forgot the date on which the declaration was promulgated? Would he have confused a set of resolves setting up a system of government to replace the overthrown royal authority with a declaration of independence? Could he have thought, just twelve years afterwards, that Mecklenburg delegates, of whom he himself had been a leading one, had on May 20 declared their country's independence when actually eleven days later they had merely enacted a set of twenty resolutions, rather than six, making arrangements for the continuation of a government that had been displaced?

Here is one bit of evidence that no person denying the declaration has ever been able successfully to refute or even reasonably reconcile with his theory of what happened during that memorable May in Mecklenburg. One effort to explain it suggested that Major Davidson named his baby "my independence boy" and the neighbors and members of the family began calling the child "Independence Ben" *after* Mr. Jefferson challenged the declaration and did it to bolster Mecklenburg's claim. This is hardly possible when one realizes that Major Davidson's little boy Ben was thirty-two years old when the authenticity of the document was first challenged. And his "senile" father was fifty-two when his last child was born, this same "Independence Ben."

Ten years before any controversy arose, a young fellow named James Wallis made a speech at the closing exercises on June 1, 1809, of the Sugaw Creek Academy. This speech was printed on August 10, that year, in the Raleigh *Minerva* and a portion of the speech was carried years later in the *Catawba Journal* of July 11, 1826. Here is a part of the youth's speech:

"On May 19, 1775, a day sacredly exulting to every Mecklenburg bosom, two delegates, duly authorized from each militia company in the county, met in Charlotte. After a cool and deliberate investigation of the causes and extent of our differences with Great Britain, and taking a review of probable results, pledging their all in support of their rights and liberties, they solemnly entered into and published a full and determined Declaration of Independence, renouncing forever all allegiance, dependences or connection with Great Britain—dissolved all judicial and military establishments emanating from the British crown and established others on principles corresponding with their declaration which went into immediate operation, all of which was transmitted to Congress by express and probably expedited the general Declaration of Independence."

Where did young James Wallis get his facts?

It would be many years before either Martin's history or Garden's *Anecdotes of the American Revolution* would be published. But there were then many participants in the convention still living and vigorous. Too, and this is significant, the head of Sugaw Creek Academy was the Reverend Samuel C. Caldwell. And who was Caldwell? He was the son-in-law of John McKnitt Alexander, the husband of Alexander's daughter Abigail Bain. He lived in the Hopewell community near his father-in-law until 1805, when he gave up the pastorate of Hopewell Church and became pastor of Sugaw Creek Church, in whose nearby Academy four years later young Wallis made his speech about the Mecklenburg declaration. And who was James Wallis? He was the son of John McKnitt Alexander's daughter, Jean Bain, the wife of the Reverend James Wallis. Where, indeed, did young Wallis get the information?

Governor Swain and other students of the declaration controversy believed that enactment of the set of twenty resolutions on May 31, eleven days *after* the promulgation of the declaration answers several questions.

The May 20 declaration positively asserts Mecklenburg's freedom from Great Britain. The language is blunt, almost angry . . .
"Resolved, That we, the citizens of Mecklenburg County, do hereby dissolve the political bonds which have connected us with the
mother country, and absolve ourselves from all allegiance to the
British crown, abjuring all political connections with a nation that
has wantonly trampled on our rights and liberties and inhumanly
shed innocent blood of Americans at Lexington. . . . Resolved,
That we do hereby declare ourselves a free and independent people
. . . a sovereign and self-governing people under the power of God
and the General Congress . . ."

There was no equivocation about this May 20 document. The
British rule in Mecklenburg was ended, not conditionally ended.
At the passage of the document Mecklenburg had no laws and no
legally constituted officers.

So, in Resolution IV and Resolution V on May 31, the delegates,
in order to provide a government to fill the vacuum, decreed "That
we do hereby ordain and adopt as rules of conduct all and each of
our former laws, and that the crown of Great Britain can not be
considered hereafter as holding any rights, privileges, or immunities
amongst us," and "That all officers, both civil and military, in this
county, be entitled to exercise the same powers and authorities as
heretofore; that every member of this delegation shall henceforth be
a civil officer and exercise the powers of a justice of the peace, issue
process, hear and determine controversies according to law, preserve peace, union and harmony in the county, and use every exertion to spread the love of liberty and of country *until a more general and better organized system of government be established.*"

Highly important among the John McKnitt Alexander documentary materials that escaped the disastrous fire at Alexandriana,
his home nine miles north of Charlotte, on April 6, 1800, is the half
sheet of foolscap containing notes in the old secretary's handwriting. Some of the paper is torn and no longer are many of the words
legible, but enough has survived to give strong support to the
declaration. Writes Mr. Alexander:

On the 19th May 1775, pursuant to the Order of Col. Tho. Polk to
each Captain of Militia in his regiment of Mecklenburg County, to

elect nominate and appoint 2 persons of their Militia company, cloathed with ample powers to devise ways & means to extricate themselves and ward off the dreadfull impending storm bursting on them by the British Nation &c. &c.

Therefore on s^d. 19th. May the s^d. Committee met in Charlottetown (2 men from each company) Vested with all powers these their constituents had or conceived they had &c.

After a short conference about their suffering brethren beseiged and suffering every hardship in Boston and the American Blood running in Lexington &c. the Electrical fire flew into every breast and to preserve order Choose Abraham Alex. Esquire chairman & J.McK. A. Secretary. After a few Hour free discussion in order to give relief to suffering America and protect our Just & natural right

adjured

1st. We (the County) by a Solemn and awfull vote, Dissolved our allegiance to King George and British Nation.

2nd. Declare our selves a free & independent people, having a right and capable to govern ourselves (as a part of North Carolina)

3^d. In order to have laws as a rule of life—for our future Government We formed a Code of laws, by adopting our former wholesome laws.

4th. And as there was then no officers civil or Military in our County We Decreed that every Militia officer in s^d. County should hold and occupy his former commission and Grade.

A comparison of these notes by the convention secretary, made before the fire at Alexandriana, shows that they parallel the declaration rather than the May 31 Resolves, even in the order of recital.

But Mr. Alexander continues, and this notation is highly significant:

But in a few days (after cooling) a considerable part of s^d. Committee Men conveened and employed Captn. James Jack (of Charlotte) to go express to Congress (then in Philadelphia) with a copy of all resolutions and

s^d. Laws & a letter to our 3 members there, Rich^d. Caswell, W^m. Hooper & Joseph Hughes in order to get Congress to sanction or approve them &c. &c.

Captn. Jack returned with a long, full, complasent letter from s^d. 3 members, recommending our zeal perserverance order & forebearance &c.—(We were premature) Congress never had our s^d. laws on their table for discussion, though s^d. Copy was left with them by Captn. Jack.

And further along in the notes Alexander observes:

N.B. allowing the 19th. May to be a rash Act [Here the original is torn] effects in binding all the middle & west [torn] firm whigs—no torys but [torn]

After discussing events in Mecklenburg following the convention and during Cornwallis' invasion, he asserts: [torn] "& foregoing extracted from the old minutes &c. J. MK. Alexander."

Still clearly in the convention secretary's handwriting, the notes refer again to the indignation in Mecklenburg that flared into anger and resulted in the "rash act" that was the May 20 declaration:

[torn, probably Su]ch were the feeling and sympathetick sensations of the Mecklenburgers, when they knew their brethren of Boston were beseiged by General Gage & in a state of Starvation, that in each Captn. Militia company a subscription was signed for their relief—many subscribed one Bullock—other 2 joined for one Bullock—and none was suffered to sign but what the officers and leading men admited, & for whom they were responsible, &c. And had there been a plan of government for their driving to Boston, 100 would have been given in the county in one week—the next news we heard—Boston had got relief— We were thanked for our goodwill—

And soon afterwards we smelt and felt the Blood & carnage of Lexington which raised all the passions into fury—and revenge which was the immediate cause of abjuring Great britain on May 19 1775.

April 19. 1775 wa[s] the battle at Lexington.

Could these notes, made by one of the principal participants in Mecklenburg's pre-Revolutionary history, have referred to a set of resolves that did not declare independence, did not mention the battle at Lexington, evidenced no outburst of emotion at the assault upon citizens in Massachusetts, but calmly set up a system for governing a county already free of Great Britain?

Honest, yes; men of good character, yes; say critics of Alexander and Major John Davidson and Captain Jack, General Joe Graham, and the others; but senile, forgetful and confused, unable to remember the nature of a document that literally they ventured their lives in signing, unable to remember when they adopted it.

This indictment of senility is farcical. And it was never made until *long after* every participant in the events of May 1775 in Mecklenburg was dead. Almost two-thirds of a century had gone by before this explanation of the "myth" was even suggested. And some years later a notation by Alexander himself, wrongly read, was advanced in support of the contention that the convention secretary twenty-five years after the convention was in his dotage. It was not until Peter Force's discovery in 1838 of the May 31 Resolves in the Massachusetts paper that this novel explanation of senility, confusion, and forgetfulness was advanced.

Doubtless a large proportion of Mecklenburg's male population was present at that convention, and certainly the delegates were the picked men of the section, the most forceful leaders, the most intelligent. Could the whole group, every man and boy inside or about the little court house on that memorable day when the express rider brought the inflammable news from Lexington, have been confused about what happened and when it took place?

The May 20 declaration, to reiterate, refers angrily to "a nation that had wantonly trampled on our rights and liberties and inhumanly shed innocent blood of Americans at Lexington."

Was it not natural then that Mecklenburgers, already deeply aggrieved over the trend of affairs in the Carolinas, should be enraged at the news of Lexington?

But the May 31 Resolves *have no mention of Lexington.* They are a calm set of resolutions *aligning Mecklenburg with the colonies* under the "direction of the Great Continental Congress" but, in view of "the exigencies of this county," which had just declared itself free and independent of Great Britain, setting up "certain rules and regulations for the *Internal Government* of this county, *until such laws shall be provided for us by the Congress.*"

Why did the May 31 Resolves make no reference to the battle at Lexington, the news of which when received in Mecklenburg had provoked a veritable storm of invective against Great Britain? The very logical answer is that no mention of this battle was made in the Resolves because that battle had been referred to in the more heated declaration of eleven days earlier.

And why is the May 31 document comparatively restrained and judicial? Because, says John McKnitt Alexander, it was drafted "in a few days (after cooling)" and in the realization that the May 20 action, in which Mecklenburg had stepped forth alone of all the communities in the colonies to defy Great Britain, had been, indeed, "a rash Act."

And why, ask proponents of the declaration's authenticity, would the May 31 Resolves have been enacted to supersede laws of a government that no longer existed if that government had not been overthrown? It had been overthrown, they insist. The declaration had done that. The May 31 Resolves followed as a necessary action, namely, the establishing of a government to take the place of one no longer in existence.

But then, why the preamble to the Resolves declaring that:

"Whereas, By an address presented to His Majesty by both Houses of Parliament in February last, the American colonies are declared to be in a state of actual rebellion, *we conceive* that all laws and commissions confirmed by or derived from the authority of the King and Parliament are annulled and vacated, and the former civil constitution of these colonies for the present wholly suspended. To provide in some degree for the exigencies of this county in the present alarming period, we deem it proper and necessary to pass the following resolves, viz:-"

The Mecklenburgers by May 31, had cooled considerably, as Mr. Alexander wrote in his notes, and realizing that they stood alone in all America in rebellion against the British government, were now, in a paper they were expecting to send to the Continental Congress aligning themselves with the rest of the colonies. But the other colonies had not rebelled formally. So Mecklenburg in the May 31 Resolves preamble declared that this county conceived all the others actually to be in a state of rebellion through action of King George in his address to Parliament declaring them in rebellion.

We have ourselves revolted, Mecklenburg is saying in substance, but you are also in rebellion by declaration of the King; we stand together in that our laws and commissions are null and void, and in Mecklenburg "to provide in some degree for the exigencies of this county in the present alarming period" we are establishing a new government to take the place of the one dissolved.

In other words, Mecklenburg, standing alone since May 20 by her own action, joins the colonies also in rebellion, as Mecklenburg conceived it, according to the King's declaration.

Those who contend that the May 20 declaration was authentic and that "the true declaration" was not the May 31 Resolves insist, therefore, that a study of the alleged declaration and the established twenty Resolves will impel the researcher to reach the conclusion that passage of the May 31 resolutions was an action supplemental to the declaration and made necessary by its adoption.

That was the conclusion of the committee of the North Carolina General Assembly that prepared and published the State Pamphlet of 1831.

4

VERIFYING THE FACTS

THE PAMPHLET published by the legislature of North Carolina in 1831 sought to answer all questions then being asked about the Mecklenburg declaration. It introduced documentary evidence to support the Mecklenburg claim. "By the publication of these papers," the committee appointed by the General Assembly to undertake that task officially finds, "it will be fully verified, that as early as the month of May, 1775, a portion of the people of North Carolina . . . did by a public and solemn act, declare the dissolution of the ties which bound them to the crown and people of Great Britain. . . . The first claim of Independence evinces such high sentiments of valor and patriotism, that we cannot, and ought not, lightly to esteem the honor of having made it. The fact of the declaration should be announced, its language should be published and perpetuated, and the names of the gallant representatives of Mecklenburg, with whom it originated, should be preserved from oblivion, which, should it involve them, would as much dishonor us, as injure them. . . . The committee are aware that this assertion has elsewhere been received with doubt, and at times met with denial; and it is therefore believed to be more strongly incumbent upon the House to usher to the world the Mecklenburg Declaration, accompanied with such testimonials of its genuineness, as shall silence incredulity, and with such care for its general diffusion, as shall forever secure it from being forgotten. . . ."

This pamphlet of 1831 contains a copy of the declaration and the names of its signers, the article from the *Raleigh Register* of April 30, 1819, the reprint of which in the *Essex Register* was forwarded by Adams to Jefferson to initiate the controversy, and a number of certificates. This *Raleigh Register* article begins with the statement:

It is not probably known to many of our readers, that the citizens of Mecklenburg County, in this State, made a Declaration of Independence more than a year before Congress made theirs. The following document on the subject has lately come to the hands of the Editor from an unquestionable authority and is published that it may go down to posterity.

Then follows a story of the May 19-20 convention, the adoption of the declaration, and a copy of that document, and a recital of subsequent proceedings in Charlottetown, the sending of Captain Jack to Philadelphia with the Mecklenburg papers. The article continues:

On the return of Captain Jack, the delegation learned that their proceedings were individually approved by Members of Congress, but that it was deemed premature to lay them before the House. A joint letter from said three Members of Congress (Richard Caswell, William Hooper and Joseph Hewes) was also received, complimentary of the zeal in the common cause, and recommending perseverance, order and energy . . .

At the end of this article is a certificate:

The foregoing is a true copy of the papers on the above subject, left in my hands by John McKnitt Alexander, dec'd. I find it mentioned on file that the original book was burned April, 1800. That a copy of the proceedings was sent to Hugh Williamson, in New York, then writing a History of North Carolina, and that a copy was sent to Gen. W. R. Davie.

J. McKnitt

The signature was Dr. Joseph McKnitt Alexander's customary way of signing his name. An accompanying certificate, referring to the Davie copy, reveals:

State of North Carolina,
  Mecklenburg County.
  I, Samuel Henderson, do certify, that the paper annexed was obtained by me from Maj. William Davie in its present situation, soon after the death of his father, Gen. William R. Davie, and given to Dr. Joseph McKnitt by me. In searching for some particular paper, I came across this, and knowing the handwriting of John McKnitt Alexander, took it up, and examined it. Maj. Davie said to me (when asked how it became torn) his sisters had torn it, not knowing what it was. Given under my hand this 25th Nov., 1830.

Sam. Henderson

Many other certificates attesting to the authenticity of the Mecklenburg declaration from participants in the May 1775 convention follow. Among them are those made by Captain James Jack, then living in Georgia, and General Joseph Graham, who as a youth had been present at the Mecklenburg convention. The Reverend Humphrey Hunter's manuscript memoirs provide an extract giving the declaration text and detailed particulars of the action on May 19-20. A certificate signed by four men who as youths were present at the convention attests to the authenticity of the declaration then promulgated; another, by Isaac Alexander, gives similar testimony; so does one by Samuel Wilson. And one of the strongest is that of John Davidson, himself a signer, dated "Beaver Dam, October 5, 1830," in which the venerable leader in the fight for independence declares unequivocally:

. . . When the members met, and were perfectly organized for business, a motion was made to declare ourselves independent of the Crown of Great Britain, which was carried by a large majority. Dr. Ephraim Brevard was then appointed to give us a sketch of the Declaration of Independence, which he did. James Jack was appointed to take it on to the American Congress, then sitting in Philadelphia, with particular instructions to deliver it to the North Carolina Delegation in Congress (Hooper and Caswell). When Jack returned, he stated that the Declaration was presented to Congress, and the reply was, that they highly esteemed the patriotism of the citizens of Mecklenburg; but they thought the measure too premature.

I am confident that the Declaration of Independence by the people of Mecklenburg was made public at least twelve months before that of the Congress of the United States.

I do certify that the foregoing statement, relative to the Mecklenburg Independence is correct, and which I am willing to be qualified to, should it be required.

This certificate, in the form of a letter, is addressed to "Doct. J. M. Alexander."

Publication of the General Assembly's pamphlet was considered to have clinched the case for the May 20 declaration, which seems to have been challenged up to that time only by Jefferson and his friends who felt that the Mecklenburg paper was itself a challenge to his July 4 national declaration. But with the finding by Peter Force in an old issue of the *Massachusetts Spy*, dated July 12, 1775, and his publication of the finding in 1838 of the preamble and the first four resolutions of the May 31 Resolves, and the later finding by Dr. Joseph Johnson, in 1847, of the complete text of the Resolves in the June 13, 1775, copy of the *South Carolina Gazette*, the modern phase of the attack on the declaration was started.

This contention, the one still being advanced by those who say there was no May 20 declaration, insisted that the May 31 Resolves constituted the "only true declaration" and argued that the Mecklenburg delegates to the convention and others present on those memorable May days had in their senility confused the alleged declaration and the actual May 31 resolutions. Though these resolutions were not an actual declaration, the critics agreed, they were, in fact, a "contingent declaration" and they maintained with insistence that they were the only paper Mecklenburgers enacted.

And then, six years later, the declaration newly challenged fell under the sharp pen of the Reverend Charles Phillips, a minister and professor of mathematics in the University of North Carolina. He was the man upon whose study of the Mecklenburg declaration controversy those who doubt its authenticity have built virtually their whole case. Dr. Phillips' contention is based upon the Davie copy of the declaration, to which the certificate given by Samuel Henderson refers.

In his certificate given to the General Assembly's committee, Dr. Joseph McKnitt Alexander in sending to that group material left by his father had further certified:

As to the full sheet being in unknown handwrite, it matters not who may have thus copyed the original record; by comparing the copy deposited with Genl. Davie they two will be found so perfectly the same, so far as his is preserved, that no imposition is possible—the one from the same original as the other is conclusive.

Dr. Phillips and all others who have denied the authenticity of the May 20 document agree, as far as they have been recorded, that the Davie copy was the work of John McKnitt Alexander's own hand. In fact, they point to that fact in support of their theory. Were it in the handwriting of someone else, their argument would have little validity. For more than a century they have used the old secretary to prove their contention that he was a confused, senile reminiscer when in 1800 at the age of sixty-seven he made the Davie copy.

And for more than a hundred years these critics have been victims of an error made by Dr. Phillips. The Chapel Hill professor-minister, in fact, through all those years has been the principal architect of the edifice in which critics have taken shelter. The story of this unfortunate mistake and its discovery eighty-six years after it was made is in itself interesting and unparalleled.

In 1853 Dr. Phillips borrowed from Governor Swain, who was then president of the University of North Carolina, material in the University library relating to the May 1775 convention in Mecklenburg. Included was the Davie copy of the declaration with the attached certificate of John McKnitt Alexander in which the convention secretary had reviewed some of the events of those early days in Mecklenburg. Then in the May 1853 issue of the *North Carolina University Magazine* Dr. Phillips wrote an article entitled *May, 1775*. In this article, which included the Alexander certificate, he contended that Mr. Alexander in providing a copy of the alleged declaration had reconstructed that document from memory and in doing so had confused what he thought was a declaration with what actually had been the May 31 Resolves.

Thinking to prove his contention, he quoted Mr. Alexander's statement in the certificate attached to the partial copy of the declaration to the effect that:

It may be worthy of notice here, to observe that the foregoing statement tho' fundamentally correct; yet may not litterally correspond with the original records of the transactions of said delegation & Court of Inquiry; as all these records and papers were burnt with the house, on April 6, 1800; but previous to that time of 1800; a full copy of said records, at the request of Doctor Hugh Williamson, then of New York but formerly a representative in Congress from this state—was forwarded to him by Col⁰. W^m. Polk in order that those early transactions might fill their proper place in a history of this State then writing by the s^d. Doctor Williamson in New York.

So, said Dr. Phillips, and so have said many historians in the years following the publication of his article, Mr. Alexander had written, by his own testimony, the Davie copy *from memory*. He was a good and patriotic man, but he had confused the so-called declaration of independence with the twenty resolutions of May 31. Thus, according to Phillips, the same confusion was true of John Davidson, James Jack, General Joseph Graham and all the others who had testified specifically to the authenticity of the May 20 document.

And that article, published more than a century ago, is the basis of the burden of all argument opponents of the declaration's factualness have offered. There the controversy stood for many years.

Then, in 1904, some fifty years after Dr. Phillips published his article, O. J. Lehman of the Bethania community discovered in the archives of the Moravian Church a sketch of events of the period from 1775 through 1779. A paragraph in the record devoted to 1775, translated into English, declares:

I cannot leave unmentioned at the end of the 1775th year that already in the summer of this year, that is in May, June, or July, the County of Mecklenburg in North Carolina declared itself free and independent of England, and made such arrangements for the administration of the laws among themselves, as later the Continental Congress made for all. This Congress, however, considered these proceedings premature.

This record was made in 1783 by Traugott Bagge, described by Miss Adelaide L. Fries, able historian of the Moravians in America, as "the most able man of affairs in Wachovia during the War." Miss Fries in her study, *The Mecklenburg Declaration of Independence as Mentioned in the Records of Wachovia*, published in 1907, emphasizes the importance of the Bagge entry in confirming the Mecklenburg claim. Particularly significant is the fact that Bagge's notes support the statement of John McKnitt Alexander in his notes and elsewhere, even to the use of the word *premature*. Bagge evidently alludes also to two papers rather than one; one paper declares Mecklenburg *"frey u. independent von England"* and the other makes "such arrangements for the administration of the laws among themselves, as later the Continental Congress made for all."

Where did Traugott Bagge get his information?

Another entry in this *Salem Diary* records:

July 7, 1775. This afternoon a man of Mecklenburg, who had been sent as an express from there to Congress in Philadelphia, upon his returning journey delivered here a circular addressed to Mr. Traugott Bagge; the same was signed by Hooper, Hewh, and Casewill; it actually contains an ENCOURAGEMENT to take up arms, etc. . . .

Who was this "man of Mecklenburg" but Captain Jack returning through the Moravian settlements to Charlottetown from his mission to Philadelphia?

Meanwhile, for more than half a century the Davie copy, admittedly a document in the handwriting of John McKnitt Alexander with his fatally damaging admission that "the foregoing statement tho' fundamentally correct; yet may not litterally correspond with the original records . . ." etc., had been lost. What had become of it since Dr. Phillips used it in writing his article for the May, 1853, issue of the *University Magazine?*

William Henry Hoyt had wondered. He wrote Dr. Kemp Plummer Battle, who in 1875 had become president of the University, to inquire about it. Dr. Battle replied that the copy had disappeared in the dispersal of important papers after the death of Governor Swain in 1868. So, in preparing his book-length assault upon the authenticity of the declaration, Mr. Hoyt *did not see the*

Davie copy. As the basis for his discussion of the Davie copy, he used Dr. Phillips' copy of that copy.

And there the mystery of what had happened to the Davie copy remained until, ten years after the Hoyt book was published, Dr. J. G. deRoulhac Hamilton, history professor in the University, in 1917 announced that he had discovered the long lost Davie paper. He had found it among the papers of Dr. Battle, a nephew by marriage of Dr. Phillips. It had been put away with some papers unrelated to Mecklenburg. So the Davie document, vastly important in the declaration controversy, was recovered. But the tremendous significance of this bit of paper was not to be revealed for another two decades. Dr. Hamilton, himself a challenger of the declaration and a supporter of Dr. Phillips in his belief that the alleged document was a myth, failed to discover the startling story plainly revealed in the paper he had uncovered. He perhaps did not carefully examine the old paper; at any rate he failed to notice a notation and a deletion on the face of the paper, plainly in John McKnitt Alexander's handwriting, that would be the most significant and sensational discovery in the entire period of the controversy.

It remained for Dr. Archibald Henderson of Chapel Hill, internationally famous mathematician, historian and biographer, to announce this find. Dr. Henderson for years has been interested in the Mecklenburg declaration question and his researches had led him more and more to a confirmed belief in that document's authenticity. The year before Dr. Hamilton's discovery of the long lost Davie copy Dr. Henderson had published what he termed "a scientific demonstration" that the news of the battle at Lexington actually did reach Charlotte on May 19 rather than on May 30 or 31. Were some incontrovertible evidence to be found that this news did not come to Charlottetown until the last day or two in May, Dr. Henderson pointed out, the argument for the May 20 declaration would immediately be insupportable. But if it could be shown that the messenger arrived in the little Mecklenburg village on the afternoon of May 19, as many witnesses were to declare in later years, the date of declaration would be set positively as the twentieth.

Thereupon Dr. Henderson set out to show that a messenger coming south with the alarming news of the British assault upon the citizens of Massachusetts would very likely arrive very nearly on May 19. He showed that an express rider bearing the news reached Philadelphia on April 24, that on April 30 the story had come southward to Petersburg, Virginia, and on May 6 was in New Bern, North Carolina, and on May 29 away across the mountains in Boonesborough, Kentucky. If he could only find a record showing news of the battle arriving in Salisbury by May 18 or Salem by May 17, he reasoned, he would virtually establish the probability that the express reached Charlotte on May 19. And after long research he found it! In the *Salem Diary*, for the year 1775, he read:

May 17, 1775: This afternoon Brother Richter brought from Bethabara a packet of letters and Church periodicals and papers from Bethlehem and Lititz which Christel Conrad, who got back today from Pennsylvania, brought with him; the letters were of dates April 25 and May 1, among other things they announced the unpleasant news that about April 19 there occurred a skirmish near Boston between the Royal troops and the Provincial Militia.

From Salem to Charlottetown was but an easy two day's ride. Surely, he reasoned, such desperately alarming news would not have been thirteen days reaching Mecklenburg from the Moravian settlements.

But his discovery in examining the Davie copy of the declaration found by Dr. Hamilton was far more valuable. In the North Carolina newspapers of April 9 and May 7, 1939, Dr. Henderson revealed that after an intensive study of the *Davie copy* he had found that Dr. Phillips in his consideration of that original source instrument had made a series of mistakes that completely nullified the conclusions of his article in the May, 1853, *University Magazine*. Mr. Alexander, Dr. Henderson had discovered, contrary to the assertion of Dr. Phillips and to the utter confounding of his position in the 1853 article, had *not* said he had written the copy of the Mecklenburg declaration from memory; on the contrary, Dr. Henderson had discovered Alexander's assertion, plain to see in the

Davie original, that *the section devoted to the declaration* itself *had not been written from memory, but* from *"the journals and records of sd. Committee."*

Following the section in which he gives the text of the Mecklenburg declaration of May 20 and tells of the expressing of the "s^d. proceedings" to Philadelphia by Captain Jack and of the captain's return with the announcement that Congress had deemed the Mecklenburg action premature, etc., appears the highly significant notation in Alexander's handwriting: "Thus far from the Journals & Records of sd. Committee." (Underlining is Alexander's.)

Just below the convention secretary's notation and written in another hand is the statement, also underlined, "here the copy of the record ends."

Most significant of all, perhaps, or equally as important, is the deletion from Alexander's writing of two words, "delegation &." The line through the "delegation &.," heavily scratched, is in the same ink and evidently was done at the same time the writing was. The secretary at that point (and on this statement Dr. Phillips based his assumption, now shown clearly to have been wrong, that Alexander was writing *everything* in the Davie paper from memory) had written: "It may be worthy of notice here, to observe that the foregoing statement tho' fundamentally correct; yet may not litterally correspond with the original records of the transactions of said delegation & Court of Inquiry . . ."

If this statement had stood—and this is the way Dr. Phillips quoted it in his *University Magazine* article and the way Hoyt and other critics of the declaration claim thought that Alexander had written it—then Alexander would have certified that everything said in his foregoing statement "though fundamentally correct; yet may not litterally correspond with the original records . . ." But Mr. Alexander, evidently in scanning what he had written or perhaps at the very moment of writing had realized that he had written something in error, and so he heavily scratched out the "delegation &" with the result that the statement then said "may not litterally correspond with the original records of the transactions of the Court of Inquiry . . ." But as to the other facts, namely, the original records of the delegation—the convention delegates who wrote and ratified the declaration—the Davie paper was *not* a writing from memory.

Why did Dr. Phillips *restore* two words? These were the most significant ones—plainly scratched out by the person who wrote them. And when restored, they completely reversed the meaning of the sentence, so that instead of validating the text of the declaration, as Alexander in eliminating them clearly had meant to do, they actually invalidated it by making him say he had written that text from memory! Dr. Phillips must have seen other changes made by Alexander, one of them being the scratching out of a word for which a substitution was made, changes made with the same pen and ink that scratched out the "delegation &." which Phillips restored.

Dr. Phillips' action in thus changing this key statement to make it say exactly opposite to what Alexander did say must remain a mystery of North Carolina history. Certainly it is indefensible if he did it in order to further his contention; if innocently he overlooked the fact that the words had been eliminated by their author, he demonstrated himself to have been in that research careless and unreliable. But in any event and whatever the explanation, his gross error has done more to rally the myth-contenders than any one other contribution.

Since Dr. Henderson made public his discovery—that the convention secretary was transcribing from the records of the convention—no one has gone on record with any theory attempting to refute Dr. Henderson's conclusion. But there are some who still insist on being shown contemporaneous documentary evidence.

Five years after Dr. Phillips made his inexcusable error, President Swain of the University, in his "special verdict" given at the request of Mr. Bancroft, declared his belief that a May 20 declaration was made. And James H. Moore in his very able and convincing *Defence of the Mecklenburg Declaration of Independence*, subtitled *An Exhaustive Review of and Answer to All Attacks on the Declaration*, published in 1908, declares in his preface that "Mr. Hoyt has done the friends of the Declaration more service by the presentation of many facts and documents hitherto unknown or neglected than he has damaged their cause by his argument." This statement is all the more justified following the invaluable discovery by Dr. Henderson of the Phillips error.

Dr. Henderson, having given much mature study to the declaration controversy in the years before and since he made this discovery, agrees that the verdict of Governor Swain was correct. Says Dr. Henderson:

"With all Swain's conclusions I concur. I have faith in the honor and veracity of the participants and eye-witnesses, about a dozen of whom were ruling elders and ministers (one) in the Presbyterian Church. I am inclined to accept the versions of those who were there and took part in the events described, in preference to people living 179 years later who regard the whole historical episode as an almost miraculous mass-myth. I rely upon the scientific support of documentry evidence and the rewarding wisdom of common sense."

This verdict of Dr. Henderson, delivered in May, 1955, is the conclusion of the great majority of those who with objectivity have explored that intriguing and inspiring May 1775 in Mecklenburg. They require no further documentation in support of the declaration. Many great and significant happenings in the world's long story have had far less contemporary documentation than Mecklenburg's declaration of independence.

5

ENTER ANDREW JACKSON

HARDLY had the business of the May meetings been completed before Mecklenburgers began planning for their participation in the session at Hillsboro in August of the North Carolina Provincial Congress.

In naming delegates to represent them at Hillsboro, Mecklenburg's citizens once again chose trusted, veteran leaders. John H. Wheeler, in his *History of North Carolina*, released in 1851, names as delegates: "Thomas Polk, John Phifer, Waightstill Avery, Samuel Martin, James Houston, and John McKnitt Alexander." Significantly, the list contains the names of four signers of the Mecklenburg declaration. They took with them a set of instructions on how to implement the county and state governments in light of their new freedom from English rule.

But, at Hillsboro, Mecklenburgers once more were premature. At this session in the autumn of 1775 North Carolina did not declare its independence, though at the subsequent session in the spring, held at Halifax, the body unanimously adopted a resolution "that the Delegates from this Colony in the Continental Congress be empowered to concur with the delegates from the other colonies, in declaring Independence and forming foreign alliances; reserving to this colony the sole and exclusive right of forming a constitution and laws for this colony."

This resolution, adopted on April 12, 1776, almost three months before the adoption of the national declaration, recorded North Carolina as the first of the American colonies officially in favor of breaking with England. It gave the state flag the second of its two dates. The other is May 20, 1775. Both dates represent actions inspired in large part by freedom loving pioneers of the Mecklenburg back country.

But although the August and September session the year before produced no outright declaration of independence, it did see the establishment of plans for the raising of military forces and the setting up of a civil government. The delegates provided for the raising of troops, committed North Carolina to pay its due proportion of expense in the training of a continental army, and named a committee to set up a system of civil government. This government would be vested in a provincial council for the entire province, a committee of safety for each district, and a committee for each town and county in the province.

The provincial council was to be composed of one man elected by the Congress, who would serve as governor, and two persons from each of the six districts. From the Salisbury district, which included Mecklenburg, Samuel Spencer and Charlotte's Waightstill Avery were chosen.

Hezekiah Alexander and Benjamin Patton represented Mecklenburg on the newly organized committee of safety, which was composed of a president and twelve members from each of the six districts. Larger committees were named for each of the counties and towns.

Meanwhile, determined efforts were being made to organize an efficient military force in the province and Mecklenburg was fully represented both in leadership and troops provided. But though soldiers from Mecklenburg in the next several years would be fighting far from home, actual invasion by the British would not come to Mecklenburg until late in the war.

The Provincial Congress first provided for the organization of two regiments of the Continental Line, with George Davidson a captain and George Graham an ensign in the first. The plan provided also for the enlistment from each of the six districts of militiamen, designated as minutemen. At the meeting the following December of the Provincial Council two other battalions of minutemen were authorized and Thomas Polk was made colonel of the second. The next spring the Provincial Congress, meeting at Halifax, created four new regiments and named Thomas Polk colonel of the fourth, with William Davidson a major. Colonel Polk had been serving as colonel of the county militia. Other officers included Adam Alexander as lieutenant colonel, and John Phifer and John Davidson first and second majors. Hezekiah Alexander of Sugaw Creek was named paymaster of the new fourth regiment. Mecklenburg's political leaders were fast becoming the region's military commanders.

And before the year that had seen Mecklenburg delegates meet in convention in the log court house was ended, Mecklenburgers had marched off to war, though this expedition, which was against a group of Tories called Scoffelites, would gain little place in history except for an amusing, if characteristic, action taken because of it by the young ladies of Mecklenburg. This was a compact entered into by them agreeing that they would not "receive the addresses" of any young man who had not served in that campaign. The *South Carolina and American General Gazette* of February, 1776, revealed the Mecklenburg misses' determination:

The young ladies of the best families of Mecklenburg County, North Carolina, have entered into a voluntary association that they will not receive the addresses of any young gentlemen of that place, except the brave volunteers who served in the expedition to South Carolina, and assisted in subduing the Scovalite insurgents. The ladies being of opinion, that such persons as stay loitering at home, when the important calls of the country demand their military services abroad, must certainly be destitute of that nobleness of sentiment, that brave, manly spirit which would qualify them to be the defenders and guardians of the fair sex. The ladies of the adjoining County of Rowan, have desired the plan of a similar association to be drawn up and prepared for signature.

The next summer a company of Mecklenburg militia under the command of Captain Charles Polk, son of Colonel Thomas Polk and husband of Hezekiah Alexander's daughter Mary who would long be recalled among the early families as "Devil Charlie" Polk, was among the nineteen hundred troops led westward by General Rutherford into the Cherokee country to subdue those tribesmen. Among Mecklenburg officers on this expedition were Dr. Brevard and three other signers of the Mecklenburg declaration, Colonel

Adam Alexander, Lieutenant Colonel John Phifer, and Major John Davidson.

Mecklenburgers were also numerous and prominent in the brigade of more than 9,000 troops organized about that time at Wilmington, which the next summer went north. They arrived early in July at Philadelphia, fought in the battles at Brandywine and Germantown, and starved and froze with General Washington that disastrous winter at Valley Forge. It was during their stay in Valley Forge that a group of them instituted Charlotte's Phalanx Lodge of Masons, members of that body point out with much pride.

And when the fighting moved southward, Mecklenburgers were participants. With the surrender of Charleston to the British in May 1780, Mecklenburg soldiers were captured and imprisoned. Among them was Dr. Brevard, who was then serving as surgeon in the American forces. But the individual who would survive to achieve greatest fame was a youngster who though not old enough to be a soldier would become involved with the Redcoats in their push northwestward from Charleston. This Mecklenburger, then only thirteen, was a red-headed, obstreperous boy named Andrew Jackson.

Jackson was born March 15, 1767, in the Waxhaw settlement within a few hundred yards of what later would be the North Carolina-South Carolina line. He was naturally familiar with that section, its back roads and trails, and when Major William R. Davie in his efforts to slow the advance of the British in this region below the Waxhaws required scouts and mounted messengers, he was able to use young Jackson to advantage. But the youthful ranger was captured and imprisoned at Camden; it was during that time that he was struck across the head with the flat of a British officer's sword when he refused to clean the Redcoat's boots. Very probably the fiery red-head in his refusal had added what the Englishman considered an insolent remark. It was also at that time that Andrew's brother Robert died of smallpox; already his brother Hugh had been killed in the fighting. And when, after his mother's tearful pleading, he was released, he himself was sick and half-starved, "a skeleton," he described himself, "not quite six feet long and a little over six inches thick."

Years later he would still be giving the British concern and his biographers—and countless interested persons in the intervening decades—cause for controversy. And to Mecklenburgers the question of where he was born would become, next to the Mecklenburg declaration of independence, their most warmly debated historical controversy. Was the seventh President born at the McKemey cabin in North Carolina or across the road at the Crawford plantation in South Carolina?

6

...AND ANOTHER GREAT CONTROVERSY

PERPLEXING to the motorist traveling along the highway from Charlotte to Lancaster, South Carolina, paralleling the eight-mile stretch of the north-south boundary line between the Carolinas, are two signs but a few miles apart.

The first, an official North Carolina historical marker, proclaims: "ANDREW JACKSON. Seventh President of the United States, was born a few miles southwest of this spot." The marker refers to the site, on a now little used road, of the George McKemey cabin in which Jackson was born March 15, 1767.

The second marker, placed by the South Carolina Historical Commission, asserts with equal assurance that the seventh President was born, less than three miles from the McKemey cabin, on the Crawford plantation.

The McKemey site is in North Carolina, the Crawford site in South Carolina. Can it be, the startled motorist asks himself, that one President could have been born in two places? Yet two sovereign states have so proclaimed.

On the Capitol grounds in Raleigh, North Carolina, proud North Carolinians have erected an imposing statuary group to the three Presidents born in North Carolina—Andrew Jackson, James Knox Polk and Andrew Johnson. And at the South Carolina Crawford "birthplace" equally proud South Carolinians have established an Andrew Jackson historical park.

Manifestly, despite the solemn asseverations of the official markers, Andrew Jackson was not born in both houses. But in which?

The question has been debated ever since the red-headed Wax-

68

haw youth attained national fame. Like the Mecklenburg declaration controversy, in all probability it will never be settled to everyone's satisfaction.

There are even varying views of what the controversy involves. Most students of the subject contend—and many do whether they are students of the Jackson story or not—that he was born in the McKemey cabin (the name is variously spelled, including McCamie and McAmey) and therefore in North Carolina or in the Crawford house and therefore in South Carolina. But there are some, too, who agree with the contention of Gerald W. Johnson, distinguished North Carolina writer, as revealed in his *Andrew Jackson: An Epic in Homespun*, that Jackson indisputably was born in the McKemey cabin, but that the little log structure may have been in South Carolina. On the other hand, Marquis James in his *The Border Captain*, the first of his three-volume biography of Jackson, declares that whether his birthplace was the McKemey or the Crawford house, Jackson was born in South Carolina—what was South Carolina at the time of his birth.

But if the question was debated in his lifetime, what did Jackson himself say about it? Manifestly, he couldn't have known of his own knowledge where he was born, but did he not have a definite opinion about it, based on what he had been told?

Evidently he had no firmly fixed opinion. When the controversy arose, his mother had been long dead, and many others who would have known. He had left the Waxhaw community at an early age. Perhaps he had taken for granted that he was born in the Crawford house, though he did not actually say so, since from his earliest remembrance he was living there with his widowed mother. Yet there is also evidence to indicate that as a child he thought he was born at McKemey's.

He often described himself as a native South Carolinian, and it is on such statements that supporters of the Crawford birthplace contention seem mainly to rely. But could he not have thought he was born in the McKemey house and in South Carolina?

In the time of Jackson's birth the boundary line was not known; it was but vaguely traced through this section of the Waxhaws. Not until May 5, 1813, was the line actually run. It was on the occasion of the surveying of this line that the Governor of North Carolina reportedly observed as he mopped his perspiring brow that "it's been a long time between drinks."

The establishment of the boundary put the McKemey cabin 407 yards east of it, in North Carolina; at the same time the Crawford house some three miles down the road, was a few hundred yards west, in South Carolina. Remains of the McKemey cabin, including large chimney stones, to this day determine its location.

The capstone of the South Carolina birthplace argument is the letter that Jackson wrote on August 11, 1824, to James H. Witherspoon of Lancaster, South Carolina, who had asked him where he was born. Jackson replied from Nashville:

D'r Sir, your letter of the 24th ult. is Just recd, and altho an entire stranger to you feel a lively interest in your prosperity and that of your family your lady being the descendant of a distant relation by mariage, I mean your Ladies mother.

I have a great wish to revisit my native state, and once more mingle with those friends of my Juvenile days who may still be living. . .

As to the question asked, I with pleasure answer. I was born in So Carolina, as I have been told at the plantation whereon James Crawford lived about one mile from the Carolina road [crossing] of the Waxhaw Creek, left that state in 1784, was born on the 15 of march in the year 1767.

yr mo obdt. Servt.
Andrew Jackson

In 1767 the plantation "whereon James Crawford lived" was owned by James's brother Robert and the deed placed its eastern boundary at the State Line. The McKemey house likely, it is argued, was a part of the Crawford plantation. Mrs. Jackson, Mrs. Crawford, and Mrs. McKemey, as well as Mrs. Sarah Lessley, the midwife at Andrew's birth, were sisters and with their husbands had come into the Waxhaws some two years before from Ireland. So Jackson, it is contended, could have been referring to the McKemey house on "the plantation whereon James Crawford lived." This view is supported by an affidavit of James Craig, "formerly of Waxhaw, then of Mississippi," as quoted in James Parton's monumental biography of Jackson, in which Parton says Craig related that once while sleeping with Jackson in the McKemey house, young James Faulkner, Andrew's cousin, was told by Andrew that he had been born there.

Perhaps as a result of having seen published Jackson's letter of August 11, 1824, to Witherspoon, someone who signed himself "K" wrote a letter to the Columbia, South Carolina, *Telescope,* and this letter was copied by the Charleston *Courier* in its November 24 issue. This letter, summarized by Dr. Archibald Henderson in his monumental *North Carolina: The Old North State and the New,* refuted General Jackson's assertion that "I was born in So Carolina, as I have been told. . ."

"There has been much uncertainty in regard to General Jackson's birthplace," this letter said. "I am glad that I have it in my power to settle this question. . . . After the death of his father, his mother . . . went to live with her brother-in-law, a Mr. Mc-Amey. . . . General Jackson was born at the house of Mr. Mc-Amey, and therefore in the State of North Carolina. When he was about six weeks old his mother removed with him to the house of Mr. James Crawford, another brother-in-law, on the South Carolina side of the road."

Some four years after Jackson wrote Witherspoon, a letter from Craig was published, on July 11, 1828, in the *United States Telegraph,* Washington, in which he asserted that "General Jackson was born 2 miles of this spot; there are living witnesses yet remaining."

This was the year of the lively Presidential campaign and already scurrilous stories were being circulated about Jackson, some of them concerning his birth and parentage. Evidently having seen the Craig statement, George Nevills of Ohio, chairman of a committee supporting the Jackson campaign, wrote Craig and asked him to obtain affidavits with which to refute the scandalous reports. This Craig proceeded to do. After making abstracts of the certificates, he sent the originals to Nevills. The originals disappeared, but the abstracts are now in the North Carolina Historical Commission's archives.

But even in that era the documents obtained by Craig did not settle the controversy. And years later a July 4 oration delivered by Samuel H. Walkup, a leading lawyer of Union County, North

Carolina, which in 1842 had been formed from Anson and Mecklenburg, stimulated renewed argument because of his reading the signed testimonials of two elderly men of the Waxhaw community. In these certificates Benjamin Massey and John Carnes each affirmed that Mrs. Sarah Lessley [sometimes spelled Leslie] Lathan [sometimes spelled Lathen], the President's cousin, said that Jackson was born at McKemey's, that as a girl of seven she had gone there with her mother, Mrs. Sarah Lessley, Mrs. Jackson's sister, that she well remembered having walked the nearer way through the fields, and that she was present when Andrew was born.

In 1858, Colonel Walkup, an uncle of the late William Henry Belk, noted merchant of Charlotte, who would later be colonel of the Forty-Eighth North Carolina Regiment in the War Between the States, continuing his interest in the Jackson birthplace argument, wrote to Mr. Craig, who some twenty years before had moved to Mississippi, for further information substantiating the contention that the McKemey cabin was the birthplace. And on September 23 of that year the North Carolina *Argus,* a weekly newspaper of Wadesboro, North Carolina, published a series of affidavits obtained by him. A copy of this newspaper was kept by C. C. McIlwaine of Union County, and when in 1891 it was seen by R. B. Redwine, a student at the University of North Carolina, young Redwine borrowed it and had the article about Jackson's birthplace published in the *University Magazine.* Copies are on file in the University library.

"I think it can be as clearly demonstrated as any such thing can be at this distance of time that General Andrew Jackson, the late President of the United States, was born at the house of George McKemey, or McCamie, in Mecklenburg County, North Carolina, after his father's death, on Twelve Mile Creek, North Carolina," declares Colonel Walkup, after an introductory paragraph, and he then launches into his discussion. Transcripts from a number of the affidavits were used by Parton in his biography, which was published in 1861. Each document is offered to support the McKemey site version; each was made by a person familiar with the Waxhaw region and the Jackson story. In fact, most of those testifying were related to the seventh President.

Andrew Jackson, Sr., had moved into the Waxhaws not long before his death. On September 21, 1766, he had applied for a patent to 200 acres on Twelve Mile Creek. It was while engaged in clearing his land, according to the traditional story, that he ruptured himself; he died within a few days after the injury. The body was prepared for burial, and since a heavy snow had fallen before it could be carried to Waxhaw Presbyterian Church graveyard, it was placed on a sort of sled and the funeral party, several of them reputedly well fortified with refreshments provided in those days at proper wakes, started through the snow to the church several miles away.

When the party arrived, it was already growing dark. And to make things infinitely worse, it was discovered that the sled bore no body. But several members of the party quickly retraced their journey and upon coming to a small creek, found the coffin. It had slipped from the sled as the horses had plunged across the little stream. The body was placed on the sled again and a short while later, after a service by torchlight, was committed to the earth. A tombstone stands in the ancient churchyard over what is purported to be the elder Jackson's grave.

Andrew Jackson died only a few days before his son's birth. On the return from the funeral, Elizabeth Jackson stopped at either the Crawford house or the McKemey house and gave birth to her third son. But in which house?

Colonel Walkup, though a native South Carolinian, felt that the evidence supported the McKemey site. But he wished to see the controversy settled, and so, three decades after Jackson had been elected to the highest office in the nation, he determined to collect evidence that would end the controversy.

"This is oral tradition," he says, "among the near neighbors and nearest relations of Jackson himself in Waxhaws, North Carolina and South Carolina, as is shown by the certificates of Benjamin Massey, Esq., and Messrs. John Carnes, taken in 1845, and John Lathen (his second cousin), James Faulkner and Thomas Faulkner (also second cousins of Jackson), who all testify that old Sarah Leslie and Sarah Lathen, the aunt and cousin of General Jackson, often asserted that 'he (Jackson) was born at George McCamie's, and that they were present at his birth,' that Mrs. Leslie, his (Jackson's) aunt, 'was sent for on the night of his birth,' that 'it was at her brother-in-law's, George McCamie's, in North Carolina, close by where she (Mrs. Leslie) lived in North Carolina,' and that she 'took her little daughter, Mrs. Lathen, with her,' and 'recollected well of walking the near way through the fields in the night time.'

"In addition to this positive testimony," Colonel Walkup's article continues, "we have the testimony of Mrs. Elizabeth McWhorter and her son, George McWhorter, and Mrs. Mary Cousar, who state that they were 'near neighbors, and present on the night of the birth of General Jackson,' or were there on the next day, and have a distinct recollection that 'he was born at the house of George McCamie, in North Carolina'; which testimony rests upon the statements of Samuel McWhorter, the grandson of Elizabeth McWhorter, Thomas Cureton, Senior, and Jeremiah Cureton, Senior, who heard these old persons very often speak of these facts in the most positive terms, and who gave many circumstances in corroboration of its truth. And all these witnesses, and those whose traditions they relate, were persons of unimpeachable honesty and veracity, who had the very best opportunities of knowing the truth of all the facts they narrated, who were near neighbors, near relatives, and intimate associates with Jackson in his youth."

Colonel Walkup also presented some interesting testimony from the immediate relations of General Jackson and persons living in South Carolina who had direct knowledge of the birth and events leading up to it.

Benjamin Massey's affidavit, dated August 5, 1845, affirms:

Sir: Agreeable to your request, and to fulfill my promise to you, I herewith send you Mrs. Lathen's history of the birth of Andrew Jackson, as related to me by herself about the year 1822, as well as my memory now serves me. Mrs. Lathen states that herself and General Andrew Jackson were sisters' children; that Mr. Leslie, the father of Mrs. Lathen, Mr. McCamie, Mr. Jackson, the father of Andrew, and Mr. James Crawford, all married sisters; Mr. Leslie and Mr. McCamie located themselves in Mecklenburg, N. C., Waxhaws; Mr. Crawford located in the Lancaster District, S. C., Waxhaws; Mr. Jackson located himself near Twelve-Mile Creek, Mecklenburg, N. C.; that she was about seven years older than Andrew Jackson; that when the father of

Andrew died, Mrs. Jackson left home and came to her brother-in-law's, Mr. McCamie's, previous to the birth of Andrew; after living at Mr. McCamie's awhile, Andrew was born, and she was present at his birth; as soon as Mrs. Jackson was restored to health and strength she came to Mr. James Crawford's, in South Carolina, and there remained.

I believe the above contains all the facts as given by Mrs. Lathen to me.

Benjamin Massey

Perhaps the strongest of the affidavits bolstering the McKemey claim was given by John Lathan, son of Mrs. Sarah Lessley [Leslie] Lathan. Said he:

The following is about what I have heard my mother, Sarah Lathan, say in frequent conversation about the birthplace of Andrew Jackson, President of the United States. She has often remarked that Andrew Jackson was born at the house of George McCamie and that she, Mrs. Lathan, was present at his birth. She stated that the father of Andrew Jackson, viz., Andrew Jackson, Sr., lived and died on Twelve Mile Creek, North Carolina, and that soon after his death Mrs. Jackson left Twelve Mile Creek, North Carolina, to go to live with Mr. Crawford in Lancaster County, South Carolina. That on her way she called at the house of George McCamie, who had married a sister of hers, Mrs. Jackson, and while at McCamie's she was taken sick and sent for Mrs. Sarah Leslie, her sister, and the mother of Mrs. Sarah Lathan, who was a midwife, and who lived near McCamie's. That she, Mrs. Lathan, was a young girl, and recollects going with her mother; they walked through the fields in the night; and that she was present when Andrew Jackson was born. That as soon as Mrs. Jackson got able to travel after the birth of Andrew Jackson she went on to Mrs. Crawford's, where she afterward lived.

The maiden names of my grandmother and sisters (Mrs. Jackson, Mrs. McCamie, and Mrs. Crawford) were Hutchison. One of them married Samuel Leslie, my grandfather, one married James Crawford, one married George McCamie, and one married Andrew Jackson, Senior. Jackson lived on Twelve Mile Creek, North Carolina; Leslie lived on the north side of Waxhaw Creek, North Carolina, on the east side of the public road leading from Lancaster Court House, South Carolina, to Charlotte, North Carolina, about one mile east of said road, and east of a large branch, and near George McCamie's, as I understood, but not so near the public road as McCamie's. I don't know where McCamie lived—Crawford lived near Waxhaw Creek South Carolina.

My mother, Sarah Lathan, was the daughter of Samuel and Sarah Leslie, and died about 35 years ago, and was over 60 years old at her death. My mother lived near me until her death, and we lived about seven or eight miles from Samuel Leslie's and William J. Cureton's place, and about two miles from old Waxhaw Church, in South Carolina. I am 70 years of age and have a very distinct recollection of all facts above stated as true and correct, as stated by my mother, and as recollected by myself.

John Lathan.

In another affidavit, Thomas Faulkner, described as Jackson's second cousin, who said he was seventy years old and had lived all his life in the Waxhaws, testified substantially to the same facts. So did James Faulkner, grandson of Mrs. Sarah Lessley [as it was generally spelled in her day], the midwife and Mrs. Jackson's sister, who affirmed that often she had heard his aunt, Mrs. Sarah Lathan, say that as a seven-year-old child she had gone in the nighttime through the fields with her mother, Mrs. Sarah Lessley, to the McKemey house and that she was there when Andrew was born.

James Faulkner testified that he had heard his aunt, Mrs. Sarah Lathan, say she was present at McKemey's house when her cousin Andrew was born.

One of the affidavits from the Craig collection was made by a Mrs. Mary Cousert [variously spelled Cowsar, Cousare, etc.], who affirmed that she was "at McKemey's the morning Jackson was born and before he had been dressed."

The affidavits present a very strong case for the McKemey cabin as the Jackson birthplace. In fact, Parton declares without question that Jackson was born there, as Johnson does, and others who have given careful study to the question. Marquis James, too, agrees that the evidence is very strong. But he points out that Mr. Walkup may have "put words in the mouths" of the persons testifying; he says that the Parton quotations do not agree altogether with the affidavits and adds that the affidavits as presented are abstracts rather than the originals.

James, after making a stronger case for the McKemey house, it appears, than for the Crawford plantation, concludes: "My opinion is that neither party has proved its case, but that the Crawford house has a little better of it on Jackson's own testimony."

But Marquis James, strangely, makes no reference to Jackson's Murfreesboro letter. And that letter weakens, almost to the point of nullifying it, the case of the Crawford site supporters based upon the Witherspoon letter. It is an interesting letter and it gives weight to the contention that Jackson actually knew little, or cared, about where he was born.

Evidently—to return to the campaign of 1828 and the efforts of Nevills to refute nasty rumors about the President's birth and ancestry—Jackson saw the affidavits sent to Nevills by James D. Craig and was convinced by them that he was born in the McKemey cabin in what by then had been established to be North Carolina. At any rate, apparently from then on, as his correspondence tends to prove, he considered North Carolina his birthplace.

On February 26, 1831, a committee representing Murfreesboro, North Carolina, wrote to President Jackson requesting that he visit their village on his expected southern tour. They referred to North Carolina as the state of his nativity.

Replied Jackson, in a letter dated Washington, March 8th, 1831:

Gentlemen:—I have the satisfaction to acknowledge the receipt of your letter of the 26th ultimo.

Should my official duties permit me to visit my native state during the recess of Congress, I will with great pleasure accept the flattering invitation which you have so kindly presented me in behalf of its inhabitants to visit Murfreesboro. The State of North Carolina is a portion of our country endeared to me by the earliest associations. It was upon her bosom and among her citizens I first entered the career of life. The people were the patrons of my youth as they have been the true and zealous supporters of my political course. Their generous confidence and kind regard will ever be remembered with feelings of the warmest sensibility.

Allow me gentlemen to present to you individually and through you to the citizens of Murfreesboro an expression of the gratitude and esteem of

Your fellow citizen,

Andrew Jackson

So, seven years after he had written Witherspoon the letter upon which those who contend he was born at the Crawford house mainly rely, President Jackson himself renders that evidence virtually valueless by his letter to the citizens of Murfreesboro in North Carolina, declaring upon "her bosom and among her citizens," he "first entered the career of life."

But that was in 1831. And the preceding half century would have advanced his career far beyond his native Waxhaws. In 1780, with the British pushing northwestward in the up-country from their victory at Charleston, nothing could have been of less concern to the thirteen-year-old red-head than in what house he had been born.

7

A WELCOME FOR CORNWALLIS

THREE weeks after Charleston fell and the British started toward the Waxhaw settlements, General Griffith Rutherford assembled nine hundred militiamen in Charlotte. The situation in the South, he told them, was desperate. "Go home, boys," he said, "and get all the powder and balls and flints you can find, and be ready when I call you."

The call was not long coming. In June the militia assembled in Mallard Creek east of Alexandriana. Major Davie took charge of the cavalry, other leaders were assigned troops, and Colonel William Lee Davidson was given command of three hundred light infantrymen.

Rutherford was watching closely the advance of British General Rawdon toward upper South Carolina when he learned that a force of perhaps more than a thousand Tories was assembling across the Catawba at Ramsour's Mill. At once he sent orders to Colonel Francis Locke to plan to attack the Tories; he would join him shortly and they would fall on the Loyalists. But Locke did not get the message; instead, he notified the general that he was marching to attack the Tories. And before Rutherford could reach the battleground, Locke's men had fought the Loyalists, killed many, utterly defeated the others.

More victories over loyalist groups followed. A month after the Ramsour's Mill battle, other Loyalists were defeated at a place called Colson's Mill on the Pee Dee, and on July 31 Major Davie swept down on another band of Tories near the British garrison at Hanging Rock and defeated them. But a week later, though he did heavy damage and inflicted many casualties, Davie was not able to overwhelm the defending garrison there.

The British continued to advance, despite the victories over Tory groups, and deep gloom, like the sweltering heat of August, lay heavy upon Mecklenburg and the back country. Then, before daylight August 16, Cornwallis and the inept Gates came together near Camden. And before the day was ended, the two forces had clashed and those Americans who had not been killed or captured were running. It was, military students say, the worst American defeat of the Revolution. Ahead of the fleeing men, racing northward towards Charlotte, were Gates and North Carolina's Caswell. Nor did Gates stop for long until he was at Hillsboro. Caswell paused in the village; his task was to rally whatever forces might be available in the desperate necessity of stopping Cornwallis. But that was a vain hope. The road to Charlotte was wide open, so Mecklenburg feared at any rate.

But General William Lee Davidson's men, including Davie's hard-riding horsemen, were determined to make the Redcoats pay dearly for every mile of advance into North Carolina. Employing guerrilla tactics, they swept down upon detached groups, harassed foraging parties, and all the while kept vigilant eyes on the advancing main body.

General Davidson, who had been wounded severely in the fight at Colson's Mill, had been recuperating at his home in the Centre community. On the last day of August, upon the petitioning of the militia itself, he had been named a brigadier-general to succeed Rutherford, who had been captured at Camden. Now he commanded the militia of the Salisbury district, which embraced the western third of the state and was by far the largest militia district.

On the seventh of September Cornwallis started northward from Camden. Meanwhile Mecklenburg militiamen were assembling at a camp on McAlpine's Creek some seven or eight miles south of Charlotte. Immediately upon receiving his commission, General Davidson reported there and assumed command. He had some 400 back country men with nondescript weapons and few supplies. But many of them possessed their rifles—long barreled, small-bored weapons—and they knew how to shoot them. Some of these rifles had been made in Charlotte. The militia general sent out calls for volunteers to join him. Two weeks later, however, he had enlisted no other county militia, and Cornwallis was hardly twenty miles south of him in the Waxhaws. His men, he reported to General Gates, were in "high spirits" and "determined to stand out to the last extremity rather than submit to the fate of So. Carolina." Support was coming, however, and on the night of September 21 General Jethro Sumner arrived with his brigade. The day before, the partisans' spirits had been raised by the exploit of Colonel Davie and Major George Davidson, who with their horsemen had darted in to surprise a force of Loyalists pillaging the home of a patriot named Wahab (later the name would be Wauchope and then Walkup). The colonel reported that of the Tories there were "Killed 12; on the ground, wounded by our best intelligence, about 60." One prisoner was taken, and the Davie forces captured some much needed horses, saddles, and other supplies.

But at best these small victories could do nothing more than delay the British troops' arrival in Charlotte, from where Cornwallis was hopeful he could rally Loyalist support that would enable him to subdue North Carolina and perhaps end the war.

And then, early on the morning of September 25, news came into the camp on McAlpine's Creek that Cornwallis had left the Waxhaws and was coming toward Charlotte. Quickly Davidson ordered a retreat; the troops came up through Charlotte and continued several miles past the village along the road to Salisbury. But they were not going to leave the county seat to the Redcoats without a fight. Davidson directed Colonel Davie to do what he could to delay the British advance, and Joe Graham, a youngster who had been in heavy fighting both north and south in previous months but for some time had been on his mother's farm nearby, joined Davie. Sumner continued his retreat toward Salisbury, but Davidson some five miles beyond Sugaw Creek Church paused to await his Lordship's arrival.

Shortly before noon the next day, September 26, 1780, the British entered the village. It would be Charlotte's first—and to this day, at any rate, last—enemy invasion.

Many accounts of the skirmish have been recorded, some by participants, including Cornwallis' Commissary Stedman. Historians have given considerable attention to it. *Piedmont Partisan*, the story of General Davidson, by Chalmers G. Davidson, includes one of the most entertaining as well as authoritative discussions of the fight. These writers agree that though it was no more than a small skirmish, it was important; they look upon it as the turning point of Cornwallis' campaign in the Carolinas. Less than two weeks later at Kings Mountain the fortunes of the British would begin their swift decline.

The British came into Charlotte from the southeast and approached the court house along East Trade Street. A British account of the skirmish, published in 1794 in London, states:

In the center of Charlotte, intersecting the two principal streets, stood a large brick- or stone-pillared building, the upper part being the court-house, and the under part the market-house. Behind the shambles a few Americans on horseback had placed themselves. The legion was ordered to drive them off: but upon receiving a fire from behind the stalls, this corps fell back. Lord Cornwallis rode up in person, and made use of these words:— "Legion, remember you have everything to lose, but nothing to gain;" alluding, as was supposed, to the former reputation of this corps. Webster's brigade moved on and drove the Americans from behind the court-house; the legion then pursued them; but the whole of the British army was actually kept at bay, for some minutes, by a few mounted Americans, not exceeding twenty in number.

Other contemporary accounts declare that Tarleton's cavalry, with one Major Hanger commanding and the Redcoat infantrymen in support, approached within three hundred yards of the little court house before the horsemen were ordered to charge. But when the defenders from behind the wall beneath the court house greeted them with a deadly accurate fire, they turned precipitately and fled. Two other charges were made before the Americans were dislodged by the British infantrymen pressing up the street and firing from the safety of the houses and outbuildings. They withdrew in orderly fashion out past Sugaw Creek Church, where in further fighting Captain George Locke was killed and young Joe Graham went down under an avalanche of saber cuts and bullets.

Tradition says that the widow Wilson and her daughter Susannah, who in later years would be known affectionately as Aunt Susannah Alexander, had gone in search of their cow and found the wounded soldier. They got him to the widow's home and treated his wounds, and then hid him away in the loft. The next day the wife of a British officer out seeking to buy chickens came to Mrs. Wilson's and in some way learned of the presence there of a wounded American. She promptly offered to send a British surgeon to attend him. Graham heard her and when she had gone, slipped away to his mother's home.

This is one of Mecklenburg's more dramatic stories of a dramatic period, but to improve on it, some believe that young Andrew Jackson was with the widow and her daughter that evening. Jackson and his mother about that time did come to live with Mrs. John Wilson, the niece of Mrs. Jackson and daughter of Margaret McKemey, wife of George McKemey. The Jacksons had fled from their Waxhaw home when the Tory marauders in that region became so frightening with the advance of the British northward. And certainly it would not have been out of character for this redhead, whose rough handling by a British officer whose boots he had refused to polish would gain him added fame, to have been prowling about the Sugaw Creek section where that day the fighting had been so intense.

That the British had encountered fierce opposition was readily admitted by the British. Tarleton, summarizing the Charlotte fighting, in his *History of the Southern Campaign, 1780 and 1781,* wrote:

Earl Cornwallis moved forward as soon as the legion under Major Hanger joined him. A party of militia fired at the advanced dragoons and light infantry as they entered town, and a more considerable body appeared drawn up near the court-house. The conduct of the Americans created suspicion in the British; an ambuscade was apprehended by the light troops, who moved forward for some time with great circumspection; a charge of cavalry under Major Hanger dissipated this ill-grounded jealousy, and totally dispersed the militia. The pursuit lasted some time, and about thirty of the enemy were killed and taken. The King's troops did not come out of this skirmish unhurt; Major Hanger, and Captains Campbell and McDonald were wounded, and twelve non-commissioned officers and men were killed and wounded.

But the fierceness of the Redcoats' reception did not end with their capture of the village and Cornwallis' establishment of his headquarters at Tom Polk's home across from the court house. The British commander, who had envisioned the flocking to him of people of the region to seek protection of the Royalists, found that they would not be intimidated. A broadside, printed in Charleston, with the date of September 27, 1780, in type rather than filled in by hand, shows that his Lordship was confident of enlisting the support of the people in this section of North Carolina. Either by design or accident, the dating of the broadside was perfect, for it had been set for issuance on the day after his arrival in Mecklenburg's tiny county town. The proclamation is interesting and revealing both for what it said and the manner of its expression, but more so because it discloses the British commander's complete misunderstanding of the citizens of Mecklenburg County and those others in the general region of the back country.

In this unique paper Earl Cornwallis urged the inhabitants of North Carolina to deliver up what arms they possessed and give a military parole "to remain thenceforth peaceably at Home, doing no Offence against His Majesty's Government," for which they would be "protected in their Persons and Properties. . ."

The broadside said:

NORTH-CAROLINA
By the Right Honourable
CHARLES EARL CORNWALLIS
Lieutenant-General of His Majesty's Forces
&c   &c   &c

A PROCLAMATION

WHEREAS THE ENEMIES OF HIS MAJESTY'S GOvernment continuing to practice every Artifice and Deceit to Impose upon the Minds of the People, have, as industriously as falsely propagated a Belief among the People of this Country, that the King's Army indiscriminately makes War and commits Ravages upon the peaceable Inhabitants, and those who are in Arms and open Rebellion against His Majesty's Authority: I think it proper, in order to remove such false and injurious Impressions, and restore as much Peace and Quiet to the Country as may be possible, during the Operations of War, hereby do assure the People at large, that all those who come into the Posts of His Majesty's Army under my Command, and faithfully deliver up their Arms, and give a Military Parole to remain thenceforth peaceable at Home, doing no Offence against His Majesty's Government, will be protected in their Persons and Properties, and be paid a just and fair price in Gold or Silver for whatever they may furnish for the Use of the King's Army; it being His Majesty's most gracious Wish and Intention rather to reclaim His deluded Subjects to a Sense of their Duty, and Obedience to the Laws, by Justice and Mercy, than by Force and Terror of His Arms.

GIVEN Under my Hand and Seal at Headquarters in Charlotte-Town, this Twenty-Seventh Day of September, One Thousand Seven Hundred and Eighty, and in the Twentieth Year of His Majesty's Reign.

CORNWALLIS

By His Lordship's Command,
J. MONEY, Aid-de-Camp.

GOD SAVE THE KING

* * * * * * * *

CHARLESTOWN : Printed at WELLS Office. No 71 Tradd Street

But his Lordship's efforts to lure Mecklenburgers into his service were without success. His stay in Charlotte would be recorded as one of his most humiliating experiences in the Revolution.

Davie hovered about the village and harassed the British, and up on Rocky River, Davidson was sending out small detachments that struck at the enemy's foraging parties, intercepted messages sent by Cornwallis and other British officers in their efforts to keep in communication with one another, and seized and sent away Tories to prevent their reporting to the British invaders information of American troop movements. They gave Cornwallis no peace. Tarleton would write further of this backwoods village:

Charlotte town afforded some conveniences, blended with great disadvantages. The mills in its neighborhood were supposed of sufficient consequence to render it for the present an eligible position, and, in future, a necessary post, when an army advanced; But the aptness of its intermediate situation between Camden and Salisbury, and the quantity of its mills, did not counterbalance its defects. The town and environs

abounded with inveterate enemies, the plantations in the neighbour-
hood were small and uncultivated; the roads narrow, and crossed in
every direction, and the whole face of the country covered with close
and thick woods. In addition to these disadvantages, no estimate could
be made of the sentiments of half the inhabitants of North Carolina,
whilst the royal army remained at Charlotte town. It was evident, and
it had been frequently mentioned to the King's officers, that the counties of Mecklenburg and Rohan were more hostile to England than any
other in America.

The most dramatic example of this inveterate hostility, and also
of the advantage of the militia's style of fighting over the close-rank
method of the British, was the skirmish some eight miles north of
Charlotte on the Beatties Ford road, which has come to be known
as the battle of McIntyre's farm. Cornwallis had been in Charlotte
one week. Already his supplies were dwindling. The Redcoats' foraging parties were being so harassed by the straight-shooting Mecklenburgers that the commander had been forced to send out large
detachments in search of supplies. On Tuesday, October 3, or as
some records indicate, the next day, Cornwallis dispatched a force
of several hundred men up the twisting red road toward Hopewell
Church. At the McIntyre farm, called in a report made October 5
by General Davidson "Mr. Bradley's on Long Creek," the marauding Britishers were fired upon from the nearby woods by a group
of some dozen young farmers of the neighborhood. In the words
of the correspondent of the *Pennsylvania Packet*, happily writing
back to his paper, "Captains Thompson and Knox, with fourteen
men, attacked above 300 of a foraging party, who were entering
Mr. Bradley's plantation (eight miles from Charlotte) with near
60 waggons, and drove them back with such precipitation that, as I
am well informed, many of their horses fell dead in the streets on
their return."

Though the report must have been colored by the correspondent's enthusiasm, the fight at the farmhouse was of much significance; doubtless it convinced Cornwallis that his proclamation was
to have little if any effect in this rebellious region. "So inveterate
was their rancour," Commissary Stedman observed, "that the messengers, with expresses for the commander-in-chief, were frequently murdered; and the inhabitants, instead of remaining quietly

at home to receive payment for the produce of their plantations, made it a practice to waylay the British foraging parties, fire their rifles from concealed places, and then fly into the woods."

The McIntyre farmhouse, with the bullets of the Americans in its log walls, was very probably the oldest structure in Mecklenburg County and certainly one of the most historic. But after standing for almost two centuries, the old house was purchased several years ago by a resident newly come to Mecklenburg. And, despite efforts being attempted to have it purchased and preserved as the county's oldest historic shrine, he had it razed. Now the site is a tangled, densely overgrown spot known to hardly any of the thousands who stream by it daily over the asphalt highway that has succeeded the narrow clay road of Revolutionary days. Its destruction was another example of modern Mecklenburg's indifference to perpetuating historical sites for coming generations.

On the Saturday following this skirmish at the Beatties Ford road farmhouse, however, disaster overtook the British invaders of the back country. General Davidson was three days hearing of it; it was on Tuesday when a courier rode into the camp on Rocky River and brought him the startling and joyous news of the battle at Kings Mountain. Colonel Patrick Ferguson, commanding a force of upcountry Loyalists, in the main, had been attacked atop Kings Mountain by American militiamen; Ferguson was dead, scores of the Tories were dead with him and other scores wounded, and the others were captives. Cornwallis' trusted lieutenant, said to have been the best shot in the British army, had been completely whipped and his invading force destroyed.

When Davidson got the inspiring report, he sat down and wrote General Sumner. Some of his figures were wrong, based upon inaccurate information brought him, perhaps, but the letter was generally correct, and in the succeeding days it was widely circulated; in Philadelphia, Congress ordered its publication and soon it was copied even in England. The general wrote Sumner:

Camp Rocky River, October 10, 1780

Sir—I have the Pleasure of handing you very agreeable Intelligence from the West. Ferguson, the Great Partizan, has miscarried. This we are assured of by Mr. Tate, Brigade Major in General Sumpter's late

Brigade. The particulars from that Gentleman's Mouth stand thus: that Colonels Campbell, Cleveland, Shelby, Sevier, Williams, Brandon, Lacey, etc., formed a Conjunct Body near Gilbert Town consisting of 3000—From this Body were selected 1600 good Horse, who immediately went in search of Colonel Ferguson, who was making his way to Charlotte—Our people overtook him well posted on King's Mountain, and on the evening of the 7th Instant at 4 o'clock, began the attack which lasted forty seven minutes; Colonel Ferguson fell in the action, besides 150 of his men—810 were made prisoners, including the British —150 of the prisoners are wounded—1500 Stands of arms fell into our Hands. the enemy surrendered We lost about 20 men among whom is Major Chronicle of Lincoln County, Colonel Williams is mortally wounded, the number of our wounded cannot be ascertained. This blow will certainly affect the British very considerably. The designs of our conquering Friends near King's Mountain not certainly known, it is most probable that they will secure their prisoners in or over the mountains and proceed toward Charlotte—The Brigade Major who gives us this was in action. The above is true. The Blow is great and I give you Joy upon the Occasion.
    I am, Etc.,

                                        Wm. Davidson

    The victory at Kings Mountain was one of the greatest of the Revolution. Many historians account it the turning point of the war. Bancroft declared it "was the fatal blow which utterly disconcerted the plans of Cornwallis, and forced him into that change of policy which had its end at Yorktown."
    Because American militiamen had been so effective in disrupting communication between Cornwallis and Ferguson, it was perhaps several days before the beleaguered British commander in Charlotte learned of the catastrophe at Kings Mountain. It was staggering news. Already the British were in a most difficult situation. Food was becoming scarce and hard to obtain; many of the men were ill; worst of all, perhaps, Cornwallis was isolated in the region of a desperately hostile people. Little Charlottetown, his Lordship had found, was indeed "an agreeable village, but in a damned rebellious country." He had been correct in describing it as a hornets' nest.
    On Thursday afternoon following Saturday's fight at Kings Mountain Cornwallis began evacuating Charlotte. Late that night

General Davidson heard of the withdrawal, and promptly he sent a dispatch rider to General Sumner with the good news:

We have a Report from a Man of Veracity just arrived from within 6 Miles of Charlotte that the Enemy have evacuated Charlotte & that last Night at 10 O'Clock the Rear of the Army passed Barnet's Creek 5 Miles below Charlotte on the Road to Bigger's Ferry.

The general added that he was confident Colonel Davie "had a Sufficient Force to gall the enemy in their Rear."

It was to Barnett's mill that a Charlotte merchant, one William McCafferty, had led the Redcoats. This McCafferty, like another merchant there named Duncan Ochiltree, had favored on the British to protect his property and now, with the Redcoats leaving, was fearful that the patriots would wreak vengeance upon him. So after having led the British into a swamp in the vicinity of that mill, he slipped away and rushed to Davidson's camp to report. But the general sent him under guard to Sumner with the observation to that officer that "His late Conduct is to me a demonstration that he is not a friend to his country."

It was while Cornwallis was retreating from Mecklenburg that another incident is said to have occurred that provides us with one of Mecklenburg's best Revolutionary stories. According to legend, marauding British soldiers came to the home of Captain McDowell on the York road. Mrs. McDowell talked the soldiers out of committing any damage, when she found that they too were under the command of a Captain McDowell—of His Majesty's forces.

As soon as the foraging British Captain McDowell and his men left, Jane Parks McDowell picked up her two-year-old son John, wrapped him in a blanket, and mounting her horse, rode northward into the darkness, on past Charlottetown and out the Salisbury road to the camp of the Americans, where she notified her husband and his comrades of the Redcoats' retreat toward the Catawba.

So Cornwallis and his Britishers slipped away from the hornets' nest. But he would return within less than four months for one further skirmish on the red soil of Mecklenburg. He had been in Charlotte sixteen days—from September 26 to October 12.

8

DEATH AT COWAN'S FORD

H IS LORDSHIP's venturing into North Carolina had been disastrous. The carefully thought out southern campaign upon which he had embarked so hopefully was shattered never to be reshaped. The backbone of the British offensive against the South was broken.

Cornwallis had envisioned a three-pronged drive northward to overpower what he considered would be feeble resistance in North Carolina. He had ordered the capture of Wilmington, to be held as a port city through which he could receive supplies and also as a right wing protection of his own forces in their drive toward Charlotte and on to Hillsboro. And to the west he had dispatched Ferguson from Ninety-Six to move northwestward to enlist Tory supporters and subdue rebels. Cleared of resistance on the wings and in the rear, his Lordship would sweep through North Carolina and roll on into Virginia to end all American resistance to His Majesty's government.

That had been Cornwallis' plan. But now, hardly more than five weeks after he had left Camden, his grand strategy was a shambles. The capture of Wilmington would come too late to help Cornwallis. To the west Patrick Ferguson was dead and buried at Kings Mountain and his forces, regulars and Tories, were dead, wounded, or captured. And in the center his Lordship, chagrined, fearful, bitter, was running southward in disorganized retreat.

The correspondent of the *Pennsylvania Packet* in a subsequent analysis summarized the Redcoats' ill-fated two weeks in Charlotte:

Whilst the enemy lay at Charlotte they were confined within their lines by our riflemen, who nabbed them if they set out their heads. In short, his lordship never found himself so far from home as at that place; and it may appear strange that although we were more than two weeks in surprizing distance with our raw militia, yet the enemy never attempted it, owing, I suppose to the great attention of our commander in preventing them from obtaining intelligence, and moving his troops every night.

The British had left Charlotte in virtual panic; in their rush to leave the camp at Barnett's mill they had abandoned some twenty wagons, a large quantity of clothing, many tents and other equipment, and a number of guns. They had heard that General Davidson had some 5,000 soldiers and was pursuing them; actually the brigadier general had hardly more than 300 men, but Davie with a part of Davidson's cavalry was harassing the fleeing Redcoats and the number of their pursuers must have seemed frightfully large.

General Davidson wanted to attack Cornwallis, particularly after a heavy rain had swollen the Catawba with Tarleton's Tory forces on the west side and Cornwallis' not yet across. He sent a message to Sumner suggesting that they join in an assault on the British, but the rain slowed Sumner and Cornwallis outdistanced his pursuers and withdrew to Winnsboro, where seventy miles south of Mecklenburg's pestiferous hornets he established headquarters.

The battle of Kings Mountain had electrified American hopes, which after Camden had been at perhaps the lowest point since the Revolution's beginning. In the Salisbury district General Davidson was busy enlisting men to take the places of those whose terms of service had expired. By the middle of November, the deeply concerned Colonel Davie wrote General Smallwood, "The torments of the damned are scarcely equal to the torture of my feelings these five or six days past, from the rage of the militia for returning home. Most of them deserted before the last evening."

But down in South Carolina General Sumner added to the confidence of the Americans in the Carolinas by a victory over Tarleton at Blackstock's plantation, though in doing so he was himself severely wounded. General Davidson in writing his congratulations expressed deep concern:

My anxiety for you (least your Wound be fatal) is such that I have scarcely spirit to congratulate you on your glorious victory. I sincerely wish you a speedy recovery, and in the meantime regret the Want of your services in the field, at this critical and important Juncture. Gen'l Gates with the Continental Troops will be at Charlotte tomorrow. We lie at the old post a dead weight on the Publick. I think I am possessed of all the patience necessary to my profession but I assure you it is nearly exhausted. . . .

In the last week of November General Gates brought what was euphemistically called the southern army into Charlotte. On December 2 General Nathanael Greene took command of this force, numbering, according to a field return made just before the march to Charlotte, more than 1,100 militiamen and upward of a thousand Continentals, with some 400 under command of Morgan. But it was what Greene aptly termed "only the shadow of an army." Several hundred of them had no arms and were almost without clothing in the dead of this winter of 1780, and half of the entire force were untrained militiamen. Too, the fighting in the vicinity of Charlotte had used up all the supplies in that region. Greene decided to leave Charlotte. But before he could get his army moving, heavy rains set in and kept his troops from marching. It was December 20 when he divided his forces and went with one group to the Cheraw region on the Pee Dee in South Carolina, where he made camp the day after Christmas. The other group was sent toward Ninety-Six under Daniel Morgan.

Cornwallis, too, was on the move. He sent Tarleton to meet Morgan; they clashed at Cowpens on January 17 and Morgan gave the British cavalry a resounding defeat.

Now Cornwallis, smarting at this new setback, started in determined pursuit of Morgan, who began retreating toward Mecklenburg. As Morgan kept safely ahead of the British commander, General Greene at Cheraw ordered his force under Huger to march northward toward Salisbury and he himself rode northwestward toward Charlotte to join Morgan, who had written him that a continuing ailment in his hip would make necessary his taking a leave of absence from his command. "I am not unacquainted with the hurt my retiring will be to the service, as the people have so much dependence in me," he wrote Greene; "but the love I have for my country, and the willingness I have always showed to serve it, will convince you that nothing would be wanting on my side were I able to persevere. So that I must beg leave of absence, till I find myself able to take the field again." He assured the General that "Gen. Davidson, Col. Pickens and Gen. Sumter" could "manage the militia better than I can, and will well supply my place."

Meanwhile, during the preceding many weeks General Davidson had been riding the district enlisting recruits to fill the places of those men whose terms of enlistment had expired. On learning that Cornwallis was again on the move, he had sent out orders for the militia to meet at Charlotte on January 10. The victory of Morgan at Cowpens a week later, in which many of the men sent by Davidson to Morgan had fought, had given to the Americans a resurgence of hope and confidence. But even yet, two weeks after the Charlotte muster and a week after Cowpens, Davidson wrote Greene that he was "distressed on account of the Smallness of our Resources and the Want of propper Ecconomy." But he was still anxious to attack the enemy, even though by Greene's appointment of Colonel Davie to be his commissary-general, Davidson would not have the services of that daring and resourceful cavalry leader.

In this new venture into North Carolina Lord Cornwallis was careful to avoid a second encounter with the Mecklenburg hornets. He swung to the left and came northward west of the Catawba. It was late in January now. For three days he camped at Ramsour's Mill, where he was joined by Tarleton. On the twenty-eighth he marched eastward toward the river to Jacob Forney's; there for another three days his hungry Redcoats feasted on the affluent Forney's cattle and sheep, hogs and chickens, while they waited for the swollen waters of the Catawba to subside. Before establishing his camp at Forney's, some four miles from the river, he had ventured to Beatties Ford but had found it impassable because of the raging current. On the other side of the river, too, he had been informed, were Americans awaiting him at all the fording places. Above Beatties were McEwen's and Sherrill's, and below were Cowan's, Tool's, and Tuckaseege.

The task of the Americans, spaced thinly along the eastern bank, was to anticipate Cornwallis' crossing strategy and slow his advance in order to give Morgan, already impeded by the prisoners and supplies he had taken at the Cowpens, more time to conduct an orderly retreat. Cornwallis, on the other hand, would be trying by a surprise maneuver to get across the river with a minimum number of casualties and as quickly as possible.

On Monday, January 31, Cornwallis made his move. It had begun to rain again and the British commander felt that to delay longer might mean the loss of any chance to overtake and destroy Morgan's forces. He made a move to indicate he was planning to cross at Beatties Ford by sending Lieutenant Colonel Webster and a detachment of Redcoats to "make every possible demonstration by cannonading and otherwise, of an intention to force a passage there," he would write some six weeks later. But at one o'clock on the morning of February 1 he would march down the river to Cowan's Ford, where he planned his major drive to cross the stream.

Meanwhile, General Greene had arrived at the Catawba and with Colonel Washington had visited Morgan and Davidson at Beatties Ford and planned his strategy. Though no records of this meeting reveal what was said, it is evident by what immediately followed that Greene directed Davidson, who had placed his men at the various fords along the eastern bank, to do what he could to slow Cornwallis' crossing. And then he and Morgan set out towards Salisbury.

Soon after they left him, Davidson dispatched a company of cavalry under Joe Graham, who had by now recovered from his wounds at Sugaw Creek in late September, and infantry led by Colonel William Polk, southward four miles to Cowan's Ford. Graham was to keep a patrol on the move to see that the British did not make a surprise crossing under cover of darkness. Toward nightfall Davidson himself led a detachment to Cowan's Ford and set up camp a half mile or so back from the river, but he assigned a picket to watch from the water's edge the Cowan's crossing point.

At one o'clock in the morning of February 1, Cornwallis reveals in his own account of the skirmish at "McCowan's ford," the British general began his march to the river, which was reached after much difficulty and the loss of some of their cannon, "the morning being very dark and rainy & part of our way through a wood where there was no road." But instead of going to Beatties Ford, which his actions there during the day had indicated he would try to force, he moved down the river to Cowan's. This was actually two fords; one, the horse ford, though shallower than the other, was longer, because it crossed the stream obliquely; the other, called the wagon ford, went straight across the river.

Davidson evidently feared that Tarleton's troops might, in the darkness of a winter's night, slip across the Catawba and get behind him, from which position they could attack him as the British infantry began its crossing. So he stayed well back from the river bank opposite to the point where the horse ford emerged on the Mecklenburg side. Meanwhile, the pickets huddled on the bank at the eastern end of the wagon ford.

It was nearing daybreak when Cornwallis reached Cowan's Ford and, hardly hesitating, began crossing the swollen stream. A man named Frederick Hager, a Tory who lived in the vicinity, was serving as the Redcoats' guide. Hager led them straight across along the wagon ford and soon the horses were over their heads in the raging torrent. The pickets on the eastern bank were asleep, according to the story related years later by one of them, Robert Henry, a boy of sixteen at the time. But the noise of the Redcoats' crossing awakened them and their firing brought General Davidson and his men racing toward the wagon ford.

For a few minutes the action was lively; the militiamen were picking off many Britishers struggling in the water. The return fire was heavy, and hardly had Davidson arrived when he was struck from his horse. In a few minutes, several other Americans were killed. The British loss was greater, but the skirmish proved a defeat for the Americans. Their resistance hardly slowed Cornwallis' advance. It would be recorded, however, as the last battle with an invader on Mecklenburg soil. And in the fall, on October 19, Cornwallis would surrender at Yorktown.

February 1, 1781, was a dark day in Mecklenburg. General Davidson, an amazingly successful organizer, had been the driving force of the area's resistance. His death, as General Washington and the Congress would testify, was a great blow.

Late that evening the General's body, stripped and rain-drenched, was found by David Wilson, brother-in-law of his kinsman, Major John Davidson, and Pastor Thomas McCaule of Centre Church, and Richard Barry. They took it to the home of David's widowed stepmother, Mrs. Samuel Wilson. Fortunately, they were able to dress it in a suit left there by Captain James Jack, Mrs. Wilson's brother. That night by torchlight, with Pastor McCaule conducting the brief service and with Mary Brevard Davidson standing stalwart beside the red clay grave, William Lee Davidson was buried in Hopewell churchyard.

General Davidson had been killed by a rifle ball through the heart. Frederick Hager's rifle, said the neighbors, shot such a ball. Hager went west, and died in Arkansas in 1814. Tradition persists in naming the Tory as Davidson's slayer.

Today the Duke Power Company's huge Cowan's Ford dam spans the Catawba almost at the exact point of the British crossing.

9

"A TRIFLING PLACE"

WITH independence, so boldly proclaimed in 1775, securely established by 1781, Mecklenburgers were free to contribute their energies to the peaceful pursuits of building a nation. The overthrow of British rule had been hardly noticeable in those six years of Mecklenburg's local government; the change had been in authority, not personalities. The same officials who had served under the King had continued to serve after Mecklenburg revolted.

So after Yorktown, they, like their comrades in the various provinces along the Atlantic seaboard, came home to undertake the tasks of peace. They repaired the little court house in Charlottetown, damaged in the Cornwallis invasion of September of the year before; they undertook to build new schoolhouses or give added support to those already started in such communities as Sugaw Creek, Rocky River, Poplar Tent, Steele Creek, Hopewell, Beatties Ford, Providence, Clear Creek, and Charlottetown; and they began to increase materially their crops of small grain, corn, and cotton.

Perhaps no period in Mecklenburg's two-hundred-year history has been of greater significance in shaping her course than the period between the ending of the Revolution and the beginning of the nineteenth century, particularly the last decade of it. Even some of the less significant happenings of that era are memorable.

Hardly more than a year after this decade began, for instance, tiny Charlottetown entertained the infant nation's first President at a gala picnic supper in the yard of Colonel Thomas Polk's home at the northeast corner of Tryon and Trade streets. It was on a Saturday afternoon sixteen years after Tom Polk had read the

Mecklenburg declaration from the court house steps—May 28, 1791. General Washington arrived about three o'clock that afternoon to be greeted by the villagers and many other Mecklenburgers who had come in from farms miles around. That Charlottetown was no pretentious place is plainly revealed in the diary kept by one William Loughton Smith, a South Carolinian, who in his entry of May 6—three weeks before Washington's arrival—observed: "Near Charlotte are some finely cultivated fields. This place does not deserve the name of a town, it consists only of a wretched Court House, and a few dwellings falling into decay. There is a good tavern kept by Mason, where, however, I paid the dearest bill on the road."

The President was on the return journey of his southern trip that had taken him as far south as Savannah and Augusta in Georgia. He and his party had left Crawford's at four that morning and after traveling eighteen miles had reached Harrison's, some three miles south of Pineville. After a brief rest there the party came on into the village and the President was escorted to the house that the year before for two tumultuous weeks had been the headquarters of Earl Cornwallis. There an elaborate feast had been prepared and doubtless many of Mecklenburg's notables were present, including members of the convention of May 19-20, 1775, and leaders in the Revolutionary War.

President Washington had been met near the Carolinas border by a group from Mecklenburg and Rowan who after welcoming him had escorted him and his party northward to the village. In this group was a nineteen-year-old youth from Salisbury who had been chosen to welcome the President on behalf of a military company from Rowan. Fortunately this young man, Charles Caldwell, who would later become a distinguished physician and teacher of medicine, recorded in his diary a detailed account of his meeting the President. He had been sent ahead of the Salisbury company in command of a detachment of thirteen riders. Delightfully he tells how he was so awed at his first sight of General Washington that for several minutes he was unable to speak. But he at length recovered his power of speech, he relates, and in reply to Washington's question, "Pray, sir, have you lived long in this part of the country?" he assured the President that he had since his childhood.

"You are then, I presume, well acquainted with it?" Washington asked, and when he told him he was, the President added the observation, "During the late war, if my information be correct, the inhabitants were true to the cause of their country, and brave in its defense."

Then young Caldwell, garrulous now, his diary discloses, sixteen years and one week after the May convention of 1775, made this significant observation to the President:

"Your information is correct, sir. They were, almost to a man, true-hearted Whigs and patriots, and as gallant soldiers as ever drew swords or pointed rifles in behalf of freedom. In Mecklenburg County, where we now are, and in Rowan, which lies before us, a Tory did not dare to show his face—if he were known to be a Tory. It was in a small town, which we shall pass, that Lord Cornwallis lay encamped, when he swore that he had never been in such a d-m-d nest of Whigs, for that he could not, in the surrounding country, procure a chicken or a pig for his table, or a gallon of oats for his horse, but by purchasing it with the blood of his soldiers who went in quest of it."

"Pray, what is the name of that town?" General Washington asked, says the Caldwell diary.

"Charlotte, sir, the county town of Mecklenburg, and the place where independence was declared about a year before its declaration by Congress. . . . We shall arrive at Charlotte tomorrow morning, where you will be received by five hundred at least—perhaps twice the number—of the most respectable inhabitants of the country, a large portion of whom served, in some capacity, in the Revolutionary war. . . When I passed through the town yesterday morning a large number of them had already assembled, and the crowd was rapidly increasing. And they are exceedingly provident." His diary entry goes on to give this picture of early Charlotte's preparing to entertain a President: "Convinced that they cannot all be supplied in the town, with either food or lodging, many of them have brought with them large and well-covered farm-wagons for their bedchambers and enough of substantial food, already cooked, for a week's subsistence. Others again have already erected, and are still erecting, for their temporary residence, in the midst of a beautiful and celebrated grove (where a victory was gained by a company of militia riflemen over a party of Tarleton's dragoons), the very tents under which they slept as soldiers, in the service of their country. And they are about as obstinate and noisy a set of gentlemen as I have ever met, or ever wish to meet again—especially when in a hurry. I was obliged, much against my will, to hold a long parley with them, yesterday morning, when I wished to be in motion to meet you, lest you might anticipate me in reaching the boundary line of the State.

"The General was evidently pleased with my narrative, and so diverted by the increased freedom and ease of my manner (for I was now perfectly myself)" he adds quite unnecessarily, "that though he did not actually smile (for he rarely smiled), he seemed, at times, as I fancied, more inclined to a little merriment than to maintain unchanged his habitually grave and dignified aspect."

The diary, as reproduced in Dr. Archibald Henderson's comprehensive study of that Presidential journey, *Washington's Southern Tour, 1791,* continued in considerable detail to record the conversation of the President and the youthful Caldwell:

"He at length inquired of me whether he might expect to meet at Charlotte any of the leading members of the convention which prepared and passed the Mecklenburg Declaration of Independence, and especially whether my father would be there. I replied that my father was dead, and that Dr. Brevard, the author of the declaration, was also dead; that of the members of the convention still living, I knew personally but two—Adam Alexander, who had been president of the body, and John McKnitt Alexander, his brother, who had been secretary . . . that they lived at some distance from Charlotte, but that I felt confident their ever-green spirit of patriotism, united to their strong desire to see him, would bring them there, should they be able to travel."

This diary, therefore, provides additional testimony in support of the Mecklenburg declaration.

An article published January 9, 1898, written by G. R. Prowell, further records little Charlottetown's reception of the President:

"On this eventful Saturday, crowds of people on foot, on horseback, and the better order of the peasantry in vehicles, came to the little village of Charlotte to catch a glimpse of Washington. It was the first and only time that many of them had seen the tall and dignified form of the man who will always be marked as the greatest American. The streets and adjoining roads were lined with men, women, and children for hours before his arrival, for it was not as a certainty known when he would reach Charlotte."

That night President Washington and his party were put up at the inn on the north side of West Trade Street, a few paces from the intersection with Tryon, operated by a Captain Cook. Early the next morning the party started northward toward Salisbury. In his haste the President neglected to return his powder box to his dressing case. After he had gone, Mrs. Cook discovered that he had left it behind, and when several young ladies of the village hastened to the inn after the great man's departure, she powdered their heads with the President's powder. "Now you can always remember," she told them, "that you have had the distinction of having your hair powdered from General Washington's box."

The President, however, evidently was not particularly impressed with the county town of Mecklenburg. In his own diary of the southern trip he described Charlottetown as "a trifling place."

In the same year that President Washington visited Mecklenburg another man moved here. He, too, in his own way must have been a sturdy character, and he also recorded his coming, and his living here, succinctly and withal charmingly. His arrival likewise was significant, for he might well be pointed to as typical of a great proportion of Mecklenburgers of the closing years of the eighteenth century whose descendants would provide the county a staunch citizenship through succeeding generations.

His name was Sugar Dulin; he was a son of Thomas Dulin and his brother was Rice Dulin. Rice, appropriately enough, as a young man moved to Charleston, South Carolina. Sugar came to Mecklenburg in 1791, bought a large tract ten miles east of Charlottetown, and lived there until his death about 1845. But Sugar Dulin tells his own story more effectively:

N.B.—I was Born in Onslow County, No. Carolina, the 23rd Day of April, 1763 as my parents sd any How Before I Mind & they Settled within Two miles of where Trentown in Jones County stands, & they sd Before I Mind they moved Ten Miles Higher up within one mile of old Daniel Shines & there I was Raised & lived until I went to the army & never farther from Home than to Nubern until I went to the army & then I made it my Home until I was married, and then I lived in sd County until 1791. I Removed to Mecklenburg County on the place I now live on. Now this the 1st Day of April, 1835 against the 21st of this Instant I have lived in Mclinburg County, No. Carolina, Forty Two years, &.

Done with my own Hand & the leading men of this County may Due the Ballance as to my Carretter, &.

Sugar Dulin.

I have lived with one wife going on 51 years & we Have Raised Five Sons & five Daughters & we this Day counted our Grand Children & we make them 94 that our Sons & Daughters has had & we Counted 13 great grand Children. This the 20th of March, 1837.

Sugar Dulin.

Mr. Dulin, like the great preponderance of Mecklenburgers in that day and for many decades afterwards, was a farmer, and doubtless raised some cotton, though in those years cotton was grown sparsely. There were several reasons. One important one was that producing cotton entailed much work. And after it was raised and picked, it required the separating of the lint from the seed, a tedious task. Cotton grown then, therefore, was generally for home use. Cotton would not become commercially of great value until ample slave labor permitted its extensive cultivation.

But the back country of the Carolinas had never been particularly favorable to the slave trade. The Rowan Committee of Safety almost a year before the Mecklenburg declaration's promulgation, in fact, had declared that "the African trade is injurious to this colony, obstructs the population of it by freemen, prevents manufacturers and other useful emigrants from Europe from settling among us and occasions an annual balance of trade against the Colonies."

The people of the back country were pioneers; most of them had traveled the long and arduous way from Pennsylvania and Maryland to open a new country, and bringing slaves, even had they owned them, hundreds of miles into a wilderness would not have been feasible. But these pioneers were not persons of wealth; few of them owned any slaves. They were in the main young people seeking an opportunity in a new land. They would themselves hew their living out of this wilderness.

So in the early days Mecklenburgers had few slaves. By 1790, two years after he had built his new brick mansion house, Rural Hill, Major John Davidson owned 26 slaves. The Polks and the Springses counted slightly more. John McKnitt Alexander's Cato, on the Alexandriana plantation, would perhaps be the best remembered; his name survives because it was to him that Alexander gave strict orders to burn down his barns and granary rather than permit the foraging Britishers in 1780 to plunder them.

But in this last decade of the century young Eli Whitney came down to Georgia from New England to teach school. Soon he realized the need of a machine to separate the cotton lint from the seeds, and he made a little boxlike contraption that would pull the lint from the seeds about as fast as five to ten people would be able to do it by hand. In 1793 he finished his working model and the next year he patented it. Some two years later a man named Holmes brought out an improved model, and litigation followed. But soon the gin was being manufactured and farmers were increasing their acreage devoted to cotton. And with the growing of more cotton, the holding of slaves became profitable, or seemingly so. Some historians would even maintain that invention of the cotton gin led to the War Between the States.

As cotton became king, a landed gentry grew up in areas that had been the homes of hard working small farmers and artisans. Soon the wealthier began to rely on their overseers and slaves and devoted themselves to the arts, sports, and the social graces. They hunted, raced their horses, attended balls and dinners, visited in Charleston, tidewater Virginia, and Philadelphia, even built up large libraries. In 1817, for instance, a generation after the Revolution, the still back country region organized the Centre Library Society, and six years later the General Assembly granted a charter to the New Providence Library Association, whose laudable purpose was to promote "general reading and literary culture."

So Mecklenburg, as the South did generally, gradually embarked upon the ruinous one-crop system that depleted the soil and enervated much of the citizenship. The smaller farmers and skilled artisans became competitors of the slaves. And soon many Mecklenburgers, both of the landed families and the less privileged, began to move farther south and west in pursuit of more land and greater opportunities. In Mecklenburg the developing aristocracy lived in the main outside the still unpretentious village of Charlotte, especially in the Hopewell, Sugaw Creek, Steele Creek, and Providence sections, and northward in the Centre community, and up and down on both sides of the twisting channel of the Catawba. But before the century was ended—in the last year of it, in fact—over near the present Concord in Cabarrus, which seven years before had been cut from Mecklenburg's eastern side, something else occurred that soon would prove of great significance in the life of this region.

On a Sunday morning while his parents were at church, twelve-year-old Conrad Reed, with his little sister and younger brother, slipped down to nearby Meadow Creek to try to spear fish with his bow and arrow. In the water he saw a shining bright object that he first thought was a fish. But when he investigated, he discovered that it was a very heavy object about the size of the flatiron his mother used. He took it home. His father carried it to a silversmith, but he did not know what the pretty "stone" was, and Reed took it home, where for two years or longer it was used as a doorstop.

Then in 1802 Mr. Reed carried the strangely heavy stone to Fayetteville and showed it to a jeweler, who asked him to leave it there so that he might flux it; it was gold, he explained to Reed. And upon Reed's return, the jeweler showed him a bar of gold six or eight inches long, and asked him if he would sell it. Reed, thinking he would ask a high price, offered to sell it for $3.50! The jeweler promptly bought it.

On his return home, John Reed began to search for gold in the creek and the next year found a nugget weighing 28 pounds, said to be the largest ever found in the United States. Other large nuggets were found, some of them weighing as much as 16 pounds down to 13, nine, and two of eight pounds, and many smaller ones.

Discovery of gold in this section of old Mecklenburg and subsequently in various sections of present Mecklenburg, including Charlotte, started a new industry. In the six decades before the War Between the States completely disrupted the life of the nation, mining came to be one of the region's most important industries.

Charlotte became the mining capital of the United States, and prospectors, engineers, technicians accomplished in methods then in use, and laborers skilled in mining operations came here from all over the country and even from foreign countries. For an even half century from Conrad Reed's discovery until the California gold rush of 1849, Mecklenburg was the center of the nation's mining activities.

So large did the mining industry of this community become that it was decided to erect a United States mint in Charlotte, and the cornerstone was laid in 1836. The structure was erected on the site of the present west wing of the Federal Building on West Trade Street, where it stood for a century. In 1936 the building was dismantled and then reassembled, stone by stone, in Eastover as the Mint Museum of Art.

In the first year of operation the Charlotte mint accepted deposits totaling more than $130,000, and coined gold of a total value of about $85,000. On May 20, 1861, it was occupied by Confederate militia, the Charlotte Grays. It was used as a hospital during most of the war. After the war it was reopened as an assay office, and it continued to operate until about 1913. During its service as a federal mint, coinage amounting to more than $5,000,000 was produced. In the two decades before it was razed it was used for various federal purposes, including Army and Navy recruiting, employment, and other services of the government.

The Mint, one of Charlotte's handsomest structures, was designed in the Federal style of the Republican period by William Strickland, Philadelphia architect who designed many famous buildings in that city. Its most prominent decoration was the great golden eagle over the door. Of this eagle, Stuart Warren Cramer, assayer at the mint from 1889 to 1893, once wrote that "This eagle was a landmark in Charlotte when I first came here, and a pet of Charlotte people, as well it might be, for it was perhaps the largest eagle in the world, being fourteen feet from tip to tip, and five feet high. When I had to redecorate it, it took over 165 books of gold leaf and ten books of silver leaf to cover it."

Extensive though intermittent operations were continued in Mecklenburg for a century and a half after Conrad Reed's original discovery, and although it is now considered not rich enough to warrant further mining, much gold-bearing ore remains. Charlotte streets, visitors are often told, are paved with gold. Actually some of the low-value ore brought up from mine tunnels burrowed beneath the city was used in paving some streets. A mural, sixty feet long and ten feet in height, on the south wall of the North Carolina National Bank's branch at North Tryon and Ninth Streets, done by Kenneth W. Whitsett, native Mecklenburger, vividly reviews the story of gold in old Mecklenburg.

But the last decade of the eighteenth century saw also the beginning in this area of another mining industry. Iron mining and processing along the Catawba River on the Lincoln County side quickly grew into an important business and several Mecklenburg families were to become affluent in it. Major John Davidson and two of his sons-in-law, Joe Graham, who had almost lost his life in the skirmish with the British in Charlottetown, and Alexander Brevard, purchased interests in the iron business in Lincoln County, and Vesuvius Furnace and Mount Tirzah Forge came to be widely known. Their products were sold as far away as Charleston.

Midway of this same decade, on November 2, 1795, a baby would be born in Mecklenburg who fifty years later would become President of the United States. During the administration of this Mecklenburger, who has been described as "one of the most completely successful presidents of the United States," the republic would expand to the Pacific coast; Texas, Iowa, and Wisconsin would be admitted to the Union; gold would be discovered in California; the United States Naval Academy would be established at Annapolis; and many other developments significant in the life of the new nation would be recorded. And, perhaps not strangely, about his birthplace a controversy would arise, as it had in the case of Andrew Jackson. But this argument does not involve any other state or any other county. It is agreed that James Knox Polk, eleventh President, was born in the present boundaries of Mecklenburg County. But where? Was it near Pineville or near Huntersville?

Some years ago an unpretentious monument purporting to mark the birthplace of Polk was put up at the site just south of Pineville of the cabin in which Samuel Polk and his wife Jane Knox lived.

But substantial evidence can be presented to support the contention that Polk was not born in the Polk cabin, although he was taken there as an infant as soon as his mother was able to make the thirty-mile journey from the Knox home some two miles and a half southwest of Huntersville.

Like the Jackson controversy, the one over Polk's birthplace likely will never be settled to everyone's satisfaction. The D. A. Tompkins' *History of Mecklenburg County*, Volume I, published in 1903, makes the statement that "November 2, 1795, James Knox Polk, eleventh President of the United States, was born between Hopewell and Huntersville, at the home of his mother's parents, Mr. and Mrs. James Knox. His father, Samuel Polk, was a son of Ezekiel Polk, and in 1806, when James Knox Polk was eleven years of age, moved with his family to Tennessee."

But near the end of that same volume Tompkins also declares that "James Knox Polk, eleventh President of the United States, was born eleven miles south of Charlotte, near Little Sugar Creek church, November 2, 1795." And on a page facing the President's portrait two pages farther on, beneath the fanciful drawing of a one-room cabin, is the legend:

Cabin Near Pineville, Mecklenburg County, in Which James Knox Polk, Eleventh President of the United States, was Born November 2, 1795.

John H. Wheeler in his *Historical Sketches of North Carolina*, published in 1851, says that Polk was born "about eleven miles south of Charlotte on the land now owned by Nathan Orr, about two hundred yards south of Little Sugar Creek." He gives no supporting details.

In 1897 Dr. John Brevard Alexander, Mecklenburg physician-historian, a native of the northern section of Mecklenburg, in his *Biographical Sketches of the Early Settlers of the Hopewell Section*, declared that ". . . Samuel Polk married Jane Knox, a daughter of Captain James Knox, who lived four miles northeast of Hopewell Church. The Knox house has disappeared, but the foundation stones are still visible, and the spring that supplied the Knox family with water still runs." The site, says he, "was made historic more than a century ago by being the birthplace of President James K.

Polk. . . . At this home of James Knox, the father of Jane, who married Samuel Polk, was the child born who was afterwards President of the United States. How long Sam Polk lived here, or whether Mrs. Polk only returned to have her mother's care during her first trying ordeal, we are not informed. But we are informed there was a muster ground here known as 'Polk's old field.' This has very much the appearance that Sam Polk lived here for a while at least."

Dr. Alexander goes on to tell the story that "Peggy Alcorn, an Irish girl who came from Ireland with her mother when six years old, people of good character but very poor, was, when 13 years old, hired by Sam Polk to wait on his wife and nurse the baby, their first child. . . . This girl afterwards married Eli Alexander, who lived four miles southwest of Davidson College, where they raised a family, of which each member proved to be a good citizen. Ezekiel, Martin, Moses, and Eli were all staunch Presbyterians, and the two daughters, Malissa married John Bell and Mary married E. A. McAulay. No people in North Carolina have a better reputation for honesty, integrity and truthfulness, and they say it, and have told their children that their mother often spoke of the time she waited on Mrs. Polk and nursed the baby who afterwards became President."

In his *History of Mecklenburg County*, speaking of Peggy Alcorn, Dr. Alexander says that "Many years afterwards, when the girl had become an old woman, she said it was a common thing for a young woman to go back to her mother to be confined with her first child," and adds that "This very plausible version of his birthplace was given by my venerable friend, E. A. McAulay, Esq., who married a daughter of the nurse of the President."

Dr. Alexander also refers to a possible birthplace of Polk in Charlotte in reporting that Susan Barnett, who as Susan Smart was present May 20, 1775, at the Mecklenburg convention, had been quoted as having said that Polk was born "in the house occupied by Richard Carson, now owned by L. W. Sanders."

A memorial stone in the old Hopewell graveyard gives support to one version of the Huntersville birthplace contention. It marks the grave of "CAPT. JAMES KNOX—Who in hope of a glorious resurrection to eternal mark, deceased October 10th in the year of the Christian era, 1794. Aged 42 years."

James Knox Polk's maternal grandfather, therefore, died a year before his namesake was born. One tradition says that the widow Polk's daughter and her husband then came to live with Mrs. Knox and remained there until after the birth of their son. The other version is that Jane Knox Polk left her Pineville home shortly before the expected arrival of her child and came up to her mother's to await the baby's birth. Either version fits well the tradition, which declares the Alcorn child was employed to attend the young mother and care for the infant. In the Gilead community in northwestern Mecklenburg the story of Peggy Alcorn's being the future President's first nurse has persisted through the century and a half since Polk's birth. And even now an old spinning wheel thought to have been made in Ireland is pointed out as once having belonged to an Alcorn girl who first nursed James Knox Polk after his birth in the Knox home.

10

"THE COUNTY TOWN OF MECKLENBURG"

INVENTION of the cotton gin had an almost immediately discernible effect upon the economic life of the South, including Mecklenburg, and, despite the fact that Charlotte, significantly and fortunately, would continue to develop as an industrial center, for the first several decades of the new century cotton would be the unchallenged king.

Charlotte's population in September, 1786, totaled 276, of whom 123 were Negroes. In 1790 the village had grown to 325 and the county's population was recorded at 11,395. Ten years later, as the new century began, the county's total had dropped to 10,439—but some 4,000 had been taken from Mecklenburg with the forming in 1792 of the new county of Cabarrus. Midway of the century the county's population would have advanced to but 13,914; but once more Mecklenburg had lost by the lopping off of a part of her territory, for some 5,000 had been lost to Union, set up in 1842.

Ten years later the 1860 census showed 17,374. In the century since 1860, Mecklenburg's growth has been more than 1500 per cent. Why the slow development during the first century of the county's history?

Some students of history insist that the expansion of cotton production with the attendant dependence upon unskilled slave labor is largely responsible. The Mecklenburg region lost in this era to the deep South and Southwest many of its best citizens, who left in search of more extensive and productive land on which to raise cotton.

Major John Davidson's twenty-six slaves at Rural Hill in 1790—to go back to the era just before the invention of the cotton gin—decreased to nineteen by 1800, but ten years later would be thirty, despite the fact that Major Davidson had found them unprofitable for employment in the operations of his iron industry. The increase in the number of slaves evidently reflects his need of added labor to work his expanded cotton acreage. And the Major's two sons, Robin and John, on nearby plantations owned another thirty given them by their father. Later Robin himself would own more than a hundred at Hollywood and be the largest slaveholder in the county.

Major Davidson's extensive plantation, which has been estimated to have embraced up to 20,000 acres, though doubtless not so large as neighboring Alexandriana, was, like many another plantation of that era, a little feudal empire almost self-supporting. All food, with the exception of coffee, sugar, tea, and a few other staples, was produced on the acres spreading out from the mansion house. Clothing, too, was made from materials grown at home. Cotton bales were hauled on wagons to Charleston, and some were shipped down the Catawba on flat-bottomed scows to Cheraw. Other Mecklenburg produce was sold as far away as Philadelphia. Major Davidson's operations paralleled those of other large landowners of the county, such as the Polks of Willswood and the Frews of Frew's Folly, two prosperous plantations whose handsome mansion houses are among the county's oldest landmarks. Willswood, on Caswell Road at Providence Road, is one of Charlotte's handsomest homes; Frew's Folly, now known as the Craighead Davidson place, is near Sugaw Creek Presbyterian Church.

But as the decades passed and slavery began to be less profitable, the economic emphasis in Mecklenburg shifted from the production of cotton to its manufacturing. Even in the early days of the resurgence of cotton growing, in fact, Charlotte had been industry-minded. As the new century opened, the village had a flour mill, a blacksmith shop, a saw mill, a gunsmith, several tailors, hatters, weavers, and probably other establishments, in addition to several stores and taverns. An authentic, even though brief, view of one of these taverns, as well as the court house at the square, evidently Mecklenburg's third, is provided by William D. Martin's diary, *A Journey from South Carolina to Connecticut in 1809*, published (1959) in Charlotte.

"We breakfasted this morning late in Charlotte," Mr. Martin wrote, "the county town of Mecklenburg. The village consists of two streets crossing in a square; in the center of the town stands a tolerably elegant Brick Court House with a cupola. In my host & lady, Mr. and Mrs. Huston, were united the rare qualities of attention, politeness & kindness. As the lady having prepared a genteel breakfast, when she observed us setting out again, with all the hospitality of a friend & kindness of a mother, she presented & insisted on my accepting some biscuit and cheese, which, said she, 'will serve as a repast at Noon.' Such disinterested goodness among strangers raised into action the most lively sensations of gratitude . . ."

One of the principal reasons for the continuation and development of industry in the village of Charlotte was the advantage of location. As the economy of the region advanced, Charlotte's situation in the center of it had much to do with its becoming the economic hub about which industry would turn. And not only manufacturing but distribution would become a more important factor in Charlotte's and Mecklenburg's advancement. Within one century after the establishment of the Republic, cotton manufacturing would be gaining ascendancy and within another several decades the Mecklenburg-Cabarrus-Gaston area would be the nation's textile manufacturing center.

The second decade of the nineteenth century was hardly under way when the young Republic again became embroiled in a war with England, and Mecklenburg contributed to the American forces 433 men from its population of about 15,000. And some three decades after the ending of this conflict, during the administration of Mecklenburg's James Knox Polk, a company organized in Charlotte saw lively action in the Mexican War.

But Mecklenburg in the first half of the nineteenth century did not achieve the place in history that the preceding fifty years had earned. And the principal celebrations in that period would commemorate the signing of the May 20, 1775 declaration, as they would likewise in the first half of the twentieth century. Remarkably, at the fiftieth anniversary, according to the account in the weekly *Catawba Journal*, "a band of Revolutionary veterans, wearing badges with the figures '75 stamped on them," were present, and at the meeting in the Presbyterian church, the orator's "address to the patriotic band whose venerable forms were before him, and whose snowy locks and bended frames formed such a striking contrast to the picture he had sketched of their youthful strength and vigor, was peculiarly appropriate and pathetic, and excited emotions in every breast which may be easily imagined but not described."

In the afternoon "about 4 o'clock p.m., a large number sat down to a dinner prepared by Dr. Henderson in the beautiful grove of the college green," the article continues in the flamboyant style of that day, "and after the cloth was removed, numerous toasts were drunk. The first was to 'the day we celebrate' and the next to 'the patriots who signed the Mecklenburg declaration of independence of May 20, 1775.'"

At least two of the document's signers were still living; David Reese was in Cabarrus and Major John Davidson, his beloved Violet now dead, had left Rural Hill to live with his youngest daughter, Betsy, the wife of William Lee Davidson, son of the general killed at Cowan's Ford, at their home, Beaver Dam, two miles east of what soon would be Davidson College.

Historian John Brevard Alexander states in his *Reminiscences of the Past Sixty Years*, published in 1908, that he himself was present as a boy of ten at the celebration in 1844. One had been held, too, in 1835, at which some persons had related recollections of happenings on the day being commemorated. At the 1844 May 20 celebration, says Dr. Alexander, "a table was set, a fine dinner was spread, and enough of room was made for fifty guests. Each plate was five dollars. The object was to raise money to build a monument to the signers of the Declaration of Independence of May 20, 1775. . . . This table was set just inside of Wm. Julius Alexander's yard, where the monument to the signers now stands [on the site of First Union National Bank's building at the southeastern corner of Tryon and Third Streets]. . . . At the head of the table a large armchair was placed, and was occupied by Maj. Tommy Alexander, a Revolutionary soldier, in his 85th year. There were but two more Revolutionary soldiers living at this time in the county, and they were not able to be present."

Dr. Alexander describes in connection with this celebration one of the earliest recorded civic campaigns in Charlotte. At the close of the eloquent address of James W. Osborne, he reports, "the chief marshal, Ephraim Brevard, came forward and called up the descendants of the Davidsons, the Alexanders and the Grahams and Brevards, and whoever else had the blood of heroes in their veins to come forward and cover an XX bill he laid upon the table, and a large number responded. Then he called for those who felt able to give a ten, to which a like number responded. But when he called for those who were not able to give ten dollars to give five, the whole multitude would march up and cover his five. This appeared to my youthful mind as a wonderful pile of money."

But though for the first half of the century population growth was slow in Mecklenburg and there were no movements as memorable and significant as those of the preceding decades, that era was in no sense a drab, colorless, and unexciting time. Before the War Between the States would destroy the pattern of life, a calm but pleasant culture existed in Mecklenburg. Dr. Alexander, who did more than any other one citizen to record it, saw life full and satisfying. "Fifty years ago," the 74-year-old Dr. Alexander wrote in 1908, "we had a civilization that has never been excelled. It is true that a half century ago the millionaires in America might have been counted on less than the fingers of one hand; now they are estimated at many thousand. But then fifty years ago it was a rarity to see a case of poverty, save from sickness or some misfortune. How is it now? From fifty to one hundred in the county home, and double as many more are fed by the city in the cold months of winter."

It was surely a more unhurried existence Mecklenburgers lived in those days. "Sixty years ago," the good doctor went on to recall, "we had much more time than we have now. Then we loved to visit our friends; stay all day, or longer; it was not called a visit unless you tarried for at least one meal. If it was six or ten miles, you were expected to stay two or three days. If it was only a mile or two, the good wife would go in the morning horseback and the husband would go after dinner and come home together after supper. The good women of that day would always take their sewing or knitting with them. I have seen them knitting on a sock while being driven to Charlotte. As a contrast we now see but little visiting and then they have but time to stay only a few minutes; don't even take off their bonnets."

Of education a century ago in Mecklenburg, Dr. Alexander says: "Fifty years ago there were not a half dozen school houses in Mecklenburg worthy of the name. But little money was appropriated for the benefit of public schools, and none for building houses. The school house was built near a spring; the house was generally built of small logs, notched close, but one door, and one long window; beneath it augur holes were bored and long pins inserted to hold up one or more planks for a writing table. The rudest kind of seats for pupils to sit on, without backs, so that there would be nothing in the way of the ever present rod. This was regarded as a necessary piece of furniture. It used to be said by the teacher when hunting a school, 'you furnish the boy and the book, and I will furnish the hickory.' The pendulum has now swung to the opposite extreme. Palaces now occupy the places once filled by hovels. The time was when the State gave by the hundred, now gives thousands; the rod is seldom used, and a golden road is now being marked out as the only way to learning. We can hardly keep up with the changes time forces upon us."

And this, also from the doctor: "It is now considered almost as essential to be a good football player as it is to be a good Latin or Greek scholar, or be able to work a problem in Euclid. Fifty years ago if a chap would leave Chapel Hill or Davidson to play a ball game in Columbia, Raleigh or Wilmington, he would have been considered only fit for the mad-house."

But listen to Dr. Alexander in this gem delivered long before television was ever imagined:

"I would call attention to the fact that fifty years ago the modesty of the good people was not shocked by flaunting before their faces the advertisements of certain patent medicines, what they will accomplish; they are too nauseous to talk about. Modesty has not the sway that it formerly wielded, or these advertisements would be ruled out of this civilization."

Times—in Mecklenburg as elsewhere—have changed, and the face of the city and county, but the people have changed little, a study of the forefathers of the present residents will reveal.

But the mode of life in Mecklenburg changed less, perhaps, in the six decades or so preceding the beginning of the War Between the States than in any other period. The change since 1920 has been greater than it was in all the previous century and a half of the county's existence.

It wasn't so long ago, in Mecklenburg County, for instance, that all cooking utensils were primitive and scarce. Pots, ovens, spiders and lids were obtained at the iron furnaces in Lincoln County. Cooking was done on the open hearth. A boiled dinner had to be cooked in a pot hung on a potrack, suspended over the fire. The cook was a master of dexterity. She stood before the big fireplace, "with the coffee pot at one side, the chicken frying in a stew pan, the biscuits in a spider, the sweet potatoes baking in an oven, and a pot hanging over the fire with the universally enjoyed dish of hog-jaw and turnip greens, or that never-to-be forgotten dish of o'possum and sweet potatoes . . ."

And nearly everybody drank hard liquor in early Mecklenburg. Corn whiskey was the standing drink, for both winter and summer. Even the poorest could afford it, at ten cents a quart, or thirty cents a gallon. It was wholesaled for eleven cents a gallon. And it was pure corn, four gallons out of every bushel. But though everyone took their toddy, very few got drunk. Corn whiskey was kept in the homes, and offered on all occasions.

In sports, horse racing and cock fighting were popular. Not infrequently a considerable part of the male population was entertained by bare-knuckled fighters who beat each other into gory pulps in improvised rings; often the bouts would go for dozens of rounds and until one of the maulers yelled "Enough!" Shooting matches, with sections of beef as prizes, were frequently held, with one dollar for four shots being the usual charge.

Amazing, almost unbelievable, to young Mecklenburgers of today, was the slowness of communication in the early years of the nineteenth century. There were few daily newspapers in the nation and the cost of subscribing was high. Dr. Alexander remembered having seen the stage coach passing Sugaw Creek Church with a white flag on the back with the announcement in large lettering: HARRISON ELECTED PRESIDENT. The election had been held six weeks before.

It was in the first third of the nineteenth century that Charlotte, still a village, set aside a large section across Trade Street from the site of old Pat Jack's tavern, which had been burned by the British in 1780, for a church to be used by all denominations that might wish to share it. In 1832 the Presbyterians paid off a debt on the building and acquired possession. In succeeding years the present beautiful Norman-Gothic structure was built and later remodeled and enlarged. Stories were told that during Reconstruction times members of the Ku Klux Klan met in the basement.

Behind the church was laid off Charlotte's first cemetery, in which are buried many persons prominent in the early days, including Thomas Polk and his wife, Susan, Governor Nathaniel Alexander, who had been a surgeon in the Revolutionary army and was Governor from 1805 to 1807, Major George Graham, and others of Mecklenburg fame. In 1833 the Baptists erected a house of worship at College and Third Streets. This church did not thrive, but in 1855 a successor built at Brevard and Seventh Streets established the organized denomination in Charlotte, and in the declining years of the Reconstruction the present First Baptist Church was built. In 1908 it was remodeled to its present Byzantine style; in recent years substantial facilities have been added.

When Charlotte's first church was erected, Mecklenburgers for two generations had been worshipping in churches scattered throughout the section, including notably the seven original Presbyterian churches and the Providence congregation of that denomination, organized about that period.

Fine homes, elegant in structure and appointment, were also being built. Perhaps the finest surviving residence of that day, the Torrances' Cedar Grove in northern Mecklenburg, rivaled the Davidsons' Rural Hill. But there were others in which gracious living would not be interrupted until the ordeal of the War Between the States and the Reconstruction that followed that desperate struggle. "The home of Robert Wilson," for instance, writes Dr. Alexander, who knew it well, "was better known to fashionable people fifty years ago than any other place in Mecklenburg County. The family was educated, refined, wealthy, and their hospitality was held as a princely virtue. Their daughters were fond of music and dancing, inheriting this propensity from both ancestors." Around this old homestead, the historian adds, "clusters so many fond memories of a civilization that has passed, much of it into oblivion, but enough has been recorded in history to preserve the truth that the grand race of men who governed for the first seventy-five years of our political history were, indeed and in truth, leaders of men." The Robert Wilson house was erected about 1819. Long unoccupied, it fell into decay, but the drawing room was removed about a decade ago to a north Mecklenburg home and restored to its original appearance.

This was the period also in which Charlotte's methods of transportation began to show themselves inadequate to the developing community, and during the middle of the century the stage coaches were supplemented by railroads connecting Charlotte with the regions north and south. Banks, too, were beginning; in 1834, a branch of the North Carolina Bank was established. In 1853 the Bank of Charlotte was chartered with a capital stock of $300,000. Soon textile mills began operating and little Charlotte was establishing its economic leadership of a vast region.

11

A GREAT CITY EMERGES

MECKLENBURG's steady, if slow, development through the early and middle decades of the last century was halted, however, with the outbreak of the War Between the States. It would be many years before the South would show an appreciable recovery.

The Presidential campaign of 1860 in Mecklenburg, as many subsequent campaigns would be, was a bitter one. When the votes for President were counted, it was found that John Breckinridge had received 1,101; Bell, 826; Douglas, 135, and Abraham Lincoln, none.

But although South Carolina had seceded in 1860, it was not until a year later, on May 20—Mecklenburg's independence day—that a reluctant convention in Raleigh voted North Carolina's withdrawal from the Union. The Confederates' firing on Fort Sumter and Lincoln's call for troops with which to suppress the Southern "insurrection" had hastened the secession of North Carolina. In Charlotte the United States Mint was taken over for use as Confederate headquarters, and soon Mecklenburg young men were drilling. The First North Carolina Volunteers, who later were to achieve fame as "first at Bethel, farthest at Gettysburg, and last at Appomattox," within a few days after the surrender of Fort Sumter would embrace two Charlotte militia companies, the Hornets Nest Riflemen, an organization that would survive to the present, and the Charlotte Grays. Young students of the Charlotte Military Academy, whose cornerstone had been laid hardly three years earlier, and their faculty leaders entrained as a body for Raleigh to begin rigorous training as troops and to lead in the training of

119

green recruits. The Charlotte Military Academy, as the D. H. Hill School, survived until a few years ago as a part of the Charlotte school system. It stood on the approximate site of the new Charlotte Y.M.C.A. building at East Morehead Street and South Boulevard. With the closing of the Academy at the beginning of the war, the school building shortly became a hospital in which hundreds of sick and wounded Confederate soldiers were treated.

The next year, when the Confederate Naval ordnance facility at Norfolk was being threatened by Federal forces, it was moved 250 miles inland to Charlotte and established at the foot of the gentle slope on East Trade Street some two hundred yards from the Square. The selection of Charlotte as the site of the Confederate Navy Yard, as the ordnance depot was called, was probably due to the excellence of its railroad connections.

Though many naval weapons were fashioned here for the Confederate Navy, the ordnance depot had a short life, for on January 7, 1864, its warehouses and other facilities were destroyed by fire and explosion that consumed supplies and munitions valued at some ten millions.

Little action during the War Between the States occurred in the vicinity of Charlotte, though in the last days Union raiders pillaged the undefended area. But Mecklenburg, like North Carolina in general, contributed heavily of all her resources to bolster the Southern cause.

The assassination of Abraham Lincoln, the only strong arm in the Federal government to whom the South could look for fairness and decent treatment, ushered in a period that succeeding generations were to record as the most shameful in the history of the now reunited nation.

Charlotte has a peculiar connection with this tragedy, too, for it was while Jefferson Davis, President of the Confederacy, was a guest at the Bates home on South Tryon Street, near the site of the North Carolina National Bank, that he was informed of the assassination of President Lincoln. President Davis and members of his Cabinet, with several military aides, were retreating southward from Richmond and had just arrived in Charlotte on the afternoon of April 18, 1865. Lincoln had been shot the Friday night before, April 14, at Ford's Theatre in Washington, and had died the next day. This was Tuesday afternoon, and Mr. Davis was addressing a crowd that gathered at the Bates home to welcome him, when he was handed a telegram. He read it in silence. "Can this be true? This is dreadful, horrible! Can it really be true?" he is reported to have said to those beside him. He then handed the telegram to Colonel William Johnson, who read the news to the assembled crowd.

Two days later, on Thursday, April 20, President Davis presided at a meeting of the Cabinet in the Dewey Bank, which stood in the first block of South Tryon Street's western side where the present Bank of Charlotte is now situated. Later the meeting adjourned to the Phifer home on North Tryon Street—it stood on the present site of the Sears, Roebuck store—in order that Secretary of the Treasury Trenholm, who was ill there, might take part in the discussion of the South's situation, infinitely worse now that Lincoln was dead.

In June, Charlotte was occupied by Federal troops of the 180th Ohio Regiment commanded by Colonel Willard Warner. A few weeks earlier, however, a company of New Jersey troops under the command of Captain M. C. Runyan had entered Charlotte and established what he would later describe, in a letter to the adjutant of the Ninth New Jersey Volunteers, as "good order." This letter, written from "Greensborough, N. C., May 13, 1865," reveals, from a Federal soldier's viewpoint, the situation in Charlotte at the end of a disastrous war that had drained Mecklenburg, as well as the entire South, of virtually all its resources. This county had furnished to the Confederate armies more than 2,700 men, more than the number of qualified voters, approximately one of every six people in the county, adult and children, white and Negro.

Of the arrival of the troops taking command in this area and of the citizens encountered, General Thomas H. Ruger reported, in part: ". . . I arrived here and established my headquarters on the evening of the 13th. Portions of the division have arrived from time to time until now nearly the whole division is here. I have been issuing such orders and regulations as I have thought proper for the maintenance of order. I find the citizens generally disposed to accept the new situation without complaint, and apparently desirous of resuming a condition of peace and observance of law. This region of country is strongly rebel, however."

Almost a century before the forefathers of these Mecklenburgers had been similarly described by the invading Redcoats. But then the invaders had remained less than a month. This time they would remain, coming and going, for a decade. And the decade would be recorded as the worst in the county's history. Mecklenburgers who lived through those days of the Reconstruction—notably Dr. Alexander, whose bias and exaggeration, no doubt, are both understandable and forgivable—would never be able to put out of their visions those Reconstruction times that "will forever stand alone, wrapped in political blackness, when crime stalked through the land unabashed by the light of day."

Nevertheless, the Northern troops and the citizenry generally maintained friendly relationships and here and there even romance between a Northern youth and a Southern belle flourished. And in 1867, when Captain H. M. Lazelle and his troops left Charlotte, the board of aldermen thanked him and his men for their good conduct and even expressed regret that they were leaving. But at its best the decade following the war was an ordeal to the citizens generally and a nightmare to many.

It was during these critical days, more trying even than during the war itself, that the Ku Klux Klan was organized. Established to protect a defenseless area that was being exploited shamefully by politicians and adventurers who had come south to foist themselves upon a stricken people—and who were to earn the shameful epithet of "carpetbagger"—the Klan was composed of the best citizenry of the community. It bore no resemblance in membership or motive to the group that in recent years without right appropriated an honorable name. The original Klan, though it doubtless committed excesses at times, of a certainty did much toward saving Southern civilization at the time of its most desperate need.

Charlotte's population in 1860 was recorded as totaling 1,366. The abolition of slavery that followed shortly, and the influx into the village of impoverished landowners from the farms had much effect, no doubt, in launching the development that within three-quarters of a century would see Charlotte's population increased a hundred times.

Landowners now without slaves to work their acres and unused themselves to farm labor came to town and sought work in trades, business, and the professions. The county's old agrarian system was ruined; it would never again achieve its antebellum status. Such great plantations as the Torrances' Cedar Grove and the Johnstons' Walnut Grove, which were being operated on their most lavish scale at the outset of the war, would never again be small feudal principalities.

But out of the destruction of the agrarian system would begin to develop the new South, and in North Carolina the backbone of this development would be its Piedmont area, with Charlotte as the center. Within the first six months of 1867, it is recorded, a dozen stores and some 75 other buildings, many of them residences but others erected for industrial use, were built in Charlotte. For that day, when Mecklenburg and the entire South were desperately stricken, such a growth was a phenomenal achievement for so small a town. And within the five-year period following the ending of the war, Charlotte continued to grow remarkably, with money from reopened gold mines and capital supplied by Northern industrialists providing the energy to speed that development. Charlotte's fourth bank was established in 1871 to join the First National, Dewey's, and the Bank of Charlotte. It was the Merchants and Farmers, and its establishment was a further indication that Charlotte was fast becoming an important center of the South's slowly expanding industrial activity.

Four years after the last Federal troops withdrew from Charlotte—that was 1876—Zebulon Baird Vance, who had been North Carolina's war governor and was then living in Charlotte, was elected governor in a bitterly contested campaign with his Republican rival, Thomas Settle. At one of the Vance-Settle debates, held in Charlotte, an audience estimated at 4,000 attended. That was for those days a tremendous throng, but the year before had seen the gathering in Charlotte of the greatest crowd said ever to have overrun the town, whose population was now expanding rapidly. The attraction was Charlotte's celebration of the centennial of the Mecklenburg declaration of independence. Thirty thousand persons jammed in for the parade, the speaking, the fireworks. *Harpers Weekly* sent its staff artist to cover the event and he drew several illustrations, one of them showing the Square crowded with celebrating Mecklenburgers and persons from distant counties.

Like the event it was commemorating, the 1875 celebration was a two-day occasion. It began at noon on May 19 with the raising of the Confederate stars and bars to the top of a high flagpole at the Square. Governor C. H. Brogden spoke as Mecklenburg's honor guest and the New Bern band played *The Old North State* and a number especially composed for the occasion, *Mecklenburg Polka*. The re-established Union was recognized at the end of the program with the firing by the Raleigh Light Artillery of thirty-eight guns in salute to the thirty-eight states of the nation. The military was more prodigal with its powder, however, when the great day dawned; the Raleigh company and the Richmond Howitzers joined in firing one hundred guns. Trains, wagons, buggies, saddled horses and mules continued to bring thousands into the little town. At nine o'clock the procession for the parade began forming, but it was nearly noon, contemporary reports disclose, when the march to the fair grounds started. A dozen military companies and eighteen fire companies were in the parade, led by marshals on galloping horses, with bands playing and cannon booming. For those days it was a tremendous parade, and it would herald innumerable processions through the streets of Charlotte during the coming decades. More music and old-fashioned oratory enlivened the formal occasion at the fair grounds, which was recessed in the afternoon for another speaking that night at the Square. Here orators from many states, even as far away as Indiana, which sent her Governor Hendricks, extolled the courage and patriotism of the early Mecklenburgers.

One of the principal speakers was Governor Vance. Four years later he was elected to the United States Senate, where he remained in office until his death in 1884. He was North Carolina's beloved war Governor and would continue to be one of the state's political idols whose name for many a decade would work magic in politics.

But the celebration on May 20, 1898, would eclipse even the centennial commemoration. On that occasion, the *Charlotte Daily Observer* would devote virtually its entire space to a report of the celebration, which centered about the dedication of the monument to the signers of the declaration. The principal speaker of the day was former Vice President Adlai E. Stevenson, a descendant of the

Brevards and grandfather of the Illinois Governor who a half century later would be the Democratic candidate for President.

"May 20th, 1898, dawned auspiciously," the *Observer* reporter began his lengthy story of the celebration. "Not a cloud was in the sky. The sun shone brightly. The streets were free from dust. The complicated machinery of the great celebration worked smoothly. There was no hitch, no jarring, no unpleasantness. All went merry as a marriage bell.

"The procession feature of the day was splendid," the report continued. "Probably there was never a longer or more enthusiastic one in any North Carolina celebration before. It was at least a mile long. It rendezvoused on South Tryon Street and the formation of the line began as early as 8 or 8:30 o'clock. The compact mass of veterans, horsemen, carriages, floats, etc., reached from the Square back as far as Morehead Avenue. . . ."

The speaking was in the First Presbyterian churchyard. "No more beautiful spot could have been found for the ceremonies," the reporter wrote. "The church occupies the center of a square, shaded with magnificent elms, which yesterday seemed conscious of the beautiful historical drama going on beneath their wealth of beauty and foliage. . . ."

On the speaker's platform were many Mecklenburg celebrities of that day, including Mrs. Stonewall Jackson and Mrs. Rufus Barringer, widows of Confederate generals. As the veterans passed by, "Mrs. Jackson waved a Confederate flag, which she held in her hand constantly, as a response to the reverential affection and regard expressed in the faces of all who passed. . . ."

After the prayer by Rev. J. R. Howerton, D.D., pastor of the First Presbyterian Church, the reading of the Mecklenburg declaration and a prize-winning poem on the declaration by Rev. W. W. Moore, D.D., the speaker was presented by J. P. Caldwell, editor of the *Observer*.

"The speaker was interrupted numbers of times by applause," the report continued. "The patriotic sentiments, handsomely turned phrases, strength of thought and logical sequences, drew forth the appreciation of a patriotic, cultured, and discerning people."

The paper carried Mr. Stevenson's address in full. It was a lavish recital of Mecklenburg's colonial and Revolutionary history, emphasizing the action of the May 20, 1775 convention and reviewing the development of the nation during its first century's existence. "So, my countrymen, at this shrine," Mr. Stevenson closed, "the generations yet to come will learn the sublime lessons of patriotism anew; will, beneath the shadow of the noble column your hands have reared, swear again their allegiance to the holy cause of freedom and of country—the cause for which the signers of the Mecklenburg Declaration lived and died; will, in the words of the great statesman, find here 'something that will remind them of the liberty and the glory of their country.' As—'the centuries fall like grains of sand'—this monument, charged with its sacred message to the ages, will endure. History will be just, as God is just, and the names inscribed here will not perish from the memories of men."

The monument, a drawing of which occupied the front page of the paper, stood in front of the court house on South Tryon at East Third Street. When the court house was built on East Trade Street a quarter of a century later, it was moved to the esplanade in front of the new structure.

Eleven years after this celebration, Mecklenburg had as guest at another great May 20 event President William Howard Taft, and in 1916 President Woodrow Wilson was the speaker. But by then Charlotte citizens were beginning to put the emphasis on looking to the future potentialities as well as to the past's accomplishments.

Charlotte, in fact, was growing steadily during the late 1880's and into the 1890's. Numerous municipal projects were launched and private enterprise provided other needed facilities. Telephone lines were erected and hand-cranking telephones installed. Electric lights supplanted kerosene lamps; horse cars appeared along the streets and in a few years the horses were retired and electric power was substituted; new city and county buildings and a new post office building were erected; the Charlotte National Bank, with a capital stock of $125,000, was organized in 1897 and joined Charlotte's other banking houses.

At the turn of the century there was the short-lived war with Spain, to which Mecklenburg contributed four companies. Two of these companies were members of the First North Carolina Regiment, which landed the first American troops in Havana; one was a member of the Second North Carolina Regiment; and the fourth was a company of Negro troops. The census of 1900 reported Charlotte's population was 18,091. It was in this period that an industry was shaping that would be of tremendous significance not only to Mecklenburg but to the entire Piedmont region in providing power to operate innumerable industrial enterprises that over the next few decades would transform the economic life of that area. Under the leadership of James B. Duke this hydroelectric power development would expand quickly to giant size and importance; within a half century the construction of great dams and power plants along the Catawba River would materially change even the geography of the entire river region.

The new century would record Charlotte's emergence into a position of leadership among the cities of the Carolinas and a topmost rank among the municipalities of the southeast. And as the city grew, the proportion of its population to that of Mecklenburg County went up rapidly. In 1900 its 18,091 population, in fact, was hardly one-third of the county's 55,268. Six decades later almost three of every four Mecklenburgers would live within the city limits.

12

OF THINGS MEDICAL

THOUGH in no phase of Mecklenburg life would two centuries bring a greater advancement than in the field of medicine, Charlotte's present-day importance as one of the foremost medical centers in the South had its beginning in the early days of the region's settlement.

The first recorded visit of a resident physician in Mecklenburg was that of Dr. Joseph Kennedy in 1766, though earlier Dr. John Newman Oglethorpe of Rowan and a Dr. Cantzon, who is reported to have treated a man living in what is now Lincoln County, had practiced in this section. By far the most distinguished physician of the county's colonial years, however, was Dr. Ephraim Brevard, who earned his right to the acclaim of history as a leader in the fight for independence and as the principal author of the May 20, 1775, declaration. Dr. Brevard's practice was brief; he died on the eve of the achievement of independence.

A year before Dr. Brevard's death in July, 1781, Dr. Thomas Henderson, who had been a school teacher, began to practice medicine in little Charlottetown. He was the forerunner of other Hendersons who would establish themselves in Charlotte medicine in succeeding generations. He practiced for almost two score years.

Up in Hopewell about that time Dr. James R. Alexander, who would be the first of many Alexanders to become doctors in Mecklenburg, was establishing a large practice. In 1780, according to Tompkins' history of the county, "when the smallpox was epidemic in the county, having been brought here by the British and American armies," he vaccinated many of the people of his section.

"In one family he vaccinated ten persons, charging one pound currency for each 'innoculation'—probably depreciated continental currency." The doctor must have used the scab method of inoculation in which scabs from a smallpox sufferer were employed to infect the patient with the dread disease. It was a dangerous method, though usually the case developing from such treatment was much less virulent than the regular cases. In 1796 Dr. Edward Jenner developed from animals infected with cowpox what is considered the progenitor of the modern method of vaccination against smallpox, and shortly after the beginning of the nineteenth century his method was brought to America.

Treatments commonly prescribed by the doctors of a century ago seem strangely primitive. Dr. J. B. Alexander in his county history in discussing medicine in Mecklenburg tells of the methods employed by two notable doctors of the early decades of that century, Dr. McKenzie and Dr. D. T. Caldwell, who formed a partnership about 1822. "One of the partners would go and see the patients on the south of town, and the other would go and see those on the north side. They would see all the patients every other day. This was the era of bleeding. Dr. Caldwell said that if he met a fresh case and failed to bleed from any cause, he felt sure McKenzie would bleed him tomorrow. If any case was doubtful, they would compromise by leeching. . . . It was a common sight to see two or more jars two-thirds full of water with a quantity of leeches floating about ready for use, in the drug store."

Doubtless similar treatments were given their patients by two other physicians of the early days, one of whom achieved distinction in politics rather than in medicine. He was Nathaniel Alexander, who became a member of the House of Commons and later the Senate in the General Assembly, a member of Congress, and Governor. The other was Dr. Joseph McKnitt Alexander, son of the May 1775 convention secretary and the county's most noted practitioner of the early eighteen-hundreds, whose practice extended to his death in 1841.

And these methods of treatment likely changed little in the first half of the nineteenth century.

Bleeding, which evidently was the method used in the treatment of many ailments, even anemia, doubtless hastened the deaths of some patients who might have survived had they escaped it. In 1845 a hog drover from Kentucky stopped overnight in Mecklenburg at the home of a man described as a "steam doctor." In the night the Kentuckian developed a violent chill that was followed shortly by a high fever. His host promptly bled him. When he quickly became violently ill, this steam doctor sent for a regular physician. This practitioner, another Alexander, Dr. M. W. Alexander, found the man suffering with erysipelas. Dr. Alexander declared the man should not have been bled, that the bleeding would hasten the patient's death. "Don't blame him, Doctor," the hog drover said; "the damned fool had no better sense." The story indicates that at least there were some physicians even in those early days who knew that bleeding was not always advisable. The hog drover died and Dr. Alexander soon was a victim of the dread disease, and in the epidemic that followed, hundreds died in the northern section of the county.

What doctors in Mecklenburg prescribed, and what they charged for their medicines and services, in the period of the War Between the States is revealed in the records of a family of the Gilead community of northwestern Mecklenburg. The physician was the historian, Dr. Alexander himself, and the family was related to him. The statement, written on a pale blue sheet of account paper, is headed: "R. F. Blythe in account with J. B. Alexander for Medicines and Medical attention, 1868."

In the physician's careful handwriting the statement lists:

Jan.	2d.	To quinine 12 grs.	.50
"	25th	Visit & prescription	1.25
		Blue-fill & morphia	.25
"	26th	Visit & Prescription	1.25
		Morphia	.25
"	27th	Visit & prescription	1.25
		quinine	.25
"	28th	Visit & prescription	1.25
		quinine, morphia, & chloroform	.50
"	30th	Visit & prescription	1.25
		quinine	.25

Feb.	2d.	To quinine 10 grs.	.50
"	26th	To blue-fill, & calomel	.25
May	26th	To quinine	.25
"	"	To calomel	.25
"	27th	Visit & prescription	1.00
"	"	calomel, Powder & quinine	.50
Aug.	5th	To quinine	.25
Oct.	10th	Visit & prescription	1.25
		cal. & quinine	.25
"	11th	Visit & prescription	1.25
		Swt. Spts. Nitre, & quinine	.50
"	12th	Visit & prescription	1.25
		quinine	.25
"	13th	Visit & prescription	1.25
"	15th	Visit & prescription	1.25
		cal. Morphia & Nitre	.25
"	15th	Visit & prescription	1.25

$20.00

In 1896 a great advancement in the science of medicine had its beginning in Mecklenburg County. It has been contended that the first X-ray picture made in America was made at Dartmouth College "on Saturday evening, either January 24 or February 1, 1896, probably the latter," according to an article in the Dartmouth Alumni Magazine of April, 1930. But such a picture was made on January 12, 1896, at Davidson College, the late Osmond L. Barringer, Charlotte automobile pioneer and historian, pointed out, and he was positive of both the date and the fact that the X-ray picture was made. In the first place, it was on a Sunday night, not the proper time for such activities in a strict Presbyterian community, and in the second place, he was one of the students who made the picture.

With young Barringer were Eben Hardie of New Orleans and Pender Porter, who later became a physician in Brooklyn. The boys had heard of the experiments of Wilhelm Conrad Roentgen at the University of Wurzburg in Bavaria. In November of the fall before, Roentgen while experimenting with some of his laboratory equipment had noticed mysterious X-radiations. Puzzled, he continued to experiment and on January 4 he announced that he had been able to make pictures through solids, and the X-ray was born.

The Davidson students had heard of the Roentgen experiments. So this Sunday night they decided to see if a contraption they had in the laboratory, called a Crookes tube, would take a picture like Roentgen's. It appeared by the information available that the equipment was quite similar.

They located the janitor and bribed him to let them have the keys. Then they went to the dissecting room—Davidson at that time had a medical school—and with a pocketknife sawed the finger from a cadaver. The finger still had a cheap ring on it. In the science laboratory they laid out on a photographic plate beneath the Crookes tube, the finger, with two straight pins stuck through it, a folding pocket magnifying glass, two cartridges, a pin, and two rings in a pill box, and a few other small articles. Then they turned on the current. Three hours later they turned off the electricity and young Barringer developed the picture. They had, those who have given much study to the subject of the X-ray are confident, the first X-ray photograph ever made in America! It was a clear picture; it has been reproduced many times in the two-thirds of a century since it was made.

The three boys at that time said nothing of their experiment, however. But, on February 27, 1896, the picture of an X-ray photograph made by Dr. H. L. Smith was published in the *Charlotte Observer*. The picture and the accompanying article were sensational. This picture was of the hand of a cadaver. "The hand," the newspaper article revealed, "was cut off a few inches above the wrist, Dr. Smith said, and he fired a pistol ball into the fleshy part of the palm. He recalled that he then placed the hand over the photographic plate and exposed it to the ray for 15 minutes. When he developed the negative, he found that he had a perfect picture of all the bones in the hand and the bullet lodged between the third and fourth fingers in the palm."

Some weeks afterward Dr. Smith was instrumental in saving the life of a little girl who had swallowed a thimble. By using his crude X-ray equipment he was able to locate the thimble, which later was removed by three Charlotte surgeons in one of the first operations of the sort ever performed.

In 1903 Mecklenburg doctors organized the Mecklenburg County Medical Society, and it was hardly three years old when it was host to the physicians of North Carolina at the fifty-third regular annual session of the Medical Society of the State of North Carolina. The official record of the convention would describe the Charlotte meeting as "not only numerically the largest attended and with the largest number of papers ever presented, but with a professional esprit de corps manifest on every hand to an extent never before surpassed in the history of North Carolina medicine."

Dr. Edward C. Register of Charlotte was president of the state society that year; there were 41 other Mecklenburg physicians on the county society's first roster. Dr. Annie Lowrie Alexander, daughter of Dr. J. B. Alexander, one of the first women physicians in the South, presented a paper at the state meeting. A paper was also presented by Dr. James R. Alexander, who survived the meeting a half century, on the subject then being widely debated, "Physicians' Use of Automobiles." Dr. R. L. Gibbon was chairman of the committee on arrangements and called the session to order on May 29, 1906, in the Mecklenburg court house. Scores of papers on every phase of medicine were offered during the three-day convention. But the annual dinner—it did not begin until 10:30 that night—must have been the climactic event. The official journal of the convention summarizes the evening in a page and a half and describes it as "a most sumptuous banquet."

Covers were laid for 600 in the O'Donoghue Hall, the report discloses. The seats "were filled by the visiting doctors and their friends, the local doctors, and distinguished citizens of Charlotte." Fifteen toasts were offered. Charlotteans toasting and the subjects were: Dr. R. L. Gibbon, "Southern Medical Literature"; Dr. John R. Irwin, "The Age of Medical Research"; Dr. J. P. Munroe, who then lived at Davidson, "Southern Medical Schools"; D. B. Smith, Charlotte lawyer, "Medical Jurisprudence"; and W. C. Maxwell, "Our Ancestors and Ourselves." Charlotte's Dr. R. J. Brevard was toastmaster.

Revealing, if also highly amusing, was the discussion in those early days of the twentieth century of the use of the automobile by the physician. At the same time the state society was meeting in

Charlotte in 1906 a 35-page article in the Journal of the American Medical Association was being widely read and discussed; in this article 66 American doctors listed the advantages and disadvantages of using the automobile in medical practice. One Carolina physician declared "there is no question about the usefulness of an automobile to a physician. It is so much quicker and can be left standing anywhere without an attendant. It can easily cover twice the ground in a day that a horse can. . . ." Another declared that "for the overworked doctor the auto is better than medicine, vacation, or religion," and added that "it makes one forget he is living or that one day he must die." Still another in describing the proper car for a doctor's use said, among many things, that "it must *not* have pneumatic tires. . . . It must be air cooled. . . . It should have at least two cylinders. . . ." One physician reported that the cost to him of a car and one year's operation was $840.80. . . . Time saved in making trips, said he, was 40 per cent. Speed, he said, was immaterial. "Fifteen miles an hour is fast enough. There should be a law forbidding a manufacturer from building an auto that would go faster than 20 miles an hour."

In November, 1953, in a two-day program rivaling the convention in Charlotte in May, 1906, the Society commemorated the fiftieth anniversary of its founding. The scientific program was developed around papers and motion pictures discussing the use of the heart-lung machine in the surgical treatment of heart ailments.

On its fiftieth anniversary the Society's original list of forty-two physicians, of whom five were still living and a sixth, Dr. Parks M. King, its first secretary-treasurer, had just died, had increased to upward of 200, and in 1960 the membership had grown by some fifty per cent to more than 300.

The Mecklenburg Bar Association, which lists a membership almost as large as the medical group, through the years has included lawyers and members of the state and federal judiciary who likewise have achieved wide distinction. From the first lawyer of more than community esteem, Charlottetown's Waightstill Avery, to the late Judge John J. Parker, senior judge of the United States Fourth Circuit Court of Appeals, Mecklenburg has had many lawyers of unusual ability.

Perhaps no lawyer or jurist who ever lived in Mecklenburg attained the international distinction earned by Judge Parker, who came to Charlotte from his native Union County shortly after receiving his license to practice. As a comparatively young man he was recognized for his learning in the law and was nominated by President Hoover for a seat on the United States Supreme Court. But unfortunately and unfairly, he was refused confirmation by the United States Senate. By one vote, though his own Republican party could easily have confirmed the President's nomination, he lost. But without bitterness and with renewed application of his keenly analytical legal mind to the problems brought before him, he continued to serve with great distinction on the Circuit Court of Appeals. Long before his death Judge Parker was recognized throughout the nation as the ablest jurist in the federal system, including the members of the Supreme Court bench itself. His most widely publicized assignment, no doubt, was that of serving as one of the two American judges at the Nuremberg war trials.

13

A CITY NEEDS BOOSTERS

MECKLENBURG staged one of its most notable independence day celebrations with the 1916 visit of President Woodrow Wilson. After a parade from the Southern Railway station on West Trade Street, Mr. Wilson spoke from a platform at Phifer Avenue and North College Street in front of the Presbyterian College. It was on this occasion that Charlotte's Mayor T. L. Kirkpatrick addressed a standing throng for some forty minutes in reviewing the illustrious history of Mecklenburg. For years the mayor would be scolded for having spoken twice as long as the President, and many years later in her memoirs Mrs. Wilson, who sat on the platform that memorable day, would refer to the mayor's long speech. But Colonel Kirkpatrick always insisted that Mr. Wilson told him he was not feeling well and asked him to stretch out his remarks. Governor Locke Craig in introducing the President did so in one brief sentence. The Kirkpatrick-Craig-Wilson speaking sequence would long be recalled by Charlotteans who stood packed together in the warm sunshine that day to hear Mecklenburg's pioneer patriots extolled in flaming bursts of oratory. The visit of the President brought thousands of visitors to the city; it was the largest celebration of the May 20 declaration to that date in the county's history.

That afternoon President and Mrs. Wilson visited Davidson College, where Wilson had been a student during the academic year of 1873-1874. When the President walked into his old room, No. 13 on the first floor of the old Chambers Building, the freshman who was rooming there at the time, it was reported, was so dumbfounded that he dived out the window as Mr. Wilson came in through the doorway.

Less than a year after Mr. Wilson's Mecklenburg visit, the United States was officially at war with Germany. In the nineteen months before the armistice of November 11, 1918, Mecklenburg supplied some eighteen hundred inducted service men and other hundreds who enlisted in the various branches of the military and naval forces or contributed their services to the nurses' corps, the Salvation Army, the Red Cross, the Y.M.C.A. and Y.W.C.A., and other groups engaged in the nation's gigantic war activity.

Charlotte became a name known in countless American homes through the establishment on the western outskirts of the city of a great Army training camp that at times housed more than 50,000 troops. The camp was named for the Revolutionary General Greene, who on December 2 in that desperate winter of 1780 in little Charlottetown had taken command of what was optimistically termed the American Army of the South.

And to those who knew their Revolutionary War history, that winter of 1917-1918 in Charlotte would remind them of the rigorous 1777-1778 at Valley Forge. One of Charlotte's strong arguments in the city's bid for the camp was the mildness of the winter climate that would permit efficient training of the recruits. But hardly had winter begun when these young men, coming south with visions of tanning themselves in warm southern sunshine, stepped from their trains into snow deeper oftentimes than that they had left in New England or other northern or eastern sections. It snowed intermittently throughout the winter and the frozen ground made both construction of camp facilities and the training of inductees difficult. But despite the terrors of the weather and, in late 1918, a disastrous influenza epidemic that killed hundreds, Mecklenburg's reception of these young men was so warm and generous that after the war many returned to Charlotte to marry and establish homes and become influential citizens. One such soldier was Herbert H. Baxter, a Bostonian who would become mayor of Charlotte and a long-time member of the city council. Recorders of the Mecklenburg story will doubtless agree that these years marked the beginning of Charlotte's emergence as a cosmopolitan community. From World War I days on, Charlotte would continue to attract as residents citizens from many sections of the nation. Never again would the community be the leisurely paced and provincial region it had been during the first century and a half of the republic's existence.

It was in the period following shortly upon the ending of World War I that Charlotte began an expansion that within a few decades would see the population double and redouble until the 1960 census would reveal it had passed the 200,000 figure. But historians seeking the causes of this tremendous expansion would find it necessary to go back into the years before the war's beginning, for as the new century began, civic-minded citizens already were looking ahead to a burgeoning metropolis pushing outward from the crossing point of those straggling red roads of Revolutionary Charlottetown. One of the evidences of this awakening to the opportunities ahead was the meeting on October 20, 1905, of a group of such citizens in the office of a young lawyer named E. Randolph Preston and the organization of the Greater Charlotte Club, whose slogan was "Watch Charlotte Grow." And although the war interrupted this growth to some extent—in bringing soldiers to Camp Greene who would return as residents it also helped spur the city's development —Charlotte shortly began an expansion that soon thrust the Queen City into the very forefront of southeastern municipalities.

The Greater Charlotte Club, however, was not the first organization designed to promote the development of Charlotte. Three decades before its organization there had been a Charlotte Board of Trade that within a few years came to be known as the Chamber of Commerce. But the Chamber was ineffective and about 1893 ceased to function. About a decade after the Greater Charlotte Club was launched, however, it became a revived Chamber of Commerce. When the new Chamber was organized on June 17, 1915, one of the members of the board of directors was a College Street-born business man who as a boy had been employed to light the gas lamps along Tryon and Trade Streets. His name was Clarence Otto Kuester.

Four years after formation of the organization, Mr. Kuester would be prevailed upon to become its full-time executive as vice-president and business manager, and until his death on March 12, 1948, as "Booster" Kuester he would be known throughout the nation as this section's most enthusiastic and successful promoter.

The tireless energy of Clarence Kuester and the wide support his enthusiastic leadership was able to command kept the city and the Piedmont Carolinas under the appraising scrutiny of national leaders of business and industry. One of the principal reasons for the success of these efforts was the fact that the advantages of the Piedmont section as Charlotte's greater trading territory were just as enthusiastically presented as those of the city itself. Countless speeches in the larger industrial centers of the nation, innumerable brochures describing Charlotte and the Piedmont, motorcades carrying Charlotte and Carolina delegations to other cities, and receptions in Charlotte for visiting captains of business and industry hammered insistently the theme of Charlotte's importance as the center of a developing region of superior advantages.

One of the objectives of the Chamber was the promotion of the good roads movement. Mecklenburg had long been North Carolina's foremost exponent of good roads. In fact, about the time the first Chamber of Commerce was being formed in 1879 the pioneer good roads acts was passed by the General Assembly, which was applicable to Mecklenburg only, making the county the unit and levying a special tax for the construction and maintenance of roads. Mecklenburg soon became known for its macadamized roads. In 1915, the same year the modern Chamber was organized, the General Assembly established the State Highway Commission. And shortly after his election as Governor, Charlotte's Cameron Morrison led the movement to build highways connecting every county seat and principal town in the state. In all these activities in promotion of good roads, Charlotte's Chamber, led by Mr. Kuester and with the enthusiastic support of many other civic leaders, gave determined aid. Their goal was good roads not only in North Carolina but throughout the southeast and the nation. The leadership of Charlotte's Colonel T. L. Kirkpatrick in the good roads movement received national recognition with his election as president of the United States Good Roads Association. During these early years of the road building movement the Chamber sent motorcades into other states to help develop interest in the construction of connecting highways.

Charlotte's situation in almost the exact geographical center of the Carolinas was one of its more important advantages. The great network of state highways begun in the administration of Mecklenburg's Governor Morrison, who later would become both United States Senator and Representative in Congress, was carried forward under subsequent administrations. Furthermore, during the four years in office of Governor W. Kerr Scott virtually every road of more than small local importance was paved, so that North Carolina's pioneer good roads county in 1960 continues the foremost in the state in both the length of its permanent roads system and the enthusiasm of its support of highway construction and maintenance. This development of highways leading out in every direction from Charlotte to connect the city with all parts of the nation was one of the factors, of course, largely responsible for this city's becoming a motor transportation center second only to Chicago in importance in the nation.

14

...AND ARTISTS

A MERICA was plunged into World War II with the assault of the Japanese upon Pearl Harbor on December 7, 1941, and once again Charlotte was selected as the site of war facilities. Morris Field was established six miles west of the city as a military air base, the huge Ford Motor Company former assembly plant on Statesville Avenue was converted and greatly expanded into a quartermaster depot from which training camps and other military facilities in the Carolinas were supplied, and ten miles southwest of Charlotte on York Road a tremendous shell-loading plant was built to produce ammunition for the Navy. This great facility at times employed some 10,000 men and women. Before World War II ended with the capitulation of Japan, Mecklenburg furnished more than 21,000 men and women to the services, of whom nearly 600 gave their lives.

World War II and the Korean conflict of 1950-53 slowed but did not halt the advance of Charlotte and rural Mecklenburg. During the decade of the '50's the city and county entered upon the most notable phase of their accomplishment in the two-century history of the community. This development was not entirely an expansion in population and economic enterprise. Not only would business already established record remarkable growth and new industry move into Mecklenburg to bring citizens and add millions in payrolls, but also this period would mark a tremendous advancement in the other phases of community life, including the cultural.

As Charlotte through the years has gained a more pronounced leadership in the business and industry of North Carolina, there have been those, even Charlotteans, who have contended that

141

Mecklenburgers have been little interested in phases of life not related directly to economic and industrial expansion. The Chamber of Commerce and other civic groups, they insist, have limited their promotional activities to bringing in new business, building new manufacturing plants, obtaining enlarged and improved transportation facilities, and in other ways developing the financial structure. Bank clearings, carloadings, sales volume—these things, say such critics, have been emphasized to the almost complete neglect of cultural activities.

But such indictment cannot be sustained. Even the Chamber of Commerce, established primarily to foster such growth, through the years has given considerable attention to the advancement of the community's cultural life. In 1925, the one hundred and fiftieth anniversary of the promulgation of the Mecklenburg declaration, the Chamber led in sponsoring the production of what until that year had been the largest dramatic spectacle ever to commemorate the Mecklenburg independence day. Several hundred people participated in the planning, producing, and staging of *The Pageant of Charlotte and Old Mecklenburg,* written by Thomas Wood Stevens and staged in the amphitheatre of Independence Park, then a delightfully landscaped outdoor theatre upon which a few years later the city's American Legion Memorial Stadium was built. Clarence Kuester effectively coordinated the activities of the various patriotic societies and other groups promoting this sesquicentennial celebration.

And twenty-three years later Mr. Kuester was the guiding spirit in originating and organizing efforts that culminated in the staging of *Shout Freedom!* at the Southern States Fair Grounds nightly, with the exception of Sunday, from May 20 through June 3. This production was staged on an outdoor set, the largest ever built in America. A half dozen or more full-size reproductions of the buildings of Charlottetown in 1775 were erected along a stage front of two hundred yards width and across the lake from the grandstand. Some 50,000 persons saw the play in which a cast of several hundred persons presented in drama, music, and dancing a lively story of Mecklenburg's fight for freedom. This huge production was largely written, planned, promoted, and produced by Mecklenburgers, many of whom were descendants of the colonial men and women they were portraying. Mr. Kuester, who had retired from his post of executive vice-president and general manager of the Chamber of Commerce on January 1, 1948, died March 12 a few minutes after his return home from a meeting of the general committee planning the May 20 commemoration. When the play opened in May one of the performances was designated as a memorial to Charlotte's lifelong loyal son and most enthusiastic promoter.

Shout Freedom! was directed by Thomas B. Humble, who eighteen years earlier had come to Charlotte as director of the newly organized Little Theatre. This institution in the thirty years of its uninterrupted activity has produced scores of plays of importance in highly professional manner and hundreds of Charlotteans have had parts in the casts.

In this same period, too, theatrical groups, musical organizations, including the Charlotte Symphony Orchestra, the Charlotte Community Concert Association, the Charlotte Opera Association, the Charlotte Community Christmas Chorus, and numerous other organizations in the world of the arts combined to give Mecklenburg wide recognition as a center of culture as well as commerce.

Several Mecklenburgers became famous as entertainers. The best known of this group came into the national spotlight from college bands they had organized or in which they had played, including Hal Kemp and John Scott Trotter of Charlotte, left-handed violinist Johnny Long of Newell, and Betty Johnson of Paw Creek, who went from the Johnson Family singers into radio and television. Cowboy hero Randolph Scott played on Charlotte's streets in his boyhood.

Charlotte would gain added distinction as a center of cultural activities through the removal of the old United States Mint from its original place beside the post office on West Trade Street to a site in Eastover. In the movement to preserve and move the historic structure and transform it into a museum of art, many Charlotte citizens provided support, and through the years its work has been advanced with enthusiasm by such leaders as Mrs. H. C. Dwelle and Mrs. Lewis C. Burwell.

The modern interest in art might be credited to a group of artists whose contributions were made in the early decades of this century. Among them were Miss Blossom Lucas, whose studio behind her home on the corner of East Avenue and Davidson Street was a favorite meeting place of the Charlotte colony of painters. Miss Lucas was known throughout the country for the excellence of her chinaware painting, which was very much the vogue in those days. A Dr. Ortell, an Austrian, who later became an Episcopal rector and left some of his work to Sewanee, was another Charlotte resident distinguished as a painter. For a time Charlotte had as a resident, also, an artist, William Funk, who later became a favorite painter of Kaiser Wilhelm's family. Another painter of that period was Miss Annie Rankin, a pupil of the celebrated William Chase.

In recent years three native born contemporaries would be among Charlotte's more widely recognized painters, portraitists, and cartoonists. Kenneth Whitsett and Eugene Thomason work extensively in both water colors and oils, and Russell Henderson chiefly in water colors. In recent years Dayrell Kortheuer and Charles Clement Tucker, residents though not native Charlotteans, have achieved distinction as portrait painters. And in the years before these men were working, Andrew Hutchinson was widely known as a cartoonist who contributed drawings to the old humorous magazine *Life* and other notable periodicals of his day. In sculpture Professor Charles Bentine was the first resident to receive national recognition. His work included the Andrew Carnegie bas relief for the Charlotte Public Library and other Carnegie libraries in the nation and busts of Isaac Erwin Avery and John Charles McNeill. Sarah Everett Toy's work in sculpture presently has won her considerable recognition, and there are many Charlotteans doing excellent work in painting, among them Katherine Kortheuer, Alice Steadman, Dorothy DeLaney, and others probably not as well known in their fields. As Mecklenburg approaches the last third of the twentieth century, the participation of its citizens in the various arts, either as amateurs or professionals, multiplies as interest increases and broadens.

The greatest single example of such interest, even to the point of active participation, was the planning, promotion, and production of the largest symphonic drama ever staged in North Carolina. The Presbyterian bicentennial commemoration's *Voice in the Wilderness*, a play with music, song, dance and pantomime, was staged on June 14-16 and 19 in 1955 at the Southern States Fair Grounds.

The site is within a few hundred yards of old Sugaw Creek Church, where two centuries before much of the action of the drama had taken place. Significantly, a great majority of the more than 400 members of the cast—men and women, boys and girls, babies in arms, actors from a few months of age to past eighty years—were descendants of Mecklenburgers they were portraying, and many of the thousands watching likewise were descendants of those pioneer patriots and churchmen.

More than two dozen committees under the general chairmanship of A. Grant Whitney, with John McDowell as production coordinator, Dr. R. H. Stone, clerk of Mecklenburg Presbytery, as secretary-treasurer, and Rufus A. Grier as chairman of the Presbytery's bicentennial committee, directed the project from inception to completed production.

The first recorded effort in the field of arts in Mecklenburg, however, was in writing. It was titled *A Modern Poem* by *The Mecklenburg Censor*. Reputed to have been written by Adam Brevard, brother of Dr. Ephraim Brevard, it lampoons in saucy rhyme certain prominent citizens of Mecklenburg. A rare old manuscript of this poem of some 245 lines was preserved in the Charleston, South Carolina, Library. It was distributed, perhaps in a few handwritten copies, in Mecklenburg in 1777. *A Modern Poem* is published in full in the concluding pages of James H. Moore's *Defence of the Mecklenburg Declaration of Independence*.

In those early years the principal writing activities were by ministers developing subjects of a theological character, extensive research by Dr. Chalmers G. Davidson has revealed. The authors of these pamphlets were men like the Rev. James Wallis of Providence and the Rev. Samuel Craighead Caldwell of Sugaw Creek and Hopewell. The purpose of these men primarily was to refute the wave of French deism that gained a foothold in this section in the last decade of the eighteenth century. And until the period of the War Between the States the little writing that appears to have been done in Mecklenburg was in the general field of religion, including such works as collected sermons of eminent divines, or treatises on political and governmental or educational subjects. The only writer of what could be termed belles-lettres in that day in Mecklenburg, Dr. Davidson finds, was a native Mecklenburger, Philo Henderson, who wrote poems. He attended Davidson College and the University of North Carolina, returned to Charlotte as a lawyer and editor of *The Hornet's Nest* and died young, heartbroken at the death of his beautiful fiancee, tradition declares.

In 1866 General D. H. Hill returned to Mecklenburg and established in Charlotte the first literary periodical in this county. He called it *The Land We Love*. It contained poems, fiction, and essays; its primary purpose was to insure the recording of the war in a manner fair to the Confederacy.

General Hill, in his earlier career as a teacher at Davidson College, had written an algebra textbook. Some of the problems he had devised indicated quite clearly his strong Southern attachments. One problem, quoted by Dr. Chalmers Davidson in his study of Mecklenburg literature, is illustrative:

A Yankee mixes a certain number of wooden nutmegs, which cost him ¼ cent apiece, with a quantity of real nutmegs, worth 4 cents apiece, and sells the whole assortment for $44; and gains $3.75 by the fraud. How many wooden nutmegs were there?

One of the frequent contributors to General Hill's *The Land We Love* was Mecklenburg's first resident novelist. Though a native of Portsmouth, Virginia, Mrs. Fanny Murdaugh Downing came to Charlotte when the Federal forces overran the Norfolk-Portsmouth region. She continued to live in Charlotte until 1869, and it was during the period spent in this community that she wrote countless long and short poems, including many published by General Hill, and the first novel, titled *Nameless*, written in this county. It was published in Raleigh in 1865; the setting of the story is England.

For the next half century little was written in Mecklenburg, however, except of a biographical or historical nature. Among these were the books of Dr. J. B. Alexander and D. A. Tompkins that provide much of the information available concerning the first century and a half of Mecklenburg life. In 1897 Clement Dowd wrote *The Life of Zebulon Baird Vance*.

But it was in the first decade of the new century—when the Alexander and Tompkins books and the declaration arguments were published—that writing newspapermen in Charlotte would emerge from the columns of their newspapers to do books that would bring them more than local fame. Three reporters on the staff of *The Charlotte Observer*, edited by the widely known and still remembered J. P. Caldwell, would be in the forefront of a company of newspapermen who during the next half century would produce scores of volumes, several of which became international best sellers. Two of the three, Isaac Erwin Avery and John Charles McNeill, came to *The Observer* from other communities, but the third, H. E. C. Bryant, widely known as "Red Buck" Bryant, was a native of the Providence community in southern Mecklenburg. Mr. Avery's volume of essays, *Idle Comments*, published in 1905, and Mr. McNeill's *Songs Merry and Sad* and *Lyrics from Cotton Land*, would be recalled by appreciative readers decades after the deaths of the authors. Each died at the age of thirty-three, Mr. McNeill of what the physicians termed a "wasting illness."

Mr. Bryant, who wrote *Tar Heel Tales*, went from *The Observer* to other newspapers and for many years was chief of the Washington news bureaus of the New York *World* and *The Charlotte Observer*. In retirement after a distinguished career, he continues to write newspaper columns in which he reminisces entertainingly and nostalgically of the Mecklenburg of long years ago.

From the Caldwell era of Mecklenburg journalism through World War I and to the rising shadow of Hitlerism, newspapermen kept busy at their chores. But this dearth of publishing was broken in 1937 with the publication of *Marshal Ney: A Dual Life*, by LeGette Blythe, which subsequently was published in Great Britain and Germany, and for the next two decades Mecklenburg's production of books—novels, biographies, plays, books of verse, volumes on religious subjects, analytical works—kept pace with its advance in the economics of business and industry.

In this period of resurgence in writing in Mecklenburg the North Carolina Mayflower Cup, awarded annually for the best book of non-fiction and for years given for the best book in any field written by a resident of the state, was awarded to four persons closely rooted to this county. The first winner was W. J. Cash, whose book, *The Mind of the South*, earned the plaudits of critics everywhere as one of the most brilliant volumes of analysis and interpretation done in that era in the nation. Mr. Cash, though not a native Mecklenburger, wrote his book while engaged as associate editor of *The Charlotte News*. He died the year the book was released, 1941, and the Mayflower award was made posthumously. In 1958 a former editor of *The News*, Burke Davis, won the cup with his *To Appomattox*. But Mr. Davis had begun his publishing during his newspaper career in Charlotte. His first book, a novel titled *Whisper My Name*, had a Charlotte locale; it would be the forerunner of several important novels and biographical works by Mr. Davis.

The other two Mayflower Cup winners, however, were Mecklenburg natives and one has been a lifelong resident of the county. The book, *Miracle in the Hills*, by Dr. Mary Martin Sloop and Mr. Blythe, was awarded the cup in 1953. It is the account of Mrs. Sloop's unique mountain school at Crossnore. She was a native of Davidson, though much of her life was spent in the North Carolina mountains. A Japanese translation of the book carried her story into that ancient land. Mr. Blythe had served many years on the staffs of the Charlotte newspapers.

Marian Sims of Charlotte wrote both novels and short stories for the largely circulated popular magazines. Her novels, particularly *The City on the Hill*, which has a locale and characters bearing a strong resemblance to Charlotte and Charlotteans, are authentic and believable reflections of the current scene. Her *Beyond Surrender* was a venture, unique for her, into historical fiction; it is the story of the War Between the States. Other Sims titles are *Morning Star*, *The World with a Fence*, *Call It Freedom*, *Memo to Timothy Sheldon*, and *Storm Before Daybreak*, published over a decade and a half between the early nineteen-thirties and 1946.

It was a young Mecklenburg newspaperman, however, a resident though not a native, who would in the early years of World War II write a book of non-fiction that within a few months after publication became a sensational best seller and the basis of a successful motion picture. *See Here, Private Hargrove*, was a compilation of columns Marion Hargrove had sent back to *The Charlotte News*, on which he was working when he went into the Army. The book sold into the millions, and is listed as one of the twenty-one best sellers of all time. From his Army experience Mr. Hargrove went to New York, where he continued to write, and from there to Hollywood. Other books followed, none comparable in success to the first.

Before young Hargrove was scoring his amazing success, however, another *Charlotte News* writer, Tim Pridgen, had begun publishing. His first book was *Tory Oath*, a story of the Revolution in his native Bladen County. *Courage*, a story of modern cockfighting, followed. *West Goes the Road*, another novel tracing the early movement into Tennessee, was published shortly after Mr. Pridgen's moving to that state.

Two other Charlotte newspapermen collaborated to do an intriguing novel concerned with Indians thought by some to have been descendants of Croatans and members of John White's lost colony of Roanoke Island. Written by John Paul Lucas, Jr., and Bailey T. Groome, the novel is titled *The King of Scuffletown*. It was published in 1940.

In that same year one of two historical novels with locales in Mecklenburg was published. It was *Alexandriana*. The time of the story was early Mecklenburg just prior to and during the Revolution. This novel, by LeGette Blythe, was followed in 1949 by Chalmers G. Davidson's *Cloud Over Catawba*, a story, done with the care of a professional historian, about the antebellum planters living along the banks of that stream. But for the novel that would outsell all other books written by a native of the county, LeGette Blythe went for his locale to the other side of the world in the time of Christ. His *Bold Galilean* is a story of Palestine in the ministry of Jesus. Other Biblical novels by him would follow, among them *A Tear for Judas* and *The Crown Tree*.

But Mecklenburg authors with little or no newspaper writing background also produced many books. The majority of these volumes were written by ministers on subjects related to religion. This group of authors included Dr. G. Ray Jordan; Dr. Clovis G. Chappell; Bishop Herbert Spaugh, who for many years also was contributing a daily newspaper column of counsel; President Walter L. Lingle of Davidson College; Dr. John A. Redhead, Jr.; Dr.

Ernest Lee Stoffel; Rev. J. G. Garth; Bishop Costen J. Harrell; Dr. John R. Brokhoff; Dr. J. S. Nathaniel Tross; and Rev. J. A. Baldwin. In that period, too, Mary Bledsoe Gillett published a novel, *Shadows Slant North*. And Dr. Davidson added several biographies, including *Major John Davidson of Rural Hill* (which preceded his *Cloud Over Catawba*), *Friend of the People*, and *Piedmont Partisan*.

In that period, also, books of a local character, including several family journals, were published by Mecklenburg citizens. J. B. Ivey, noted Charlotte merchant who had gained distinction also as a flower grower, published his memoirs. Some years later David Ovens, his associate in merchandising, penned his memoirs under the title *If This Be Treason*. And through the years Mrs. Ethel Dabbs Thomas brought out several light novels related to the lives of textile operatives of the area.

The newspaper writing fraternity, either active journalists or of former long experience in that field, continued to produce books that propelled Mecklenburg farther into the front rank of southeastern communities distinguished for their writing achievements. In the decade of the nineteen-fifties, these writers were particularly busy; certainly no other ten years in Mecklenburg's history produced as many Mecklenburg-authored volumes, and they were in many fields.

But it was in this decade, as it neared the end, that another resident of Mecklenburg would have startling success as author of three best selling books that would attain tremendous national distribution. In hard covers and paperbacks they would sell into the millions. He was Harry Golden, and he had come to Charlotte—he was born in New York's lower East Side—and launched a unique periodical called *The Carolina Israelite*. His three books were collections of short editorials, criticisms, and essay-type articles taken in the main from the issues of his paper. Much of the selecting and editing was done by his son, Harry Golden, Jr., who had worked for several years on *The Observer*. The first book, and the most successful, was his *Only in America*. Two others, following shortly upon the first, also quickly gained enthusiastic reception. They were *For 2 Cents Plain* and *Enjoy, Enjoy!* Each book upon publication shot upward in the best selling lists and mounted to a phenomenal sales total.

And certainly not to be overlooked in the listing of Mecklenburg writers is one who in this generation surely has become the best known native of the county, the Reverend William Franklin Graham. Many books have been written by or about him. Billy Graham, reared on the dairy farm of his parents on the outskirts of the Charlotte of his boyhood, has preached to countless millions throughout the world. He will be recorded as the most noted evangelist of the era.

Significant in Mecklenburg's cultural advance in the nineteen-fifties, too, was establishment in Charlotte midway of the decade of a publishing house designed to manufacture and publish books, particularly of a community or sectional interest.

In this time of resurgence in writing, Mecklenburg was also reading. This would be shown in the mounting sales volumes of the book stores, but even more noticeably in the surging monthly circulation reports of the Public Library of Charlotte and Mecklenburg County's main library, its various branches and stations, and its traveling bookmobile. Under the leadership of Director Hoyt Galvin, the library, which enjoyed a tremendous expansion of plant in the middle years of the fifties, became an institution fulfilling an increasingly important function in the day-to-day life of Mecklenburg's citizenship. The handsome and highly functional main library on the North Tryon Street site of the old Carnegie Public Library was recognized immediately as one of the finest library facilities in the South, and the several branches in the city and at Davidson, Cornelius, Huntersville, Matthews, and Pineville, each a building planned and constructed to serve the library needs of its community, have contributed greatly to the general advancement of the arts.

So, as the 'fifties ended and emerged into the 'sixties, Mecklenburg had satisfactorily refuted the frequently heard contention that all its interests and efforts centered upon gaining population, increasing its manufactured products output, and enlarging wholesale and retail sales volumes through widening their distribution. Though the city and county were giving much emphasis to the accomplishment of these laudable economic goals, they were not doing so, it was becoming more abundantly evident each year, to the exclusion of the advancement of the cultural.

EPILOGUE

THROUGH the cabin window he watched the car coming up the lane. Then he went outside. "Light, and come in, John," he said, as the car slowed to a stop on the leaf-dappled parking circle. "Welcome to north Mecklenburg's woods."

"You've got a wonderful place here," his visitor said, climbing out to shake hands. "That drive up here through the woods, and now this house—" John paused, looking around, intrigued. "This is just the sort of writer's retreat you read about in novels, eh? But say, where's the water? I thought you were going to build on the lake."

He laughed. "The lake just hasn't got here yet." He pointed. "See those stakes? That's where the shoreline will be at high water when the lake fills up. Seven hundred sixty-foot level, top of the Cowan's Ford dam. When the lake fills, I'll be sitting right on the shore."

Inside, they stood on the wide rock hearth with their backs to the fire and talked. John twisted around to face the blazing logs. "Nothing more cheerful than an open fire," he observed. "Say, what is this?" He pointed toward an odd-looking iron piece standing in the fireplace jamb.

"It's a potrack, John. Colonial fireplaces used to be high enough for a person to stand up inside them, with a long bar from one side to another on which they would hang the potrack. See, this is two flat pieces of iron attached together so that this one slides past this other. They put this hooked end over the bar and hung the pot on the hooked end of this other piece. Then they could slide the bar up and down according to how hot the fire was. This particular potrack was made by John McKnitt Alexander. See the date: 1785? And these initials, I. P .and C. P., are thought to have been the initials of a newly married couple to whom he gave this potrack as a wedding gift."

"You like antiques, don't you?"

"Well, yes, if there's some significant history relating to them. That old candlemold there, for instance"—he nodded his head to indicate—"came from the McIntyre log cabin where that little group of Hopewell boys had the skirmish with Cornwallis' foragers—"

"Say," John interrupted, "you really should do that history of Mecklenburg. With all these books"—he waved a hand toward the filled shelves that reached the ceiling along one paneled wall—"and you must have a lot of source books among them, you should be able to write it without leaving your hideaway, eh?"

Now it was his turn to point. "I'll tell you something, John," he said. "See that typewriter-paper box over there? I've done it—the story of Mecklenburg. It's inadequate, of course; it would take several volumes to tell the story fully. But I decided to write my story of our county, as you suggested."

"And you've finished it?" John was beaming. "It's ready for the printers?"

"Except for a little trimming here and there. I'm taking it to town this week." He grinned. "Nowadays we don't have to go to New York to get a book published. But, as I was saying, this one leaves out much more that it might well include were there space available to do it. What I have tried to do is hit the high spots of Mecklenburg's amazing story. I know many readers will be disappointed that I have left out this person and that incident, but it has been necessary to make this book highly selective; I have tried to tell a readable story, giving emphasis to important highlights of Mecklenburg history rather than trying to cover the whole two-hundred-year range since colonial days."

"Good. I think that's the way to handle it. After all, as you've just said, it would require several big books to provide a history in any great detail." John paused, turned back to face the dancing flames. "Say," he said, looking over his shoulder to confront his host again, "now that you've had a fresh look at Mecklenburg over the long span of its history from colonial days to the present, what's your verdict about this—this genus *Mecklenburgus,* I believe you called him?"

He laughed. "Reviewing Mecklenburg's story from before the little log court house in the dirt roads' crossing to the new county office building on Fourth Street has been a rewarding experience. Mecklenburg had a great story in her early days, she has a tremend-out story right now, and the coming years should provide an even greater one. And, to answer your question, I think the reason is that her type of citizenship has changed very little, if any, through those two hundred years. The hard core of that hard-headed, inde-pendent, industrious, determined citizenship that was the Mecklen-burger of 1775 has come right down through the generations." He clapped his hand on his friend's shoulder. "Yes, sir, John, the genus *Mecklenburgus,* despite importations from Boston to Beaumont, from Michigan to Miami, has persisted. Snatch almost any modern day Mecklenburger from his station wagon, exchange his gray flannels for knee breeches and cocked hat and set him astride a horse, you'd never know him from one of the Alexanders or David-sons or Brevards"—he paused, grinning—"riding off through the woods to that May 19 convention!"

BOOK TWO

THE STORY OF CHARLOTTE
and
MECKLENBURG COUNTY

Topically Told by

Charles Raven Brockmann

1

EARLY SETTLERS

I N America there were centuries of frontiers. The Piedmont frontier of the Carolinas was first described by an explorer sent out, in 1670, by Governor Berkeley of Virginia. To this traveler, John Lederer, belongs the credit for opening the trading path used later by the colonists of Virginia for trading with the Indians of the Carolinas. Originally known as the Occoneechee Trail, the Catawba Trading Path became, in the first phase of exploration and settlement, the most important route through the Piedmont.

The best available information indicates that the Catawba Trading Path had its southern terminus near the present town of Concord. Successive traders opened two branches from there, one of which led to the Catawba Indian domain on the Catawba River, a few miles beyond the present site of Charlotte. The other branch went almost directly south through Waxhaw and on into South Carolina. In the early nineteenth century minor trails began to radiate from the point where Charlotte now stands, eastward to the coast of North Carolina, southward to the Charleston area and westward to where, a few miles away, iron ore had been discovered. At the confluence of these branching highways, the city of Charlotte grew. To the gold that was discovered in Mecklenburg and surrounding counties, Charlotte owes its economic stability during the first half of the nineteenth century. To the railroads, and later to the highways which followed the original pattern by converging at Charlotte, the city owes its commercial prestige.

When Lederer directed the second of his three trips in America to the Piedmont area, the Catawbas had advanced to the point of maintaining settlements with crude housing facilities and some cleared ground for agricultural purposes. They were no longer alarmed nor surprised by the occasional appearance of white men, since many members of the tribe had drifted southward from the more populous north during the previous generation. Except for marauding groups from hostile tribes, which now and then terrorized colonists during the 1740's, 1750's and 1760's, the only Indians in Mecklenburg County were the Catawbas.

They were members of an important tribe of the Siouan stock of the north. The name *Catawba* is probably derived from the Choctaw word meaning "divided" or "separated." In 1763, following alternating periods of peace and contention over real or fancied grievances on the part of both white men and Indians, an agreement was reached whereby the white men set aside an area about fifteen miles square for the use of the Catawbas. By this time the tribe had been diminished through conflict and disease from about five thousand in 1700 to less than one thousand.

The territory allotted the Indians was on the Catawba River extending into South Carolina and with the northern boundary only a few miles from the Charlotte city limit. This reservation is shown on the maps of those days as "Indian Nation" or "Catawba Nation." From time to time the size of the reservation was reduced, and in 1950 it was composed of only a few hundred acres, nine miles south of Rock Hill, South Carolina, where about 600 members of the tribe in some 162 families made their homes.

In the summer of 1959 a number of Catawbas pushed through the United States Congress a bill allowing division of the tribal assets if a majority of the individual Indians voted for such a move. While there was some opposition, a majority voted for this division and the Secretary of Interior declared on June 30, 1960, that no Indian child born after midnight July 2, 1960, would be officially termed an Indian. Thus the tribal rolls were closed forever and the Catawba nation, last organized Indian tribe in South Carolina, ceased to exist.

Authoritative information about the history of the Catawba Indian tribe can be found in the book, *A City Without Cobwebs*, by Douglas Summers Brown (1953).

"The Lost Nation," as the Catawba Indians are sometimes described, gave way to a race of sturdy pioneers, and within twenty-five years of the arrival of the first white settlers, their numbers greatly diminished. The first such settlers were Pennsylvanians, members of the Spratt family, who arrived in the 1740's. Thomas Polk is reported to have followed these pioneers for love of Spratt's daughter, whom he subsequently married. It was the grand-nephew of this couple, James Knox Polk, who became eleventh President of the United States.

Immigrants who followed the Spratts and Polk to Mecklenburg County came from three principal sources. The largest group, the so-called Scotch-Irish, became most influential in establishing the area's culture. They rolled southward from western Pennsylvania and Virginia.

The Scotch-Irish were followed by Germans who had first settled in Pennsylvania. This group located mostly in present day Cabarrus, Lincoln, and Gaston counties. About the same time there were many arrivals from lower South Carolina who found the low country too great a contrast to their native England, Scotland, Germany, and France.

So great was the numerical superiority of the Scotch-Irish, coupled with their traditional religious fervor, that they were instrumental in organizing the first seven churches to be established in Mecklenburg. The spirit of the people who built them is, perhaps, the most significant feature to be found in the historical records of Charlotte and Mecklenburg, and has greatly influenced the lives of each succeeding generation.

Living conditions in early Mecklenburg were harsh, inconceivably so to people of the mid-twentieth century. The isolation of each family, the tiny homesites buried in almost unbroken seas of forest, helped to mold a self-reliant and sturdy people. Hardship and scarcity were their intimate companions.

All examples of early colonial architecture in Mecklenburg have long since vanished. A few homes built during the Revolutionary period and shortly thereafter still remain. Among these, one of the best known is the Hezekiah Alexander house, built in 1774. This house is built of fieldstone and is two stories in height and almost square. It is on property owned by the Methodist Home of Charlotte, but leased for ninety-nine years to the Mecklenburg Council, Daughters of the American Revolution. It contains many relics of the colonial period of American history, is kept in good condition and opened occasionally for public inspection.

The most admired early home still standing in this section is the Craighead Davidson home, built by Archibald Frew in 1780. This is a white frame house on North Tryon Street, surrounded by a well-kept lawn, attractive garden flowers, trees and boxwoods. It has been occupied for many years by the family of Mr. and Mrs. Craighead Davidson and is now maintained as the home of their daughters, the Misses Mary Louise and Alice Davidson. These and other examples of early architecture to be found in the Mecklenburg area are described by James Stenhouse in his *Exploring Old Mecklenburg* (1954).

By 1760 the population of Mecklenburg was well, if sparsely, distributed and the establishment of Mecklenburg as a separate county took place in 1762. Once the county was established the necessity for selecting a county seat became a problem.

Residents of the Rocky River community sought to have the county seat in that section and, toward this end, had a bill introduced in the legislature. Citizens living nearer the spot variously named on old maps as "Charlotteburg" and "Charlottetown" hastily constructed a log structure which they designated as a courthouse, as an inducement to having their village made the county seat. In 1768 Charlotte was named "temporary county seat for 7 years," and in March 1774, it became the permanent county seat.

Charlotte began its corporate being on November 7, 1768, occupying a plot of 360 acres. This property had been deeded by Henry E. McCullough, agent for Lord George Augustus Selwyn, to Abraham Alexander, Thomas Polk and John Frohock as "trustees and directors aforesaid of a town, etc."

As their first official act, the trustees of the town laid out 100 of the original 360 acres into half-acre lots, sale of eighty of which had already been arranged. Roughly, the 100-acre plot which furnished the nucleus for Charlotte was bounded on the north by present-day Fifth Street, on the south by Fourth Street, on the east by College Street, and on the west by Church Street.

The usual house among the first built in Charlotte was built of sawed or hewn logs with cracks filled with mud or straw. There would be a large room about twenty feet square with a high roof and one or two bedroom areas partitioned with curtains or planks. Light came from only one window in each room. The common chimney was made of stone, though a few better ones were made of brick, and the roof was clapboard fastened with home-made nails.

2

MECKLENBURG COUNTY

M OST authorities on the earliest known facts about Mecklenburg County rely on *Lawson's History of North Carolina*,
by John Lawson (1714) and on *A Journey to the Land of Eden*, by
William Byrd, written about 1733 but unpublished until 1841. Of
the two, Lawson's book is the more enlightening as to the immediate vicinity of Mecklenburg County.

John Lawson was one of the incorporators of Bath Town, the
first town to be established in North Carolina. During the eight
years he remained in America, he occupied himself as a surveyor
and explorer. His principal journey carried him from Charleston,
South Carolina, via the eastern edge of the Santee, Wateree, and
Catawba rivers to the vicinity of Mecklenburg. Continuing in a
northeasterly direction along the Catawba Trading Path, he went
through Rowan, Guilford, and Alamance counties to the vicinity
of Hillsboro. From there, he moved in a southeasterly direction
toward the settlement on the coast.

While it is not certain that Lawson actually traversed the present
county of Mecklenburg, he came near enough for his comments
upon natural resources and the Indians to apply to this county. He
termed it "a delicious country."

William Byrd, whose account was based on his travels through
North Carolina in 1728, also liked what he saw: "The course from
Roanoke to the Catawba lies through a fine country that is watered
by several beautiful rivers. . . ."

It was into this favored land that Thomas Spratt and others came.
During the 1740's there was such an influx into this section that by

1762 the legislature, meeting in New Bern, granted a petition for a new county to be formed from Anson County. The act creating Mecklenburg County was passed December 11, 1762, to become effective February 1, 1763. The county was named Mecklenburg in the hope of pleasing King George III of England and gaining favor, since his Queen was a native of the district in Germany bearing the name.

In 1768 Tryon County was formed from Mecklenburg, and in 1792 another large slice of Mecklenburg went to create Cabarrus County. These losses were followed by several minor changes in boundary lines between counties, the final area to be removed from the original Mecklenburg going to form Union County in 1842. This left Mecklenburg an irregularly shaped 549 square miles, or 347,520 acres, lying in the south central part of North Carolina. The southern boundary of Mecklenburg rests on the South Carolina border. The county lies on the eastern edge of the Piedmont section of the Carolinas. Typical of southern Piedmont, the county's general surface consists of a series of gently rolling slopes to almost level interstream areas, becoming more broken and hilly as the larger streams are approached.

Elevations throughout the county vary considerably. From 300 feet above sea level along bottom lands of the river, the elevation ranges to 795 feet at the western edge of Charlotte. The city's average elevation is 750 feet, dropping to 570 feet at Pineville, fifteen miles to the southeast.

The average annual temperature of Mecklenburg is about 60 degrees F., with about 100 degrees for the hottest day and 5 degrees below zero for the coldest. The annual precipitation ranges from 35 to 68 inches. The latest date for a killing frost is about April 1, with the first frost in the fall about November 1, permitting agricultural and horticultural activities to be pursued with only a short interruption during the winter months. Average monthly precipitation is from three to six inches with maximum rainfall in June, July, and August, at which time it is most needed for growing crops. The wind blows from a southwesterly direction most of the time with average velocity of about six miles per hour, carrying considerable moisture. These winds are seldom severe enough to cause appreciable damage.

The county is well drained. Its general slope is to the south and southwest except along the eastern border, which slopes to the east. There is a ridge extending from the northern boundary to the northeastern (Derita) area of Charlotte, thence to the Mint Hill area. All of the water to the east of this ridge flows into Rocky River, while all to the west flows eventually into the Catawba River, largest stream in the county, falling 190 feet between the northern and southern boundaries of the county. The principal tributaries of the Catawba River are Davidson, McDowell, Long, Paw, and Steele creeks. Those draining into Rocky River are West Branch, Clarks, Mallard, and Clear creeks.

In Mecklenburg County more than a quarter of a million people make their homes, most of them within the 65 square miles that is Charlotte. In the county are five towns: Huntersville, Cornelius, Davidson, Matthews, and Pineville, and the villages of Newell, Derita, Mint Hill, and Paw Creek.

Government

Prior to the Civil War, the government of Mecklenburg County was conducted largely by Justices of the Peace, who acted through a county court. The General Assembly set forth certain necessary functions for the operation of the county and authorized the county court to engage personnel to perform the duties of the various positions created.

In 1868, the government of the county was placed in the hands of five commissioners elected by the people. This form is still in use. In actual operation, the Chairman of the Board of Commissioners is the chief executive of the county. His duties correspond to those of a city manager in a municipality, in that he carries out mandates of the board of which he is chairman.

To such obvious responsibilities in the early days as entering settlers on land and connecting them with roads; recording deeds, mortgages, and conveyances; settling estates and policing the county, there was added in the 1830's the duty of providing a "system of common and convenient schools." The 1880's saw the beginning of public health activities, and about 1900 public library service was begun. By 1960 there were about 700 people in the employment of Mecklenburg County.

It took increasingly large amounts of money with which to pay these people as their services became necessary, and to perform governmental functions. The money had to come from taxes.

Year	Property Valuation	City tax rate per $100 value	County tax rate per $100 value
1925	$163,744,296	$1.92	$1.00
1950	$259,659,145	$1.97	.97
1960	$794,500,000	$1.50	$1.56

The first courthouse in Mecklenburg was located on what later became Independence Square, where Trade Street crosses Tryon Street in Charlotte, boastfully renamed by some, the "crossroads of the Carolinas."

The first crude log courthouse was replaced in 1810 by a brick building of about the same size constructed on the same site. This building was overhauled about 1829 and served until 1845 when a substantial two-story building was erected on the northeast corner of Trade and Church Streets, later identified for sixty or more years as the location of the Selwyn Hotel. For some months in 1865 the records of the State Department of the Confederacy, including the Great Seal, were stored in this courthouse.

The fourth courthouse in Mecklenburg, built in 1896 and occupied in 1897, was located on the southeast corner of Tryon and Third Streets. For that period it was quite a pretentious building and one that was expected to serve indefinitely. However, by the early 1920's, it became apparent that so much more room would be needed that enlarging it was out of the question. Much of Charlotte's early history occurred on the spot where the courthouse stood. This was the site of Queens College, later Queens Museum and, still later, Liberty Hall Academy. On this lot were buried a number of Cornwallis' troops who were killed in the Battle of Charlotte, September 26, 1780. Some of their bones were found when excavations were made for the courthouse .

Bowing to necessity in 1925, the commissioners acted with dispatch in acquiring property and erecting a new courthouse, the fifth for Mecklenburg. The building occupies the greater part of a city block bounded by Trade Street, Fourth Street, Alexander Street, and Myers Street. The cost of the new building with added equipment was approximately a million dollars, about half of which was raised from sale of the property which had been vacated. This building, 700 East Trade Street, was formally opened in the spring of 1928 and is still in use, notwithstanding even more crowded conditions than existed in the building relinquished in 1928.

The present courthouse is in a beautifully wooded square and adjoins a like block on which is located the Charlotte City Hall.

To alleviate the inconveniences incident to crowded conditions in the present courthouse, Mecklenburg voters on November 4, 1958, authorized bonds in the sum of two million dollars for the purchase of property on which to build an annex to the courthouse, or more properly, a county office building, and 500 thousand dollars for modernizing the main building.

There has never been a serious scandal with any city or county official or office. Even with this enviable record and the excellent manner in which Mecklenburg public affairs have been handled, the news of improved methods elsewhere has led many people to advocate consolidation of the county and city governments, in the hope of decreasing costs and improving efficiency. One of the early leaders in this movement in North Carolina was Miss Carrie McLean, a member of the Mecklenburg delegation to the legislature in 1927.

The trend toward consolidation began in Mecklenburg in 1929 when public library service became jointly financed. Then, more from necessity than with the idea of promoting city-county consolidation, the health departments of Charlotte and Mecklenburg began joint operations July 1, 1953. Later, and probably because of the success of the health departments, arrangements were completed for submitting both city and county tax statements together, and receiving payment in one place. Then, on June 30, 1959, the voters of Charlotte and Mecklenburg took a major step toward eventual complete consolidation, by authorizing the combining of the two public school systems. At the same election a large bond issue was approved for the purpose of increasing physical facilities throughout the consolidated public school system.

The consolidation of the school systems of Mecklenburg came just ten years after the completion of a survey made by the Institute of Government of Chapel Hill. This survey was ordered by the County Commissioners and the City Council in order to "find out whether or not it is feasible to consolidate the City Government of Charlotte and the County Government into one governing body for Charlotte and Mecklenburg County." Miss McLean's dream may indeed come true, as have those of so many other progressive spirits whose names adorn the pages of Charlotte and Mecklenburg history.

3

CITY GOVERNMENT IN CHARLOTTE

S INCE its birth two hundred years ago the crossroads village that
was once known as Charlottetown or Charlotteburg has grown
into the largest city in the Carolinas and one of the most important
industrial and distribution centers in the nation. One of the distinctive features of this growth has been the thoroughness with which
newcomers have been assimilated. An observant writer once
said: "One adopts Charlotte ways or one does not, in which latter
event, one soon moves on." And many did, both native born and
newcomers. Charlotte actually lost about one-third of its population between 1830 and 1850. At the end of the Civil War, however,
Charlotte was one of the first towns to catch the vision of an industrialized South. Hydroelectric power from the Catawba River
made it the heart of a large textile area, while its business leaders
were working energetically to attract new and diversified
industries.

Notwithstanding acceptance of the new industrialism, older residents had a tendency to cling to the past. Modern Charlotte was
considerably behind other Southern cities in relenting before
mounting pressure for open Sundays, legalized liquor and the liberal behavior pattern which followed World War I. It was not
until June 4, 1941, that the City Council, defying the vociferous
opposition of a die-hard group, passed, by a vote of 8 to 3, an ordinance permitting Sunday motion pictures and outdoor sports.

In strange contrast to Charlotte's reputation as a church-going
center are its persistently high crime rate and traffic death toll.
Remedial measures for this state of affairs are among the most discussed subjects at meetings of religious, civic, and study groups.

For a city of its size, Charlotte may still be described as conservative, but not unreasonably so. Twenty years ago a research specialist, reporting on Charlotte's governmental affairs, wrote: "The state tax limitation for parks and recreation necessitates the present niggardly budget of $22,000, but it is unlikely that the council would be willing to appropriate more if it could." The 1960-61 budget of the Charlotte Parks and Recreation Commission was $768,044.25. The same earlier authority said, "The city has no swimming pool ... there are no city hospitals etc." Today, there are three swimming pools and the 352 bed and 36 bassinet Memorial Hospital. If more need be said, consider the mildness of Charlotte's shock over the Supreme Court's desegregation decision, and the city's graceful acceptance of the solution to public school integration devised by local school authorities.

The history of the city began in 1767 when a courthouse was built in Mecklenburg County, where the Catawba Trading Path crossed the trading route of pioneer settlers. On November 7, 1768, the state assembly created the town of Charlotte in "An Act for Establishing a Town in Mecklenburg County." This act, which was equivalent to Charlotte's first charter, required less than two printed pages, whereas the present city charter fills forty-two pages, supplemented by a Code of Laws requiring about 600 pages. The quaint, original charter reads, in part, as follows:

"I. Whereas it has been represented to this Assembly that 360 acres of land granted to John Frohock, Abraham Alexander, and Thomas Polk, As Commissioners for the County aforesaid, for erecting a courthouse, prison and stocks; which 360 acres was afterwards laid off into a town and commons . . . on some of which good and habitable houses have been erected, and that by reason of the healthfulness of the place aforesaid and convenient situation thereof for trade, the same might become considerable if it was erected into a town, by lawful authority."

With some slight alterations, such as changing the title of the Chairman of the Commissioners to Intendent and, later, to Mayor, the commission form of government established by this enabling act was used until the Civil War. During this war, a few volunteers acted as patrolmen, and these were followed for a few years by the Federal troops occupying Charlotte. It was in the beginning of this latter period that a town official was thoughtful enough to close the city's books and hide them until some time after the war. The entry in Minute Book 3, Page 38, of the town council, reads:

"No further meetings of the board were held after March 23, 1865, events culminated so rapidly. Most of the store houses in town were filled with sick Confederate soldiers sent from Virginia and elsewhere to get out of the way of the advancing Yankee army.

"The town books and papers were sent off to the country, the clerk betook himself to the woods with the valuables of the Bank of North Carolina, Richmond fell, Lee's army surrenders, Johnston's army surrenders.

"The Confederate President and his cabinet held their last meeting in the Br. Bank Building in Charlotte, then departed Southward and the Confederacy was at an end." The minutes were signed by T. W. Dewey, town clerk at the close of the Confederacy.

Following the withdrawal of Federal troops, an aldermanic form of government was adopted with aldermen and mayor elected by the people. The number of aldermen varied from time to time, reaching a total of twenty-two in 1907. Political reforms, necessitated by Charlotte's industrial growth, were accomplished by a change from the aldermanic to commission form of government in 1917. At that time, three commissioners replaced an assortment of elected officials which included the mayor, twenty-one aldermen, the city clerk, tax collector, and water commissioners.

While the commission form worked well in comparison with the preceding aldermanic government, it failed to keep abreast of the needs of a growing city. In 1929, by a vote of 4,436 to 2,496, a city manager and council plan of government was instituted, whereby a professional city manager was employed to execute policies and instructions issued by a board of seven elected councilmen. Hardships imposed by the depression of 1929-1933 shook the faith of many in the city's new form of government, but during the incumbency of Mayor Ben Douglas, 1935-1941, and City Manager James B. Marshall, faith was restored, and has since been happily maintained.

The boundary lines of the original 360 acres which the first commissioners governed were, roughly, Brevard Street on the east, Poplar Street on the west, Seventh Street on the north, Third Street on the south; in all, about seven-tenths of a square mile. Slowly and not at all steadily, the city has grown to its present metropolitan status:

Year	Sq. Miles	Population	Density Sq. Mile
1815*	.74	Est. 450	608
1850	1.68	1,065	634
1885	2.23	8,405	3,769
1910	12.76	34,014	2,664
1930	19.36	82,675	4,270
1950	29.79	134,042	4,499
1960	65.10	201,564	3,095

*City limits first registered in 1815.

These extensions have brought into the city many real estate subdivisions which once ringed the city. Dilworth, Charlotte's first adventure into suburbia, was built by Edward Dilworth Latta. The Elizabeth section, including Elizabeth Avenue, was named for Mrs. Ann Elizabeth Watts, wife of a Durham tobacco magnate, and mother of Mrs. Charles B. King. It was Mrs. King's husband who founded a Lutheran college, largely with funds provided by his father-in-law, and named it Elizabeth College in honor of his mother-in-law. The name was given to the residential area that grew up around the college. Myers Park was once the farm of Jack S. Myers, while Eastover was given its euphonious name by the developer, Mr. E. C. Griffith. The Belmont section takes its name from an ancient spring which was a popular picnic ground, but no one knows why the spring was originally named Belmont.

Seversville was named for the Severs family, early residents of the vicinity. Biddleville grew up around Biddle University, named for early benefactors, members of the Biddle family of Philadelphia. The institution was later renamed Johnson C. Smith University. Wilmore honors Messrs. Wilson and Moore, two Charlotte mayors who formerly owned the property. Wesley Heights was named for a church which, in turn, took its name from a former favorite pastor. Chantilly was named by its developer, Paul Chatham, for a province in France, but no special significance seems to be attached to the names of most sections.

Charlotte was late in acquiring a separate building for use as a city hall. Few early officials devoted their entire time to municipal affairs and, quite naturally, performed such duties wherever most convenient. In 1879 the city clerk had an office in a building next door to the courthouse which then fronted on Trade Street at the northeast corner of Church Street. At the time the mayor had a small office on East Trade Street in a building which housed the Hornet Fire Company, the city's first fire-fighting force.

During the 1880's the building (demolished in 1960) at the northwest corner of Tryon and Sixth Street came to be known as the City Hall and housed the city clerk, tax collector, Police Department, and city jail. In 1891 a new city hall was built on the southeast corner of Tryon and Fifth Streets, and served until the present building at 600 East Trade Street was occupied in 1927.

Like the government of Mecklenburg County, the government of the city of Charlotte has not only been free from scandal, but the men who have held office have been conservatively energetic in handling the city's affairs. Regardless of honesty or ability of successive officials, however, Charlotte, in common with other North Carolina cities, has very little home rule. Officials must work under an outmoded legal and constitutional system which requires the state legislature to authorize all acts of consequence involving municipal affairs.* When the new city hall was built, a special act of the legislature was necessary in order to sell the old building, even though the proceeds were to be applied to the cost of the new.

In the early years of organized government in Charlotte, all policing, fire fighting, and road building were on a voluntary basis, or on assignment by the commissioners. Whatever revenue the town received came from the sale of lots and the imposition of fines and penalties. The first city tax was levied in 1824 when each male was required to pay "$1 in lieu of street work." The next year a tax of ten cents was levied on each $100 worth of property, and in 1839 license taxes were required of grocery stores, liquor dealers,

---

*When the Public Library was offered an opportunity to publish this history, a special act of the legislature was needed to amend the Library's charter.

merchants, peddlers, and entertainment groups. Thereafter, taxable items and rates were fixed annually to meet the needs of a town which grew very gradually until about 1900, more rapidly for the next few years and with breathtaking speed after 1940.

As succeeding governmental bodies were confronted with the necessity for providing new services, there have been instituted various departments, commissions, and authorities.

Charlotte City Government in 1961

Charlotte is governed by a council-manager system. The council, or legislative body, is composed of a mayor and seven residents, elected for two-year terms by voters of the city in odd-numbered years. The council member receiving the largest number of votes becomes by custom the mayor *pro tem*. These positions are sought and held through other than financial motives since the annual salary of the mayor (1960) is $3,600, and that of councilmen $1,200 per year.

The mayor is the titular head of the government, serves as official representative of the city, and presides at council meetings. He makes appointments to boards, commissions, and other positions authorized by the city charter. The council sets the policies, in open weekly meetings, under which the city government operates, and appoints a city manager at a 1960 salary of $17,500 annually, whose duty it is to carry out the policies.

The city manager has authority to appoint and dismiss all department heads and employees except those appointed by the council. (Job titles and salaries in 1960 were as follows: City Clerk, $7,092; City Accountant, $9,250; Collector of Revenue, $8,500; City Treasurer, $9,000; City Attorney, $10,600; Judge of Recorder's Court, $9,750; City Solicitor, $7,500; Judge of Domestic and Juvenile Court, $9,750.)

City employees and advisors work under or for departments, commissions or boards, and authorities. The chief administrative departments are police, fire, building inspection, health,[1] engineer-

---

[1] See Chapter 11.

ing, motor transport (garbage collection and street cleaning), taxes and licenses, and water.

The principal boards and commissions, all members of which serve without compensation, are: Airport Advisory Committee, Boxing and Wrestling Commission, Electrical Advisory Board, Fireman's Relief Board, Health Advisory Committee, Park and Recreation Commission,[2] Charlotte-Mecklenburg Planning Commission, Zoning Board of Adjustment, Civil Service Commission, Redevelopment Commission.

The following are responsible for municipally owned properties but conduct their affairs separately and apart from the city's other financial operations: Mecklenburg County Board of Education,[3] Memorial Hospital Authority,[4] Rehabilitation Hospital Board,[5] Charlotte Housing Authority, Auditorium-Coliseum Authority,[6] Veterans' Recreation Authority, Board of Trustees of the Public Library of Charlotte and Mecklenburg County.[7]

Law Enforcement

On November 15, 1933, four members of the notorious Touhy Gang from Chicago robbed a mail truck of $120,000 in one of Charlotte's most spectacular crimes. This case skyrocketed Chief of Police Frank N. Littlejohn to national fame when his discovery of a Chicago laundry ticket near the scene of the crime led to the arrest of the gangsters and recovery of some of the money.

Such spectacular crimes are not "normal" for Charlotte. But Charlotte people are responsible for more than their share of heinous crimes, as explained below. The following news item is reprinted in full from the *Charlotte Observer* for February 28, 1960:

"MURDER RECORD LOOMS. Charlotte, which set a 19 year record for murder in 1959, is off to a fast start this year.

---

[2]See Chapter 12.
[3]See Chapter 5.
[4]See Chapter 11.
[5]See Chapter 11.
[6]See Chapter 9.
[7]See Chapter 5.

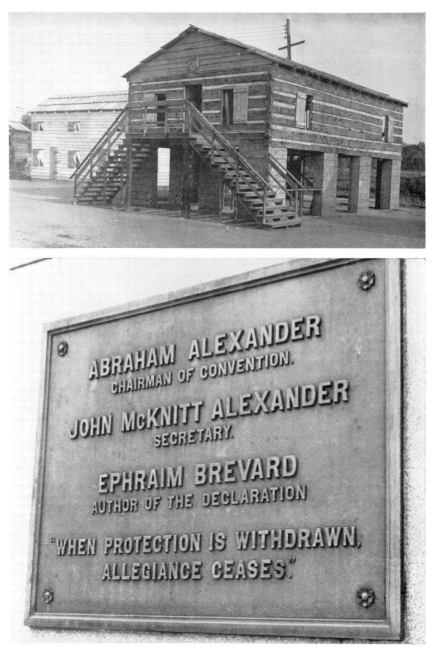

Above: Reproduction of Mecklenburg's first courthouse erected for the pageant, *Shout Freedom!* *Below:* Plaque on the Signers Monument honoring signers of the Mecklenburg Declaration of Independence.

Charlotte's third courthouse on the northeast corner of Church and Trade
Streets, showing "standpipe" in rear, about 1890.

Occupied in 1897, the fourth Mecklenburg County Courthouse was on the site of Liberty Hall, southeast corner of Tryon and Third Streets.

Charlotte City Hall in the 1880's on the northwest corner of Tryon and Sixth Streets.

Charlotte's first real City Hall, built in 1891, on the southeast corner of Tryon and Fifth Streets.

Above: Charlotte City Hall, 600 East Trade Street, occupied in 1927.
Below: The fifth Mecklenburg County Courthouse, occupied in 1928.

Above: United States Post Office and Court House, built during World War I at Mint and West Trade Streets and enlarged in 1934. *Below:* The United States Mint in its original location on the present Post Office site. Shipp Monument in foreground.

Queen Charlotte, 1713-1784, wife of George III of England. Before her marriage she was Princess Charlotte of Mecklenburg-Strelitz. Charlotte and Mecklenburg County were both named in her honor.

"Five people have been murdered here so far. At the same point last year, only one murder had been committed.

"The greatest proportion of Charlotte murders are classified as 'crimes of passion,' and usually are the result of a fight or sudden outburst of temper.

"And, in the past, weapons used have varied.

"But all of the five people killed this year have died of gunshot wounds.

"In 1959, 33 people were murdered here. This set a record topped only in 1940, when the Queen City became known as 'the murder city' of America.

"Harassed policemen investigated a total of 46 murders in that year."

The great proportion of such crimes are committed by Negro citizens. An analysis would undoubtedly disclose that the Negroes who commit crimes of violence are not much more improved educationally or economically than they were as slaves, a condition to be regretted and corrected as speedily as possible. To some degree it was unavoidable in a locality impoverished by the Civil War and Reconstruction. Charlotte's prosperity is of comparatively recent origin. In like manner, the high rate of crime among white persons in Charlotte most certainly is influenced by the group experiences responsible for the violence of their reaction to all patriotic, religious, and other human emotional situations.

Modern police protection began with the organization of a Police Department on January 11, 1866, with an Intendent at $1,000 per year, and eight patrolmen who were paid $50 per month. There were no appreciable changes until 1901 when sixteen additional patrolmen were employed. Since then, the growth in both equipment and personnel has been rapid.

Today the Charlotte Police Department consists of six divisions: Patrol, Traffic, Detective, Juvenile, Research, and Training. There are approximately 300 officers with minimum monthly pay of $300, 30 civilian employees, 40 patrol cars, 25 motorcycles, a patrol wagon, and a mobile crime laboratory. Since 1925 the Police Department has occupied its own building at East Fourth and Alexander Streets, adjacent to City Hall.

Fire Protection

The American LaFrance fire engine, now on display at 1903 East Boulevard, served as Charlotte's most useful piece of fire-fighting equipment from about 1896 until 1925. No phase of life in Charlotte has as much sentiment attached to it as that of the volunteer firemen. The memories crystallized by that old fire engine will never die for those who experienced the excitement of fire fighting before the days of motor vehicles.

From the founding of Charlotte until late in the nineteenth century, all fire fighting was done by volunteers. The most important days in each year to firemen were those upon which the annual Fireman's Tournament was held in the various cities of the state, for staging contests between all types of equipment. Few events in the world of sports today can compare with the excitement of steam fire engines, drawn by charging steeds in double or triple harness, racing over the prescribed course, belching flames and smoke; the fast hose coupling and plug connecting by the hose companies, the rapidity and hazard of the climb up extended ladders, or the speed with which reelmen raced on foot to the finish line, where unwound hose was coupled to the "plug" and the dramatic yell given for "Water." The climax of each tournament was the grand parade of all equipment, bands, celebrities: participating firemen in the traditional red belts, blue shirts, metal hats, and other regalia of the fire-fighting profession, proudly displaying trophies won in past events.

No one who has heard the eerie sound of the midnight alarm tolled by the bell in the courthouse yard will ever forget the tense moments that followed, while the awakened populace counted the taps of the bell in order to locate the section of town from which the alarm originated; nor the ear-splitting, staccato blasts as the flames became visible to the first locomotive engineer, and the din as other engineers spotted the danger. It was the custom until well along in the twentieth century for locomotive engineers to awaken the populace whenever and wherever a burning building was seen, a custom credited with saving many lives, especially in rural sections. Volunteer firemen were men of strong sentiment and proud of their organizations. A few are still around to indulge in spells of nostalgia when reading of the activities, in outlying sections of Mecklenburg, of organizations similar to the old-time fire-fighting units in the city.

Some of these senior ex-firemen still gather around fire stations on summer afternoons to regale their highly trained and expensively equipped successors with accounts of past incidents and achievements. A favorite story concerns Neptune No. 2, a hand-pumped fire engine which was perhaps Charlotte's first piece of fire equipment. After serving from 1866, first with a white unit and then with the Negro "Neptune" unit, until 1891, the engine was sold to Marblehead, Massachusetts, for $100. In 1906 it was resold to Westfield, Massachusetts, for exhibitions and tournaments. At Westfield, this sturdy piece of equipment suffered the most humiliating experience possible when it burned in a fire which consumed the garage in which it was housed.

Charlotte's most dramatic fire story has to do with the burning of the Belmont Hotel, upon which occasion Neptune No. 2 saw its last local service. This fire, in 1891, occurred on a night when the temperature was near zero. After fighting most of the night, firemen had to cut away the ice which had formed on the front of the building, in order to get at the flames beneath. All through the day and far into the second night the Neptunes and other volunteers fought to subdue the flames.

The Belmont Hotel fire was notable for the series of fatalities that followed in its wake. The woman who overturned the lamp which started the fire was burned to death. Mr. Cul Eagle received a broken leg by falling over a piece of lumber, from which injury he died. One Negro fireman smashed an egg in the pocket of a brother fireman who whipped out a pocket knife and sank it in the jugular vein of the offender, causing almost instant death.

Nearly a quarter of a century later, July 1, 1914, Charlotte lost its only fire chief to be killed in action. Chief J. H. Wallace and Captain W. B. Glenn died instantly when powder exploded in the burning barn of Contractor John B. Hawkins on South Cedar Street. Three other firemen were injured. This accident was recalled on July 9, 1959, when exploding chemicals injured a number of firemen in a building being demolished at 300 Templeton Street.

Among Charlotte's disastrous fires, the largest occurred January 7, 1864, when the Confederate Depot and Ammunition Warehouse was burned with an estimated loss of ten million dollars. On December 17, 1922, the six-story Trust Building at 212 South Tryon Street, housing the Academy of Music and many offices, was almost completely burned, as was the three-story building next door occupied by Brockmann's Book Store. Charlotte's most horrible fire occurred March 15, 1940, when the Guthery Apartments on North Tryon Street burned, killing eight persons and injuring six others. Of all Charlotte fires, the most spectacular was that of the 54-year-old, block-long Southern Railway Freight Station, June 24, 1954.

Such distinctive names as Hornet Steam Fire Engine Company, Pioneer Steam Fire Engine Company, Independence Hook and Ladder Company, Neptune Hand Fire Engine Company (Negro), and Yellow Jacket Fire Engine Company (Negro) are gone now. They have given way to prosaic Station No. 1 through Station No. 12 in 1960. Personnel has increased from not more than twenty-five volunteers to 352 in 1960. Equipment now consists of about twenty engines of various types, six ladder companies and fourteen miscellaneous pieces. The first piece of motor equipment was acquired April 1, 1912.

W. Hendrix Palmer, fire chief from 1927 until 1948, was president of the International Association of Fire Chiefs in 1940, and his successor, Chief Donald S. Charles, president of the same international organization in 1957.

Charlotte Water Supply

Before 1900 Charlotte's water, which now comes from the Catawba River, originated in a spring-fed reservoir of two small lakes on land which is now Independence Park. Later, water from Sugaw Creek was pumped into the reservoir and from thence into a tall standpipe in the rear of the courthouse, then located on the northeast corner of Trade and Church Streets, where the Selwyn Hotel now stands. Facilities were increased from time to time to meet the growing needs of the city. A huge filtering plant was built just beyond Johnson C. Smith University, at the highest point in the city; today the city's water comes through one of the most modern filtration plants in the South, on Oakdale Avenue.

Housing Authority

A little more than a year following passage of the United States Housing Act, the Housing Authority of the City of Charlotte was created with five members, sworn in by Mayor Ben E. Douglas on December 7, 1938. On February 16 following, Harold J. Dillehay was appointed executive director, assuming office March 1, 1939, a position he has since held with marked success.

The first project of the Charlotte Housing Authority was the securing of a loan of $2,104,000 with which Piedmont Courts, for white families, and Fairview Homes, for Negro families, were built. Later, with passage of the National Housing Act in 1949, an additional loan was secured for construction of Belvedere Homes and Southside Homes.

Charlotte-Mecklenburg Planning Commission

The Charlotte-Mecklenburg Planning Commission was established September 8, 1954, at a joint meeting of the City Council and Board of County Commissioners. The new organization succeeded the Charlotte Zoning Commission which had been in operation since June 1946. William E. McIntyre, a professionally trained planner, became the first Planning Director and has since served with distinction, employing several trained assistants whose duty it is to chart the physical growth of Greater Charlotte.

Zoning Board of Adjustment

In accordance with the requirements of the state enabling act covering property zoning, the Charlotte Board of Zoning Adjustment, consisting of five members, was created June 28, 1947. On January 28, 1956, the membership of the board was increased to ten, five members each from the city and county, a provision made necessary by the forthcoming annexation of a huge perimeter area by the city.

A concurring vote of four-fifths of the members present at any meeting is necessary to reverse any order, requirement, or decision made by the Chief Building Inspector.

Pet Department

Created July 10, 1944, and administered during the first fifteen years by Thomas J. Revelle, Superintendent, the Pet Department of the City of Charlotte serves society by protecting the interests of pets, especially dogs, of which there are more than 40,000 in Mecklenburg County. As of 1960 the Pet Department enforces a City Ordinance of eighteen sections, and for that purpose requires an executive office in the City Hall, an animal shelter on Shuman Avenue, and personnel consisting of a superintendent, four day wardens, one night warden, three clerical workers, two cleaners, and one night watchman.

Charlotte Politics

The presidential election of 1928 will serve to tell a lot about the political and social make-up of Charlotte and Mecklenburg County. Democratic nominee Alfred Emanuel Smith, lawyer, governor of New York State, acknowledged liberal, was a foe of prohibition and a Roman Catholic. The Republican nominee was Herbert Clark Hoover, mining engineer, Secretary of Commerce during the Coolidge administration, conservative personally and by political inheritance, and Protestant (Quaker).

Charlotte, in common with the rest of North Carolina, hadn't voted Republican for nearly a generation and was in no mood to do so in 1928. The city was predominantly Protestant; in fact, it had been only a few years since the people had first permitted the employment of a Roman Catholic as a teacher in the public schools. Fortunately for the collective Protestant conscience of the community, there was also the question of the repeal of the Eighteenth (Prohibition) Amendment to the Constitution of the United States. So, no Protestant had to vote against Al Smith because of his faith. Smith advocated repeal of the Prohibition Amendment and Charlotte was a dry community, notwithstanding the two favorite cliches of the day are said to have described voters who "voted dry as long as they could stagger to the polls," or "voted dry and drank wet."

Smith was badly defeated in North Carolina and in Charlotte. In the state the vote was Hoover, 348,923; Smith, 286,227. In Mecklenburg the vote was Hoover, 12,041; Smith, 9,690; and in Charlotte, Hoover received 8,941, Smith, 7,082.

The campaign divided the Democrats of Charlotte into two armed camps, figuratively speaking. The battle of words was fought furiously for weeks on local platforms, through the mails, in newspapers, and otherwise. Words were spoken that would have severed forever life-long friendships almost anywhere except in Charlotte where, fortunately, passions are quickly heated and almost as quickly cooled. The great depression, coming just a year later, hastened the process of reconciliation when all thoughts were turned to the relief of community miseries.

Sufficient time may now have elapsed for those who made some of those hasty and harsh statements at that time to forgive the inclusion of a few of them here. They are needed for the sake of accurate reporting and to shed light upon certain characteristics of the people. The following brief quotations are representative of very many which appeared in both Charlotte newspapers for weeks preceding the election.

In the *Charlotte News*, Friday, November 2, 1928, seventy-two of Charlotte's most prominent Democrats paid for a full page advertisement which carried their names and in which the following lines, typical of the whole, appeared: "Protest against the whispered campaign of hate, bigotry, intolerance and misrepresentation that is being waged in behalf of Mr. Herbert Hoover."

The opposition came back with a page in the *News* signed by one hundred Democratic men and women, of equal prominence, who also signed their names and headed "The County that Braves a British King will never cringe 'neath a Tammany lash," and which read, in part: "We resent to the depths of our being the insult to the intelligence and integrity of the Democratic men and women . . . which was contained in a full page ad which appeared in Friday's *News*."

The following day the *News* carried another full page advertisement, signed by a leading attorney who was one of the signers of the page published Friday. Excerpts from this page: "You either wilfully or ignorantly misrepresented history in your 'hymn of hate' against the supporters of Al Smith . . . you grossly slander the patriots who signed the Mecklenburg declaration of independence, May 20, 1775, when you compare yourselves to them . . . they rebelled against the British King in order that they might have religious liberty. You have rebelled against the Democratic party's nominee in order that he and his followers may not have religious liberty." Which shows that Mecklenburgers, as in 1775 or in the 1960's, are capable of strong feeling and powerful argumentation.

With a singleness of purpose, but with frequent differences as to methods, the area's pioneers and their descendants have molded the governmental structures and laws under which they live and have lived. An article in the *Charlotte Observer* for November 1, 1959, and an editorial in the same paper for December 7, 1959, described accurately how this has been done.

Captioned "Old time city fathers harassed too—Blue laws are a chronic Council pest," the article of November 1, 1959, reads, "Blue Laws have given Charlotte City Councils troubles as far back as the city's records go. And city records show no blue law has ever lasted in any form more than a few years.

"But they also show that total repeal has been a long time coming even though several close votes have barely saved the blue laws. Minutes of Council meetings also show that the ministers or ministers' organizations have been the principal supporters of blue laws.

"One of the first references to blue laws in the city's records was on January 15, 1866, when the board of aldermen passed an ordinance prohibiting the sale of whiskey, beer or wine on Sundays. Three years later an ordinance was passed closing barber shops on Sunday. The sale of cigars and tobacco on Sunday was banned in 1877 and, although there were protests against the move, the ordinance was not repealed.

"Special laws concerning observance of Sunday reached something of a peak in 1880 when an ordinance prohibiting any manner of work or sporting event was passed. The history of blue laws since that time is simply one of naming exemptions, making the laws more liberal. And there was a fight at every turn.

"It was during the 1930's that the issue began to appear more and more frequently. More demands for exemptions and more demands for repeal appeared. Sunday baseball and Sunday movies took the spotlight. Pages of minutes are devoted to these subjects and to the delegations which appeared before the City Council.

"By early 1938 enough demands for Sunday recreation were heard and some restrictions lifted. The old minutes show that the same arguments were made at that time that were made at public hearings in October, 1959. All so-called 'Blue Laws' were abrogated on November 2, 1959, though Sunday amusements for profit cannot begin before one o'clock in the afternoon on Sunday."

The editorial of December 7, 1959, in the *Observer* is captioned, "Another Local Controversy Marks the Tide of Progress," and reads: "To the long-time observer of Charlotte's turbulent history, the current fuss about overhanging street signs stirs nostalgic memories.

"Few, indeed, are the worthwhile civic improvements that have not been accompanied by hassles before the City Council, complete with delegations and the lawyers hired to speak for them.

"It dates way back, but there was actually a terrific hue and cry when the underpass on E. Trade Street was constructed. Merchants vowed they'd be ruined.

"Through the years other public furors were stirred up by the widening of Morehead and Graham streets, the selection of a site for Douglas Municipal Airport, the routing of Independence Boulevard (critics said it would never be used. Hah!), a ban on country buttermilk, taxicab meters and rates, any number of parking bans on busy streets, liberalizing the blue laws, ABC Stores, the first zoning ordinance, efforts to eliminate street name duplications.

"Somehow, the city managed to struggle through these great issues, all of them argued emotionally and vociferously at the time. And few thoughtful citizens would now undo a single one of the improvements.

"So it is that we feel not unkindly toward the small group of merchants who are in a last-ditch fight against the ordinance requiring them to tear down signs which overhang the sidewalks in the main business district.

"They are acting in historical character and they will make their views known to the City Council today, as they have every right to do.

"It does not follow, however, that the Council should do more than give them a courteous reception. However sincere and well-motivated, they are a minority, and a small one. Beyond that they are short of vision, for it is in their own long-range interest, to make the central business district as trim, uncluttered, and as visually attractive as possible. Elimination of the garish and blatant signs, many of which lose their effectiveness entirely because of the competition from others, will do much to attain that objective.

"The ordinance was passed two years ago. It is a good ordinance. There has been ample time for compliance.

"We urge the protesting merchants to accept the Council's decision in good spirits and with full understanding that this temporary hardship for them will be in the best interest of the whole Charlotte community."

Elections in Charlotte

Municipal elections in Charlotte are, for the most part, non-partisan, though for many years a candidate who had been prominent in state or national Republican politics has been at a considerable disadvantage, to say the least. In state and national politics Charlotte and Mecklenburg usually follow the statewide pattern, but with variations. For instance, in the Republican landslide of 1928, the Republican candidate for Congress from the Charlotte district, Charles Andrew Jonas, was one of the two Republican congressmen elected from North Carolina. He displaced Alfred Lee Bulwinkle, Democrat. Bulwinkle was re-elected to his old seat in Congress in the next election. Upon his death he was succeeded by Hamilton C. Jones, Democrat, of Charlotte, who was, in turn, defeated by Charles Raper Jonas, Republican, son of the Republican representative in 1928. Since his election in 1952 Jonas has been the only Republican from North Carolina serving in Congress, having received the following votes in Mecklenburg:

1952	Jonas 42,845	Jones 32,298
1954	Jonas 21,824	Sedberry 13,291
1956	Jonas 45,686	Douglas 24,544
1958	Jonas 24,245	Clark 22,640
1960	Jonas 49,405	Clark 36,195

Presidential elections in recent years have brought out the fact that Republican political sentiments have been on the increase in North Carolina, and markedly so in Mecklenburg County.

	Mecklenburg		North Carolina	
	Democrat	Republican	Democrat	Republican
1932	18,167	4,973	497,566	208,344
1936	26,169	4,709	615,151	223,284
1940	28,768	7,013	609,015	216,633
1944	25,950	9,434	527,399	263,153
1948	14,353	11,518	459,070	258,572
1952	33,044	44,334	652,802	558,107
1956	27,227	44,469	590,530	575,062
1960	39,362	48,250	713,136	655,420

Leaders: Past, Present, and Future

One of the most authoritative lists of men who helped bring the city to its present stature politically and otherwise, prior to 1900, is contained in Volume II, *History of Mecklenburg County and the City of Charlotte*, by D. A. Tompkins. The list contains brief biographical sketches of eighty men, of whom the following, mostly members of the legal profession, are best remembered:

Abraham Alexander, who presided over the meeting on May 20, 1775, which adopted the Mecklenburg declaration of independence and who was one of the signers of that document; Colonel Adam Alexander, a signer of the declaration; Captain Ezra Alexander, a signer; Hezekiah Alexander, a signer and member of the Provisional Constitutional Congress; and John McKnitt Alexander, a signer and secretary of the convention which adopted it. Of the twenty-seven signers, five bore the name of Alexander.

Others in Mr. Tompkins' list are: Waightstill Avery, a signer, prominent lawyer and progenitor of many bearing his name who have distinguished themselves in politics; General Rufus Barringer, a native of Cabarrus County who located in Charlotte following the Civil War and became an influential lawyer and citizen; General Daniel Harvey Hill, editor and educator who, like General Barringer, married one of the Morrison girls and, thus, became a brother-in-law of "Stonewall" Jackson; Thomas Jefferson Holton, owner and editor of Charlotte's leading newspaper, *The Journal*, later *Whig* (1828-1860); Colonel William Johnston, lawyer and railroad financier; James W. Osborne of Salisbury, admitted to Charlotte bar in 1833 and prominent in civic affairs; Thomas Polk, most prominent man of Charlotte when the town was founded and host to President Washington upon his visit to Charlotte.

When the final quarter of the nineteenth century began, three of the most influential men in Charlotte were W. P. Bynum, Hamilton C. Jones, Sr., and Clement Dowd. Staunch Republican Bynum served on the Supreme Court of North Carolina; Jones, who was severely wounded in the Civil War, served as United States District Attorney; Clement Dowd was a lawyer, president of the Commercial National Bank, and author of a book-length biography of Zebulon Baird Vance.

During the last decade of that century a number of lawyers, who later contributed much to the city's legal and political history, began their practice in Charlotte. In 1892 Charles Walter Tillett, Sr., James A. Bell, Edwin T. Cansler, Sr., Heriot Clarkson, Charles H. Duls, Johnson D. McCall, H. N. Pharr, and George E. Wilson were prominent. Frank M. Shannonhouse and Chase Brenizer began making their mark a few years later. Mr. Brenizer was chairman of the Mecklenburg County Board of Elections for many years. Most of these names are to be found among today's leading lawyers in the persons of the sons of these nineteenth century leaders.

Among lawyers who began their practice in Charlotte during the first years of the twentieth century were Thomas C. Guthrie, Sr., A. B. Justice, Thomas LeRoy Kirkpatrick, Frank R. McNinch, Plummer Stewart, Jake Newell, W. F. Harding, Edwin Randolph Preston, John A. McRae, Brevard Nixon, Thaddeus A. Adams, Norman A. Cocke, Robert S. Hutchison, Cameron Morrison, Paul

Whitlock, F. Marion Redd, Louis B. Vreeland, and John J. Parker.

By 1910 most of the lawyers who were practicing in Charlotte before the turn of the century were dead. Their places were filled rapidly, as openings were created through the needs of a growing population, by such men as J. Frank Flowers, W. S. O'B. Robinson, James L. DeLaney, Claude A. Cochrane, Edgar W. Pharr, Carol D. Taliaferro, H. L. Taylor, Charles Walter Tillett, Jr., W. Hunter Marshall, John R. Kenyon, Miss Julia Alexander, Marvin L. Ritch, Miss Margaret L. Berry (Mrs. Robert B. Street), Henry C. Dockery, and C. H. Gover.

During the 1920's the profession added such able personages as Walter Clark, Jr., D. E. Henderson, Frank H. Kennedy, Uhlman S. Alexander, J. A. Lockhart, Miss Carrie L. McLean, Frank W. Orr, Edwin B. Bridges, Fred B. Helms, Tom P. Jimison, William H. Bobbitt, John D. Shaw, Wade H. Williams, and John H. Small, Jr.

The high caliber of men and women who have made the law their profession and who have elected to practice in Charlotte has been fully maintained during the second quarter of the twentieth century. The District Bar Association of the Twenty-Sixth Judicial District for 1959-1960 boasts approximately 300 members, many of whom are, comparatively speaking, newcomers. They give promise of becoming as well and warmly remembered in the years to come as those mentioned in preceding paragraphs are now regarded.

Charlotte Minutiae

Charlotte has an attractive and meaningful historical seal, or coat-of-arms, but neither the name of the artist nor exact date of its adoption are known. The only official reference to it is contained in the minutes of the City Council for May 6, 1929, which reads: "The flag shall have a blue field with the Seal in white, which was designed during the term of Mayor Bland from May 1911 to May 1915." The historical seal bears the words, "City of Charlotte—Mecklenburg County, North Carolina," on the border. The arms are a bough of a tree (indicating growth), a liberty cap, a hornets' nest, two hands clasped (indicating friendship), and the date, 1775 (the year the Mecklenburg declaration of independence was signed). All city stationery bears the coat-of-arms.

The official flower of the city of Charlotte is the red rose, adopted by action of the City Council May 5, 1948.

Blue and white are the official colors of the city, but the date of their adoption is not known. The shade of blue is between old blue and royal blue.

In 1960 Charlotte passed the 200,000 mark in population. "Spearhead of the New South," shouts the Chamber of Commerce, and "the end of an epoch" say the authors of this history, nervously. It is a good stopping point. Future historians can pick up the story with the year in which Charlotte really emerged from the status of a town to that of a city. The figures prove it, as the Chamber of Commerce was quick to note.

It was the year when, on April 16, preliminary figures for the eighteenth decennial census of the United States gave Charlotte, for the first time, a population of more than 200,000 people. The next day the *Charlotte News* commented editorially upon this event in typical Charlotte fashion, as follows:

"Swelling her chest like a lady trackster, Queen Charlotte broke the 200,000 tape officially yesterday morning. She had 878 souls to spare, by the census figures. It was a photo finish.

"An enthusiastic group of city fathers learned the news from the district census supervisor at 11 o'clock Monday morning. City Manager William J. Veeder summarized the feelings most Charlotteans have. Two hundred thousand people means, more than anything else, an entirely new state of mind. 'It's a magic figure,' Mr. Veeder said. It is just that. It is a psychological shot in the arm. Wisely husbanded, its offshoot will be real civic progress.

"What the figures show is that Charlotte's economic boom has been accompanied by a population boom. The city's bounty since 1940—new industry, new distributors, new merchants, new professional services—is distributed among 100,000 new citizens.

"Charlotteans need not be reminded that bigger does not always mean better. Urban America is littered with the corpses of once proud, pleasant small towns whose life-force vanished with growth because growth was never disciplined and never channeled properly.

"For the most part Charlotte has avoided that fate splendidly. Civic-minded citizens, conscious that mere growth is a necessity but not a sufficiency for municipal greatness, have kept Charlotte's expansion disciplined.

"The challenges will grow. The day when the 200,000 tape was broken should bring not only exhilaration but a rededication to the principles by which mere gatherings of people and buildings become great cities. Cities must bear in mind these needs:

"Recreation—from play to serious enjoyment of the arts.

"Social stability—from sound government and law enforcement; and by guarding against the disintegration wrought by slums, unrejuvenated business centers, and run-down housing.

"Educational and civic growth—which can be obtained only by imaginative fiscal management and sound long-range planning and financing.

"Leadership.

"But in the last resort, cities are raised to greatness by a spirit—always difficult to touch but as old as the wandering Athenians and Romans who believed that their city was the center point of the world. And it was."

The year 1960 will also be remembered as the year the city and county school systems were consolidated. It was the year in which the huge First Baptist Church began to think seriously of leaving its downtown location. Construction of the campuses of Charlotte College and Carver College was well under way. Early in the year, the American Commercial National Bank announced plans for consolidating with the Security National Bank of Greensboro to form the North Carolina National Bank, second largest banking chain in the Carolinas and fourth in the South. The $2,500,000 Y.M.C.A. building was officially opened in the spring. Notwithstanding the uncertainty usually associated with an election year, Charlotte business firms were enjoying unprecedented prosperity.

In examining Charlotte papers for 1960, researchers will be impressed by the amount of space given to racial discrimination, juvenile delinquency, illegitimacy, the divorce rate, the aging population and underfed school children. They will note that slum clear-ance, urban redevelopment and similar symptoms of municipal growing pains occupy the attention of officials and citizens. Some will smile over the consternation caused by the changing of more than 500 street names in order to eliminate duplication that had become monstrous. They may grieve that no improvement was made in 1960 in the matter of public concern about the significance of "Evacuation Route" signs along the highways, or attention to the occasional "alert" sounded by the Office of Civil Defense.

Among the more hopeful signs that brighten the horizon of a new decade in Charlotte should be noted the city's extensive par-ticipation in teacher-pupil exchange arrangements with overseas countries. Future historians can report upon the success of this phase of the attempt to settle international differences through human friendships and understanding. In educational circles, also, 1960 will be remembered as the year in which standards were re-examined with the idea of returning to some of the older methods of teaching in the hope of finding an answer to the problems of apparent laxity among our youth.

Upon the success of these and other serious 1960 projects depends the caliber of men and women who will adorn the pages of Char-lotte history during the final decades of the twentieth century. The names and achievements of their forebears who brought the city this far along its way in the fields of religion, education, busi-ness and industry, culture, health, and welfare are recorded in the following chapters, and offered as examples worthy of emulation. It is worthwhile to hope and plan so that each new generation may be able to say, with Kipling,

> "Surely in toil of fray, under an alien sky
> Comfort it is to say, 'Of no mean city am I.' "

First Presbyterian Church

St. Peter's Episcopal Church, erected in 1892,
is a North Tryon Street landmark.

First Baptist Church

First Methodist Church, home of the congregation formed by
consolidation of Tryon Street and Trinity Methodist churches.

St. Patrick's Roman Catholic Church

First Church of Christ, Scientist

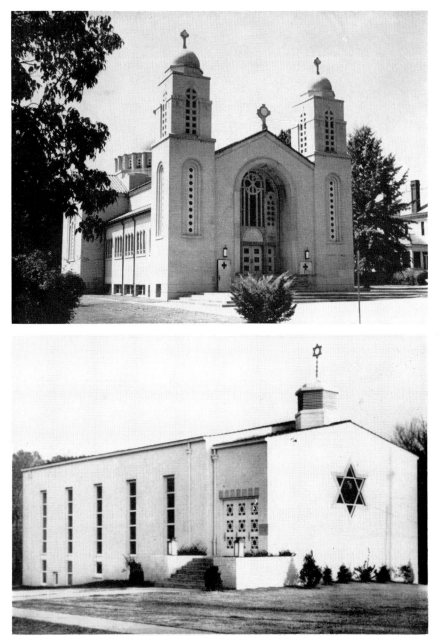

Above: The Greek Orthodox Cathedral on East Boulevard is the seat of the Southern Diocese of the Greek Orthodox Church. *Below:* Temple Beth El.

St. Mark's Lutheran Church

4

CHURCHES

FROM its earliest beginning, Mecklenburg has attracted a church going people, and its society has long been church-centered. But even so, the growth of Charlotte's religious groups in more recent years is remarkable.

An 1875 directory lists nine white churches: two each for the Methodists and Presbyterians, and one each for the Baptists, Episcopalians, Lutherans, Associate Reformed Presbyterians, and Roman Catholics. There were six Negro churches: two Baptist, three Methodist, and one Presbyterian. By 1910 the figures were thirty-five white and twenty-four Negro. The list of denominations remained constant until 1918, when a synagogue was listed. A Seventh Day Adventist Church was added about 1914, the Christian Science Church in 1920, and the Moravian Church in 1925.

Until 1940 the white and Negro churches were listed separately, but after that they were listed together but still classified according to denominations. However, the list of non-denominational churches had grown to twenty-two, of which the most familiar are Garr Auditorium and Brethren Assembly. This form of listing continued until 1957, after which all Charlotte's nearly three hundred churches were listed in one alphabetical arrangement.

Since a complete treatment of all denominations is obviously impossible here, a short sketch of the mother church of the three leading denominations will be given, and brief mention made of others, in the hope of conveying an overall picture of the extensive and important place religion has had, and now holds, in Charlotte and Mecklenburg County.

Presbyterian

The earliest settlement in Mecklenburg County was in the Rocky River community, later to become a part of Cabarrus County, and, according to tradition, the first settler was John Rodgers, who arrived in 1732. If this is true, then his arrival antedated by several years the coming of Thomas Spratt, earliest known settler at Charlotte. Rodgers and those who followed him to this vicinity were predominantly Presbyterians. These people soon felt the need for a minister, and they gladly welcomed Rev. Hugh McAden, an itinerant Presbyterian minister. To him belongs the credit for holding the first regularly conducted religious service in the Rocky River section.

The exact date is unknown, but it was about 1750 that a Presbyterian congregation was formed at Rocky River, probably through the influence of Mr. McAden, who held a number of services in various homes of the community. Definite records begin with the installation of Alexander Craighead as minister of the Rocky River congregation on Monday, November 6, 1758. He thus became the first pastor of the first church of any kind to be established in Mecklenburg County.

Another group of pioneers settled nearer the present site of Charlotte and organized the Sugaw Creek Presbyterian Church in 1755, with Rev. Mr. Craighead serving as pastor of both the Rocky River church and the Sugaw Creek church from the time each was organized until 1766. Details of his long, eventful, and sometimes turbulent life are recorded in numerous places, notably *The Presbyterian Church at Rocky River*, by Thomas Hugh Spence, Jr. (1954) and *A History of Sugaw Creek Presbyterian Church*, by Neill Roderick McGeachy (1954). Mr. McGeachy writes: "Time and talent both fail as we try to assess the worth and contributions of this man whose life and work set the mold for Sugaw Creek Church and whose family and descendants have extended his influence through a large part of our Southland, and its institutions. Alexander Craighead, faithful servant and minister of Jesus Christ and His church, fighter for freedom and self-government, your spiritual descendants rise up through the centuries and call you 'blessed.' "

In the few years that followed the establishment of these first two churches in Mecklenburg, six additional Presbyterian churches were organized: Steele Creek (1760), Hopewell (1762), Poplar Tent (1764), Center (1765), Providence (1767), and Philadelphia (1770). Each of these churches has a long and inspiring history of its own, and some have had book-length histories written about them. All have been the subject of newspaper feature articles from time to time. These churches are still active in 1960 and, with the exception of Rocky River Church, take important roles in the affairs of Mecklenburg Presbytery. Most of them still make use of all or portions of their original structures, though rebuilding in varying degrees has been found necessary, and many have modern additions for educational, recreational, and social purposes.

Alexander Craighead's successor at Rocky River Presbyterian Church was Hezekiah James Balch, who later was one of the signers of the Mecklenburg declaration of independence. Joseph Alexander became the second pastor of Sugaw Creek Presbyterian Church, to be followed in 1780 by Thomas Craighead, son of Alexander Craighead, supply minister for two years. In 1791 Samuel Craighead Caldwell, grandson of Alexander Craighead, became pastor of Sugaw Creek Church and served two terms spanning 35 years, and in 1837 John Madison McKnitt Caldwell, a great-grandson of Alexander Craighead, served as pastor.

Some of these and many other founders of Presbyterianism in Mecklenburg were dramatically portrayed in *Voice in the Wilderness*, written and staged to celebrate the bicentennial of the founding of Presbyterianism in Mecklenburg. It was viewed by many thousands when presented in Charlotte June 14-19, 1955.

That the city did not always dominate Mecklenburg is illustrated by the fact that almost fifty years elapsed between the building of the first seven churches in Mecklenburg County and the building of the first church of any kind in Charlotte. Initial efforts to erect a church in town were not taken until 1819, when the town commissioners set apart a lot on Trade and Church Streets to be used for a church and cemetery. Begun in 1819, the building of this church was not completed until 1823. When the church was finished there remained a considerable debt from an original sum the commissioners had borrowed from the Charlotte branch of the

Bank of New Berne. For some years thereafter the building was used by various denominations, but principally by the Presbyterians who had organized a church in 1832. When payment of the remaining sum, $674, became due in 1835, because of the expiration of the bank's charter, John Irwin, a prominent Presbyterian, paid off the debt and became owner of the property. On March 24, 1841, members of the congregation reimbursed Mr. Irwin and he deeded the property to the Presbyterian Church, by whom it has been owned ever since.

Formal organization of the Presbyterian Church of Charlotte took place on the fourth Sunday of August, 1832, with some thirty-six members enrolled. The pastor was Rev. Robert Hall Morrison, pastor of Sugaw Creek Presbyterian Church, who devoted one-third of his time to the Charlotte church, receiving from it $200 of his total annual salary of $800. Dr. Morrison resigned in January 1833. On May 3, 1834, Rev. A. J. Leavenworth was installed as the first full-time pastor of the Charlotte church.

The small, original church was replaced November 17, 1895, by an edifice which has been enlarged and improved from time to time. Today it is one of the larger church properties of Charlotte, and retains the architectural charm of an earlier period. Prior to 1873 most members of the congregation owned and held deeds to the pews, a custom not uncommon at the time. The original tract of land occupied by this church and still intact prompted one visitor to comment in print:

"I have visited many cities in this country, in Europe, in parts of Asia and Africa and I have not found anything more impressive than the sight of your magnificent city square with its majestic trees and green grass surrounding a church building of striking architectural design. One city block in this commercial age reserved for God. My, how unusual and how beautiful."

Known only as the Presbyterian Church from its founding, the church automatically became known as First Presbyterian Church with the organization of the Second Presbyterian Church in 1873. The history of Charlotte's First Presbyterian Church is long and filled with brilliant accomplishments and the names of distinguished men and women. Davidson College was established by Rev. Robert Hall Morrison, pastor of the church and first president of Davidson

CHURCHES   197

College; and Barium Springs Orphanage, some forty miles from
Charlotte, is the outgrowth of a little home established in Charlotte
largely by women of the First Presbyterian Church. The First
Church is conceded to be the mother church of some forty Presbyterian churches now in Charlotte.

Among distinguished men and women who have been active in
the First Presbyterian Church were General Daniel Harvey Hill
and his wife Isabella, General Rufus Barringer and his wife Eu-
genia, Colonel John Brown and his wife Laura, and Mrs. T. J.
"Stonewall" Jackson (the four ladies were daughters of Rev. Robert Hall Morrison); Governor Zebulon Baird Vance and his first
wife, Harriet Newell Espy; Edward Kidder Graham, later president of the University of North Carolina; Dr. Walter Moore,
president of Union Theological Seminary; James W. Osborne, Sr.;
Judge Victor Barringer, and General John A. Young.

The centennial celebration of the First Presbyterian Church was
observed by a series of meetings held November 16-20, 1932. At
that time the minister was Albert Sidney Johnson. The governing
bodies were no less worthy than their illustrious predecessors.
Session: George M. Rose, clerk; Frank H. Andrews, M. E. Boyer,
W. B. Bradford, E. T. Cansler, W. M. Wilcox, McAllister Carson,
Robert A. Dunn, F. O. Hawley, Morgan B. Speir, Sr., J. W.
McClung, Dr. J. P. Munroe, Jesse M. Oldham, H. H. Orr, and
Thomas J. Smith. Diaconate: C. M. Carson, J. A. Fore, Dr. Robert
L. Gibbon, C. W. Johnston, John M. Scott, W. B. McClintock,
A. S. Orr, H. B. Patterson, Ivey W. Stewart, W. N. Ward (treas-
urer), Albert T. Summey, Dolph M. Young, and J. W. Zim-
merman.

No description of the First Presbyterian Church of Charlotte
should be concluded without recording the achievements of Mrs.
J. A. Fore and Miss Madeline Orr in compiling histories of the
church, its ministers, members, and activities, from its beginning
until the present. Mrs. Fore's *Scrap Book* and Miss Orr's *Collection
of Historical Materials* repose, for safekeeping, in the Historical
Foundation of the Presbyterian Church at Montreat, North Carolina. Copies on microfilm are available to the public for reference in
the Public Library of Charlotte. More than a record of one church,
Miss Orr's history throws much light on life in the nineteenth

century as lived in Charlotte. Some idea of the wealth and variety of her notes may be gained from the following samplings:

A quotation from the *Catawba Journal*, August 22, 1826, reads: "People are invited to assist in throwing up ditches to keep hogs out of the Presbyterian cemetery."

A note in 1874 implies that organization of the Second Presbyterian Church aided the First Church inasmuch as in October of that year, the deacons asked members to surrender the deeds to their pews, so that pews might be free.

A news note dated April 29, 1873, reads, "The bell for the Presbyterian Church arrived yesterday. The old bell of the Presbyterian Church is now used for the town clock. It was the only bell in the city not sacrificed for the Confederate cause."

A quotation from the *Charlotte Observer* for May 19, 1876, reads: "The picnic of the First Presbyterian Church held at Moore's Ferry on the Catawba River . . . not a single untoward occurrence during the day." The manse of the church was built in 1876 and in 1912 the paling fence, seen in many old pictures, was removed and afterwards replaced with one of iron.

Organization of the Second Presbyterian Church became necessary when the congregation of the original church outgrew the building, the date being October 22, 1873. Pending completion of the $10,000 church building in 1875 at 224 North Tryon Street, the new congregation used the county courthouse as a place of worship. In 1894 an imposing sanctuary was built, to which a commodious educational building was added in 1921.

After a hectic and somewhat poverty-stricken start, as recorded by Robert S. Hutchison in *The Earliest Members of the Second Presbyterian Church of Charlotte, North Carolina* (1951), the new church proved a worthy companion to its distinguished parent in furthering the cause of Presbyterianism in Charlotte and throughout the world. Detailed information, including biographical and genealogical sketches of officers and many members of the Second Church, is recorded in *History of the Second Presbyterian Church of Charlotte, North Carolina*, by Robert H. Lafferty (1953).

The Second Presbyterian Church sacrificed its identity, as did the Westminster Presbyterian Church, when they united in June,

CHURCHES 199

1947, to form the Covenant Presbyterian Church. Covenant has the most imposing group of religious buildings in Charlotte. Sometimes, teasingly, it is referred to as "The Little Vatican."

From these two original churches have come the inspiration and much of the money for a long list of thriving Presbyterian churches convenient to all sections of the city. The list of pastors who have attained fame in these churches is entirely too long for inclusion here, but a few are so well remembered that they must be mentioned.

Still loved in memory by many elderly citizens is Dr. J. R. Howerton, pastor of the First Presbyterian Church, 1897-1906. He was the father of Phillip Howerton, lay moderator of the General Assembly of the Presbyterian Church U. S., 1958-9. Among others who served the same church with distinction was Dr. Albert Sidney Johnson, 1918-41. Rev. Charles E. S. Kraemer, 1945-54, resigned to become head of the Presbyterian School of Christian Education. From June 20, 1896, until April 5, 1903, Dr. J. W. Stagg was the beloved pastor of the Second Presbyterian Church. Very popular among citizens of all denominations was Archibald A. McGeachy, who served as pastor of the Second Church from September 1, 1908, until his death September 24, 1928. Participating in his funeral service were Dr. Albert Sidney Johnson, Rev. Father Jerome, Dr. J. R. Bridges, editor of *The Presbyterian Standard*, and Dr. W. H. Frazer, president of Queens College. More recently, Dr. John A. Redhead, 1937-1945, and Dr. Warner L. Hall, April 28, 1946, to date, have enjoyed the warm fellowship established so firmly by their predecessors. The first pastor of Myers Park Presbyterian Church was Dr. Edgar L. Gammon, 1927-1939, who resigned to become president of Hampden-Sydney College. Dr. James A. Jones succeeded Dr. Gammon, winning for himself a host of admiring friends throughout the city before he resigned to become president of Union Theological Seminary. Many ministers who have served Presbyterian churches in Mecklenburg County, outside of Charlotte, will be long remembered but none with more genuine affection than Rev. John M. Walker, pastor of Steele Creek Presbyterian Church, 1920-1948, and Rev. John W. Grier, for almost fifty years pastor of the Huntersville Presbyterian Church.

Presbyterian Foundation

As a leading center of Presbyterianism in the South, it is fitting that Charlotte should have been selected as headquarters for the Presbyterian Foundation of the Presbyterian Church in the U. S. (Southern). The present name was chosen in 1957 to replace the former cumbersome title under which it was chartered by the State Legislature on February 19, 1866, "The Trustees of the General Assembly of the Presbyterian Church in the United States and the Presbyterian Foundation, Inc."

The purpose of the Presbyterian Foundation is "to receive, hold, employ, and dispose of all of the estate and property, real, personal and mixed which may, from time to time, be acquired by gift, devise, bequest, purchase or otherwise." By 1957 operations became so extensive that the services of a full-time director were required and the first to fill this position was Dr. John R. Cunningham, former president of Davidson College.

Methodist

The first Methodist sermon and probably the first sermon of any kind ever preached in Mecklenburg was delivered by Reverend George Whitfield in October 1742 on what is now the campus of Davidson College. A quarter of a century later, the Methodists were sufficiently numerous in North Carolina to form a Carolina Circuit.

From that time on, influenced by "the great awakening" (1775-1778) membership in Methodist societies in North Carolina multiplied four times in two or three years. Today, it is estimated that every eighth Mecklenburger is a Methodist. The pioneer Methodists originally settled near the present town of Pineville. By 1785 these people had formed a small congregation, worshiping for the first twenty years in an open arbor, served by circuit riders and itinerant preachers.

This congregation met on Catawba Indian land, before it was made generally available by the government. A large tract had been bought by Harrison Hood, a wealthy Presbyterian, lately from Virginia, who, when approached by the Methodists for permission to erect a church on his land, not only donated the land but supplied most of the required lumber, logs, and slave labor.

The church was referred to as Harrison's Church, but there is some confusion as to whom that name honors. It may have been Harrison Hood, or Samuel Harrison, a prominent Methodist who lived nearby. George Washington's diary, for May 28, 1791, records his breakfast at "Harrison's" before going on "to Charlotte, 13 miles further along by 3 p.m."

The first structure at Harrison's Methodist Church was erected some time between 1805 and 1815. It was built of hewn logs notched up in the old-fashioned way and covered with oak boards with the cracks between the logs filled with clay mortar. Harrison's Methodist Church community had, in addition to President Washington, another distinguished visitor in the person of Bishop Francis Asbury. In an account of his travels is recorded: "Monday, November 14, 1808, Rode 33 miles hungry, cold and sick to Harrison's, Mecklenburg County. I came unwell and taking medicine to Robert Hancock's, Waxhaws. I suffer but it is the will of God. 1800 miles since leaving Baltimore, I have ordained Hancock a local deacon."

Few small communities were so honored as to have had visits from both the "Father of the Country" and the "Father of American Methodism." No local church has had a more interesting history written about it: in 1955 Rev. Orion N. Hutchinson wrote *A History of Harrison Methodist Church*, which is still in manuscript form only. Mr. Hutchinson summarizes the activities of Harrison's to the end of the nineteenth century by stating, "The church has moved from brush arbor to two buildings, from a circuit of 16 or more societies to a circuit of 4 churches. All in all it was a good hundred years and 'the best is yet to come.' "

Over the years many other Methodist churches have been organized throughout the county and in the five incorporated towns. The second oldest is Trinity Methodist on Beattie's Ford Road. Hickory Grove Methodist Church was organized in 1844; its fourth building was dedicated on Sunday, March 17, 1935.

Methodism in Charlotte began in 1814 when Dr. David R. Dunlap, a practicing physician and a Methodist, located here. When Methodist ministers visited Charlotte, many of them complied with

Dr. Dunlap's request to preach at services which were held in the courthouse. A few years later the little group of Methodists who had settled in Charlotte secured the occasional services of a preacher, Rev. William B. Barnett, who was the first minister of the newly-formed Sugaw Creek Circuit. The first class, or congregation, was formally organized in 1818, with Dr. Dunlap as leader, in time to share the community church which had been built by the town council.

In 1833, the junior preacher on the Sugaw Creek Circuit, Rev. David J. Allen, became the first full-time minister to the Charlotte congregation and in 1834 the first Methodist Church was built. This small building served until 1859 when a sizable church was built at the southwest corner of Tryon and Sixth Streets, and the name Tryon Street Methodist Church adopted. This, then, was the beginning of one of the two churches that were united to form the First Methodist Church of Charlotte, largest Methodist body in the city and mother church to many of the 48 Methodist congregations of Mecklenburg in 1960. The other of the two churches forming the First Methodist was Trinity Methodist Church, organized in 1896 and located at 401 South Tryon Street. Both churches had grown rapidly and at the time they were merged Tryon Street Church reported a membership of about 1,400 and Trinity Church, approximately 1,100 members.

Tryon Street Methodist Church and Trinity Methodist Church were officially united into the First Methodist Church on October 28, 1927 by Bishop Edwin D. Mouzon. The Bishop delivered the first sermon on Sunday morning, October 30, 1927, in the $900,000 structure on the corner of Tryon and Eighth Streets. In less than a year, the depression began. For some years it appeared that the church property might be lost but by 1944 the congregation had cleared the indebtedness. Dedicatory services were held March 9-19, 1944, with the formal dedication being made by Bishop Clare Purcell, and the dedicatory sermon preached by Bishop W. W. Peele.

The First Methodist Church and the two churches from which it was formed have numbered among their members some of Charlotte's most distinguished men and women. Charles J. Soong, father of the famous Soong sisters of China, was ordained a Methodist minister in the old Tryon Street church. This occurred during the annual conference, November 30, 1885. During his visit Mr. Soong was entertained at dinner in the home of the W. W. Hagood family, among the oldest and most faithful members of the church.

Other large Methodist congregations meet at Dilworth Methodist Church, founded about 1907, and the Myers Park Methodist Church, founded in 1925. The original building of the Dilworth church was on the corner of Worthington and Cleveland Avenues, until 1926 when the impressive sanctuary at 605 East Boulevard was completed. To this building, there was added in 1941, a large educational building, named for its donor, James Addison Jones.

Members of the Myers Park Methodist Church worshiped in the chapel of Queens College pending occupancy of their own church in 1930. Founders of this church, memorialized in a monograph published in observance of the 25th anniversary of the church, were: H. Connor Sherrill, Robert I. Dalton, George H. Moore, Fred Anderson, Dr. R. T. Ferguson, J. J. Akers, Dr. P. C. Hull, W. J. Stultz, D. D. Traywick, and Louis Asbury, who was not only a founder, but donated his services as architect of the building.

Many ministers and officers have brought the Myers Park Methodist Church to its present prestige. Rev. C. Excell Rozzelle, first pastor (1925-1927), laid the foundation upon which his successors built so well; J. Luther Snyder transferred his membership from Hawthorne Lane Methodist Church, contributed an organ and the $115,000 educational building; under Dr. Richard L. Owenby (pastor 1932-1941) the church indebtedness was paid in full and dedicatory services held (May 18, 1941); Dr. Embree H. Blackard (pastor 1941-1945) completed the organization of a competent staff; Dr. James G. Huggin (pastor 1945-1952) brought well deserved recognition when he became District Superintendent in 1956-1958.

Baptist

Of the three largest Protestant denominations, the Baptists were the last to become organized in Charlotte. Their growth has been most impressive, however, and they have more than made up for their late start. The 1957 Charlotte City Directory lists 76 Baptist churches, 48 Methodist and 40 Presbyterian, the figures including both white and Negro congregations, and missions of all kinds. The Baptists have also been diligent in preserving their local church history, as a reading of the accompanying bibliography shows.

The first Baptist church in Charlotte was constituted in 1833. The church consisted of only 11 members dismissed from Flint Hill Baptist Church, about 12 miles from Charlotte, just across the South Carolina line. It did not prosper and after a decade passed out of existence. The first permanent Baptist church in Charlotte was constituted in June 1855 and named Beulah Baptist Church of Christ. The first service was held September 7, 1856. Thus, with many evolutionary steps began the First Baptist Church of Charlotte which today probably has the largest single congregation in the city. The history of this church is recorded in *First Baptist Church of Charlotte 1832-1916*, by Carrie L. McLean. It makes fascinating reading:

"November 1861. The pastor tendered his resignation. Is it any wonder? Not able to get together even five men for a business meeting and $360. annual salary, only $140. of which had been paid." (In 1959 the *Charlotte News* listed the salaries of Charlotte ministers as: Baptists, from $2,000 to $15,000; Methodists, $3,500 to $12,500; Presbyterians, $4,200 to $12,000.)

"1865. A source of great annoyance and a subject that occupied much time at business meetings was the church bell. Committee after committee was appointed to try to have the bell fixed so that it would ring better. A solution to the problem was offered by the war, the bell was made into bullets with which to shoot the Yankees ... But the next bell was worse than the first and numerous attempts to get it fixed failed. Since the church has been on Tryon Street, it has never had a bell."

"1867. A salary of $500. was pledged the Pastor."

"June 1868. Letters were granted to all colored members recommended by the colored deacon and fifty-five of them ... were formed into a regular colored Baptist church. Prior to 1867 the colored members had no surnames and were listed as, 'Moses, servant of Grier,' or 'Peggy, servant of Jenkins.' "

"1883. At this time, so poor was the church, that they were unable to buy hymn books for the Sunday School. One of the duties of the Assistant Superintendent was that each week he procured a piece of muslin and spent each Friday night in stencilling on the muslin the hymn from the hymnbook owned. This was placed before the school . . . so that all could see."

"1892. It was resolved that membership should be withdrawn from members engaged in dancing."

The First Baptist Church is regarded as the mother church of 76 Baptist churches and missions in Charlotte and vicinity, some of which are beginning to rival the parent in membership, physical plant and achievement. The oldest of the mission churches began as the Ninth Avenue Baptist Church (1895) with Dr. L. R. Pruette as pastor. It was relocated in 1949 and named Midwood Baptist Church. The Pritchard Memorial Baptist Church, formed November 10, 1901, was the outgrowth of a Sunday School established by Dr. Pruette and Dr. T. H. Pritchard in 1895. St. John's (1922) and Myers Park (1943) have grown rapidly.

To those who know Charlotte best, certain names are synonymous with the Baptist faith: Thaddeus A. Adams, Henry B. Benoit, James R. Bryant, Dr. Amos S. Bumgardner, W. W. Crymes, John L. Dabbs, F. B. Davant, R. S. Dickson, Henry C. Dockery, William Carey Dowd, Sr., W. F. Dowd, J. A. Durham, J. B. Efird, Albert L. Faul, W. R. Foreman, Thomas S. Franklin, R. L. Goode, Brodie S. Griffith, V. J. Guthery, J. P. Hackney, L. L. Hackney, H. G. Harper, Fred B. Helms, Herman D. Horton, Dr. J. G. Johnson, A. B. Justice, Z. V. Kendrick, Clarence O. Kuester, Sr., Marshall E. Lake, Frank D. Lethco, B. Arp Lowrance, Carl McCraw, R. E. Mason, Lex Marsh, Dr. John Q. Myers, J. M. McMichael, J. B. Oates, Dr. C. N. Peeler, D. L. Probert, J. R. Purser, Dr. W. S. Rankin, E. E. Redfern, A. P. Rucker, W. J. Senn, John C. Shepherd, N. J. Sherrill, Cyril G. Smith, Junius Smith, Dr. Raymond Thompson, R. L. Vernon, J. M. Woodside, M. F. Wooten, and J. A. Yarbrough.

Biographical sketches of all pastors of the First Baptist Church are contained in *Biography of a Thriving Church*, by John Marvin Crowe (1953). Within the pleasant memory of many who are now living were Dr. A. C. Barron (1896-1905); Rev. H. H. Hulton (1906-1912); Dr. W. M. Vines (1913-1917). Dr. Luther Little (1917-1943), who served through two major wars and the country's most severe depression, will be long remembered for his monumental Christian achievements in Charlotte. Dr. Casper C. Warren succeeded Dr. Little and, because of his outstanding ability as demonstrated locally and throughout the South, was president of the Southern Baptist Convention, 1955. Dr. Claude U. Broach, scholarly pastor of St. John's Baptist Church, has been one of Georgia's great contributions to Charlotte, especially in the fields of inter-church cooperation and in work with the younger people of the community. Under the pastorate of Dr. George D. Heaton, the Myers Park Baptist Church grew rapidly from an idea to one of the most beautiful church structures in the city.

From April 1928 until forced by advancing age into graceful retirement, the pastor of Pritchard Memorial Baptist Church was Dr. William Harrison Williams. On his retirement, in 1958, Mayor James S. Smith said, "If Baptists had a bishop, Dr. Williams would certainly be it."

Episcopal

The first recorded service by a member of the Protestant Episcopal Church in Charlotte was held in a church erected for the common worship of the community and unconnected with any denominational organization. This church occupied the site of the present First Presbyterian Church on West Trade Street. The Rt. Rev. John Stark Ravenscroft, first bishop of the diocese of North Carolina (1823-1830) was in Charlotte and preached in that community church building on the first Sunday in November 1824.

St. Peter's Protestant Episcopal Church was established in Charlotte, first as a mission in 1834, later to become a parish of the diocese in 1844. An Episcopal visitation was made June 25, 1834 by the Rt. Rev. Levi Silliman Ives, the second bishop of the diocese of North Carolina (1831-1853) and at this time four persons were confirmed.

The first church building for St. Peter's Episcopal Church was a small brick edifice erected on a lot opposite the Post Office on West Trade Street. This property was sold later and a new site purchased on North Tryon Street, the present location. The cornerstone was laid by the Rt. Rev. Thomas Atkinson, the third bishop of the diocese of North Carolina (1853-1881) on May 21, 1857 and the building was completed in 1858.

During the War Between the States members of the parish participated in the importation of Bibles and prayer books from England for use by the Confederate soldiers. On April 23, 1865 Jefferson Davis, President of the Confederate States of America, with members of his cabinet worshiped in St. Peter's Church following the surrender of the Confederate Army at Appomattox.

The small old church was dismantled and the present church erected in 1892. The Parish House was added in 1911-12.

Since its early beginning in 1834, the following parishes and missions have been established: St. Michael and All Angels; St. Martin's; Church of the Holy Comforter; St. Andrew's; St. Mark's, near Huntersville; Chapel of Hope; St. Mary the Virgin at Thompson Orphanage; Christ Church; St. John's; and St. Christopher's. There are presently sixteen members of the clergy serving the church in Charlotte and Mecklenburg County.

Four rectors of St. Peter's have become bishops: the Rt. Rev. Joseph Blount Cheshire; the Rt. Rev. Edwin Anderson Penick, D.D., consecrated bishop-coadjutor of this diocese October 15, 1922 and becoming bishop on December 27, 1932; the Rt. Rev. John Moore Walker, D.D., consecrated bishop of the diocese of Atlanta September 22, 1942; and the Rev. Gray Temple, bishop elect of the diocese of South Carolina, 1960.

The first rector of St. Martin's Episcopal Church was Rev. John Long Jackson who later became bishop of Louisiana and whose successor, Rev. C. Alfred Cole, became bishop of Upper South Carolina. At Christ Church, now largest in the diocese, the first rector was Rev. George M. Henry, who later became bishop of Western North Carolina. The longest pastorate of an Episcopal church in Charlotte was held by Rev. Robert Bruce Owens, rector of the Church of the Holy Comforter, 1916-1945, a man of many talents all of which he contributed liberally to the intellectual and spiritual life of his adopted city. An equally well known and respected Episcopal clergyman is Rev. William H. Wheeler, who served 1922-1940 as superintendent of the Thompson Orphanage.

He later became assistant minister at St. Peter's Church in charge of some of the missions throughout the city, hospital visitor, and "friend of man."

As with all Charlotte churches certain names become identified with the denomination. In Protestant Episcopal circles, especially St. Peter's Church, some of these names are represented by members of the families of such past and present members as Fred Bonitz, W. Irving Bullard, Lewis C. Burwell, Edwin Clarkson, Judge Francis Clarkson, H. T. Cosby, Stuart W. Cramer, John H. Cutter, Harold C. Dwelle, Burt Fitch, Rupert Gillette, Jeremiah Goff, Mrs. Patsy Goodwin, Dr. W. A. Graham, E. C. Griffith, Thomas Griffith, Thomas Guion Griffith, John W. Labouisse, John B. London, Henry McAden, William McLaurine, E. C. Marshall, Dr. W. B. Mayer, M. M. Murphy, Frank Shannonhouse, E. A. Terrell, Dr. John Hill Tucker, James H. Van Ness, and J. Frank Wilkes.

Roman Catholic

The cornerstone of St. Peter's, the first Roman Catholic Church in Charlotte, was laid on St. Patrick's Day 1851, and the church was dedicated in 1852. This small church on the southeast corner of Tryon and First Streets was replaced in 1892 by a new and much larger building which, with additions and improvements, is still in use. The second and more imposing Roman Catholic Church, St. Patrick's, on Dilworth Road, was dedicated in 1939. It was the first Roman Catholic Church in North Carolina to be consecrated immediately upon completion. St. Patrick's Church was made possible largely by the gift of John Henry Phelan of Texas, whose ancestors were from Charlotte. The first pastor of St. Patrick's was Rt. Rev. Monsignor Arthur Freeman. He was followed by the present pastor, Rt. Rev. Monsignor John Patrick Manley.

Following World War II, the high percentage of Roman Catholics among the newcomers to Charlotte made necessary the formation of four additional parishes, each with its own parochial school, and one mission church. Following the 1954 desegregation decision of the United States Supreme Court, the Catholics immediately opened their churches and schools to all races.

Lutheran

Morning Star Lutheran Church near Matthews, organized 1775, antedates all other denominations in Mecklenburg except the Presbyterian. For some years it was one of the strongest rural churches in the county, but membership dwindled. Today, the church is rapidly regaining its former prestige. The first unit of a new building program was completed in 1959.

On February 1, 1959, St. Mark's, oldest Evangelical Lutheran Church in Charlotte, celebrated its centennial anniversary. It is the parent church of several congregations affiliated with the United Lutheran Church in America. The first building occupied by St. Mark's Evangelical Lutheran Church was located at College and Seventh Streets. The second, occupied from 1885 until 1960, was located midway between Seventh and Eighth Streets, on the east side of North Tryon Street. This property was sold in 1959 to the owners of the William R. Barringer Hotel. A new and handsome church building has been built on Queens Road.

The longest pastorate in the history of St. Mark's was held by Reverend John F. Crigler (1915-1948). From 1948 until 1954 the pastor of the church was Rev. Walter B. Freed, who was followed by the present pastor, Dr. John R. Brokhoff.

Among the older Lutheran churches of the city, also affiliated with the United Lutheran Church in America, is Holy Trinity Evangelical Lutheran Church on the Plaza. Now occupying an attractive new church building, this congregation was led for many years by Dr. Robert L. Patterson, who willed his extensive theological library to the Public Library. Since 1936, Rev. Olin W. Sink, formerly assistant pastor, has carried forward the work of this church.

The Lutheran Church, Missouri Synod, is represented in Charlotte by Ascension Lutheran Church, organized in 1932, currently enjoying the ministry of Rev. Leslie F. Frerking.

Associate Reformed Presbyterian

Prior to 1803, the Associate Reformed Presbyterian churches in the countryside around Charlotte were: Gilead (1787), Prosperity

(1888), Sardis (1790), Steele Creek (1794), and Back Creek (1802). In 1860 there was an attempt on the part of these churches to organize an Associate Reformed Church in Charlotte, but these efforts were disrupted by the War Between the States.

The 1873-74 Synod authorized the formation of a church at Charlotte. This brought into being the First Associate Reformed Presbyterian Church on the corner of Fifth and College Streets. As the community grew other churches were formed and by 1850 there had been added to the list Ebenezer (1869), Huntersville (1875), Tabernacle (1899), Parkwood (1908), Chalmers Memorial (1908), Statesville Avenue (1908), Glenwood (1919), Craig Avenue (1949).

The First Associate Reformed Presbyterian Church, located now on North Tryon Street, divided in 1952. One group remained the First A.R.P. Church and retained the property. The other group formed the Westminster Church of the Presbyterian denomination U. S. (Southern) on September 14, 1952. On July 15, 1952 the Sardis A. R. P. Church became affiliated with the same denomination, making a settlement with the A. R. P. Synod for the church property.

Jewish Congregations

While Jewish congregations and houses of worship are of comparatively recent origin, there have been religious and benevolent activities by Jewish citizens in Charlotte for a hundred years. Temple Israel, older of the two Jewish congregations, is the outgrowth of the Hebrew Benevolent Society which, in 1875, was a flourishing Charlotte organization. That year they gave a charity ball and raised $100 for an old age home.

An early Jewish leader in Charlotte was Samuel Wittkowsky, a warm friend of Governor Zebulon Vance, and probably the inspiration for Vance's famous address, "The Scattered Nation." There was a branch of the Baruch family living in Charlotte and Bernard M. Baruch, financier and friend of Presidents, spent a good deal of his time as a boy with his uncle in Charlotte. Some other Jewish citizens of the late nineteenth century whose names and whose descendants are familiar include Samuel and Solomon Cohen,

H. Bumgarten, A. A. Nathan, David Goldberg, Jay Hirshinger, and Louis N. Schiff.

From this social group, and another which was formed to provide a Jewish cemetery, there evolved a congregation and synagogue. Actual formation of the congregation occurred about 1895, and the first building on West Seventh Street came into existence about 1916. The 60th anniversary was celebrated in 1955 in a new synagogue on Dilworth Road, completed in 1949. On that occasion there was only one of the founding members present, Mrs. David Ben Silverstein, who shared honors with the 1955 officials: Rabbi Aaron Tofield, Dr. Albert Kossove, president; Ben Jaffa, vice president; S. S. Fligel, treasurer; and Leon Kraft, secretary.

The newer Jewish congregation in Charlotte, Temple Beth El, was organized in 1942 and shortly thereafter built a synagogue on Providence Road. The first rabbi selected by this congregation was Philip Frankel.

Seventh Day Adventist

The Seventh Day Adventist congregation in Charlotte dates from 1914. By 1947 its membership had increased sufficiently to build a church at 1011 East Morehead Street. This building was dedicated in December 1951.

Moravian

The Moravian congregation in Charlotte was formed on November 7, 1920, and on October 19, 1924 the first service was held in the newly built chapel, since known as The Little Church on the Lane.

The Little Church on the Lane is the fulfillment of a dream of Mr. and Mrs. W. T. Wohlford, members of the original group. They donated the property on which the parish house and parsonage stand. Dr. Herbert Spaugh came to the church as resident pastor and is still (1961) pastor. It is generally agreed that Dr. Spaugh is the best known Protestant minister in Charlotte. Outstanding among his contributions are his long and effective service as Chairman of the Charlotte School Board, and quarter century as author of "The Everyday Counselor," popular daily feature of the *Charlotte News*. This column is also carried in other southern newspapers.

In 1959 Dr. Spaugh was elected a bishop of the Moravian Church. He continues as pastor of The Little Church on the Lane, with Rev. James L. Johnson as assistant.

Christian Science

A group of students of Christian Science began holding regular services in Charlotte homes in 1900. As the number grew, services were held in rented halls. In 1905 the group was organized as a Christian Science Society. In 1911 this Society had fulfilled requirements of the mother church, The First Church of Christ, Scientist, of Boston, Massachusetts, and became known as the First Church of Christ, Scientist, of Charlotte. In 1919 the church purchased property at Cedar and West Trade Streets and services were continued there until 1940 when a new edifice of New England Colonial architectural design was erected on East Morehead Street. This building was dedicated in 1945, free of debt.

A Christian Science Reading Room, where may be obtained the Bible, Christian Science textbooks, and all authorized Christian Science publications, is maintained by the church in downtown Charlotte.

Unitarian

Although it is among the oldest religious denominations in America, the Unitarian Church was an unknown organization in conservative, Protestant Charlotte until recent years. The rapid expansion of Charlotte following World War II brought Unitarians to the city in increasing numbers, and in 1947 they began to hold services.

Pending construction of a church on East Boulevard, services were held in the Broadway Theatre. The first leader in Charlotte was John Morgan, a gentleman of such personal charm and sincerity that the new organization soon became firmly established and has since continued as an aggressive and influential institution.

Mormon

One of the newest church edifices in Charlotte was occupied October 1, 1959 by members of the Church of Jesus Christ of Latter Day Saints, more commonly known as the Mormon Church. Membership in the Charlotte branch has gradually increased over the past 20 years from a handful to more than 250 people. This growth is due principally to the efforts of young missionaries making house to house visits.

Greek Orthodox

In 1923, following a gradual increase in Charlotte's population of Greek origin dating from about 1900, a Greek Orthodox Community was organized, with the blessings of the Greek Orthodox Archdiocese of North and South America. Between forty and fifty charter members attended the organization meeting and elected Gus Kokenes as president; Charles Michaels, secretary; George Plumides, treasurer. To serve with them were Chris Leventis, Charles Anagnos and Sam Wallace as board members.

By 1929 the new church had grown sufficiently to justify the purchase of a building on South Boulevard which had been vacated by Westminster Presbyterian Church. This building served until 1954 when the imposing edifice at 600 East Boulevard was occupied. It was the first of several units. This Community Center also serves as headquarters for the Southern Diocese of the Greek Orthodox Church which was created in the early 1940's to administer the affairs of the church in the South. Since 1939 Rev. Chrys Papalambrou, a graduate of the Theological School of Halki, Constantinople, has been the spiritual head of the Community.

Quakers or Friends

In the spring of 1960 the small group of Quakers in Charlotte became organized as the Charlotte Friends Fellowship. The board of trustees was composed of Dr. Elizabeth Corkey, Miss Sally Southerland, J. C. Rush, Dr. William Beidler, and Carol B. Mullis, with Donald Bruce Thornton as clerk, Miss Helen Stroupe as recording clerk, and John Charles Rush, treasurer. This group laid plans to begin the formal and official Monthly Meetings of the Religious Society of Friends.

Negro Churches in Charlotte

Despite the fact that the local Christian Ministers Association is an interracial group and has had a Negro minister as its president, Charlotte's Protestant and undenominational churches were still almost entirely segregated in 1960. In the sphere of religion no appreciable effort toward universal desegregation had been made by either white or Negro citizens. The reason is, apparently, that since the churches of the two races were separated in the South following the War Between the States, the Negro church has become the most significant influence in the Negro community.

The history of Negro churches and their activities in Charlotte largely parallels that of white churches. In 1875 there were five Negro churches: Ebenezer Baptist and one unnamed Baptist church; Zion Methodist and one unnamed Methodist church; and one Presbyterian church. It is interesting to note that the pastor of the Presbyterian church is listed as Stephen Mattoon. He was, at that time, president of Biddle Memorial Institute, later Johnson C. Smith University. This Stephen Mattoon was the grandfather of Norman Thomas, himself an ordained Presbyterian minister, who was on several occasions nominee for president of the United States as a candidate of the Socialist party. The number of Negro churches increased at about the same rate as white churches and in 1925 there were thirteen Baptist churches, sixteen Methodist, five Holiness, two Lutheran, and seven Presbyterian. There was also a Congregational, a Seventh Day Adventist, and an Episcopal church serving the Negro community.

Among the undenominational churches, by far the best known is the Church of the Rock of the Apostolic Faith, organized in 1924 by Bishop C. M. Grace, known to his followers as Daddy Grace. Throughout the years this sect grew into a national organization and currently, in Charlotte, the congregation occupies the largest single Negro church structure in the city. Known as The House of Prayer for All People, it is located on South McDowell Street.

Bishop Grace made it a custom to visit Charlotte each summer and, following a spectacular parade by members of his congregation, baptised a large group of converts in a small lake.

Daddy Grace died in Los Angeles, California in January, 1960. His body was brought to Charlotte where it lay in state for 24 hours, to be viewed by thousands of his grief-stricken followers. The following paragraphs, written by columnist Kays Gary, appeared in the *Charlotte Observer:*

DADDY GRACE 'TOOK ROCK NO ONE WOULD USE AND BUILT HIS CHURCH.'

How can the phenomenon of Daddy Grace be explained?

A learned and widely respected Negro minister of an established faith has this answer:

"Grace took a rock no other builder would use and made it the cornerstone of his church."

The rock was Brooklyn.

Brooklyn had always been Charlotte's slum ridden section.

The name was leprous. It represented crime, poverty, shiftlessness and was populated, in the public eye, by untouchables.

"But he gave those people there," the minister said, "a new self-identity. They had somebody who wanted them. He gave them hope and something to be happy about."

Echoing the words of former Police Chief Frank Littlejohn, the minister added that "you will find no member who is not industrious and none who does not respect right and the law."

Others may judge the purposes of Grace as they will, but this minister doubts that the bishop's primitive flamboyance was the product of complete self-interest.

He suggests that Grace knew what would appeal most to those who could be drawn to his church . . . that there is member pride in his Cadillac, diamonds, mansions and vast property holdings all in the church's name.

Moreover, he says, that which appears undignified and in bad taste and selfish by standards of accepted society can be genuine and sacred to those who never found this society particularly kind.

This minister believes that the cult's by-laws provide for election of a titular head to administer the vast property and bank holdings which only Grace could touch. And he declares that he knows this wealth is used in part to build more Houses of Prayer and to give material aid "to any member in dire circumstances."

The minister once asked Grace why he did not use his wealth to build hospitals, schools, orphanages etc. and got this reply: "I represent all my people and all people can be lifted only a little at a time."

These observations are interesting because of the sources and especially because their sum falls between the extreme of those who regarded Grace as a repulsive charlatan and phony, and those who believed him to be a prophet.

A clearer picture of Grace and his use of all the wealth he controlled should evolve when and if the federal government files tax liens against it, as expected.

In any case the man added a historical lesson that the downtrodden, hopeless and rejected are always ripe for leadership.

Protracted Meetings—Revivals—Crusades

While activities of white and Negro churches have been basically the same, there have been two features popular with white congregations that do not seem to have appealed to Negroes. These are the related practices of protracted meetings, called revivals when held in cities, and camp meetings when held in rural areas. Because of the presence of churches in rural Mecklenburg from earliest times, camp meetings were never too important. On the other hand, the custom of holding revivals has always been popular, especially with Methodists and Baptists and, to a lesser extent, with Presbyterians. The major projects in this field have been in the nature of joint efforts by groups of Protestant churches.

There is little difference in the meaning of the words, "protracted meeting," and "revival," except that perhaps the term protracted meeting describes a series of meetings held by one church, whereas revival indicates sponsorship by a group of churches, or several Protestant denominations. Calling such meetings or revivals "crusades" is a modern idea. A meeting of this type was held in the First Presbyterian Church in 1853. The minister on that occasion was Reverend Daniel Baker of Texas who, writing of his Charlotte visit, stated: "There were 47 conversions, among them were 4 lawyers, 2 physicians, 6 merchants and a pretty large number of gay and fashionable young ladies."

The earliest city-wide revival was held in the auditorium of the

Y.M.C.A. in March 1887. The minister was Rev. R. G. Pearson. No mention was made in the local papers concerning the results of his professional appeals, but he did very well financially, raising between three and four thousand dollars for the Y.M.C.A., for which he received a fee of $1,000.

During the latter part of the nineteenth century and early years of the twentieth, the leading evangelists were Rev. Sam Porter Jones, Methodist; Rev. George Truett, Baptist; and Rev. William Black, Presbyterian. In 1915 the largest city-wide revival up until that time was held in a special tabernacle on East Avenue, seating 6,000. This was known as the Chapman-Alexander Revival, with Dr. J. Wilbur Chapman doing the preaching and Charles M. Alexander as choir director and song leader.

Rev. William A. (Billy) Sunday, the greatest evangelist of his day, conducted a very successful revival in Charlotte in December 1923 and January 1924. For this event, a huge, temporary wooden structure was erected on the southwest corner of Tryon and Third Streets. Most evangelists used their own hymn books, each containing a selection of many popular religious songs, and no one who attended the Billy Sunday services will likely forget the tremendous enthusiasm with which the congregations, led by Homer Rodeheaver, sang "Brighten the Corner Where You Are," "When the Roll Is Called Up Yonder, I'll Be There," and other favorites.

In October 1934 Mordecai Ham, the Baptist evangelist, held one of his several series of protracted meetings in Charlotte. The importance of this particular series was not fully realized until some years later when they were given credit for his conversion by Rev. William Franklin (Billy) Graham of Charlotte, who became the most noted evangelist of his time.

Following triumphant appearances in several large cities in the United Kingdom and the United States, including London and New York, Billy Graham was given an impressive reception when he returned to his own home town to lead a Crusade for Christ in 1958. The Charlotte Coliseum and Ovens Auditorium were inadequate to accommodate the multitudes attracted by the sincere and magnetic personality of their fellow townsman.

5

EDUCATION

I N HIS *History of Mecklenburg County and the City of Charlotte,* D. A. Tompkins gives biographical sketches of eighty men who were prominent in Mecklenburg during and shortly after the Revolution. The most frequent phrase in these sketches is, "he was educated at . . . ," and among the eighty, four were graduates of the College of New Jersey, later Princeton University.

Further proof that the people of Mecklenburg were well educated for that period can be seen in early letters, diaries, wills, and public documents written by people of Charlotte. To forestall contradiction based upon fragmentary evidence, it must be admitted that some local documents are as illiterate as any to be found, but generally speaking, the people of Mecklenburg were well educated and, furthermore, understood the value of education. Nearly all early wills contained a provision for the education of children or, in some cases, the apprenticing of children so that they might become proficient in some trade.

Mr. Tompkins, or perhaps his principal research assistant, Mr. C. L. Coon (later to become one of North Carolina's best known and most progressive educators), sized up the situation thus: "People in those days had practical ideas about everything. It was deemed important that children be taught the rudiments of education, and some were sent North to college, but the things most highly considered were religious and industrial training. Parents believed it essential that their children be given instruction in the Bible, Catechism and religious doctrines, and that each be trained in some trade."

With the unfolding of Charlotte's history, it will become more

218

and more apparent that in education, as in everything else, the guiding spirit has been "practical ideas about everything," or "first things first." Elementary schools there had to be, and the ability to earn an honest living, but higher education could wait.

Elementary Education

Mecklenburg County schools of 1800 and of 1860 were about the same. All schools were privately owned and conducted, largely by ministers who had space in their homes for classes. Sometimes members of the family were able to assist with teaching. There were also teachers who went from home to home on a more or less regular schedule.

Something resembling today's public school system began just prior to 1840, when $750,000 was received by the state of North Carolina as her share of funds which had been accumulated through the sale of public lands. In 1839 the legislature divided counties into school districts and each county voted whether or not to have public schools. In Mecklenburg the vote was 950 for and 578 against schools and in Charlotte, 314 for and 51 against.

The county school tax was six cents on the poll and three cents on $100 property valuation, which supplemented the income from the state fund. In 1849 Mecklenburg's portion of the public money, together with the amount raised from tax, was $2,149 and in 1850, $3,449, the second largest county fund for education in the state. When the schools were first opened in 1841 the salary of teachers ranged from $15 to $30 monthly, and the leading textbooks were Webster's Blue Back Speller, Davie's Arithmetic, and Smith's Grammar.

During the War Between the States, the income from county taxes was donated to the use of soldiers, but the state funds were used for the support of schools. There were no secondary schools other than privately owned "academies," conducted from time to time in various sections of the county. The most prominent was Bain Academy in the Mint Hill section, a name that is perpetuated in the publicly owned school of today.

By 1874 there were 46 white schools in the county with 1,702 children, operated at a cost of $4,346, and 34 Negro schools with

1,814 children, costing $2,948. In those days the schools were governed by a Board of Education, and the teachers applied to a county examiner. The Board of Education still exists, but the position of examiner has evolved into a county superintendent of education. Teachers in 1873 were paid $25 or $30 per month or, if the number of pupils was small, $1 per month for each one in attendance. Except in a few larger schools, teachers taught all subjects to pupils of all ages.

There were few changes in the field of elementary education until after the turn of the century when the constructive efforts of such men as Governor Charles Brantley Aycock, Charles Duncan McIver, and others began to be felt. Even then the progress was slow in Mecklenburg. Very gradually some of the one and two room schools were consolidated into two, three, and four teacher elementary schools. A few years later some of these were further enlarged to become Union Schools, some of which had high school grades. By the early 1920's there were a number of these Union Schools in Mecklenburg, but even as late as 1944 there were still a few one and two room schools in locations where the parents were loath to lose the convenience of a neighborhood classroom or the services of a favorite teacher.

The school consolidation movement necessitated the use of school buses, which came into use in this county in the 1920's. The problem of housing a concentration of teachers in one locality began to be solved in the fall of 1923 when Mecklenburg County opened its first Teacherage at Huntersville with Mrs. James T. Comer as matron in charge. Because of the success of this experiment, similar provisions were made for the comfort and convenience of teachers in a dozen or more locations throughout the county.

In 1950 Mecklenburg was the first county in the state to consolidate several Union Schools into one large educational plant. Today there are four of these magnificent institutions, prosaically yet wisely named North Mecklenburg, East Mecklenburg, West Mecklenburg, and South Mecklenburg high schools. Distinguished educators have headed Mecklenburg County schools and contributed their talents toward bringing the system up to its present state of excellence. The superintendents were Joseph M. Matthews,

Frank A. Edmondson, Edward L. Best, John C. Lockhart, and, since 1944, J. W. Wilson.

The first graded public school in North Carolina was opened in Charlotte October 21, 1873, by Reverend J. B. Boone. This school replaced the one room county school which had served Charlotte. Support for the new school came from $1,700 which was Charlotte's share of the county fund, $600 from the Peabody Fund, and a few private contributions. This school was continued for eight months, with an average daily attendance of 175 and total expenses amounting to $2,901.75. Lack of funds forced its closing. There were six teachers and a board of directors consisting of General Rufus Barringer, Captain John Wilkes, and Major Clement Dowd.

Among those who attended this first school were Mrs. W. W. Hagood, Sr., and Mrs. C. C. Kennedy, who sat together at the quaint little desks built for two, and both of whom grew up to become leaders in the religious and cultural life of Charlotte. A fellow classmate was James Northey, who became Charlotte manager of the Southern Bell Telephone and Telegraph Company.

Mr. Boone's school served to demonstrate the value of the public graded school. A bill to provide a special charter and levy a tax was introduced in the General Assembly, passed and ratified March 22, 1875. This act stipulated that before becoming effective it should be voted upon and a majority of registered voters should vote in favor of it. With their usual cautiousness, or should it be called callousness, the citizens of Charlotte refused to authorize the "luxury" of public schools. A similar step that must regretfully be reported was taken in the summer of 1939, resulting in the closing of the public library. There was to be no public school before 1882, just as there was no public library service from June 30, 1939, to July 1, 1940.

On the first Monday of January 1880 another election was held. The vote was 815 to 1 in favor of public, graded schools. There were 1,679 names on the registration books, but before announcing the result the board disqualified 133 names and then declared the necessary majority obtained. A taxpayer carried the matter to court. The act of the aldermen was sustained by the lower court, and finally by the Supreme Court at the fall session in 1881. And thus, with the same travail that has characterized the beginning of many of today's finest possessions, the public school system of Charlotte was born.

According to Dr. Alexander Graham, in an address delivered March 13, 1900, when the cornerstone was laid for North School at Ninth and Brevard Streets, "The white school opened for the reception of pupils on September 11, 1882, and thus was organized the school for whites in the barracks of the Carolina Military Institute. . . . The colored school opened September 25 . . . first conducted in an old tobacco barn in Ward 1."

For a period of nearly 75 years following Dr. Graham's arrival Charlotte has had only three public school superintendents. Dr. Alexander Graham became superintendent February 14, 1888, following ten years of teaching at Fayetteville. He became superintendent emeritus in 1913, when he was succeeded by Dr. Harry P. Harding, who had been a Charlotte school principal since coming from Goldsboro on October 3, 1904. Dr. Harding, in turn, was succeeded upon his retirement June 30, 1949, by Dr. Elmer H. Garinger, who came to Charlotte in 1921 as principal of Alexander Graham School and later became principal of Central High School.

Under these three distinguished educators, the Charlotte Public School System developed rapidly. In 1904 when Dr. Harding arrived, there were two white schools, known as North School and South School, with a total enrollment of 1,984 pupils, and one Negro school with an enrollment of 1,111. In July 1960, when the schools of the city and county were merged, there were 92 partially integrated schools, with a capacity of 58,594 pupils. The statistical details of this amazing growth are available in annual reports of the Charlotte-Mecklenburg Board of Education. An informal record of incidents and personalities has been preserved in a manuscript by Dr. Harry P. Harding entitled *History of the Charlotte Public School System 1882-1949.* Dr. Harding's manuscript records an event that occurred in 1880, which illustrates the tense emotionalism which has always characterized the people of Charlotte when differences of opinion develop. At that time the city officials wanted to buy the old North Carolina Military Institute building for $15,000, a step opposed by a sizable segment of the population. The opposition was so strong that members of the board of aldermen were afraid that, if they issued a check in payment, an injunction would be sought to stop payment before the bank opened on Monday morning. The whole amount, therefore, was paid in cash, including a considerable amount of silver.

In a lighter vein, but nevertheless characteristic of the city's reputation for charting its own course, is the story of the plans of the North School, opened in 1900. Among a number of plans for the school submitted by architect Frank P. Milburn of Washington were some for a new hospital building to be built in Texas. When Superintendent Graham saw the hospital plans with a large bay window in each room and other windows on the side, with space for an office, rest rooms on each of the four floors, wardrobes in each room, play room in the basement, modern heating and ventilating system, he said to the Board of Education, "That's the building we want." As of 1960, it may still be seen, still a fine school building after a half-century of use.

The consolidation of the city and county public school systems under one governing board and one superintendent in 1960 is nothing much more than the final step in a process which has been under way virtually ever since public schools were established. Specifically, the original part of the present Dilworth School was once a Mecklenburg County school and, had Central High School been built in 1904, it would have been just outside the city limits. Many other schools have been changed from county to city institutions as the city limits have been extended from time to time.

Growth of the Charlotte public school system, an orderly process from 1882, was not only halted but many gains were obliterated by the great depression which dealt its hardest blow in 1933. The seriousness of the educational situation at that time will be apparent if one contemplates the effects of a budgetary reduction from $882,912 in 1931-32 to $336,813 in 1933-34, a decrease of about sixty-one per cent. For the first time since 1882, the term was barely eight months. The twelfth grade, added in 1924, was discontinued. Fifty-four classroom teachers were eliminated and all special supervisors dropped, as well as the school dentist, six nurses, one special attendance officer, one secretary, one truck driver, and several janitorial helpers. The salary of all school employees was sixty per cent below 1930-31. The maximum annual salary for a teacher with an "A" certificate was fixed at $720, and eight years experience was needed as a requisite for obtaining that sum.

Restoration of the school system began after an election April 16, 1935, authorizing a special tax of 25 cents on the $100 valuation. On April 15, 1946, the tax for school purposes was doubled. This action was followed a week later by an election which authorized bonds in the sum of $3,980,000 for the purchase of sites and the building of schools that first led Charlotte to national prominence in the field of modern public education on both elementary and secondary levels.

Among the more significant accomplishments in the development of public school education in Charlotte, the most far-reaching was undoubtedly the establishment of "electives" shortly after the beginning of the twentieth century. A milestone, especially from the standpoint of the student body, was publication of the first high school annual, *Snips and Cuts*, at Central High School at the close of the 1908-9 season.

Compulsory school attendance became effective in Charlotte in 1919. The 6-3-3 plan, providing six years of elementary schooling and three years each in junior and senior high schools, was adopted in 1923 when the twelfth grade was added. The D. H. Hill School, which had occupied the old North Carolina Military Institute building since 1882, was abandoned as a school in 1937.

The first school cafeteria was located in the Alexander Graham High School on East Morehead Street and opened about 1921. Subsequently, space for cafeterias was provided in nearly all new school buildings. Until 1948, when management was taken over by the Board of Education and Miss Rosa Spearman engaged as director, all cafeterias were operated separately.

As for modern developments, the earliest appropriation for visual education was made in 1946 in the sum of $3,000. Charlotte high school pupils received their first television instruction in 1957.

During the eighty years that public schools have been operated in Charlotte, hundreds of men and women teachers and officials have contributed immensely to the city's intellectual life, endearing themselves in the process to thousands of pupils. The few mentioned here have been selected from the hundreds described in Dr. Harding's unpublished history.

Miss Hattie Alexander was variously teacher, principal of Highland Park School, Wesley Heights School, and Elizabeth School. Uhlman S. Alexander was principal of First Ward Grammar School, then principal of Piedmont Junior High School, and later became a successful Charlotte lawyer. Dr. Harvey P. Barret, one-time member of the Charlotte School Board, is best remembered for organizing the Central High School track team in 1923 and coaching it, without pay, for seven years. Miss Sallie Bethune was a member of the original school faculty in 1882, and was later a principal. Bethune School was named for her. Mrs. Essie Blankenship was principal of Wesley Heights School and Wilmore School. Miss Ursula Blankenship, seventh grade teacher in 1907, was principal of Dilworth School in 1913. She was a constant advocate of progressive education. Miss Dorothy Boone has been the head of the distributive education program for Mecklenburg County since about 1950, capably assisted by Miss Miriam Blair and others. Miss Ellen Brice succeeded Mrs. Blankenship at Wilmore School and supervised the growth and development of that school. Mrs. W. J. Bryan, first teacher of Bible in the Charlotte Public Schools, was a "magnetic teacher whose classes were full from the beginning." Miss Cornelia Carter was first supervisor of elementary education. Miss Willie Choate was first principal of Myers Park Elementary School and later, as Mrs. W. D. Hampton, teacher at Eastover School. Miss Gertrude Coward was first director of school libraries. She was appointed after having served as librarian at Harding High School.

Dr. Harding's list also includes Miss Bertha Donnelly, mathematics teacher; Miss Minnie Downs, head of the English Department of the city high schools; Aubrey M. Elliott, principal of Alexander Graham Junior High School; Mrs. Cornelia Wearn Henderson, principal of Parks Hutchison School and specialist in nursery school operations; Miss Cornelia Fore, teacher of history in Central High School, and later head of the History Department; Miss Florence Jamison, first principal of Zeb Vance School, later principal of Myers Park Elementary School; Miss Sara Kelley, head of the Mathematics Department, city high schools; Mrs. Ransom McMahan, secretary to the superintendent; Miss Mary Armand Nash, who in 1915 was assigned to teach art in the high school after some years of elementary teaching; Dr. John Otts, principal of Central High School (1946), later assistant superintendent of education; Miss Janet Robinson, teacher of Bible at Central High School; Forrest T. Selby, principal of Tech High School; Miss Sally Southerland, director of physical education for elementary schools; Miss Florence Thomas, head of the Home Economics Department of the city schools; Miss Isabella Wyche, principal of Myers Street School, for whom Isabella Wyche School was named.

Some of these teachers, and many others not mentioned here, will feel amply repaid for their labors as they contemplate the contributions of their students to various fields, not only in Charlotte as shown abundantly in these pages, but throughout the world. William Joseph Eudy (Billy) Arthur became a successful newspaperman and legislative authority of Chapel Hill. Dr. Julian Parks Boyd, a South Carolinian by birth, spent his school days in Charlotte. He became the librarian and historian of Princeton University. Frank Porter Graham rose to the presidency of the University of North Carolina and, later, became a United States Senator. Currently he is serving the United Nations. Herschel V. Johnson, born in Georgia, regarded Charlotte as home while holding high diplomatic posts throughout the world. Edward Herman Little, a North Mecklenburg boy, became chairman of the board, Colgate-Palmolive-Peet Company of New York. Hugh Murrill graduated from West Point and attained the rank of colonel before becoming an advertising executive. James Orr became minister of a large Presbyterian Church in Pittsburgh; Will W. Orr, president of Westminster College. J. Calvin Reid is pastor at Mount Lebanon Presbyterian Church of Pittsburgh; Charles Sylvanius Rhyne rose to the presidency of the American Bar Association; Walter Spearman is professor of journalism at the University of North Carolina; Reed Surratt became a successful newspaperman and head of the Southern Education Reporting Service of Nashville, Tennessee; Will S. Tillett is a noted physician and medical college faculty member in New York; Erskine Wakefield Smith is professor of accounting, University of Delaware; Walter Reece Berryhill is dean of the School of Medicine, University of North Carolina; Algernon Reese is an ophthalmologist in New York City.

Higher Education

Fortunately for Charlotte, every generation has produced a few people who demanded institutions of higher learning in keeping with the city's needs. For nearly two hundred years their hopes have been kept alive in the face of every obstacle. There is now some chance their hopes are to be more fully and permanently realized.

Discouragements go back to 1773 when word was received that King George had disallowed the charter for Queen's College which had been established in Charlotte two years earlier. Apparently the principal reason for this act was that the college, being in a Presbyterian stronghold, would tend to encourage more dissenters from the established Church of England.

Despite this determined opposition of the Crown, Charlotte changed the name of the institution to Queen's Museum, an appropriate name since Webster gives the derivation of "museum" as "a temple of the muses, hence a place of study." After operating successfully for three years, this unchartered college had its name changed to Liberty Hall Academy, in keeping with the revolutionary spirit of the people of Mecklenburg. Liberty Hall was located on the southeast corner of what is now Tryon and Third Streets and did well when first opened, but as the Revolution progressed, patronage was reduced and the end came when Cornwallis invaded Charlotte, September 26, 1780.

According to C. L. Hunter in his *Sketches of Western North Carolina*, "Liberty Hall Academy . . . was used as a hospital and greatly defaced. The numerous graves in the rear of the Academy, visible upon the departure of the British army after a stay of 18 days, bore ample evidence of their great loss in 'this rebellious country, the hornets' nest of America.'" Following the war, the building was used for some years as a school. Washington's diary mentions that it was "formerly a college."

From about 1800 until 1835 Charlotte and Mecklenburg were apparently without educational facilities except for small, privately conducted schools and some tutoring in individual homes. One such school, Charlotte Female Academy, was opened in 1838 by Susan

Davis Nye Hutchison. There was also a Charlotte Male Academy at this time, though little remains on record concerning it. It was during this period that the population of Mecklenburg was either static or decreasing. The frontiers to the west and south were drawing off whole families.

But even during this period, there were a few who never abandoned hope of having an institution of higher learning in the county. The subject was much talked about at a meeting of friends of education in Lincolnton, September 22, 1820. The legislature of that year granted a charter for Western College, asked for as a result of this meeting because "more western counties of the state are distant from Chapel Hill, which renders it inconvenient for their youth to prosecute their education there."

Western College failed to materialize. It was, according to one writer, "an endeavor to unite too many discordant interests." It was said that "other denominations were unwilling to do much for a college which, when founded, would almost certainly be manned by Presbyterians . . ."

Davidson College

This assumption, made some years afterwards, was evidently correct because on March 12, 1835, Concord Presbytery voted to establish an institution of higher learning in western North Carolina. This resolution bore fruit in the establishment of Davidson College. The site selected was the plantation of William Lee Davidson, in upper Mecklenburg. The presbytery agreed to pay him $1,521 for the 469 acres. Whether he accepted or not is not known as there is no record of gift or sale. From records preserved at the college, it is known that William Lee Davidson subscribed $2,000 for the endowment of a professorship shortly after the opening of the college and willed it $10,000 at the time of his death. The college bears the name of his father. The resolution, passed August 26, 1835, for naming the college reads:

"That the Manual Labor Institution which we are about to build be called Davidson College, as a tribute to the memory of that distinguished and excellent man, General William Davidson, who in the ardour of patriotism, fearlessly contending for the liberty of his county fell (universally lamented) in the Battle of Cowan's Ford."

Rev. Robert Hall Morrison, pastor of Sugaw Creek Presbyterian Church, was chosen for the first president of Davidson College at an annual salary of $1,200. He accepted notwithstanding the hesitancy expressed in this personal letter to a cousin: "am still in great perplexity by the election of President of our college having fallen upon me. I used much effort to prevent it and gave all my influence to obtain some suitable appointment beyond our bounds. I am well situated, have a fine congregation, pleasant people, good location and a family of girls. On the other hand, I know not how to get over the solicitation of friends, and the overthrow of our institution which might result from a failure to secure officers."

Teaching at Davidson began May 12, 1837 with 65 students who paid a total of $820 for tuition for five months. There were three teachers. The first complete term began in September 1837 and the first graduation class was that of 1840. Textbooks included Day's *Algebra*, Gibson's *Surveying*, Adams' *Latin Grammar*. Studies included English grammar, writing, arithmetic, geography, plane and spherical trigonometry, mental and moral philosophy, astronomy, logic, rhetoric, and politics.

The story of the school's origin and development is told in *Davidson College*, by Cornelia Rebekah Shaw (1923). Its beginnings, she says, were "typically American. The consecrated idealism of its founders, its long and losing battle with poverty and indifference, its rescue by an overruling Providence, the accumulating momentum of recent years, its present stability and far-reaching usefulness constitute a thrilling panorama of Divine Providence and human heroism." The impact of Davidson upon the region and the nation has been unbelievably greater than indicated by its modest enrollment.

Thomas Woodrow Wilson, 28th President of the United States, attended Davidson in 1873, at the age of 19, remained for one year, and ever thereafter gave evidence of fond memories of his alma mater. Miss Shaw devotes several pages to incidents in the student life of this distinguished alumnus.

North Carolina Medical College

In 1886 the Presbyterian women of Charlotte equipped a small infirmary for the use of Davidson College students under treatment of Dr. Paul B. Barringer, the college physician, who also had some private classes in anatomy and physiology which were attended by students preparing for northern medical schools. When Dr. Barringer left in 1889 to become associated with the University of Virginia, he sold his "Medical School," as it had come to be known, to Dr. John Peter Munroe, who had succeeded him as college physician.

Though never a member of the faculty of Davidson College, Dr. Munroe had long been identified with it as a student (1882) and physician, and his pre-medical classes became an important part of the village activities. These classes formed the basis for the North Carolina Medical College, chartered in 1892. In 1903 the upper classes of the Medical College were removed to Charlotte where the students could take advantage of the facilities offered by the newly-organized Presbyterian Hospital. In 1907 the entire student body of the Medical College came to Charlotte where it occupied its own building on the southeast corner of Sixth and Church Streets, a building known since 1913 as the Churchill Apartments.

During its lifetime, the North Carolina Medical College had on its faculty many of the leading medical men of Charlotte, who were instrumental in awarding the degree of Doctor of Medicine to 340 men. A complete history of this institution, listing faculty members and students, is contained in *The North Carolina Medical College*, written by Dr. Robert H. Lafferty, published 1946. When it became evident that the college could no longer meet the increasingly exacting demands of modern medical training, the college suspended operation. The entire student body was transferred in 1913 to the Medical College of Virginia in Richmond where they were entered in the regular classes and the diplomas conferred in the name of the North Carolina Medical College.

Queens College

With Davidson supplying the need for a college for the men of Mecklenburg and surrounding counties, it was not long before plans were under way for a similar institution for women. By early 1856 a group of Charlotte citizens organized a stock company and erected an attractive building at the corner of College and Ninth Streets. Rev. Robert Burwell and his wife, Margaret Anne, came to Charlotte from Hillsboro and took charge. The school was named Charlotte Female Institute. Although there have been a number of changes in ownership and name, and one inoperative period of several years, the Institute is considered the ancestor of today's Queens College.

Dr. and Mrs. Burwell headed Charlotte Female Institute until 1872, when they were succeeded by Robert Hett Chapman and Stephen Taylor Martin, jointly, and then by Dr. Martin alone. In 1878 Dr. William Robert Atkinson bought the school and conducted it until 1891, when it was closed.

Charlotte would have been left without a school for girls had not Miss Lily Long, with the aid of Mrs. Tinsley Junkin, Mrs. Bessie Dewey, and Miss Rose Franklin organized the Charlotte Seminary for Girls which was located at 510 North Tryon Street. Some of Charlotte's best known women attended Charlotte Female Institute and Charlotte Seminary for Girls, including: Mrs. John VanLandingham, Mrs. Margaret Springs Kelly, Mrs. J. P. Durant, Mrs. Bessie Myers, Mrs. I. W. Faison, Mrs. C. C. Kennedy, Mrs. W. A. Zweier, Mrs. C. M. Carson, Mrs. George Fitzsimmons, Mrs. W. H. Twitty, Mrs. J. A. Durham, Mrs. H. A. Murrill, and the Misses Alice Springs, Sallie Phillips, Laura Orr, and Charlee Hutchison.

The Charlotte Seminary for Girls was continued until 1896, at which time the Presbytery of Concord and Mecklenburg established the Presbyterian College for Women, acquiring and enlarging the building once used by Charlotte Female Institute. When the college was ready to open, Dr. J. R. Bridges was chosen as president. With Miss Lily Long as lady principal, the good will and records of the Seminary which she had organized were taken over by the new college. Thus, with the establishment of Davidson College and the Presbyterian College for Women, the Presbyterians, affiliated with the Presbyterian Church in the United States (Southern), opened the first two lasting institutions of higher learning in Mecklenburg.

The Presbyterian College for Women served Charlotte and surrounding territory well until 1912 when the name was changed to Queens College and the institution removed to the site of the present campus. The land was a gift of the Stephens Company, Mecklenburg Farm Company, Dr. William Haines Wakefield, and Mr. W. S. Pharr. Citizens of Myers Park subscribed $8,000 and this, with the proceeds from the sale of 100 acres of the original gift, provided funds for beginning the erection of Burwell Hall, Atkinson Hall, Ninniss Hall, Lily Long Dormitory, and Mildred Watkins Dormitory.

Even with these gifts, a considerable debt remained from building costs and the next ten years were the darkest in the life of the college. In 1921, Dr. William H. Frazer began an eighteen year term as president of Queens. Each year required heroic measures to assure the survival of the college, and to raise the academic standards. A look at Queens today with its spacious, well-kept campus and many new buildings, is the best evidence of the success of these efforts. This success was due to the active and financial help of such men and women as Edwin E. Jones, McAlister Carson, Hunter Marshall, David Ovens, Mrs. Cameron Morrison, the Belk families, W. Z. Stultz, H. H. Everett, Dr. James A. Jones, and many others.

Those who used these facilities to improve the intellectual and cultural life of the community are engraved indelibly on the minds and in the hearts of students. There is space to mention only a few: Dr. Ethel Abernethy, Head of Psychology Department, 1918-1954; Miss Thelma Albright, for many years Dean of the College, currently a member of the English staff; Dr. Elizabeth Blair, Academic Dean, 1924-1935; Dr. Herbert V. Carson and Dr. Charles William Sommerville, excellent counselors as well as Bible teachers; Miss Rena Chambers Harrell, Librarian for some 30 years; Miss Sarah McKee Nooe and Miss Mary Lee Taylor, who since 1934 and 1941 respectively have made numerous and devoted contributions to many phases of life on the Queens campus; Miss Laura A. Tillett, English teacher.

North Carolina Military Institute

The short-lived, but well remembered, North Carolina Military Institute appeared upon the educational scene at Charlotte in 1859. It was the brain-child of Major Daniel Harvey Hill, then professor of mathematics at Davidson College. Convinced that a national conflict was imminent and foreseeing the necessity for training young men to be ready for it, he gave up his work and came to Charlotte to establish the school.

With a loan granted by Davidson College, Hill erected a building modeled after the U. S. Military Academy at West Point, of which he was a graduate. At the outbreak of the Civil War, Major Hill was asked to take charge of the training of the Confederate troops. His first official act was to take the 150 cadets composing the student body to Raleigh. Here they are reported to have drilled 10,000 volunteers. During the war the Institute was used as a hospital for Confederate soldiers. At the close of the war, Hill, who had been advanced to the rank of General, became president of the University of Arkansas. He later returned to Charlotte where for two years he edited and published *The Land We Love*, a monthly magazine.

Mecklenburg Female College

When no longer needed for hospital purposes, the N. C. Military Institute was occupied by the Mecklenburg Female College. Rev. A. G. Stacy was the founder and president during its brief existence, October 1, 1867 through the summer of 1869. An advertisement for this school states that there were 155 students from five states who paid $103 per term of 10 months for board, tuition, fuel, light, and contingent fees. The only remaining source of information concerning this college is a complete set of four issues of a magazine entitled, *The Carrier Dove* or *Mecklenburg Female College Magazine*.

Charlotte Military Institute

In 1873 Colonel J. P. Thomas opened a private school for boys in the Military Institute building and continued it for a period of 10 years as the Charlotte Military Institute. This school was highly regarded and successful, judged by such alumni as Frank Wilkes, John G. Bryce, Charles M. Carson, Harvey Orr, Latta Johnston, W. A. Bradshaw, Heriot Clarkson, and Dr. R. L. Gibbon, all of whom were among Charlotte's most prominent citizens. The building became, after 1883, a unit of the Charlotte public school system and so remained until almost the date of its demolition in 1954.

Biddle University: Johnson C. Smith University

One of the first needs to become pressing in Mecklenburg following the Civil War was for facilities for the education of Negroes. This accounts for a movement started at a Presbyterian church meeting in Charlotte April 7, 1867 resulting in the establishment of a mission school for Negroes located on the western side of the city on a campus donated by Colonel W. R. Myers. The first large cash contribution to this mission was made by Mrs. Mary Biddle, of Philadelphia, and the institution was named for her family, Biddle Memorial Institute.

The first president of Biddle Memorial Institute was, like those who originated the movement, a white man. Dr. Stephen Mattoon, a Presbyterian minister from the North, was selected for the position because of his understanding of races other than his own gained while serving as a missionary to Siam. Dr. Mattoon served from 1870 until 1884, during which time his wife taught at Charlotte Female Institute. Dr. and Mrs. Mattoon had two daughters, both born in Bangkok. Mary remained single, but Emma married Weddington Evans Thomas in the First Presbyterian Church of Charlotte and became the mother of Norman Mattoon Thomas. Norman Thomas, minister and author, was the nominee of the Socialist party in many presidential elections. Dr. Mattoon and his wife were among the first to be buried in Charlotte's Elmwood Cemetery—Mrs. Mattoon in 1885 and Dr. Mattoon four years later.

The principal support of Biddle Memorial Institute and Biddle

University came from members of the Presbyterian Church, though from churches associated with the Northern General Assembly rather than those belonging to the Southern branch of this denomination. Thus, credit is due the Presbyterians for establishing the first three institutions of higher learning in Mecklenburg.

While Dr. Mattoon was president, the name Biddle Memorial Institute was changed to Biddle University and, on March 1, 1923, the name was again changed, to Johnson C. Smith University in recognition of generous gifts by Mrs. Jane Berry Smith in honor of her husband. Highlights in the recent history of Johnson C. Smith University include: large benefactions by James Buchanan Duke in 1923; the change to a co-educational institution in 1932; dedication of the Duke residential hall for women in 1940; celebration of the Diamond Jubilee in 1942; the president's home destroyed by fire, claiming the life of his wife, Mrs. H. L. McCrorey, and her nurse in 1944; retirement of Dr. McCrorey and inauguration of Dr. Hardy Liston as president, 1947; death of President Liston and appointment of J. W. Seabrook to serve as acting president, 1956; election and inauguration of Rufus Patterson Perry as president, 1957.

As this venerable institution, "bursting at the seams again" even with greatly expanded campus, nears the centennial anniversary, it seems appropriate to quote a few lines from the Jubilee address delivered by Dr. Julian S. Miller of Charlotte:

"If any silly skepticisms have persisted through the years as to the propriety and expediency, to say nothing of the common justice and democracy, of higher education for the Negro people, or to the capacity of this race to absorb and assimilate advanced learning, all such unfounded notions are quickly dissolved by the achievements of the graduates of this institution, and by the illustrious record of the seventy-five years of educational service rendered in this field by this University.

"If ever it is to come to pass that happy day in our national life when we, as races, will live alongside each other in cooperative and constructive relationships and just and impartial partnership, that consummation will be reached through the efforts and influence of men and women of both races who have been educated out of their narrow provincialism and who are capable in spiritual liberalism to magnify the point of similarity and to reduce the notes of differences to a diminuendo."

Baird's School for Boys

Chronologically, the school founded by Captain W. A. Barrier in 1870 follows the establishment of Biddle University. Captain Barrier operated his school for boys under the name of Macon School until his death in 1890. Then, while arrangements for the sale of the school were being made, it was "held together" by Rev. C. E. Todd and Mr. E. L. Reid, father of Virginia Reid Johnston (Mrs. Rufus) and Dr. Graham Reid of Charlotte. The interest of a former student, Major J. G. Baird of South Carolina, was aroused and he bought the school property, a large wooden building on the corner of Sixth and Poplar Streets. Major Baird introduced military tactics and, for a while, called his school Charlotte Military Institute. Later, he erected a brick building and changed the name to Baird School for Boys.

Major Baird, kindly gentleman and strict disciplinarian, was one of Charlotte's finest educators, as many senior citizens of 1960 will recall with pleasure. His school was highly rated, well patronized, and continued for about 40 years.

Charlotte Commercial College

The first business school was opened in Charlotte in December 1891 and called, by its owners L. H. Jackson and R. F. Day, Charlotte Commercial College. A period of severe financial depression began shortly after its opening, but the new business college moved bravely ahead and was well attended. In 1896, it was moved to the Y.M.C.A. and for many years was one of the important activities of that association.

Elizabeth College

Though Elizabeth College lasted less than 20 years, it holds numerous and pleasant memories. Even now, after nearly half a century, alumnae meet occasionally to relive the old days at Elizabeth.

The college was the fulfillment of a dream of Dr. Charles Banks King to establish a grade "A" college under the auspices of the Lutheran church. He had the good will and financial support of his father-in-law, Mr. Gerard Snowden Watts, wealthy tobacconist of Baltimore. There was great elation, according to the *Charlotte Observer* for May 28, 1896, because of the selection of Charlotte as the site of the new college. Charlotte people provided $9,332 cash as an inducement, and the Highland Park Land and Improvement Company donated $3,600 and twenty acres for a campus, to top the offer made by Columbia, S. C.

In an article about "Early Schools and Education in Charlotte" in the *Charlotte Observer* for June 18, 1933, Mrs. J. A. Yarbrough recalled that "In the fall of 1896, the doors of Elizabeth College, under the presidency of Dr. Charles Banks King, were opened. A Board of Trustees composed of Messrs. Charles Duls, C. Valaer, Dr. C. A. Misenheimer, and George Watts of Durham, brother of Mrs. King, aided the establishment of this school which was the first 'A' grade college in this section."

The same board of trustees served the institution throughout the twenty years of its existence. The efforts of administration and faculty met with a ready response in the hearts and minds of parents of young girls. The handsome Gerard Conservatory of Music was presented by Mrs. King's father, Mr. Gerard Snowden Watts, and the cornerstone was laid by his grandson, George Watts King, the son of Dr. and Mrs. King. Ill health influenced Dr. King to move the college to Salem, Virginia (1915) where its name was retained after consolidation with Roanoke College for Women. In 1921 Elizabeth College in Virginia was burned to the ground and all records destroyed.

The property occupied by Elizabeth College in Charlotte was acquired by the Presbyterian Hospital, the original college buildings forming the nucleus for the present larger buildings required to house that institution.

Horner Military Institute

From Oxford, North Carolina, where it was founded in 1851, the celebrated Horner Military Institute removed to Charlotte in

1914. Under Col. Jerome C. Horner, son of the founder, the institute occupied a building especially erected for its use on what was then the outer edge of the Myers Park residential section of the city. When the school closed in 1920, the building was remodeled and has since been known as the Rockledge Apartments, adjacent to the Myers Park Country Club, which uses the campus for a part of its golf course.

Charlotte and Carver Colleges

In the summer of 1946, North Carolina colleges anticipated an unprecedented increase in enrollment because of returning veterans entitled to educational benefits. The North Carolina College Conference and the North Carolina Department of Education met this challenge by sponsoring college centers, providing first year college work, in Charlotte and eleven other communities. Operation of these twelve units was to be under the Directorate of Extension of the University of North Carolina. In 1946-47, the Charlotte College Center was the largest in the state. With the addition of a second year of college work in the fall of 1947, the enrollment reached 304, making it larger than all other similar college centers combined. In the same year the Charlotte School Board organized the Second Ward Extension School, with a similar program for Negroes.

By 1949 most of the college centers were discontinued. However, the board of school commissioners of Charlotte, prompted by the continued need, and encouraged by a group of citizens led by Woodford A. (Woodie) Kennedy, absorbed the Charlotte Center and made it a tuition-paying part of the public school system. This action applied also to the Second Ward Extension School which had, by then, been named Carver College. On April 26, 1958, the value of these institutions having been clearly demonstrated, the people of Mecklenburg voted a tax of two cents on the $100 property valuation for the support of the Charlotte Community College System. The voting of this tax brought these colleges under the North Carolina Community College System and gave them their first board of trustees, members of which assumed office May 11, 1958.

From their inception these colleges have held classes in Central High School and Second Ward High School respectively. The current co-educational student body of Charlotte College is 1,500 and of Carver College 400. Miss Bonnie E. Cone became director of Charlotte College on August 1, 1947, and president in the summer of 1961. Dr. E. H. Brown served as director at Carver College for the first years of its existence.

The passage of the two-cent county-wide tax levy qualified the two institutions for grants-in-aid and capital funds from the state of North Carolina. These funds are supplemented by tuition fees. On November 4, 1958, the citizens of Mecklenburg authorized bonds in the sum of $975,000 to match a $575,000 grant from the state and to provide $400,000 with which to acquire sites for the two colleges. Of the total amount authorized by the legislature for the North Carolina Community College System during the 1959-61 biennium, the two Charlotte colleges were awarded $700,000. The trustees of the Charlotte Community Colleges acquired a tract of 262 acres on U. S. Highway 29, just north of the city, to serve the future campus needs of Charlotte College. A tract of fifty acres on Hoskins Road was purchased for Carver College.

Private and Parochial Schools

Prior to the advent of public schools and state supported colleges, all educational institutions were privately conducted by individuals or groups. That they have continued to exist, and in some cases to flourish, indicates rather clearly that there will always be a need for the non-public school.

The oldest privately conducted school in Charlotte is O'Donoghue School, established on August 27, 1887, by the Sisters of Mercy, a Roman Catholic religious order, as St. Mary's Seminary. The present name was adopted in 1905 in honor of Dennis O'Donoghue, whose bequest made possible the large building at 531 South Tryon Street, home of the school for many years.

When St. Patrick's Church was erected in 1939, a large granite-faced structure was built adjacent to it for the use of O'Donoghue School. This building was greatly enlarged in the late 1950's. With the rapid increase in the number of Catholics in Charlotte, four other parochial schools and two high schools were built. Located in different sections of the city, these facilities are now used by more than 1,000 students.

King's Business College

After the Charlotte Commercial College was moved to the Y.M.C.A., there was a need for such an institution for both sexes. In 1901 King's Business College entered upon the local educational scene. This institution had an uninterrupted and successful career for more than half a century under the management of Frederick L. Riggsbee. Since March 31, 1943, it has been managed by Milo O. Kirkpatrick, whose sons, Milo, Jr., and Robert, are also on the faculty.

A pacemaker in its broadened but still specialized field, King's Business College has recently moved into its own modern college building, with equally modern dormitory space for non-resident students. King's enjoys its distinction for the length of time served by officials and faculty members. There is Mr. Riggsbee's 35 years; Mr. Kirkpatrick's 18 years; the tenure of Bernard W. Barnett of 50 years and William F. Drinkard, more than 25 years. Mr. Barnett was honored by the Gregg Publishing Company for having taught shorthand longer than any other person in the country.

Charlotte Country Day School

A much younger private school, but one which has become a valuable addition to the city's educational facilities, is the Charlotte Country Day School. It is a state chartered, non-profit corporation. The school was founded in 1941 by Dr. Thomas Burton, who became first headmaster. The Charlotte Country Day School offers the services of a highly trained faculty of wide academic experience in its strongly academic program for boys and girls of elementary and high school age. The school recently was relocated on a 30-acre suburban campus.

Private Schools of the Past

The Charlotte University School was a college preparatory school for boys owned and headed by Professor Hiram W. Glas-

The W. S. Rankin Health Center of the Charlotte-Mecklenburg Health Department.

Charlotte Memorial Hospital is publicly owned.

Mercy Hospital, operated b

Presbyterian Hospital is maintained by the Presbyterian church.

s of Mercy of Belmont, N. C.

Above: Chambers Building at Davidson College. Martin Science Building in background. *Below:* Campus scene at Queens College, which traces its ancestry to Charlotte Female Institute, founded in 1856.

Above: First buildings on the permanent campus of Charlotte College. The Science Building is at left, Liberal Arts at right. *Below:* King's College, specializing in business training for young men and women.

Above: The Administration Building at Johnson C. Smith University. *Below:* Carver College occupied space in the Second Ward School pending construction of its permanent campus.

Above: Elizabeth College, a Lutheran institution, educated young women for twenty years, 1896 to 1916. Building is on present site of Presbyterian Hospital. *Below:* Presbyterian College, predecessor of today's Queens College. Building shown was located on North College Street between Ninth and Tenth Streets.

Above: D. H. Hill School occupied this former home of the North Carolina Military Institute from 1882 until 1937. The building stood at South Boulevard and East Morehead Street. *Below:* First Ward Graded School, one of Charlotte's early public school buildings.

gow. The school, founded in 1907, went out of existence in 1930. The Southern Industrial Institute, organized in 1903 by Rev. Jesse A. Baldwin, offered agricultural and industrial training to boys and girls. Many of the students were from needy homes, and at times this institution provided boarding space for 75 students and teaching space for 60 others. The school closed in 1925, when the needs were largely met by public educational facilities.

Parent-Teacher Associations

In 1960 the North Carolina Congress of Parent-Teacher Associations had 358,936 members and the two Mecklenburg councils had a combined membership of 38,773.

By 1917 there had been organized in Charlotte six Parent-Teacher Associations, composed of parents with children in Elizabeth School, First Ward School, Dilworth School, Wesley Heights School, Bethune School, and Villa Heights School, with a total membership of 333. These six associations then formed a Federation of Parent-Teacher Associations to coordinate the activities of various units. The name was later changed to that used at present. Dr. Harry P. Harding described the first meeting:

"The presidents and officials of the several PTA's of the city schools planned a meeting for April 1, 1917, to form a city Parent-Teacher Council. The meeting was to be held in the assembly room of the Chamber of Commerce. . . . Dr. P. P. Claxton, U. S. Commissioner of Education, who had a speaking engagement at Winthrop College, agreed to stop over in Charlotte for this initial meeting of the PTA Council.

"On the morning of April 1, I was asked to go with Mrs. Elizabeth Hoyle Rucker, Chairman of the Reception Committee, to meet Dr. Claxton at the railroad station. When the train arrived and Dr. Claxton stepped down from the Pullman car, immediately behind him came the former President of the United States, the Honorable William Howard Taft, and Mrs. Taft. They were stopping for the day with Dr. Claxton. Mrs. Rucker and I were greatly surprised and somewhat awe stricken at the sight of our distinguished guests, but she hastily telephoned Mr. David Ovens, the Chairman of the Chamber of Commerce, who caught a taxicab and joined us.

"President and Mrs. Taft took the rear seat in my new Studebaker, Mrs. Rucker and Mr. Ovens took the 'pull-out' seats, and Dr. Claxton joined me on the front seat, and away we went to the Selwyn Hotel. At eleven o'clock Dr. Claxton and Mr. Taft addressed the first PTA Council, assembled that morning to perfect an organization.

"Mrs. John Morehead entertained our distinguished guests for luncheon and then took them to the train in the afternoon. As we waited at the station for the arrival of the train, Dr. Alexander Graham and President Taft vied with each other in telling funny anecdotes. Mrs. Taft, in the meantime, was walking back and forth on the platform as if bored with it all. Never before, since he had been President, I imagine, had Mr. Taft been so informally welcomed and entertained, and he seemed to enjoy it all."

The first year's officers of the Charlotte Council were Mrs. David S. Yates, president; Mrs. C. H. Dorsey, vice-president; Mrs. Frank F. Jones, secretary; and Mrs. W. N. Jasspon, treasurer.

A similar council was formed March 20, 1926, by parents of children attending five schools in Mecklenburg County. This organization meeting was conducted by Mrs. John A. McRae, who was then president of the Charlotte Council. Mrs. Joseph Garibaldi became the first president of the Mecklenburg Council, having in 1919 served as the first president of the North Carolina Congress which originated in Charlotte, November 6, 1919. Subsequently the Charlotte Council supplied two other state presidents: Mrs. Ernest Hunter (1947-49) and Mrs. J. Zebulon Watkins (1957-60). On April 5, 1960, the Charlotte and Mecklenburg P.T.A. Councils were officially merged under the name of Mecklenburg Council of Parent-Teacher Associations. Mrs. Carlton Watkins, member of Sedgefield Junior High School P.T.A., became the first president of the new Council on May 24.

In his *History of the Charlotte Public School System*, Dr. Harry P. Harding, the man best qualified to evaluate the work of the Parent-Teacher Associations, has this to say:

"In evaluating the worth of the Parent-Teacher Associations in Charlotte much can be written of the material aid the Associations have given the needy and under-privileged children of our schools, such as providing hot lunches, free text books, first-aid supplies, dental services, pre-school clinics, and clothing.

"Much praise is due the Associations for securing library books, playground equipment, victrolas and records, radio sets, and the like for the schools, all of which at times when school board funds were too low to provide such things.

"In almost every campaign that has been undertaken in Charlotte for the improvement of educational conditions, the leadership and the greatest support have come from the Parent-Teacher Associations. . . . But to my mind the greatest contribution of the PTA has not been in material things and cannot be measured in terms of material values. The greatest value of the Associations should be expressed in terms of cooperation, support, understanding, and sympathy."

Public Library Service

The present Public Library of Charlotte and Mecklenburg County had its origin in the minds of two young citizens, Willis F. Dowd and John M. Walker, Jr. At an organizational meeting called by these two and General Rufus Barringer, J. Lenoir Chambers, Sr., and Mrs. Bessie Dewey Chambers on January 16, 1891, the Charlotte Literary and Library Association was formed, and a constitution adopted. Incorporated February 12, 1891, this association opened its doors February 20, 1891 as a subscription library with dues of fifty cents per month.

The first librarian was Mrs. Bessie Lacy Dewey, who served from March 19, 1891, until her death November 8, 1900. The library was located in the rooms over the bookstore of Stone & Barringer, 22 South Tryon Street. From 1901 until 1903, with Miss Sallie H. Adams as librarian, the library was operated from the city hall as a part of the school system and called Charlotte Public School Library.

The library was absorbed by the Charlotte Carnegie Public Library which began its official existence January 31, 1903, with Mrs. Annie Smith Ross, who began her duties November 11, 1902, as librarian. It was made possible by gifts totaling $25,000 from Andrew Carnegie, contingent upon agreement by the city to support the library with an appropriation of $2,500 annually. The charter was granted by the General Assembly January 31, 1903, the appropriation of $2,500 annually having been ratified by a vote of the people May 6, 1901. The leader in persuading Mr. Carnegie to make the gifts was Thomas S. Franklin, member of the Charlotte board of aldermen and later chairman of the board of trustees of the library. The architects were Wheeler and McMichael, and the contractors Lazenby Brothers.

The original charter provided for a public library for colored people. This library was opened in 1905 and named Brevard Street Library for Negroes. In 1929 this library was brought under supervision of the librarian of the Charlotte Carnegie Public Library and continued as a branch of the Public Library system.

In 1909 Mrs. Ross resigned and was replaced by Miss Mary B. Palmer. In 1915 Mr. Carnegie donated another $15,000 which was used to add a Children's Department and small auditorium to the original building, which annex was opened April 9, 1915. In 1918 Miss Palmer resigned and was succeeded by Miss Anne Pierce, who had been children's librarian.

In 1925, with no official action but with no objection, since Mr. Carnegie's gifts had not been contingent upon the use of his name, the term Charlotte Public Library came into use. On June 30, 1937, Miss Pierce resigned and James E. Gourley succeeded her with the title of Director. At this time the library was just returning to normal after having had its income cut drastically because of the great depression, during which the staff was reduced from 28 to 11 members.

Early in 1939 the discovery was made that for many years there had been no legal authorization for money appropriated to the Public Library beyond the annual $2,500 voted in 1901. To correct this situation, an election was held for the purpose of voting a tax levy for the support of the library. For several reasons, but principally because the vote was against registration, as required by law, the measure failed to carry and the Charlotte Public Library closed its doors June 30, 1939. Another election was held May 25, 1940, resulting in the authorization of a maximum tax levy of four cents on the $100 valuation throughout Mecklenburg County, the vote being 10,172 for and 1,966 against.

The library reopened July 1, 1940, and on November 1 following, Hoyt Rees Galvin took up his duties as director. In 1943 the position of assistant director was created, and in August of that year Charles Raven Brockmann was engaged to fill the new position. The new administration began at once to emphasize the educational, informational, and cultural phases of library services rather than the recreational aspects. Toward this end, an audio-visual section was established to lend films, records, and projectors. The first films were loaned in April 1941, and the first record albums, in December 1947.

Following a survey of the public library needs of Charlotte conducted under the auspices of the American Library Association in April 1944, the name of the institution was legally changed to Public Library of Charlotte and Mecklenburg County. On April 23, 1946, an election was held on the question of issuing $600,000 in bonds for new library buildings. Again the vote was against registration and the measure failed to carry.

When ABC stores, for the sale of alcoholic beverages, were authorized in an election, the measure stipulated that the public library was to receive five per cent of the net profits. The first check from this source was received in October 1948. This and subsequent checks made possible many improvements in library service throughout Mecklenburg that might not otherwise have been possible, notably the purchase of two mobile libraries.

On December 13, 1952, the citizens of Charlotte and Mecklenburg authorized the issuance of bonds in the sum of $1,600,000 for new library buildings and equipment. With these funds, a new main library building replaced the original Carnegie Library building at 310 North Tryon Street and was dedicated November 19, 1956. In addition, this bond issue provided funds for four branch library buildings in Charlotte and for replacing rented space with new and attractive buildings in Huntersville, Cornelius, Davidson, Matthews, and Pineville.

When completed, the new main library building was widely acclaimed as one of the most efficiently designed library buildings in America. It was pictured and described in leading architectural magazines and all American library periodicals. Architects, librarians, educators, and others from many states and foreign countries toured the building.

Children's Nature Museum

The idea of a nature museum originated with Miss Laura Owens, at the time a science teacher in the city schools. Perhaps she was influenced by the fact that her father, the Rev. R. B. Owens, was one of the city's most avid amateur lapidaries. She was the motivating force in persuading a group of prominent citizens to meet at the home of Arthur Jones for the purpose of organizing such a museum. A prospectus was prepared in May 1946. With the help of many, including members of the Junior League, Charles H. Stone, chairman of the Charlotte Park and Recreation Commission, C. W. Gilchrist, and others, the organization was formed November 11, 1947, and opened at 315 North Cecil Street. Subsequently, the present building, 1658 Sterling Road, was built with funds amounting to $68,000 raised by the Junior League of Charlotte.

Miss Owens was asked to serve as first director of the new museum but declined, though later she did serve from September 1, 1948, until June 30, 1956, when she resigned and was succeeded by James W. Manley. During its first decade the Children's Nature Museum fulfilled every hope of its originators as expressed in the original charter:

"To establish in Charlotte a Children's Nature Museum where natural science collections, literature and other training media pertaining to these collections may be housed.

"To initiate, organize and conduct programs in the natural sciences for the enjoyment and instruction of children.

"To publish and distribute pamphlets, books and leaflets to this same end.

"To increase and diffuse among children a knowledge and appreciation of natural history; to bring about a better understanding of their responsibilities in conserving the natural resources of this county; to supplement their normal school work, and to offer healthful, enjoyable, and useful occupation of leisure time."

6

COMMUNICATION AND TRANSPORTATION

Postal Service in Charlotte

THE earliest postal service to Charlotte, provided by traders and travelers, was highly erratic and expensive. Julia McNinch Slear, writing in the *Charlotte Observer* of November 25, 1934, pointed out that it was scarcely better than that reported before the beginning of the Christian era in the Books of Job, Esther, and Jeremiah.

By October 1, 1794, however, the Federal Post Office Department considered that Charlotte, with its 325 people, was large enough to justify the opening of a post office.

Prior to the coming of railroads in 1852, mail was dispatched in passenger stage coaches. These coaches were in operation as early as 1794 when the route Salisbury-to-Concord-to-Charlotte-to-Statesville and return was covered bi-weekly; by 1830 mail reached Charlotte by stage coach every other day. As railroads branched out in every direction from Charlotte during the latter half of the century, stage coaches were abandoned. The last stage route, that between Wadesboro and Charlotte, ceased operation on December 15, 1874.

Practically all mail was then transported by rail for many years. Speed in the handling of mail became somewhat of a mania and reached a climax when the Southern Railroad inaugurated a through mail train from New York to New Orleans, known as Number 97. It was probably faster than any train operating between those two points in the 1960's, but was discontinued in 1903 following one of the most famous disasters in railroad history.

247

There are several versions of what happened in *The Wreck of the Old 97:*

"... He was going down grade, making 90 miles an hour
When his whistle began to scream
He was found in the wreck with his hands on the throttle
And was scalded to death with steam.
Now, ladies you must take warning
From this time now and on
Never speak harsh words to your true loving husband
He may leave you and never return."

The post office at Charlotte, as elsewhere, quickly took advantage of motorized transportation, which became increasingly popular during the early years of the twentieth century. With the abandonment of many local railroad trains in the mid-twentieth century, the use of intercity truck routes and postal buses increased. Airmail service was begun in Charlotte April 1, 1930.

The first postmaster at Charlotte was Edward Wayne (or Waine), who served four years, beginning January 1, 1795. Between Wayne and Edward H. Thomas, the present postmaster, there were 30 postmasters and one postmistress (see appendix). Until 1833 the post office in Charlotte never did as much as a thousand dollars of annual business. In 1959 the total was $6,515,000. In 1825 the postmaster's pay was $195.35; in 1959, $10,970. Money orders were first issued here on September 9, 1867; free city delivery began September 1, 1887, and rural free delivery July 16, 1900.

Until 1881 the post office was variously located in rented space. On October 15, 1880, a contract was awarded for the erection of a building on the southwest corner of Trade and Mint Streets to serve the post office and United States Court. A lot in the rear, now occupied as a parking lot for postal vehicles, was then known as Vance Park and was popular as a playground and for occasional band concerts.

From 1915 until 1918 the post office again rented space (corner of South Tryon and Second Streets) while the building finished in 1881 was demolished and a larger one built at the same location. In 1934 a large addition was built on the adjoining property where the branch of the United States Mint had stood. The new building was dedicated on November 21, 1934, by Postmaster General James A. Farley and has since, with improvements, continued to serve postal and other governmental activities in the city.

What Hath God Wrought?

In 1844 Samuel F. B. Morse invented the electrically operated telegraph instrument; the opening of a telegraph office in Charlotte by the New York and Mississippi Telephone Company took place less than ten years later.

On April 4, 1856, the Western Union Telegraph Company was formed by an amalgamation of many smaller companies and the original office in Charlotte was continued under the new name. For over fifty years the Charlotte office of the Western Union was at 30 South Tryon Street; since January 1, 1927, it has been in the Wilder Building.

The Telephone

The first telephones in Charlotte were demonstration instruments, one in a popular drug store and the other in a nearby residence. Trial conversations resulted in the opening of an exchange with 25 subscribers on April 20, 1880. It proved unprofitable, however, and operations were suspended in 1883.

In July 1884 an improved exchange with 64 subscribers was opened under the name of Charlotte Telephone Company. Rates were $41 per year for residential service and $51 for business telephones. Growth was slow; nine years later there were only 73 telephones in Charlotte. After the turn of the century service grew rapidly and when the exchange was purchased by the Southern Bell Telephone and Telegraph Company on March 4, 1904, there were 968 subscribers.

Number of telephones in use passed the one hundred thousand figure in 1958. As of January 1960 there were 115,560 instruments in use in the metropolitan area. The Caldwell Street building was first occupied in 1929 when the dial system came to this locality. Charlotte was the first city in the Southern Bell system to have multi-office dial exchanges. By 1960 Southern Bell had an investment of about $35 million in Charlotte, an annual payroll in excess of $8 million, and was servicing nearly 25,000 long distance calls daily.

Newspapers

A saying in the library profession is: "In case of fire, let the books burn but save the newspapers and magazines." Books can be easily replaced, whereas newspapers and magazines, published by the millions, are "here today and gone tomorrow." With the coming of microfilm and microcard reproduction, the problem is nearly solved. But with the rapid disappearance of newspapers and magazines, it is almost impossible to reconstruct an accurate record of early Charlotte newspapers.

The first newspaper published in Charlotte seems to have been the *Catawba Journal*, a weekly, begun October 4, 1824, and published here for several years before being removed to Salisbury. To replace it, the *Charlotte Journal*, also a weekly, was started in 1831. This name was changed by the publisher, Thomas J. Holton, to *The Whig* on January 26, 1852. An issue dated September 17, 1861, lists Mrs. T. J. Holton as "Editress and Proprietress," so it is assumed that her husband had died, for he would have been too old for military service then required of eligible males.

Influence of the gold-mining industry in Charlotte can be seen in the name and contents of the *Miners and Farmers Journal*, established as a weekly September 27, 1830, and apparently successful for several years. The *Tri-Weekly Bulletin* appeared in 1840 and continued until 1881, though known as the *Weekly Courier* from 1865. The *Hornet's Nest and True Southron* lasted two or three years following its establishment July 7, 1849. The *Mecklenburg Jeffersonian*, weekly, began March 9, 1841, and also lasted several years.

Evidently designed to offset the influence of *The Whig*, the *Charlotte Democrat*, W. J. Yates, editor and owner, published its first issue July 10, 1852. It was published as the *Western Democrat* until 1881 and as *Charlotte Home Democrat* from February 8, 1884 until 1896, at which time it was consolidated with the *Mecklenburg Times* to become the *Times-Democrat*, and published as such until 1924.

From 1859 until 1878 there was published the *Evening Bulletin,* known from its beginning until 1868 as the *Daily Bulletin.* The *Daily Carolina Times* appeared on the scene in 1864 and remained until 1870, and the *Daily Journal* lasted from August 22, 1882, until March 25, 1883. From 1870 until 1881, General Daniel Harvey Hill published the *Southern Home* which had the appearance of a newspaper but in content was more in the nature of a magazine.

The Observer

The *Daily Charlotte Observer* began publication January 25, 1869, as the property of Smith, Watson & Company, with Francis Justice as editor. Other early editors were J. W. Wright, J. Jones and, lastly, C. R. Jones who "conducted the paper as politically independent."

In December 1886 the *Charlotte Chronicle* was started as a Democratic daily newspaper. It wasn't long before the *Chronicle* outdistanced the *Observer* and was able to announce, "The *Observer* is no more." For the next several years there was no newspaper in Charlotte with the word "Observer" in its title.

In 1892 the *Charlotte Chronicle* was sold to D. A. Tompkins and Joseph Pearson Caldwell, equally well known as an editor, and the name was changed to *Daily Observer.* Mr. Caldwell began his duties as editor on February 1, 1892, and from that day forward the *Observer* has been one of the most influential newspapers in the South. Dr. Julian Miller, editor from 1935 until his death July 28, 1946, in an article on the history of the *Observer* said: "The life story of the *Observer* dating from the Tompkins-Caldwell regime has been an epic in journalistic and industrial achievement. Its history is inextricably woven into the civic, economic and social fabric of the community."

Ownership and management of the *Observer* changed from time to time. Death and illness broke up the Tompkins-Caldwell team and in 1915, the responsibility for conducting the business was assumed by Word H. Wood and George Stephens, bankers. In 1916 these gentlemen sold all outstanding stock to Mr. Curtis Boyd Johnson, publisher of the *Knoxville Sentinel.*

In order to remain in Knoxville, Mr. Johnson sold a considerable block of stock in the *Observer* to Mr. Walter B. Sullivan, who became resident manager and president. Mr. Sullivan's illness and subsequent death made it necessary for Mr. Johnson to devote more time and attention to the *Observer* and finally to move to Charlotte in 1924. Under his ownership and management the paper enjoyed its greatest growth in size and popularity.

Mr. Johnson died on October 6, 1950, and on August 3, 1951, Ralph Nicholson was engaged as editor and publisher. This arrangement lasted until August 1953 when Mrs. Curtis Boyd Johnson became publisher. On December 30, 1954, controlling interest in the *Observer* was sold to Knight Publishing Company, owned by John S. Knight, his brother James L. Knight, and their associates, who are presently maintaining and increasing the prestige of the newspaper.

For many years prior to 1916 the *Observer* was published at 32 South Tryon Street, a location since occupied by the Bank of Charlotte and the Imperial Theatre. Need for additional space necessitated removal to Tompkins Tower, 33-35 South Church Street. Ten years later, on January 1, 1927, the *Observer* moved to its present building at the corner of Stonewall and Tryon Streets.

Growth of the *Charlotte Observer* may be judged from the record of daily circulation for ten year periods:

1916	12,986	1946	124,057
1926	37,333	1956	143,622
1936	66,212	1960	159,464

A complete story of the *Charlotte Observer* may be found in its mammoth issue for February 28, 1950. Biographical information for many of the employees is given. Following are a few of those whose services are still recalled: Joseph Pearson Caldwell, first editor and one of the foremost southern newspapermen of his time; Wade Hampton Harris, editor from 1912 until his death September 14, 1935; Dr. Julian S. Miller, editor from 1935 until 1946; James A. Parham and Rupert Gillett, associate editors; Ernest B. Hunter, managing editor 1929 until his retirement in 1958; Mason B. Hood, long-time reporter; LeGette Blythe, reporter, columnist, editorial writer and literary editor; Hazell Mizell Trotter, reporter; Haywood G. Trotter, reporter, city editor, news editor and managing editor; Haywood Thompson, features editor; Edwin Brietz, news editor; J. M. Roberts, Jr., city editor and news editor; F. Earl Crawford, feature advertising manager; P. H. Batte, business manager; D. G. Spencer and Robert P. Bell, Jr., telegraph editors; Leary W. Adams, business news editor; the famous Isaac Irwin Avery and John Charles McNeill (see Chapter 12); Mrs. J. A. Yarbrough and Mrs. Sam Presson, feature news contributors; Augustus Zollicoffer Travis, columnist; Kays Gary, columnist; Granbery Dickson, religion editor; Hal Tribble and Randolph Norton, editorial writers; Sigsbee Miller, Betty Wannamaker (Mrs. J. J. Ravers), Rita Adams (Mrs. Joseph B. Simpson), Porter Munn, and a host of others on the reportorial staff; "Dick" Banks, arts critic; Jake Houston, Jimmy Dumbell, Bruce Roberts and others of the photographic staff; Jake Wade, Wilton Garrison, Sam Miller, and many other able sports writers; Mrs. J. P. Caldwell, columnist for many years, and Mrs. Margaret Kelly Abernethy, society editor for nearly a generation.

Charlotte News

Since December 8, 1888, Charlotte has had two excellent newspapers, the *Charlotte News* having been started on that date as an afternoon competitor to the *Chronicle* which, shortly thereafter, was renamed *Observer*. The *News* was founded by Wade Hampton Harris, who had been with the old *Observer* (1869-1886). In 1895 Mr. Harris, for about $5,000, sold the *News* to Mr. William Carey Dowd, Sr., who had come to Charlotte in 1892 and acquired the weekly *Mecklenburg Times*. Mr. Dowd continued with both the weekly *Times* and daily *News*, later buying the *Home Democrat* which he consolidated with his original weekly to become the *Times-Democrat*, a weekly which he published until 1924.

Under the management of William Carey Dowd the *Charlotte News* eventually developed into North Carolina's leading afternoon newspaper. Upon Mr. Dowd's death, September 23, 1927, ownership and management of the *News* devolved upon his sons William Carey Dowd, Jr., and J. Edward Dowd. Under these gentlemen, and with the same policies and enthusiasms, the *News* kept pace with the growth of the city.

The Dowd family interest in the *Charlotte News* was surrendered on January 9, 1947, when a group of businessmen, headed by newspaperman Thomas L. Robinson, acquired complete owner-ship. Some time later, Mr. Robinson obtained almost complete ownership as well as active management of the newspaper. Under his direction, the *News* continued the fine reputation gained through its long and useful history. However, rising production costs, responsible for many newspaper suspensions and consolida-tions at the time, resulted in the sale by Mr. Robinson, August 5, 1959, of the *Charlotte News* to the Knight Publishing Company, owners and publishers of the *Charlotte Observer*.

Popular feeling in Charlotte at the time of this drastic change in the newspaper situation was one of regret that it had become impossible to continue two financially independent newspapers, but a feeling of relief and gratification that the new arrangement would apparently not jeopardize the spirit of journalistic rivalry that had existed, or diminish the vigor that had characterized the *News*.

Beginning with William Carey Dowd, Sr., there have been on the staff of the *News* many who earned deserved recognition. W. Carey Dowd, Jr., was a worthy successor to his father; so also was J. Edward Dowd, who some months after selling his interest in the *News*, became general manager of the *Charlotte Observer*. There are also C. A. "Pete" McKnight, former editor of the *News*, pres-ent editor of the *Observer;* Brodie S. Griffith, managing editor of the *News* for many years and editor and general manager of the *News* under Knight ownership. There have been reporters, edito-rial writers, feature writers and columnists galore, each with his or her personal following, including John P. McKnight, later with Associated Press and currently with the U. S. Information Agency; John Harden, head of his own public relations firm and author of several books; Cameron Shipp, who went on to become a success-ful Hollywood writer; Tom P. Jimison, who once had himself confined to a mental hospital to get the proper atmosphere for a crusading story; Dorothy Knox and Fannie Lou Bingham, feature writers; C. A. Paul and later, Julian Scheer, columnists; Tom Fes-perman, columnist, successively city editor, managing editor of the *News* and currently managing editor of the *Observer;* Harry Ash-more, editorial writer who moved on to Little Rock and became celebrated because of his editorial position in connection with desegregation news, currently editor-in-chief, Encyclopaedia Brittanica; Victor Reinemer, editorial writer who won many awards and moved on to Washington; W. J. Cash, Burke Davis, Timothy Pridgen, and Marion Hargrove (see Chapter 12); Cecil Prince, editor, whose death on May 24, 1960, at the age of 37, was a grievous shock to his associates and the community; Charles Kuralt, who may be seen frequently on national television channels; Ann Sawyer, Elizabeth Blair Prince and Martha Azer (Mrs. A. A. London), reporters; Tom Franklin and Jeep Hunter, photographers, and the two Youngs, "Dick," Sr., dean of the reportorial staff, and "Dick," Jr., managing editor. A huge jubilee edition of the *News* was published November 15, 1938, containing a mine of information and data concerning Charlotte and its people.

Charlotte Evening Chronicle

By 1903 the competition of the *Charlotte News* evidently became so acute that the *Observer* felt something should be done to offset it. There is no other way now for explaining the action of the *Observer* in establishing the *Charlotte Evening Chronicle* on May 25, 1903. This venture evidently didn't turn out as successfully as had been hoped and on May 7, 1914, the *Evening Chronicle* was sold to the *Charlotte News*, which for a time thereafter became the *Charlotte News and Evening Chronicle*.

Weekly Newspapers—Mecklenburg Times

When the *Charlotte News* discontinued its weekly edition, the *Times-Democrat*, in 1924, Mr. Bill Arp Lowrance of Forest City came to Charlotte and started the *Mecklenburg Times*. This newspaper is today a dependable source of information concerning people and events in rural Mecklenburg, and is an inexpensive medium for the publication of legal notices of all kinds.

Magazine Publishing in Charlotte

The Land We Love seems to have been the first *bona fide* magazine published in Charlotte. Volume I, Number 1, dated May 1866, lists the owners as James P. Irwin and Daniel Harvey Hill, and describes the publication as "A monthly magazine devoted to literature, military history, and agriculture." Small type and poor paper conspired to give *The Land We Love* a most uninviting appearance, while the contents seem to have been written with a "heavy hand." Publication ceased with the November 1868 issue, when the magazine was merged with the *New Eclectic* of Baltimore. This, in turn, became the *Southern Magazine* and suspended in 1875.

The *Carolina Medical Journal*, established in 1878 by Doctors E. C. Register and J. C. Montgomery, was probably the second magazine to be published in Charlotte and the one to have had the longest history. It continued until 1908 when it was absorbed by the *Charlotte Medical Journal*, of which publication Dr. J. M. Northington became editor in 1926, changing its name to *Southern Medicine and Surgery*. Publication was discontinued in 1953.

About 1895 John Cuthbertson founded the *Textile Excelsior*, changing its name a few years later to *Southern and Western Textile Excelsior*. This publication was combined with *Textile Manufacturer* about 1907 and continued until 1910.

Between 1890 and 1900 several newspapers and magazines were started but none seems to have left any greater impression than a scant entry in some issue of the city directory. Some of these were: *People's Paper*, owned by J. P. Sossaman; *Southern Industries*, owned by W. L. Scott; *Weekly Register*, owned by C. W. Peters and W. L. Yeager; *Dixie* (organ of the Order of Railway Trainmen), edited by W. B. Swindell; *Church and State*, with W. W. Bays, Jr., as business manager and Mamie Bays as editor; *Southern Success and Advertiser*, of which W. B. Swindell was editor.

In 1898 the weekly *North Carolina Presbyterian*, founded January 1, 1858, by the Synod of North Carolina, was bought and moved from Fayetteville to Charlotte by a syndicate composed of Reverend A. J. McKelway and others. Dr. McKelway became the editor and the name was changed to *Presbyterian Standard*. Dr. J. R. Bridges became editor in 1918 and in 1926 was succeeded by Rev. J. G. Garth, who served until the magazine ceased publication in 1931.

Above: Charlotte Open Air School, showing Public School Superintendent Harry P. Harding on a tour of inspection in the early 1920's. *Below:* A class in 1898, Charlotte Public School System (identifications appear on page 471).

Above: Colonel Macomb and staff in front of headquarters at Camp Greene near Charlotte, March 14, 1919. *Below:* Charlotte school commissioners in 1916 (identifications appear on page 471).

Above: Charlotte Spanish American War veterans: Walter Brem, Jr., M.D.; Bob Durham; Ernest Farrier; and Plato Durham. *Below:* A Charlotte social group taken at the turn of the century (identifications appear on page 471).

Above: President Woodrow Wilson at Charlotte May 20, 1916. By the President are Governor Manning of South Carolina, Governor Locke Craig of North Carolina, and Charlotte's Mayor Kirkpatrick. *Below:* North Carolina State Society of the Cincinnati pose at the Southern Manufacturers' Club in 1916. Charlotteans shown are F. Brevard McDowell, seated extreme right; Heriot Clarkson, standing extreme left; and Walter W. Watt, standing fourth from left.

Above: Charlotte Fire Department, January 18, 1916, located at rear of the City Hall at the corner of Tryon and Fifth Streets. *Below:* Charlotte Police Department *circa* 1910 (identifications appear on page 471).

Above: Chief W. Hendrix Palmer in the driver's seat of a steam fire engine.
Below: Steam locomotive of the early twentieth century.

Above: Funeral of Fire Chief J. H. Wallace, July 1, 1914. *Below:* Members of the Charlotte Gun Club of the 1880's (identifications appear on page 471).

Above: A typical parade float, vintage 1920. *Below:* Bus service between Charlotte and Columbia *circa* 1925 used standard passenger automobiles.

A year after the *Presbyterian Standard* located in Charlotte, Mr. George S. Escott founded the *Mill News*. This magazine was published from 1899 until 1922 when it was merged with the *American Cotton & Wool Reporter* of New York. In 1908 the *Merchants Journal and Commerce* was founded by Norman H. Johnson, an attorney, who at that time was executive secretary of the North Carolina Retail Merchants Association. When the association was consolidated with the Virginia association, the publication office was removed to Richmond.

In 1908 there was also established the *Poultry Yard*, by Elam & Dooley; the *Christian Home*, by Rev. T. J. Jenkins; the *Southern Republican*, by J. A. Smith and D. B. Paul; *The Carolina Pythian*, with Major J. G. Baird as editor, and the *Progressive Mission*.

In August 1906 Volume I, Number 1, of a literary magazine entitled *Charlotte Magazine* made its appearance. No editor nor owner is named. With the exception of an insert about Charlotte and Charlotte people the magazine might just as appropriately have been called *Asheville Magazine*, or been named for any other city. Number 2 of Volume I never appeared.

It was in 1911 that Mr. David Clark formed the Clark Publishing Company to publish the *Textile Bulletin*, the first of several publications now issued by that firm (see Chapter 7).

Another *Charlotte Magazine*, with J. Ray Shute as editor in chief, made its appearance August 1932, as a publication of the "civic clubs of Charlotte." While in every way a legitimate and attractive publication, this periodical succumbed to the ravages of depression. *The Charlotteer*, published by J. L. Dew 1937-1939, was another ambitious undertaking that failed.

In 1939 there arrived in Charlotte from New York, Mr. Harry Golden (see Chapter 12), "a likeable Jewish gentleman." After brief experiences as an advertising salesman he founded the *Carolina Israelite*, a publication with a newspaper format and contents described by *Life* magazine as, "a collection of warm essays and reminiscences with modest adjectives." Mr. Golden's success has been reflected in his paper's circulation which went quickly from a few hundred locally read copies to an international audience of more than 60,000.

The *Dairy Goat Bulletin* began its existence in Charlotte, January 1943, as a quarterly magazine, edited by Paul Palmer. In the fall of 1949 it changed hands and was afterwards published at Mena, Arkansas with a change of name, in 1951, to the *Capriculturist*.

Other Printed Communications

The mortality rate of newspapers and magazines may seem high, but does not compare with the fleeting existence of the publications of churches, clubs, and other organizations, which were started with high hopes. For a time at least, some of them had a few faithful followers. Others continued for years and since they reflect one aspect of life in Charlotte as lived in the twentieth century, a few of these latter are mentioned by way of illustrating this kind of reading material.

Charlotte: The Center was a 32 page periodical, published at irregular intervals by the Chamber of Commerce from about 1925 until early 1930. It consisted of statistics and articles aimed at prospective industries.

The *Mecklenburg Baptist* and *Mecklenburg Presbyterian* have both been published for a number of years and are typical of other denominational papers.

Bulletin of the Mecklenburg Medical Society. Volume I, Number 1 of this pocket-size magazine appeared March 1940 with Dr. Tom W. Baker as editor and Drs. Graham Reid and Allyn B. Choate, as associate editors. The business managers were Drs. Ernest W. Franklin, Walter B. Mayer and Jerome B. Hamer. Filled with professional papers which had been read at meetings of the medical profession, this was a creditable and apparently useful magazine. It suspended publication at the conclusion of Volume II when activities connected with World War II made it impossible for doctors to give the necessary time to its preparation.

Rotary Reporter, established about 1918 and still published, is typical of publications issued regularly by civic clubs. *Desert Dust*, established about 1935 and still published by the Oasis Temple, keeps the 7152 shriners posted on fraternal and other Masonic affairs.

Transportation

Charlotte is one of the nation's great transportation and distribution centers. The story of how it got that way bridges the gap between the isolation of frontier life, and the refinements of modern society.

Early transportation methods and facilities inspire admiration, but not envy, for our forefathers, whose bridle paths between neighborhoods gave way to cartways and dirt roads as villages began to spring up in the forests. Horses would sometimes carry three or four children and an adult, while proud ladies, on foot, would wear everyday shoes along the country roads and don their Sunday footwear as they neared the church.

Later came gigs, jersey wagons, surreys, buggies and carriages. A young man was judged by the horse and buggy he owned, just as today his car tells much about him. When large plantations were formed and towns laid out, families were judged by the kind of carriages owned, their horses and liveried Negro coachmen. More distant travel required stagecoaches, and for more than a half century this mode of transportation dominated, until it gave way to the railroads.

Railroads

Removed as they were from good markets, the people of the Piedmont area of North Carolina retained their self-sufficient economy for a good many years. Their logical market would seem to have been Fayetteville, but Charleston loomed just as important. The difference in distance was not great, but the two principal rivers draining the Piedmont were the Yadkin and Catawba, both running diagonally across the state into South Carolina. The easiest land routes naturally followed the water courses and up to 1850 Cheraw was the closest market to Charlotte, an eight day trip at that time.

These facts undoubtedly account for the energy with which Charlotte people joined in the agitation which began about 1825 for improved transportation facilities. On October 7, 1833, at a public meeting in Charlotte, delegates were appointed to attend a "railroad meeting" at Salisbury. At a convention on December 10, 1836 Mecklenburg and eighteen other counties were represented by 131 delegates who adopted resolutions asking the legislature to assist in the building of railroads which they stated were of great importance to western counties. About the same time Mecklenburg sent representatives to a meeting at Knoxville to consider building a road from Charlotte to Cincinnati. Other meetings occurred at intervals and a regular organization was maintained in Charlotte, after 1846, for the purpose of securing railroad transportation.

Finally, the needs became so acute that a compromise measure between eastern and western counties was passed in 1849 creating the North Carolina Railroad Company. The authorized capital was $3,000,000, of which the state was to supply two thirds and private stockholders one third. Later, the state acquired another $1,000,000 in preferred stock to complete the road.

In the meantime, Charlotte citizens had attended meetings to obtain a railroad to Columbia. Subscriptions to stock in this road were sold in May 1849, and construction began soon after. By October, 1852, the *Charlotte & South Carolina Railroad* was carrying freight though the road was not quite complete into town. The first passenger train arrived at Charlotte on October 21, 1852 and was greeted by a tremendous celebration. Crowds came from Columbia, Winnsboro, Chester and other points, and newspapers estimated there were 20,000 people present. The Columbia band furnished music and there were a number of speeches followed by a barbecue on the lawn of the Female Academy, and at night a dance and fireworks display. Henceforth there was daily passenger service between Charlotte and Columbia. The *Charlotte & South Carolina Railroad* was acquired by the *Richmond & Danville Railroad* in 1878.

The second railroad to enter Charlotte was the *North Carolina Railroad*, which ran from Goldsboro to Charlotte via Raleigh, Greensboro, and Salisbury, a distance of 219.2 miles. The first train was operated from Concord to Charlotte September 1854 and the road was completed in January 1856. The first through train ran the following day, and daily thereafter. The *North Carolina Railroad* was leased to the *Richmond & Danville* on September 9, 1871 for a period of thirty years. The *Richmond & Danville* was absorbed by the *Southern Railway System* in 1894, at which time the lease was renegotiated for ninety-nine years. The state still owns the *North Carolina Railroad* and receives compensation for its use from the lessee.

On May 19, 1870 Mecklenburg County voted $200,000 in bonds to assist in building the *Atlanta & Charlotte Air Line Railway*, and $100,000 toward rebuilding the *Atlantic, Tennessee & Ohio Railroad*, familiarly known in Charlotte as the Statesville Line. This line had been completed in 1860, but by 1864 had been torn up to provide war material. Rebuilding was completed in 1874.

All of these local railroads came together as the *Southern Railway System*, June 18, 1894. The *Southern* today has more miles of track in Mecklenburg county than there were in the entire first railroad reaching Charlotte from Columbia, which road the *Southern* now owns.

When the first passenger train arrived in Charlotte, passengers were deposited somewhere close to the present location of the Southern passenger station on West Trade Street. From one combination passenger and freight train daily in 1852 and two trains daily in 1854, passenger trains increased to a peak of about 25 to 30 trains daily in the 1920's. With the increased uses of buses, automobiles and air travel, passenger traffic then began to decline. Short railroad lines were abandoned until at present the passenger traffic in and out of Charlotte is limited to a half dozen through trains in each direction daily.

From a financial standpoint, passenger hauling has always been a minor part of the business of the Southern Railway Company, the principal business being transportation of freight. Toward this end it has devoted much effort to attracting new industries to Charlotte and vicinity. By 1900 the volume of freight business required a block-long warehouse on South College Street, between Third and Fourth Streets; the building burned in Charlotte's most spectacular fire, June 24, 1954. Later, in order to unbottle some of Charlotte's traffic arteries, the railroad built new tracks for its freight trains, skirting the business and residential sections of the city.

Passenger trains began running between Wilmington and Charlotte on December 15, 1874, via the *Carolina Central Railway*, the first section of which road, between Charlotte and Lincolnton, was put into operation April 1861. In 1900 the *Carolina Central* became a part of the basic system comprising the *Seaboard Air Line Railroad*.

From the date of its entry into Charlotte the *Seaboard* offered both freight and passenger service until November 3, 1958 when passenger service was discontinued.

The *Piedmont & Northern Railway Company*, one of the four Class I railroads now serving Charlotte, is an all-freight, Deisel line extending between Charlotte and Gastonia in North Carolina and between Spartanburg, Greenville, Greenwood and Anderson in South Carolina. It is the only railroad with its general offices located in Charlotte, and thus has the distinction of being "home grown."

The *Piedmont & Northern* was organized in 1911 by James B. Duke and his associates, as an adjunct to their various electric power and industrial developments in the Carolinas. Originally, the railroad was conceived as an interurban electric line extending through the Piedmont Carolinas.

The predecessor company of the present North Carolina Division of the *Piedmont & Northern* was the Piedmont Traction Company, organized in January 1910. Its first mission was to construct a line between Charlotte and Gastonia, connecting the street railway systems of the two cities. Interurban passenger service was inaugurated with appropriate fanfare on Independence Day, 1912. The new and fast electric passenger cars gained immediate public acceptance and for many years were the backbone of passenger transportation between the two cities. Several months after the organization of the Piedmont Traction Company, Mr. Duke and his associates obtained a charter for the *Greenville, Spartanburg & Anderson Railway*. The consolidation of the two lines was to be the first step in the ultimate connection between Gastonia and Spartanburg, and extending northward from Charlotte to other North Carolina cities. However, this plan was stoutly opposed by several trunk lines serving the area and the Interstate Commerce Commission declined to grant the company permission to complete the system. Notwithstanding the upsetting of its plan, the *Piedmont & Northern* has contributed immensely to Charlotte's industrial growth by attracting new enterprises.

The all-freight *Norfolk & Southern* extended its lines to Charlotte in December 1913, thus linking Charlotte to Norfolk through a prosperous agricultural and industrial section.

Norfolk & Southern has been especially active in acquiring sites for Charlotte's industrial expansion, and in attracting new industries.

Automobiles

Almost as exciting as the coming of the first train was the advent of the automobile in Charlotte.

An automobile is said to have been owned in Charlotte as early as 1901, but none is mentioned in the Charlotte city directory until 1904. In that year the Osmond L. Barringer Company was listed in the business section as dealer for Franklin Autocar and Cadillac automobiles. Since that time, many of the great homes of earlier citizens have been torn down to make way for service for automobiles, while many midtown lots have become parking areas, with corner positions occupied by sales rooms for automobiles and their accompanying repair shops. It seems safe to say that Charlotte automobile interests use more of the city's ground space than does any other form of business. There were upward of 62,000 automobiles registered in Mecklenburg in 1960.

Interurban Transportation

From a small beginning in 1930, the bus industry has grown to acquire its own large Union Bus Terminal, with dining and other modern conveniences to serve five bus lines: Atlantic Greyhound, Carolina Coach Co., Carolina Scenic Stages, Carolina Transit Lines, and Queen City Trailways.

Local Transportation

As the population increased and patronage became sufficient, there appeared individual public conveyances. These usually had two seats, one for the driver and the other for rider or riders. These phaetons invariably had curtains which could be unrolled for those who desired privacy. Some did, because these vehicles were used by traveling men and townsmen, who did not want their own equipment or themselves to be recognized, when visiting Charlotte's red light district, located in the vicinity of Caldwell and Second Streets, and Davidson Street, below Second. Vehicle stands were adjacent to railway stations and hotels. At the head of the line of phaetons waiting at the railway station would be an omnibus for each of the leading hotels. These were drawn by two horses and had seats facing each other, running lengthwise, and providing space for 16 to 18 passengers. A few of these horse-drawn omnibuses were replaced by motor buses from 1910 to 1915 but, with the increased use of taxicabs almost all hotel buses were abandoned by 1920.

Street Cars

In 1887 Charlotte's first horse-drawn streetcars were put into operation from West Trade Street, at the Southern Railway crossing, to the end of the line which was at the top of the hill on Elizabeth Avenue. Electric cars made their appearance in 1893 and the lines were gradually extended for the next 25 years.

There were summer cars with seats six or eight feet in length extending the width of the cars. The conductor moved along a running board, holding on with one hand and collecting nickel fares and issuing transfers with the other. The winter cars had seats which faced inward and extended the length of the cars, similar to those used for horsedrawn cars. Summer cars were abandoned about 1915, and the others converted into pay-as-you-enter conveyances.

Taxicabs and Buses

By 1915 automobiles had about replaced horses for all transportation purposes except sporting events, hauling, and agricultural pursuits. Horsedrawn public vehicles had been superseded by individual automobiles for hire and it wasn't long before some of these were grouped and became taxicab companies. The city directory of 1923 was the first to carry in its business section a classification for taxicabs. The final link between the old and new methods of local transportation broke in 1938 when motor buses replaced street cars, and the car tracks were removed, or covered over. In April 1955 the Duke Power Company, which had inherited the street car system when the Southern Public Utilities Company was absorbed, sold its buses to the Charlotte City Coach Lines.

Air Transportation

Inauguration of air transportation was announced in the *Charlotte Observer* for April 2, 1930 with headlines and a story that began, "Roaring out of the darkness of the south, Gene Brown, intrepid flier of the night skies, last night officially christened Charlotte as an air mail stop." As a pilot for Eastern Air Transport, later to become Eastern Air Lines, Brown brought the first air mail to the city before a wildly enthusiastic throng, estimated variously as from 30,000 to 50,000 people.

A group of Charlotte's most prominent citizens were on hand December 10, 1930 to welcome the first passenger flight of the same system. The 18 passenger Curtis Condor plane landed a few minutes after noon. For the first few months the passenger traffic from Charlotte averaged 30 per month on two daily flights.

The first flights into Charlotte landed at the Charlotte Airport, a privately owned enterprise provided by air-minded citizens at a cost of about $225,000. Under the management of Johnny Crowell, Charlotte's best known aviator, the airport served its purpose well. It was eventually taken over as a facility of the municipal government, and named Douglas Municipal Airport in honor of Mayor Ben E. Douglas, who spearheaded the movement for its acquisition. Subsequently, through bond issues and governmental aid, much additional land was obtained and the modern airport was dedicated and put into service July 10, 1954.

The excellent service provided by Eastern Air Lines for seventeen years was supplemented on December 5, 1947 when Capital Airlines, Southern Airways and Piedmont Airlines began scheduled flights to Charlotte, and in 1956 when Delta Airlines began its service to the community. For either short or long distances, travelers may charter private planes from Cannon Aircraft Company, Carolina Aircraft, or Southeast Airmotive.

From an average of thirty passengers monthly in 1930, air transportation has grown into a leading local industry. As of 1960, some 1,310 persons emplane daily at Douglas Municipal Airport, on 102 scheduled flights of the five airlines serving the city. In addition, 6½ tons of mail, air freight and air express are handled daily. More than 1,700 people are employed at the airport.

7

INDUSTRY AND COMMERCE

THE discovery of gold in Piedmont Carolina began the first of three important epochs which differentiate the industrial history of Charlotte from neighboring communities. For it was gold, the selection of Charlotte as a railroad junction, and the building of a network of converging highways which made Charlotte great.

During the first half of the nineteenth century, Charlotte was the gold-mining center of the United States. The official figures for domestic sources of gold in the United States for the 50 year period prior to 1848, are:

Virginia	$ 945,294.00
North Carolina	$3,933,136.00
South Carolina	$ 479,866.00
Georgia	$2,320,216.00
All other sources	$ 74,392.00

These figures may not seem impressive now, but from 1840 until the Civil War the production of gold sustained the economy of Mecklenburg and neighboring counties when other sections of the Carolinas and the South were seriously distressed. The gold-mining industry continued to function, undisturbed by diminishing activities in other lines. The coinage record of the Charlotte branch of the United States Mint showed the following amounts, tiny today but important then:

1840	$127,055	1850	$347,791
1844	$147,200	1855	$217,935

Most of North Carolina's gold came from Mecklenburg, Gaston, Anson, Cabarrus, Rutherford, Davidson and Montgomery counties. In Mecklenburg, the first discovery was made in 1799 by the small son of Conrad Reed, who found a rich nugget weighing about 28 pounds in a section of Mecklenburg which later became Cabarrus County. Soon thereafter, some nuggets were found near Rozzell's Ferry in Mecklenburg.

The first attempt to follow a seam of gold in Mecklenburg was made by Samuel McComb in 1825. His mine, known first as Charlotte Mine and later as the St. Catherine Mine, was located on what is now West Morehead Street, near the Southern Railway underpass. Its location and that of other Charlotte mines can be determined from a map drawn in 1906 by engineer Charles G. (Tommy) Hubbel, now owned by the Public Library of Charlotte. Almost a hundred mines of various sizes and quality were opened within a radius of 20 miles of Charlotte. The most important of these was the Rudisill Mine of Count Ravafanoli, who brought with him many experienced miners from Italy and other parts of Europe.

The St. Catherine and Rudisill mines were the two most profitable in Mecklenburg. Assays from these mines ranged from $24.80 to $72.41 per ton.

With increased production, there came a demand from miners for a more convenient method of disposing of their gold than that of selling to banks or merchants at a discount, or waiting for months to get returns from the Philadelphia mint. The only alternative was to take it to Rutherfordton where Bechtler Brothers had a private coinage plant. The Bechtler coins, or more properly tokens, in denominations of $1, $2.50, and $5, were honestly made but of poor wearing quality. The best collection of these rare coins in this section is owned by the North Carolina National Bank at Charlotte.

After long and persistent efforts, Congress, on March 3, 1835 authorized the erection of a branch of the United States Mint at Charlotte. This branch, opened December 4, 1837, was the first branch of the mint to be opened, though two others were authorized at the same time, one at New Orleans and the other at Dahlonega, Georgia. The Charlotte branch was designed by William Strickland, a Philadelphia artist and architect, and has been admired through the years for the simplicity and dignity of its modified Classic lines. Its only ornament was a huge eagle which rested above the front door, for years a familiar Charlotte landmark. The removal and restoration of this building, nearly a hundred years later, as the Mint Museum of Art (described in Chapter 12) is one of the most refreshing incidents of Charlotte's history.

The Charlotte branch of the mint was burned in July 1844 and notwithstanding the large volume of business transacted before the fire, Congress was reluctant to provide funds for its rebuilding. Credit is due Congressman D. M. Barringer, of this district, for securing passage of an act which resulted in the rebuilding of the mint in 1845 and 1846. Gold coins minted at Charlotte may be identified by the letter "c" and they are, of course, very scarce and valuable. The first deposit of gold in the Charlotte branch was made by Irwin & Elms on December 4, 1837, and the total coinage during the life of the mint was $5,109,443.88.

From the time it was rebuilt until the Civil War the history of the Charlotte branch of the mint was uneventful. In 1861 the mint property was seized by the Confederate authorities and held by them as military headquarters for the area until 1865. For the next two years it served very much the same purpose for the Federal authorities occupying Charlotte.

The mint was reopened May 1, 1869 as an assay office only, since the production of gold in Mecklenburg and vicinity had so dwindled that coinage could be done at Philadelphia. At the close of the War the only gold mine in operation in Charlotte was the Rudisill mine operated by J. H. Carson which, with its 350 foot shaft and 3,500 feet of levels, was the largest in this section. From then until 1903 several other mines were worked for short periods but with the rising cost of labor and materials, all operations ceased about 1900. The depression revived a slight interest in gold-mining about 1934 because labor was cheap and the government had increased the price of gold from $20.67 to $35 per ounce. The Rudisill and Capps mines closed with the return of prosperity a short time later.

By 1913 the production of gold in North Carolina had so nearly stopped that the Charlotte branch of the mint was ordered closed. From then until 1932 the building was used for a variety of purposes.

Many incidents of historic interest were associated with the

Charlotte branch of the mint. In 1901, Thomas A. Edison spent several months experimenting in the mint with methods of extracting gold from ore by the use of electricity. The first superintendent of the mint was John H. Wheeler, who is best remembered for his authoritative *Historical Sketches of North Carolina*, and *Reminiscences and Memoirs of North Carolina and Eminent North Carolinians*. Others who served as superintendent were Burgess H. Gaither, Greene W. Caldwell, William J. Alexander, J. W. Osborne, Dr. I. W. Jones and Calvin J. Cowles. The assayer during the whole period before the War was Dr. J. H. Gibbon. The assayer after the reopening in 1869 was Calvin J. Cowles and the "melter" was George B. Hanna. Stuart W. Cramer, who later became a textile leader and for whom the town of Cramerton is named, became assayer on July 29, 1899. When the mint closed on July 31, 1913 the assayer in charge, Frank P. Drane, recorded this final inscription in the guest register of the mint: "The property of the United State Government. To be held in trust by the Carnegie Library of Charlotte, subject to the call of the Director of the Mints."

Charlotte's earliest industries sprang from a demand created by the growing population. The first such need in the semi-civilized frontier area was for rifles, and the first industry was apparently a rifle factory. There came into existence by 1800 a flour mill, saw mill, and blacksmith shop, as well as several small stores. The trend in Charlotte and throughout the Carolinas was for a diversified economy, in keeping with the needs of the people. This trend was slowed and eventually almost halted when the cotton gin of Eli Whitney came into general use. This invention had a profound influence upon all aspects of life in the South, including industry and commerce in Charlotte.

Until the cotton gin, only a little cotton had been raised in Mecklenburg. It had to be tediously prepared by hand for the spinning wheel and loom. The process was so slow that only such time as could be spared from more important duties was given to the raising of cotton. The cotton gin changed this routine. Notwithstanding its crudeness, separating the seed from the lint being only about five times as fast as by hand, great impetus was given by the gin to the cultivation of cotton, and from then on the growth of the cotton industry was rapid and steady.

In the light of future developments, this new economic trend is known to have been one of very great peril to the welfare of the Carolinas and many parts of the South. The development of a sound, balanced and diversified business structure gave way before the apparent advantage of producing cotton. As the cotton gin was perfected and demand for cotton increased, the industry eventually surpassed all other lines of business. Shops, which had been productive, were closed to the public and utilized only for what was needed on the plantation. More cotton was ginned in Mecklenburg than any other county in North Carolina.

The increased demand for cotton created a greater need for slave labor and the traffic in slaves reached huge proportions. Production of cotton not only required a great deal of labor, but large acreage per capita. This course of events resulted in fewer industries requiring skill, and there was no necessity for scientific farming, or anything else scientific, since at that time, practically all cotton was shipped to the industrialized North for conversion into cloth.

The white population became quite content with this situation. By 1850 the interests of people whose minds had been occupied with miscellaneous industries and the industrial expansion, had narrowed to the development and growth of cotton. The pleasant life they lived has been told over and over again in books, plays and songs based upon the carefree and luxurious ante-bellum South. There is no denying the fact that during this period the Southern white people were happy, moderately prosperous and complacent. Those who weren't, left. This was certainly true of Mecklenburg, where the population dropped from 20,073 in 1830 to 13,814 in 1850. Thousands emigrated to the West, some because the fertility of Mecklenburg soil had been reduced by the constant planting of cotton, while others were lured by the California gold rush.

The second and probably the most important of three developments which exerted the greatest influence upon Charlotte's industrial destiny was the selection of the city as a junction for several railroads. Details of rail and other forms of transportation will be found in Chapter 6, but here we must point out their importance to Charlotte's industrial growth.

While rail transportation first became available to Charlotte in October 1852, it was not until the close of the Civil War that extensive benefits were felt. According to D. A. Tompkins, "The effects of emancipation upon all phases of industrial life was immediate and revolutionary." Subsequent events proved that Charlotte unquestionably escaped the worst evils of the reconstruction period. The relationship between Charlotte citizens and the 4,000 Northern troops sent to occupy the town following Lee's surrender seems to have been as pleasant as possible under the circumstances, and far better than in most other places.

With such an atmosphere and as the center of a production territory, and having the advantages of railroads and good government, Charlotte attracted many desirable citizens from more turbulent sections. With the arrival of these newcomers, interest in a wide range of industrial activities was renewed. The first seems to have been the repossession of the Mecklenburg Iron Works.

Though the exact date of its formation is unknown, Mecklenburg Iron Works is, without doubt, the oldest enterprise now doing business in Charlotte. The discovery, a few years ago, of a casting with the words, "Mecklenburg Iron Works 1846," leaves no room for questioning the fact that the firm is well into its second century. Unfortunately, the details of ownership and operations are unknown before 1859, when the plant was acquired by Captain John Wilkes.

Captain Wilkes, son of Admiral Charles Wilkes, was born in New York City March 31, 1827, was graduated first in his class of 135 members in 1847 from the United States Naval Academy, and for several years afterwards served, with distinction, in the navy. In April 1854 he was married and the following October located in Charlotte where, in 1859, he acquired the Mecklenburg Iron Works.

In 1861 the plant was taken over by the Confederate Government and used as a naval ordnance depot. Following the war, Mr. Wilkes regained his property and between then and the time of his death, July 6, 1908, "veritably molded the sword . . . into plowshares, emblems of peace and agriculture, predominant interests of the people of Mecklenburg at that time."

Following his death, the sons J. Renwick Wilkes and Frank Wilkes continued the business for many years but with diminishing success. In June 1950 the business was acquired by Mr. C. M.

Cox and associates, since which time production has increased considerably. Products have varied over the years from mining machinery and naval ordnance to turpentine stills; presently the fabrication of structural steel, engineered tank work and similar products come from the plant on its eleven acre tract on North Summit Avenue.

The demand for dwellings caused by the population influx after the Civil War ended was responsible for the establishment of two planing mills and a sash and door factory. These were followed by a pump manufacturer and several other small industries. Progress might have been more rapid but for the high price paid for cotton during the first few years following the war. Anyone could live by the cultivation of a few acres. Soon the increased cultivation forced the price down and then farmers and local capitalists began to realize that the only way of bettering their condition was by manufacturing the raw product at home instead of sending it away.

There were 33 cotton mills in North Carolina in 1873, but there were none in Mecklenburg. Several attempts to organize mills had failed. The Charlotte Cotton Mill, first of its kind, came into being in 1881. In 1896 there were five cotton mills in Charlotte and by 1903 the number had been increased to 17, with one each in Davidson, Pineville, Huntersville, and Cornelius.

The value of cotton seed for oil and other purposes soon became known and two mills for producing oil from cotton seed were established in Charlotte and one in Davidson. Two cotton compresses, with a total capacity of about 150,000 bales annually, were built, enabling growers to secure cash advances on cotton while holding it for possible higher prices.

Charlotte is centrally located in America's largest textile manufacturing section, but the absorption of small mills into large chains, with tremendous plants variously located according to their power and labor needs, has removed from the city proper most of the mills of which the people were so proud at the turn of the century.

The removal of the mills to nearby communities caused Charlotte's reputation to change from that of a manufacturing community to that of a financial and distributing center, a description that seems to become more and more appropriate as the second half of the twentieth century progresses. This change can be largely attributed to the third factor which influenced the industrial growth of Charlotte following the Civil War.

Had it not been for an early start in providing good roads, the chances are that Charlotte would not today be one of the nation's leading trucking and distribution centers.

Agitation for better roads in Charlotte began shortly after the Civil War, but it was not until November 8, 1887 that the city voted the first bonds in the sum of $50,000 for street improvements. Mecklenburg County soon followed by having the legislature approve the use of prisoners for road work. Daniel Augustus Tompkins, Charlotte industrialist, wrote a number of technical and inspirational pamphlets on the subject of good roads. Thomas LeRoy Kirkpatrick, lawyer, legislator and mayor, was so influential in his efforts to have more and better roads that he is given a large part of the credit for the passage of North Carolina's unprecedented $65,000,000 bond issue for good roads in 1921. Charlotte's Cameron Morrison is identified in North Carolina history as the "Good Roads Governor," although he later lamented that the use of this appellation inferred that his good deeds were limited to one field.

Beginning with the influence of gold mines prior to the Civil War, of railroads in the first decades of peace and, more recently, of highways, Charlotte has reached the pinnacle in the Carolinas as an industrial and distribution center.

Cotton, however, in one way or another is still one of the important commodities to Charlotte, notwithstanding the growth of the synthetic textile industry. Although there are not many textile plants located within the city, those within a 50 mile radius contribute substantially to Charlotte's prosperity. Because of its location the city has been selected as headquarters for sales, executive and research facilities of many large textile firms.

While most of the textile mills that dotted the Charlotte landscape at the turn of the century have moved to nearby points, a few still remain, notably Barnhardt Manufacturing Company.

Other well known textile industries of long standing in Charlotte are the Highland Park Manufacturing Company, founded June 15, 1891 and shortly thereafter acquired by W. E. Holt, C. W. Johnston, J. S. Spencer and their associates; and Nebel Knitting Company, founded by William Knebel in 1923.

So great has been the diversification of business and industry in Charlotte since 1900 that no single industry can be said to dominate the business life of the city, a factor of much importance in maintaining stable work conditions. As an indication of this variety, a few firms are mentioned here:

Agricultural Machinery

Industry in the twentieth century got off to a good start in Charlotte. First in the list of several firms that have not only weathered the intervening years, but have enjoyed continuous growth, is the Cole Manufacturing Company, organized January 1900. The company was founded by E. A. and E. M. Cole to produce seed planters, invented and patented by E. M. Cole. To date, more than two million seed planters, fertilizer distributors and grain drills have been sold in this and other countries. The Cole Manufacturing Company has followed the rule, practiced in Charlotte more than elsewhere, of retaining ownership and management in the founding family. Mrs. Jean Cole Hatcher, daughter of E. A. Cole, is currently president of the corporation.

Cast Iron Soil Pipe

The Charlotte Pipe and Foundry Company operates the oldest cast iron soil pipe plant in America. Founded by Willis Frank Dowd, Sr. in 1900, the plant has grown from 25 employees, using hand-moulding methods, to a modern plant with some 500 employees, producing more than 300 tons daily of pipe and machine-made fittings. W. Frank Dowd, Jr., succeeded his father as president of the firm and the present officials include Frank Dowd III and his brother Roddey Dowd, of the third generation in the life of the company.

Industrial Air Conditioning Equipment

Parks-Cramer Company came into existence August 27, 1918 through the consolidation of a firm founded at Fitchburg, Massachusetts in 1901 by Gilbert M. Parks, and a Charlotte firm composed of Stuart W. Cramer, William B. Hodge and others. The business, then as now, included the manufacture of industrial air conditioning equipment, trademarked "Certified Climate." It is interesting to note, in this connection, that Mr. Cramer originated and was first to use the term, "air-conditioning." His first public use of the term was in a talk which he made in Asheville, May 1906, before the Southern Cotton Manufacturers' Association. The products of Parks-Cramer Company are used by the textile industry.

Textile Machinery

The Terrell Machine Company was incorporated the same month that the United States entered World War I, so that its president, E. A. Terrell, had to turn the office over to his wife just before he entered the army. Mr. Terrell succeeded to the management of the business upon the death of his father and it has since been built into a textile machinery manufacturing plant with a worldwide clientele. During World War II the Terrell Machine Company sponsored formation of a War Production Pool, which used the services of some twenty other firms to produce military equipment. It has some 100 employees.

Peanut Food Products

Some romance is attached to the founding of many of America's leading corporations, but none more interesting than the story of Lance.

A coffee salesman named Philip L. Lance in 1913 began roasting peanuts, later grinding them into peanut butter to be used as a filler between soda crackers.

Mr. Lance was soon joined by his son-in-law, Mr. E. S. Van Every, in their second floor 14 x 22-foot plant. They first sold peanuts and peanut butter sandwiches on street corners, door-to-door, merchant-to-merchant, from baskets on the arm. Later, their progress was accelerated by a rented buggy, succeeded by a Model T Ford.

Headquarters was moved to a three story building in January 1926. By 1940, Lance had three big wings added and a fourth wing was built in 1950. Today, Lance is one of the largest and best known manufacturers of peanut butter sandwiches and other peanut food products. The firm is also known throughout the South and Southeast because of its fine Multiple Management program in which labor and management cooperate for mutual interest. Success has made the old manufacturing plant obsolete, and in 1961 construction was begun on a large new operation in Charlotte's suburban industrial area.

Chemicals

Charlotte Chemical Laboratories was formed, with the Chemical Construction Company, in 1914. Both firms had the same officers: Peter S. Gilchrist, I. Hechenbleikner, T. C. Oliver, and A. M. Webb. For a number of years the laboratories developed certain patented items and special application materials. In 1933, with the sale of the Chemical Construction Company, the Charlotte Chemical Laboratories gradually evolved from a research company to one of manufacture, development and sales. The company is firmly entrenched in the field of textile chemicals and specialties and its operations cover a wide territory. At the present time C. W. "Pat" Gilchrist is president; R. D. Long, vice president, and Peter S. Gilchrist, Jr., secretary and treasurer. Affiliated companies are Chemical Corners., Inc., Chemical Development and Estimate Corporation, Technical Processors, and Southern Products and Silica Company, Inc., of Lilesville, North Carolina.

Wholesale Trade

It is unfortunate that the Charlotte authority can't be here today who in 1875 wrote, "The wholesale trade . . . it is an immense one and promises to be larger still." He would be the first to admit that his was an understatement, insofar as Charlotte is concerned.

A description of Charlotte's wholesale trade is likely to be a little confusing because of some overlapping and changed terminology. In the last half of the nineteenth and first part of the twentieth centuries, those who sold for resale were known as wholesale merchants or jobbers. A few still are so called, but most have come to be known as distributors.

The strictly wholesale firms or jobbers in Charlotte today are represented by such companies as Allison-Erwin Company and American Hardware and Equipment Company in the hardware field; Scott Drug Company and Burwell and Dunn Division of McKesson & Robbins in drugs; Williams & Shelton in dry goods; and Biggers Brothers and Thomas & Howard in the wholesale produce and staple grocery fields.

Business firms listed as distributors are of two kinds: factory owned branches, and locally owned firms with franchises for the sale of such items as gas and electric household appliances, office machines, bulk chemicals, and other wares or commodities. By way of illustrating this point as applied to Charlotte, a few firms from each category are described:

Allison-Erwin Company

The earliest ancestor of Allison-Erwin Company was the Charlotte Hardware Company, chartered in 1875. Ownership passed in 1906 to a new corporation headed by Robert Glasgow and R. L. Erwin, father of J. C. Erwin, currently president of the firm. Two years after this incorporation, Henry J. Allison, the 1960 chairman of the board, was employed as an office boy. The second president of the firm was J. C. McNeely (1906-1912) followed by Robert Glasgow (1912-1929) and J. Starr McNeely, vice president and general manager (1921-1922).

A few years after organization, the retail and wholesale divisions of the business were separated, and the retail section eventually discontinued. The wholesale division became known as the Glasgow-Allison Company and since 1946 the Allison-Erwin Company. Growth of the firm for more than half a century culminated in the opening on October 2, 1957 of a huge new home office and warehouse properly equipped for the modern distribution of hardware, floor coverings, and major home appliances from more than 1,000 manufacturers. The company has extensive warehouses in Asheville, Goldsboro and High Point in North Carolina and Charleston, Greenville and Columbia in South Carolina.

American Hardware & Equipment Company

Founded by Charles Nuchols and James B. Duke, March 29, 1917, the American Hardware & Equipment Company is now headed by the founder's son, Lawrence D. Nuchols. The firm operates branches in Greenville, South Carolina and Wilmington, North Carolina for servicing some 3,000 accounts.

Scott Drug Company

On March 1, 1891 Mr. John M. Scott formed a wholesale drug partnership with Mr. R. H. Jordan under the name of Jordan & Scott. In 1894 Mr. Jordan retired from the partnership and the business was incorporated under the name of John M. Scott & Company, under which name it has continued as one of the South's leading wholesale drug firms. Management of the firm passed from John M. Scott and his brother Walter Scott to Walter Scott, Jr., currently president and treasurer.

Williams & Shelton Company

Mr. Charles A. Williams, Sr. founded the Williams & Shelton Company, wholesale dealers in dry goods, wearing apparel, variety store merchandise and toys, on January 1, 1898. Under the leadership of its founder, the firm soon became and has since remained one of the city's most substantial enterprises. Abandoning its downtown location in 1957 for a suburban plant, it is today headed by the founder's sons, Charles A. Williams, Jr., president, and J. Lauer Williams, vice president.

Pritchard Paint and Glass Company

In 1904 the Ezell-Myers Company, a North Carolina corporation, was formed for the purpose of operating a retail paint store in Charlotte. In 1920 T. W. Pritchard purchased control of the Ezell-Myers Company and formed the Ezell-Pritchard Company, which was later changed to Pritchard Paint and Glass Company. It is one of the largest independent dealers and jobbers of paints and glass in the South, with locations in Charlotte, Asheville, Durham and

Raleigh. In 1959 the Pritchard Paint & Glass Company erected a beautiful new building containing a large retail paint and wallpaper store, the company's general office, and a warehouse and plant of approximately 40,000 square feet.

Clark Publishing Company

Organized January 12, 1911 by David Clark to publish a weekly journal, *Southern Textile Bulletin* (now *Textile Bulletin,* published monthly) Clark Publishing Company and the later acquired Washburn Printing Company, are fixtures in Charlotte's industry. The first issue of *Textile Bulletin* was published March 2, 1911 and in January 1937, another monthly journal, *The Knitter,* was launched. In 1943, Clark-Smith Publishing Company was established to publish the monthly journals, *Southern Hospitals* and *Municipal South.* Upon the death of David Clark on November 15, 1955, Junius Smith, a long-time associate, became president of both companies.

Construction Industry

The demand for residential, industrial and road construction has brought into the picture of the city's business life a number of construction and contracting firms.

J. A. Jones Construction Company

A firm little known to Charlotte citizens but one known widely throughout the rest of the world is the J. A. Jones Construction Company. Founded in 1894 by James Addison Jones, this company had an impressive record of building accomplishments prior to World War II. By that time it had developed a large group of men with engineering and construction ability, plus experience; it was drafted to build the atomic bomb plant at Oak Ridge, Tennessee and was awarded a contract to build one shipyard for the Maritime Commission, and operate two others for them. Before the shipyards were completed Jones had contracted to build the ships and in two years launched 212 freighters (2,100,000 tons, total). The company also managed and built twelve complete camps, the equivalent of 12 cities of 25,000 population each. Construction included not only buildings, but sidewalks, water and sewage systems, streets, paving, lighting and fire protection. At times the Jones organization reached 60,000 employees.

Following World War II, the J. A. Jones Construction Company was successful bidder in monumental projects in many parts of the world, and sent trained personnel to distant points from Charlotte. On August 19, 1944, the company's fiftieth anniversary, J. A. Jones could look back on more than a billion dollars worth of construction work done by the company he founded when he was 25 years of age. What was probably more important to Mr. Jones, was the fact that five sons, Raymond A., Edwin L., Paul S., Robert J., and Johnny H. were active in business with him. Upon the founder's death, May 1950, his oldest son, Edwin L. Jones, became president of the firm. Currently, three grandsons of the founder are active in the business: Edwin L. Jones, Jr., Johnny H. Jones, Jr., and Raymond A. Jones, Jr.

Goode Construction Company

On December 11, 1960, Mr. Roy L. Goode became entitled to celebrate the golden anniversary of the Goode Construction Company, of which he is the founder. This general contracting firm can be given credit for some of Charlotte's most attractive residences as well as commercial and institutional buildings.

Blythe Brothers Company

Founded January 4, 1921 by F. J. and Joe L. Blythe, the firm of Blythe Brothers Company is now headed by F. J. Blythe, Jr. The company performs all kinds of heavy construction work and has done a sizable amount of business in all of the southeastern states, in North Africa and, for a number of years, in Puerto Rico.

McDevitt & Street Company

The firm of McDevitt & Street Company was principal contractor for many outstanding Charlotte buildings. Organized as a partnership in 1917 and incorporated in 1925 by J. J. McDevitt, the firm has been McDevitt & Street Company since March 1941. Since 1931 Mr. C. P. Street has owned controlling interest in the firm and acted as general manager.

8

BUSINESS AND FINANCE

B Y 1960, so many people had been attracted to the Piedmont section of North Carolina that the area within a 75 mile radius of
Charlotte had a larger population than an equal area around Atlanta
or other southern cities several times the size of Charlotte. As the
center of this rich trading territory, Charlotte necessarily became
"the crossroads of the Carolinas."

No history of the city would be complete without a comprehensive survey of the enterprises which have set the pattern for the
city's growth, and the individuals responsible for evolutionary steps
in its economic life.

In 1760 there were no stores in Charlotte. What the residents
could not raise or make they bought from peddlers or on infrequent
trips to Charleston or eastern Virginia.

In 1771 Jeremiah McCafferty opened Charlotte's first store, a
general store stocking such staples as whiskey, salt, molasses, cheese
and nearly everything the farmer wanted. Rafters were hung with
yarns, utensils and other wares unsuited to shelves and crude tables.

By 1776 there were three or four other stores and a rifle factory,
and in 1800 these were in addition to several general stores, a blacksmith shop, saw mill, flour mill and a number of taverns. These
served a population of only 276, of whom 123 were Negroes.

Growth for the first quarter of the nineteenth century was slow.
From 1830 to 1860, during the western migration, Mecklenburg's
population dropped by several thousand but following the Civil
War the increase in population and wealth was accelerated by the
revival of textile manufacturing, the reopening of the gold mines by
Northern capitalists and the city's improving railroad facilities.

The first city directory, published in 1875, lists six banks, three building and loan associations, five railroads, twelve boarding houses, sixteen boot and shoe dealers, fourteen dry goods stores, five hardware stores, twenty saloons and a long list of other business firms and professional services. The following firms, listed in the first directory, have been continuously in business for 85 or more years:

Mecklenburg Iron Works
Commercial National Bank (Now North Carolina National Bank)
Singer Sewing Machine Company
Western Union Telegraph Company
W. I. Van Ness & Company
Aetna of Hartford
Phoenix Mutual Life Insurance Company
Mutual Life Insurance Company of New York
Southern Railway

The oldest printing business in Charlotte was incorporated in 1893 when the Observer Printing House came into existence to take over the job printing business which had been a side-line of the Charlotte Observer since 1869. Banks R. Cates became head of the new firm and served until his death in 1941, with the able assistance of his brother Fred R. Cates, as treasurer. William J. Crichton came into the business in 1915 and was later elevated to vice president and general manager.

Formed in 1892, the Andrews Music Company grew out of the firm of E. M. Andrews & Brothers Furniture Company. Formed in 1875, this was dissolved in 1892 when Andrews Music Company was formed. Management of the firm passed successively from the founder, Frank H. Andrews, to his sons Charles S. Andrews, president, and B. N. Andrews, vice president (deceased 1957), and grandson B. N. Andrews, Jr., now vice president, and Robert E. Suther, secretary.

In 1882 Charlotte's oldest funeral firm, J. M. Harry & Bryant Company was formed. John M. Harry, the founder, began as an undertaker with the firm of E. M. Andrews & Brothers Furniture Company. In 1894 he formed his own firm, J. M. Harry & Company which, in 1938, assumed the current name when James R. Bryant came into the business.

Another venerable Charlotte firm started during this period was the Wearn Lumber Company, formed in 1883 by A. S. Summerville and later acquired by J. H. Wearn and W. R. Wearn.

The Parker-Gardner Company has been at 118 West Trade Street since 1886 when Charles W. Parker, his brother William E. Parker and others founded the retail firm to deal in fine furniture. After the depression of the 1930's the firm specialized in musical instruments. Ownership and management of the business remains with the Parker family, active management being in the hands of F. G. Parker and W. J. Parker, nephews of the two founders.

The last decade of the nineteenth century and first decades of the twentieth century were periods of quiet but steady growth. This was a period, for Charlotte, of transition from a village to something approaching the status of a city. The ravages of the Civil War had been largely repaired, and animosities were rapidly being forgotten. The brief financial stringency of 1893 did not seem to bother Charlotte citizens very much judging from the number who visited the Chicago Exposition that year. The speedy and satisfactory conclusion of the Spanish-American War in 1898 created a pleasant atmosphere in business and financial circles, and the Russo-Japanese conflict of 1903 was hardly more than an interesting topic of conversation in Charlotte.

The year 1890 brought Charlotte's first Steam Laundry Service. This business was established by Mr. A. A. Gates as an agency at which wearing apparel was collected and sent to Greenville, South Carolina for laundering. This plant was subsequently purchased by Mr. D. M. Rigler (1893) and was operated under the management of Frank D. Lethco. The Charlotte Laundry was incorporated in 1927 with Mr. Lethco as president. Upon his death in 1929, his holdings passed to his widow and daughter, Helen L. Lethco (Mrs. William F. Medearis). Shortly thereafter, Henry B. Benoit, an official of the firm for many years, was elevated to the presidency.

On September 25, 1895 Belk Brothers opened their Charlotte store. This was the fourth unit in the Belk organization established by William Henry Belk, with his brother as inactive, but not silent partner. Through several major expansions the original store of about 2,250 square feet has become the largest retail store between

Richmond and Atlanta, with nearly 500,000 square feet, and the leading unit in a group numbering approximately 400 stores. The colonial ancestry of William Henry Belk and John M. Belk is vividly recorded in *William Henry Belk, Merchant of the South*, by LeGette Blythe, as is the expansion of their mercantile and philanthropic activities. In the same source can be found a list of their descendants who so ably carry on the family tradition. Following his death on February 21, 1952, just four months before his ninetieth birthday, William Henry Belk was honored by the Newcomen Society with publication of a brochure setting forth his business accomplishments and philosophy.

Both John M. Belk and William Henry Belk have been further honored by establishment of the Belk Foundation which has made liberal contributions to more than 400 churches and educational institutions.

The year after Belk Brothers came to Charlotte, 1896, Garibaldi & Bruns, jewelers, was established by Joseph Garibaldi, watchmaker, and William L. Bruns, engraver. After the death of Mr. Bruns in 1937 and Mr. Garibaldi in 1939, the corporation became the property of the Bruns family.

J. B. Ivey & Company began business February 18, 1900 as a partnership with Joseph Benjamin Ivey as principal owner and active head of the firm, and George F. Ivey and Reverend J. A. Bowles as inactive partners. The first place of business was a storeroom located on the west side of North Tryon Street, near Sixth Street.

Today Ivey's, one of the South's leading department stores, occupies its own building, 400 feet in depth and five stories high, in the center of Charlotte's downtown shopping section. Other Ivey stores are located in Greenville, South Carolina; Asheville and Raleigh in North Carolina; and Orlando, Daytona Beach and Jacksonville, Florida.

The life of the founder of Ivey's is described in *My Memoir* by J. B. Ivey (1940) and *A Tribute*, by business associates, on the eightieth birthday of J. B. Ivey, June 8, 1944.

In these publications and elsewhere Mr. Ivey gave much credit for the success of his business to many able associates. Among these were David Ovens, who joined the firm in 1905, and remained second in authority until his death in 1957; and Mr. W. T. Buice, who joined the firm in 1929 and was second vice president until his death in 1951.

Upon the death of Joseph Benjamin Ivey, April 4, 1958, his son George M. Ivey became president and treasurer; his grandson George M. Ivey, Jr., vice president and Mr. George D. Powell, secretary and assistant treasurer.

W. I. Van Ness & Company began business in 1897 as a part-time venture in selling photographic supplies by William I. Van Ness, a partner in the photographic firm of J. H. Van Ness & Company which had been established a quarter of a century earlier. In 1900 Mr. Van Ness secured the agency for Eastman Kodak Company and established the firm which has since borne his name, now the oldest Eastman Kodak agency in the southeast. Ownership has remained with the Van Ness family, passing from the founder to his brother James H. Van Ness, Jr., to James H. Van Ness III. Frank H. Kimbrell, who joined the firm in 1902 as a clerk, is currently vice president.

No account of the retail merchandising history of Charlotte would be complete without due credit being given the Efird family for their part in the city's business history. In 1902 H. M. Efird, with cooperation of Charles A. Williams of the Williams & Shelton Company, opened a small drygoods store at 43-47 East Trade Street, operating as "The Bee Hive" but formally known as Charlotte Mercantile Company. About 1903 Mr. J. B. Efird joined the firm and subsequently Jasper W. Efird, John Roy Efird, Paul Efird, and E. L. Efird did the same. The name "Bee Hive" was dropped in 1907 and the firm became known as Efird's Department Store.

Efird's Department Store expanded rapidly into a chain of 58 stores throughout the Carolinas, led by the handsome five-story department store in the heart of Charlotte's shopping district. Business continued until 1956 when all units of the Efird chain were sold to Belk Brothers Company.

The Duke Power Company, one of the nation's ten largest utility companies in 1960, is the result of the merging from time to time of the Catawba Power Company, which began operations April 1, 1904, the Southern Power Company, and the Southern Public Utilities Company. Chiefly instrumental in the formation and growth of this huge concern, supplying electricity to approximately 3,000,000 people in a 20,000 square mile area of Piedmont Carolinas, were Dr. W. Gill Wylie, William States Lee, James Buchanan Duke, Zebulon Vance Taylor, George G. Allen, E. C. Marshall, Norman A. Cocke and their many trusted and able associates. W. B. McGuire, elected president of the company in 1959, is carrying on the same traditions.

Much of Charlotte's industrial development and prosperity has been due wholly or in part to the unceasing activity of the Duke Power Company in attracting new capital investments in the territory which it serves. From the dozens to whom credit is due for these achievements, an elderly Charlotte citizen remembers most vividly these members of the Duke Power Company personnel: John W. Fox and Charles H. Reed, industrial engineers; John Paul Lucas, Sr., who was vice president of the Southern Public Utilities Company; his son, John Paul Lucas, Jr., of the Duke Power Company; A. B. Skelding and J. A. Forney, officials of the Southern Public Utilities Company; Duncan C. Carmichael, Duncan Calder, W. S. O'B. Robinson, C. I. Burkholder, David Nabow and Frank Moser.

On October 1, 1904 S. R. Lentz opened a small grocery store at 311 North Tryon Street. More than half a century later Lentz Grocery was still located at the same address and had become the city's oldest grocery store. Upon the death of Mr. Lentz in September 1942, full ownership of the business passed to T. M. McCord, who had been a member of the firm since 1926.

In 1908 R. M. Pound and G. H. Moore went into the office supply business. With a little capital, partly borrowed, they opened a tiny store of 1100 square feet. Pound & Moore Company, Inc., celebrated its golden anniversary in a glamorous store of more than 30,000 square feet, supplemented by a warehouse of 35,000 square feet and a large printing plant. Mr. Moore retired in 1955, leaving the way clear for a close family ownership of the business still headed by one founder, ably assisted by three sons: Ralston M. Pound, Jr., vice president, Carey Pound, secretary, and a younger son, James E. Pound.

The Retail Picture: 1900-1960

In 1900 the forty-hour work week was unheard of, as were the minimum wage law, child labor legislation and many other social practices which are taken for granted fifty years later. Retail stores usually opened at eight in the morning, or before, and remained open daily until seven or eight o'clock and until nearly midnight on Saturdays. Saturday was the big day of the week in retail stores. It was a happy day for almost everybody. That was the day farmers came to town with their produce and stove-wood. Salaries of male salesmen ranged from $12 to $15 weekly (pay was somewhat less for women); and about 25 to 50 cents per day for children for a 10 hour day.

H. E. C. (Red Buck) Bryant recalls that Charlotte just before the turn of the century was becoming known as a good place to earn a living and have a home. New residents were not arriving in droves, but gradually drifting in.

"Young lawyers, doctors, preachers and business men were settling there. The city was growing and it was considered an attractive place. The people were friendly and hospitable. Newcomers got a glad hand.

"The slogan then was, 'Watch our town grow!' The population was approximately 17,000, not counting suburban areas.

"Charlotte then was old-fashioned and a farmers' town. Mules and wagons were parked along Tryon and Trade Streets during the day, horses and buggies in feed stables.

"The only noise of machinery heard was the bit of the cotton compress as it reduced five-hundred pound bales for transportation by train or ship. Much of that valuable money-making crop was then exported for foreign textile manufacturers.

"College Street was about the only nervously busy place then, during the harvesting season. Some days wagons loaded with the king crop of the county were one behind another for blocks. Many of them had come from 10 to 25 miles. They were drawn by two or four fine, well-kept mules, 16 hands high, and well groomed, most of them driven by Negro teamsters.

"During the summer season while cotton was growing, streets

Above: North Tryon Street about 1900 showing the City Hall tower at Fifth Street. *Below:* Northwest corner Independence Square, about 1890.

Northwest corner of Independence Square at the turn of the century. Wi

e the Independence Building, first skyscraper in the state, was built here.

Above: Lounge in the Manufacturers' Club, northwest corner Poplar and West Trade Streets. *Below:* A typical drug store of about 1895.

Above: Central Hotel, southeast corner of square, about 1900. It was Charlotte's leading hotel for many years. *Below:* The Casino at Lakewood Park, early twentieth century.

Trust Building which housed offices and the Academy of Music, 212-14 South Tryon Street. It was destroyed by fire December 17, 1922.

Above: The beginning of construction on Myers Park real estate development. *Below:* Carnegie Library, North Tryon Street home of Charlotte's public library service from 1903 until it was razed to make room for a larger building dedicated in 1956.

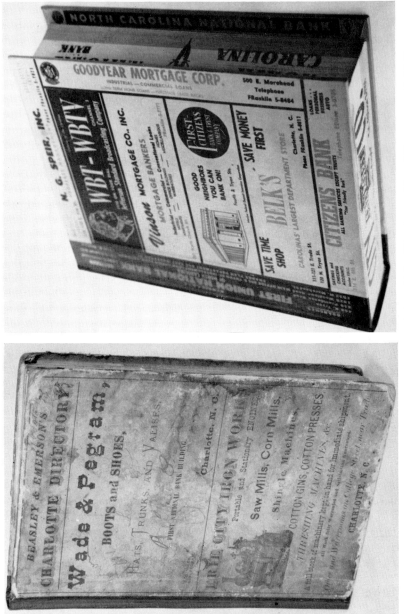

First Charlotte City Directory, published in 1875. Charlotte City Directory of 1961.

were filled with wagons loaded with watermelons, some of them weighing 100 or more pounds. Berryhill and other townships were noted for large, excellent ones.

"I saw a saloon keeper, one year, buy 20 that weighed 2000 pounds, crate and express them to a friend in New York for a special feast.

"Farmers walked the city over, peddling eggs, chickens, cows, and other food supplies. Individual producers called at private homes with butter, milk and small fruits. There were no laws or ordinances against the sale of buttermilk, turkeys, guineas or other dairy or poultry products. Many dollars went into the pockets of tillers of small farms or their wives for such things. More buttermilk was used then as a beverage or for biscuits than beer.

"Soft drinks were being sold at restaurants and drug stores. Bar rooms, Charlotte had 17, furnished hard liquor, beer and wines. People stood at counters, with feet on rails, and asked for three fingers more or less, swallowed them and took off, or stayed for more. A few bought jugs or bottles full and carried them home.

"Now and then some fellow who could not stop with less than a churn full under his shirt, got drunk or wobbly on the street, and was locked up in the city prison for 'safe keeping.' Policemen did not want to see anyone run over by a mule with a shuck collar on, or a bull or steer, escaped from a butcher's pen.

"I knew of two country dwellers who bought cots for their use in the town lock-up when arrested for too many toddys. I doubt if the liquor merchants had cocktails or highballs then. But they served mint juleps if the right sort of a patron with the right sort of pocketbook came along."

The Piggly Wiggly (1920) was the first of the innovations which changed the old time grocery into the super markets of today, with their almost unlimited variety of merchandise. In the meantime the five and ten cent stores had made their appearance, demonstrating the sales value of display and low prices made possible by volume sales for cash only. Charlotte merchants rapidly learned to adjust themselves to changing business methods.

Until the early years of the twentieth century most merchants regarded competitors as rascals or scoundrels. There was little or no cooperation between them. This mutual distrust began to give way before the common misery of "dead-beats" and the hardships imposed by the "Homestead Exemption Act." These were the two principal reasons for the forming of Merchants Associations which were organized in a number of North Carolina towns. The North Carolina Merchants Association was formed with Norman H. Johnson, a young Charlotte attorney, as executive secretary, and editor of the association's official organ, *The Merchants' Journal.* The Charlotte Merchants Association, chartered November 30, 1904 was then, as now, the largest in the state.

Since that time the growth of the Association has paralleled the growth of Charlotte's mercantile and professional life. Policies of the board of directors of the Association have been carried out by executive secretaries or executive vice presidents among whom the following have served: Mayme Moore Sifford, Vincent Paul Rousseau, L. V. Wells and Charles Council Dudley, the present executive vice president. In addition to operating an efficient credit bureau for the benefit of members, the Association cooperates with educational institutions in specialized career training programs, and sponsors many trade events, chief of which is the annual Carolinas' Carrousel, and Southern Consumer Credit Clinic.

Credit for originating the idea for a combined goodwill and sales promotion event to be held each fall belongs to W. S. Lupo, then manager of the Sears, Roebuck & Company store; Charles Council Dudley, of the Merchants' Association; P. H. Batte and F. Earl Crawford of the *Charlotte Observer.* The first celebration in 1947 consisted of a parade witnessed by some 75,000 people. In 1950 the name "Carrousel" was adopted and features increased to include princesses and bands from many points in the Carolinas, athletic events and a huge dance held in a magnificent setting. Distinguished and glamorous guests from the entertainment world are brought to Charlotte to participate and lend charm to all Carrousel activities. It is estimated that more than half a million people view the annual parade in person, and millions more enjoy the spectacle on television.

Establishment of a friendly relationship between competitors through association memberships did not, however, lessen competition between leading firms. With the growth of the Belk, Ivey and

Efird stores, competition became quite intense in the 1920's.

In 1920 the Lipinsky family, owners of Asheville's leading department store, bought the old Charlotte firm of Little-Long Company. Rejuvenated and renamed Bon Marche, it plunged into the scramble for its share of Charlotte's department store business, but after six years, Mr. Lipinsky withdrew and left the battle to his competitors. He returned in 1959 to occupy choice space in the most glamorous shopping center, Charlottetown Mall.

In the 1950's, all midtown merchants were confronted by a common enemy in the form of these centers, which began to spring up in many outlying areas. This predicament led to the formation of the Downtown Association in January 1959. Whether or not this organization will help restore the downtown prestige and popularity will remain for the closing years of the twentieth century to reveal.

Development of the community shopping centers, like many other changes in the nation's habits, resulted largely from the upsurge in automobile ownership following World War II. The greater use of automobiles for local transportation brought about a decreased use of street cars, and later, buses. Traffic congestion became so acute that by 1950 one-way streets became the rule, rather than the exception, in downtown Charlotte. Parking became a major problem. Installation of parking meters about 1942 did so little to relieve the situation that when one property owner found it profitable to convert his property into a commercial parking lot, many others did likewise. The changes thus brought about in the appearance of the downtown business section almost equal the changed view of former farm lands transformed by shopping centers into busy marts of trade.

However, native sons and daughters of Charlotte who return to the scenes of their youth after long absences will be pleased to find many familiar firms, in addition to those already named, still serving the needs of Charlotte citizens. The Southern Passenger Station will still be found on West Trade Street just below Graham. The familiar sign of Mellon's will be a welcome sight to many as they approach the "Square." Around the corner on the east side of South Tryon Street the Gilmer-Moore Shoe Company has been a familiar sight for many years. Across the street at the same old stand is Tate-Brown Company, bringing up memories of J. Caswell Tate, Claude W. Brown, Buford (Pat) Patterson, William C. Stikeleather and many others who groomed Charlotte men and women. On North Tryon Street, corner of Seventh, the drug firm founded so many years ago by T. A. Walker, still bears his name. Smith-Wadsworth Company is no longer on East Trade Street as some will remember, or on South Tryon as others saw it, but is on the outskirts of the city in a modern building.

On Fairwood Avenue is one of the largest photoengraving plants south of Washington, D. C. It grew from the Bierman Engraving Company, founded in 1915, which merged with the Charlotte Engraving Company in 1929. Everett Bierman, son of the founder, is chairman of the board of directors.

No less worthy of admiration and appreciation for contributing to Charlotte business history are members of those firms no longer active. At the beginning of the twentieth century there was the Liddell Company, a foundry enterprise, headed by W. S. Liddell; Stone & Barringer Company, booksellers and stationers who published the works of John Charles McNeill and other Charlotte writers; C. B. Flournoy, gifts and chinaware; Woodall & Sheppard, druggists; Lubin Furniture Company; D. H. Baruch, dry goods; York & Rogers, men's furnishings.

Somewhat later and until well along in the 1920's were such firms as B. F. Roark, jeweler; Miller-VanNess Company, grocers; J. N. McCausland Company, tinsmiths; Queen City Printing Company; W. T. McCoy & Company and Erskine R. Smith, Inc., furniture dealers and, last to be liquidated (1956) Smith's Book Store. It was founded by Glen Smith and upon his death, May 19, 1943, owned and managed by his nephew Carroll S. Sergeant.

Retail Liquor Traffic in Charlotte

The history of the liquor business in Charlotte differs only in detail from that in other North Carolina cities. In the early days, liquor was a staple article of merchandise in general stores. It was also available by the drink and in bottles at taverns. Later, saloons came into existence. These were forerunners of cocktail bars to be found elsewhere, but not in North Carolina, circa 1960.

In 1900 there were fifteen saloons in Charlotte but here, as elsewhere, the prohibition sentiment was growing. The "morally stunted" as the "wets" came to be described, were finally defeated. In an election held July 5, 1904, voters were given an opportunity to vote for (a) absolute prohibition, (b) a city-owned dispensary. Total prohibition carried by a majority of 485. The effective date for the beginning of total prohibition was January 1, 1905.

The legal sale of alcoholic beverages was not resumed in Charlotte until September 25, 1947, when seven Alcoholic Beverage Control stores were opened. In an election held June 14, 1947, Mecklenburg voters gave their approval for the establishment of these stores by a vote of 16,377 to 12,830.

No liquor is sold in ABC stores for consumption on the premises, nor in quantities of less than 1/10th gallon. Every precaution is taken to prevent the spread of alcoholism. Conduct of all phases of the business is regulated by law and, in Charlotte, before distribution of profits, a sum of not less than five per cent must be spent for law enforcement; a sum of not more than five per cent may be spent for alcohol education; the sum of five per cent must be given to the public library system; the remainder is divided equally between the city and county, but from the city's part five per cent must go to the Parks and Recreation Commission and from the county's part two per cent must go to each of the five incorporated towns in Mecklenburg County.

Shortly after the election authorizing ABC stores, at a joint meeting of the County Commissioners, County Board of Education and County Board of Health, a three man board was elected to manage the stores. This board consisted of Frank K. Sims, Jr., chairman, Henry C. Severs and Fred Anderson, all of whom were still serving 13 years later. In the meantime the number of stores has increased to eleven and, as of June 30, 1960, the total amount distributed to beneficiaries was $16,584,350.

Miscellaneous Retail Stores

Before leaving the field of retailing, there must be mentioned a number of businesses which have been around for a quarter of a century or more. Others of the era are well remembered but no longer in business.

Among florists, two of the better known firms doing business during the first half of the twentieth century were those of Louis Ratcliffe, Inc., and Hunter Floral Company. The firm of M. B. Smith & Company, jewelers, is one of the oldest and most highly regarded in the city. With the exception of the retail stores mentioned in this chapter, most of the old family owned and managed firms in Charlotte bowed out of the picture as the chain store movement in merchandising progressed.

Book stores gave way to book departments in department stores, but various religious denominations opened their own stores in Charlotte. The Baptists were first to do this, followed by the Presbyterians and by the Church of God. Mrs. Elizabeth Chambers Holt pleased many book-buyers by maintaining personalized service in her Charlotte Bookshop, presently located in Charlottetown Mall.

The one field that chain and department stores have not seriously affected is the office supply and equipment business. Just when other local stores began to disappear, the Kale twins and Algie Lawing formed the Kale-Lawing Company, office outfitters and printers. This firm has increased competition from Bill Shaw Company and Fowler's, and an increasing number of manufacturers who maintain their own show rooms and sales forces.

Hotels and Restaurants

A granite marker on the edge of the sidewalk in front of 209 West Trade Street indicates the site of Charlotte's first inn. It was owned by Patrick Jack, father of James Jack, who carried the Mecklenburg declaration of independence to the Continental Congress at Philadelphia in 1775. Five years later, when Cornwallis occupied Charlotte, Patrick Jack, then an old man, suffered many indignities and was stripped of most of his wealth because of the part he and his family of ten children had played in the Revolution.

The next local inn to be established also acquired historic recognition. It was Cook's Inn, 20 West Trade Street, at which George Washington stopped and left in such haste that he forgot his powder box, and later wrote in his diary: "Saturday, May 28, 1791. Set off from Crawford's by 4 o'clock and breakfasted at one Harrison's 18 miles from it and got into Charlotte, 13 miles further, before 3 o'clock. Dined with General Thomas Polk and a small party invited by him at a Table set for the purpose. It was not until I had got near Barr's that I quit the Piney and Sandy lands; nor until I got to Crawfords before the lands took quite a different complexion, here they began to assume a very rich look. Charlotte is a trifling place, though the Court of Mecklenburg is held in it. There is a school [Queen's Museum later Liberty Hall] called a college in it which, at times, have had fifty or sixty boys."

An interesting account of another Charlotte inn is found in the diary of William D. Martin who, as a young man in 1809 traveled by horseback, buggy, coach and boat from Edgefield, South Carolina to Litchfield, Connecticut, where he attended law school. After describing at some length the difficulty he had in crossing the Catawba River, he wrote on Friday April 4, 1809:

"We breakfasted late this morning at Charlotte, the county seat of Mecklenburg. The village consists of two streets, crossing in a square; in the center of town stands a tolerably elegant Brick Court House with a cupola on top.

"In my host and lady, Mr. and Mrs. Huston, were united the rare qualities of attention, politeness and kindness. As the keepers of an inn they discharged every duty. The good lady, having prepared a genteel breakfast, when she observed us setting out again, with all hospitality of a friend and kindness of a mother, she presented and insisted upon my accepting some biscuits and cheese which she said, 'will serve as a repast at noon.' Such disinterested goodness among strangers raised into action the most lively sensations of gratitude & for the moment I thought myself surrounded by my friends, a reverie at all times as pleasant as it is delusive."

Since those early days, many hotels have come and gone, leaving very little in the way of documentary evidence of their ownership or management. The hotel with the longest history was, undoubtedly, the Mansion House, built about 1840, which changed its name to Central Hotel in 1873, and continued to operate until the late 1930's.

The Central Hotel, on the southeast corner of Trade and Tryon Streets, was, for many years, considered the finest hotel between Richmond and Atlanta. Its spacious ballroom was the gathering place for Charlotte's elite. On one side of the lobby was the dining room, and the other the city's most elegant bar, until this feature was closed with the advent of prohibition, January 1, 1905. Around the huge fireplace in the rear of the office were large chairs that in summer were carried to the sidewalk, where leading citizens and "drummers" tilted them back against the walls and discussed weighty questions of the day.

For a number of years beginning about 1885 or a little earlier, the second most important hotel in Charlotte was the Buford, named for Colonel A. S. Buford, then president of the Richmond & Danville Railroad. The main part of this building, on the northeast corner of Fourth and Tryon Streets, contrary to popular belief, was not erected for hotel purposes. It was built as an office building in the 1870's by the Southern Life Insurance Company of Atlanta to house its Charlotte offices on the second floor, and the then young Commercial National Bank on the first floor. The United States Post Office and Court Room occupied the remainder of the first floor and third floor.

The building became a hotel when the insurance company had financial difficulties and sold it to a company headed by William Johnston as president and Robert M. Miller, Jr., secretary and treasurer, who immediately leased it to G. W. Kittells. Later, the wing on the Fourth Street side was added and the dining room moved from the fourth to the second floor to save elevator expense. Still later, an addition was built on the north side, facing Tryon Street, to hold the bar and dining room.

While patronized largely by traveling men, the Buford also provided living quarters for some of Charlotte's most prominent people, among them Mr. and Mrs. Walter Brem, Mr. and Mrs. Stuart Cramer and one of the city's most distinguished bachelors, Daniel Augustus Tompkins. The Buford Hotel was closed about 1915 and the lower floors converted into store rooms, the largest of which, on the corner, was occupied for many years by the Union National Bank. In 1945 the building was renovated and the upper floors occupied by the newly formed Charlotte City Club.

Modern hotel history in Charlotte begins with the opening of the Selwyn Hotel in February 1907, on the northeast corner of Trade and Church Streets. Named for the English peer from whom the land was purchased for the town of Charlotte, and built on the site of the county's third courthouse, the Selwyn was regarded as

North Carolina's finest hotel, when built, and nearly sixty years later was still numbered among the city's better hotels.

Following World War I new hotels were built in a number of North Carolina cities. Capital was usually raised by sale of stock to the business interests of the various towns. This method was used to finance the building of the 400 room Hotel Charlotte, on West Trade Street, which opened in 1923. It immediately became the city's favorite hotel.

Charlotte's most modern hotel as of 1960 is the William R. Barringer, on North Tryon Street. Opened December 14, 1940 the twelve story building with 200 rooms, was increased to 325 in 1950. In anticipation of further expansion, the Hotel Barringer Company, in 1959, acquired the adjoining property occupied for many years by St. Mark's Lutheran Church.

The Stonewall Hotel, built 1907, took its name from the occupant of the property, near the Southern station, Mrs. "Stonewall" Jackson. The 65-room hotel was closed in 1958.

The Mecklenburg Hotel, erected on West Trade Street in 1914 by Mr. W. C. Petty, a well-known hotel operator, retained in 1960 its good reputation for both dining and lodging. The Mayfair Hotel, built by Dr. James Pleasant Matheson and others, on the southwest corner of Tryon and Sixth Streets, and the Clayton Hotel, on the northeast corner of Church and Fifth Streets, served as both transient and family hotels for many years from 1915.

Just as the dominance of midtown department stores and specialty shops is threatened by the growth of suburban shopping centers, standard hotels are having to compete with modern motels. Here again, the overpowering influence of the automobile and air age is bringing about changes which may be better evaluated in another era.

It is sufficient for now to mention that this new form of hotel accommodations is the outgrowth of tourist homes. Some of these developed into groups of cottages, labeled "motels." By 1960 many motels and motor courts vied in splendor with the most lavishly equipped hotels. Confronted with this new kind of competition, some hotels began to supplement their facilities with motor courts of various types.

Public eating places, apart from lodgings, are a fairly recent development in Charlotte. In the early days, room and board all in one place, was the accepted custom. In 1900 there were 37 boarding houses in Charlotte. Today, there are none listed in the city directory.

One of the last of the old-time boarding houses to pass from the Charlotte scene was that conducted by Mrs. Margaret L. Garrison at 403 (later 419) West Fourth Street. At times Mrs. Garrison had more than 100 boarders, her principal business, and a few roomers upstairs. Meals were served "family style" in liberal quantities, well prepared and varied.

"Ma" Garrison strove hard to create the impression of being a hard-boiled business woman but she was the soul of sympathy and kindness. Six of her "star" boarders (Otto Haas, Joe Monroe, Herbert V. Brockmann, Jesse Wilcox, L. L. Ledbetter and J. R. Craven) faithful friends to the last, slipped and slid through the red mud of a rural cemetery as they bore Ma's body to its final resting place on November 15, 1935.

Older citizens remember other Charlotte eating places. There was Gresham's Southern Railway Restaurant, from about 1896 to 1914; Gem Restaurant at 19 South Tryon Street from 1900 to 1915, and the Brown Betty Tea Room, over Garibaldi & Bruns, jewelers, owned and operated by Mrs. Annie Oliver and her daughter, Mrs. Richard Pfaehler.

Modern restaurant history began in Charlotte with the opening on July 14, 1920 of the S & W Cafeteria on West Trade Street. The tremendous popularity of self-service restaurants on the Pacific Coast, where they originated about 1910, was immediately duplicated in Charlotte. Proof is to be found in the fact that the original S & W Cafeteria, now located next door to the first building, is still one of the city's most popular dining places, and is the parent unit of a large chain.

The S & W Cafeteria of Charlotte was founded by Frank Odell Sherrill and Fred Weber. Mr. Weber left the company in 1925. Mr. Sherrill remains active in the company as president and general manager. Since 1922 Emmett Crook has served as secretary and treasurer of the company and more recently three sons of the founder have come into the business.

Real Estate Dealers

In 1890 Edward Dilworth Latta began development of Dilworth, Charlotte's first big real estate subdivision. Mr. Latta's firm was the Charlotte Consolidated Construction Company, familiarly known as the 4C's Company, operators of the street railway system. The other dealer was Walter S. Alexander who, a little later, began development of the Elizabeth residential section. As a part of his promotion efforts he donated the property now occupied by Presbyterian Hospital to Elizabeth College, a Lutheran institution founded in 1897.

Early in the twentieth century George Stephens conceived the idea of developing the huge farm of his father-in-law, Mr. J. S. Myers, into a residential suburb of first magnitude in size, unexcelled in the beauty of its landscaping and with homes of unusual elegance. With the same foresight and determination that he had shown in developing Kanuga Lake resort colony in Western North Carolina, Mr. Stephens proceeded to carry out his plan.

A forgotten but interesting phase in the devlopment of Myers Park occurred September 1, 1919 when a majority of the voters living there were granted a charter making it a separate municipality. The first mayor was Charles Huntley Gover and the commissioners, Dr. John Clifford, John P. Little and J. M. Harry. The petition mentioned a number of grievances against the city of Charlotte, including complaints about roads, schools, police and fire protection. Evidently things didn't work out as well as the incorporators had hoped, for on November 8, 1924, the corporation was dissolved on petition of Paul C. Whitlock, mayor, and C. H. Gover, clerk, representing practically all of those who had sought the charter.

An important contemporary of Latta, Alexander, Stephens, and other real estate dealers of the first half of the twentieth century was F. C. Abbott, who came to Charlotte from New England in 1897. Future generations will be indebted to Mr. Abbott for recording the most important transactions of his firm and much Charlotte real estate history in his brochure *Fifty Years in Charlotte Real Estate 1897-1947.*

According to Mr. Abbott, none of the buildings occupying the four corners of Independence Square in 1900 are standing today. At that time, the Osborne home, which had long since been abandoned as a residence, on the northwest corner, housed the Woodall & Sheppard Drug Store. The Davidson home, built in 1830, was on the northeast corner and likewise converted for business purposes with Jordan's Drug Store on the first floor. The Central Hotel was on the southeastern corner, and Burwell & Dunn, druggists, on the southwest corner. The Piedmont Building at 222 South Tryon Street (demolished 1957) was considered the finest office building in North Carolina. The City Hall was on the corner of Tryon and Fifth Streets, with the city's only fire company in the rear. Presbyterian College was on North College Street and the Charlotte *Observer* at 32 South Tryon Street, now occupied by the Bank of Charlotte. Charlotte's water, about 1900, came from a small lake that later became Independence Park. The Plaza was a narrow dirt road, Chantilly a peach orchard and Eastover section the McD. Watkins' dairy farm. The 600 acre plantation that was to become Myers Park was advertised for sale at $40 the acre. The first electric light plant in North Carolina was located on the south side of the first block of East Fifth Street. Nearby was the gathering place for the horse-trading element of the community, with five or six barrooms.

The rapid and tremendous increase in Charlotte real estate values is disclosed by old deeds and other records in the Mecklenburg County courthouse. A typical example is the property at 120 North Tryon Street which was sold in 1900 for $20,000. In 1923 Efird's paid $225,000 for the same property and built a department store thereon. In 1897 the property on the southeast corner of Third and Tryon Streets, now occupied by the First Union National Bank, was bought for $12,000 as a site for a courthouse. After the new courthouse was built in 1928, the same property was sold for $425,000.

Automobiles in Charlotte

Automobiles were first mentioned in the Charlotte City Directory for 1904 when the firm of Osmond L. Barringer & Company was listed as agent for the Franklin Autocar and Cadillac automobiles.

The Buick agency has been continuously in operation since C. C. Coddington became a distributor for the Carolinas in 1909. When Mr. Coddington died in 1929, the Buick Motor Company took over the distributorship with Lee A. Folger, an associate of Mr. Coddington, as manager. This arrangement lasted until 1937 when Mr. Folger organized the firm of Lee A. Folger, Inc., and took over the retail business from Boomershine Motor Company, last of the three firms which had sold Buicks locally since 1929.

Hoppe Motors, Inc., organized in 1915 by Mr. W. T. Hoppe, has had a long and successful career as agents for Chrysler and Plymouth automobiles. The founder headed the business until 1960 when it was taken over by other interests upon Mr. Hoppe's retirement. Cadillac cars have been sold in Charlotte longer than automobiles of any other name. Since June 1, 1929 the Charlotte business has been handled by Thomas Cadillac-Olds, Inc., of which G. C. Thomas is founder and president.

The automobile industry was prominent in the news in Charlotte twice during the 1920's, once unfavorably and once favorably. It was in 1920 that the Wizard Automobile Company was organized in Charlotte and a vigorous campaign conducted to sell a million dollars worth of stock. The prospectus painted a glowing picture of the profits to be made from the sale of cars to be manufactured and sold for $395. A plant was built in the southwestern section of the city and one or two cars put together for display to prospective stockholders. That was as far as the Wizard Automobile Company got, and the bewildered stockholders were left to shoulder their losses, as were many creditors.

In 1925 the Ford Motor Company erected a large assembly plant on the Statesville road. This property was later acquired by the government as a depot for commissary and other supplies and is now, much enlarged, used as a missile assembly plant by Douglas Aircraft Company.

Small Business Firms, Then and Now

Prior to 1890 there seems to have been no white barber in Charlotte. If this seems strange in 1960 it should be remembered that in the South before the Civil War, men depended on slaves for hair cuts, beard trimming and shaves. These slaves earned extra money by serving those who owned no slaves. After the war the freed Negroes opened shops of their own.

The first white barber in Charlotte appears to have been Paul McKane who is listed in the 1891 city directory. His patronage was evidently small and uncertain for he also operated a shoe repair business in connection with his barber shop. The next white barber was apparently Mark M. Dintenfass who operated a shop at the Buford Hotel. This was in 1897 when a hair-cut cost a quarter and a shave was a dime. At that time, Thad Tate, who later became one of Charlotte's wealthiest and most esteemed Negro citizens, owned the shop in the Central Hotel. From that period on the number of Negro operated shops for white people lessened, as more and more shops were opened by white barbers. Thaddeus Tate, whose services extended from 1882 to 1944, was one of Charlotte's outstanding citizens. He held various positions of trust including that of treasurer of the Brevard Street Library for Negroes before its management was taken over by the Public Library. He was a director for more than 60 years in the Mechanics Perpetual Building & Loan Association. A sketch of his life and mention of his fine family of ten children is contained in *An Appreciation of Twenty-One Men Who Have Rendered Long and Faithful Service in One Job*, published October 13, 1946 by the Phalanx Club of the Second Street Y.M.C.A. of Charlotte. Mr. Tate died at the age of 85 on March 29, 1951.

Next in length of service among barbers was Vance M. Stine who, with Robert H. Jacobs, succeeded to the ownership of the Buford Hotel Barber Shop about 1908. Mr. Stine continued near this address until his death about 1944. Thereafter, his wife conducted the business until 1950 when it was taken over and moved to the Johnston Building by Bartley Elzie Smith, who had joined Mr. Stine in 1910, and Boyce M. Cranford. Gibson Gerry Bost, who came to Charlotte upon completion of his barbering course at Atlanta in 1910, joined Mr. Stine shortly thereafter and, as the oldest active barber in Charlotte as of 1960, continues his association with Smith and Cranford.

Among the small but important businesses that have contributed to the comfort and convenience of Charlotte people there should be mentioned first Ben F. Favell's shoe repair shop, begun in 1915 and presently more prosperous than ever; and Harry P. Murray, who has had a merchant tailoring service for about the same length of time. In 1926 there were six white and four Negro "pressing clubs" of which the City Pressing Club of D. W. Fink and J. W. Elliott was the best known. Today, the heading, "Pressing Clubs," is not to be found in the city directory. "Hair Dressers," first appeared in the directory in 1912 when the Ideal Beauty Shop of Mrs. M. M. Cross was listed. Other shops were owned by Lethia Jones and by Jessie B. Johnson. "Beauty parlors" were first listed in 1917 when Mrs. D. H. Simpson's was the only one. In 1926 there were nine beauty parlors and in 1960 nearly 300.

Banks and Banking in Charlotte

One of the earliest banking transactions to take place in Charlotte occurred when the town commissioners borrowed money from the Charlotte branch of the Bank of New Bern with which to build a church. This was between 1818 and 1823. Tompkins' history mentions that, "W. Morris was local agent for the Bank of New Bern in 1830," and he served until the bank closed when its charter expired in 1832.

Two years later, with the increased production of gold, a branch of the North Carolina Bank was opened at Charlotte. This was followed by the opening of the first locally owned bank, known as the Bank of Charlotte, with authorized capital of $300,000. The officers were H. B. Williams, president, and W. A. Lucas, cashier. The board of directors consisted of these and T. H. Brem, J. H. Wilson, D. Parks, S. P. Alexander, A. C. Steele, W. R. Myers, and H. B. Williams.

According to Tompkins' history, the Bank of Charlotte was still in operation in 1867 but it does not appear in the city directory for 1875. The directory for that year lists five banks. The three that survived for many years were the First National Bank of Charlotte, Commercial National Bank and Merchants and Farmers National

Bank. Of these three only the Commercial National now remains, though renamed, after consolidations, the North Carolina National Bank.

The First National Bank of Charlotte was incorporated in 1865. The officers in 1880 were R. Y. McAden, president; W. R. Myers, vice president, and M. P. Pegram, cashier. In 1891, Mr. Pegram was still cashier but the president was Robert M. Oates. This arrangement lasted until 1900 when Pegram replaced Oates as president, with Mr. Myers continuing as vice president. In 1904 Frank Gilreath served briefly as president, to be succeeded by Henry M. McAden, who served the bank from 1907 until its closing December 4, 1930. While Mr. Gilreath was president, the cashier was Henry M. Victor, later to become president of the Union National Bank. For many years the First National Bank was located at 20 South Tryon Street, in a building which was demolished in 1926 to make room for a 21-story building as the new home for the bank, for a number of years Charlotte's tallest building. The Commercial National Bank (North Carolina National Bank 1960), was chartered on February 18, 1874, and is the oldest national banking institution in North Carolina. During the incumbency of its first president, Clement Dowd, the cashier was Addison G. Brenizer. Mr. Dowd was succeeded by J. S. Spencer about 1890, and around 1910 Mr. Brenizer became president. In 1904, Albert Theodore Summey became a teller, later rising to become vice president. In 1911 young Ivey Withers Stewart moved from a position with Williams & Shelton to the Commercial National, eventually becoming chairman of the board of the American Commercial Bank. Following Mr. Brenizer, Robert A. Dunn served as president for a number of years, before becoming chairman of the board to be succeeded by Mr. Stewart in 1936. During Mr. Dunn's regime a number of competent young members were recruited including John P. Hobson, who became cashier and trust officer, and Herbert M. Wayne, who succeeded him as cashier.

On November 29, 1958 the Commercial National Bank was merged with the American Trust Company to become the American Commercial Bank, no longer a national bank, with Torrence E. Hemby as honorary chairman of the board; Ivey W. Stewart, chair-

Above: Ovens Auditorium, foreground, and Charlotte Coliseum. *Below:* Memorial Stadium is packed each year for the "Shrine Bowl" charity football game between high school stars of North Carolina and South Carolina.

Above: Children's Nature Museum, one of Charlotte's favorite attractions, is located at Freedom Park. *Below:* Park Center provides facilities for civic and sports gatherings.

Above: Douglas Municipal Airport. (Photo courtesy Eastern Air Lines.)
Below: Young Men's Christian Association.

Above: Home Office of the Textile Division Celanese Corporation of America. *Below:* Terminal of Akers Motor Lines, one of the many trucking firms which make Charlotte a leading distribution center.

Wachovia Building, one of the newest additions to Charlotte's skyline.

Above: The Mint Museum of Art in Eastover, formerly the United States Mint. *Below:* Main Building of the Charlotte and Mecklenburg County library system is an outstanding example of library architecture.

Above: Entrance to The Little Theatre of Charlotte on Queens Road.
Below: Easter sunrise service in Freedom Park, 1961.

Above: Piedmont Courts Housing Development. In foreground is Administration Building of the Housing Authority of the City of Charlotte. *Below:* Panoramic view of the Methodist Home for the Aged.

man; Addison H. Reese, president. Shortly after the merger, plans were announced for erecting a 16-story banking and office building to occupy the space formerly required to house the two adjoining banking establishments. In the early summer of 1960 the American Commercial Bank of Charlotte and the Security National Bank of Greensboro became consolidated under the name of North Carolina National Bank.

The Merchants and Farmers National Bank was organized about 1875, with T. H. Brem as president and J. R. Holland as cashier. The bank had a continuous existence until its closing during the banking holiday of the early 1930's.

The Charlotte National Bank was chartered in 1897 with B. D. Heath as president and W. H. Twitty, cashier. In 1908 it absorbed the Charlotte Trust Company, and in 1919 it added the Southern Loan and Savings Bank. Mr. Twitty served the bank continuously until his death in 1943, probably the longest banking record in the city's history. John M. Scott became president of the Charlotte National and was still active in that position when the bank merged with Wachovia Bank and Trust Company in 1939. Mr. Scott became chairman of the bank's Charlotte board, and John P. Watlington, Jr., was made executive head of the office. Beginning in 1948 Wachovia added neighborhood offices throughout the city and in 1958 moved to its new 15-story main office building at Trade and Church Streets. When Mr. Watlington was elected president of the statewide Wachovia in 1956, Joseph H. Robinson succeeded him as executive head of the Charlotte bank.

Wachovia was founded in Winston-Salem in 1879 as the Wachovia National Bank. In 1911, this institution merged with Wachovia Loan and Trust Company to form the present Wachovia Bank and Trust Company. The Wachovia Loan and Trust Company, under the guidance of its president, Colonel Francis H. Fries, had already become the largest bank in the state and had extended its services on a statewide basis by establishing offices in Asheville, Salisbury and High Point in 1902-03. Wachovia's Raleigh office was established in 1922, followed by a merger with the Charlotte National in 1939, to give the bank offices in most of the state's large trade and financial centers. Since 1954, Wachovia offices have been established in a number of other cities and it is presently the largest bank in the Southeast. Its trust department holds the largest assets of any trust institution in the South.

Robert M. Hanes succeeded Colonel Fries as Wachovia president in 1931. His banking career was outstanding and he was called upon to serve in virtually every high banking post in the nation. Upon Mr. Hanes' retirement in 1956, Mr. Watlington was named president and under his direction Wachovia has continued its growth, expansion and service to the region.

In 1901 Frederick C. Abbott, George Stephens and Word H. Wood formed the Southern States Trust Company. Shortly thereafter the name was changed to American Trust Company. Mr. Wood became president in 1927, a position he held until 1943; Arthur J. Draper and B. B. Gossett became vice presidents in 1923 and a little later F. W. DeArmon became assistant secretary and treasurer, and R. E. Kerr, assistant trust officer. By 1943 Mr. Wood had been elevated to the position of chairman of the board, with Torrence E. Hemby as president, and Mr. Kerr, vice president. While Mr. Hemby was president, Addison H. Reese, Arthur H. Jones, and others were added to the list of vice president, and Walter Lambeth, vice president in charge of the Insurance Department. This general arrangement continued until November 29, 1957 when the American Trust Company merged with the Commercial National Bank to form the American Commercial Bank which, in 1960, merged with the Security National Bank of Greensboro to become the North Carolina National Bank.

The Union National Bank was established in 1908. Henry M. Victor was named cashier. T. W. Wade served as president from 1908 until 1913, during which time F. B. McDowell was vice president. Mr. Victor succeeded Mr. Wade as president and at the same time Duncan P. Tillett became cashier. This arrangement lasted until 1945 when Mr. Tillett was elected president. In 1947 George S. Crouch came in as assistant cashier and in 1952 Carl G. McGraw succeeded him. Upon Mr. Tillett's death, Mr. Crouch became president, in 1947. Mr. McGraw succeeded Mr. Crouch as president in 1952. Mr. Victor became chairman of the board in 1945 and was succeeded in this position by Mr. Crouch in 1952, a position which he still holds.

On July 31, 1958 the Union National Bank merged with the First National Bank and Trust Company in Asheville and the name, First Union National Bank of North Carolina, was adopted. On November 28, 1958 the First Union National merged with the Bank of Lenoir and the Union National Bank of Lenoir. Industrial Bank of Durham and the National Bank of Wilson merged with the First Union, December 11, 1959.

In 1912 the Independence Trust Company, with Julian H. Little as president; H. A. Morson, secretary; Esley O. Anderson, cashier; and E. E. Jones, assistant cashier, opened for business. The bank owned the Independence Building on the northwest corner of Trade and Tryon Streets, and occupied the first floor during its entire existence. It failed to open after the banking holiday in the early 1930's. The stockholders continued to own the building.

On November 23, 1914 the Citizens Savings & Loan Corporation, now known as the Citizens Bank, opened its doors for business with J. O. Gardner, president; John W. Zimmerman, vice president; J. A. Fore, secretary, and James T. Porter, treasurer and manager. Mr. Zimmerman became president about 1918. Thereafter, these principal officers remained, with the addition of Zeb C. Strawn, who had joined the company in 1924 and was made treasurer in 1926. In 1946 Mr. Zimmerman became chairman of the board, Mr. Porter became president, and Mr. Strawn, executive vice president. In 1952 Mr. Strawn became president, a position which he presently holds.

The Charlotte Morris Plan Company was formed in 1918 with T. M. Shelton, Sr., president; Erskine R. Smith, vice president; Charles A. Williams, vice president and Connor H. Sherrill, secretary-treasurer. W. H. Bethea came into the firm around 1921, and Mr. Sherill became president in 1927. The affairs of this bank moved along without important changes until 1944 when the name was changed to Bank of Charlotte, headed by T. M. Shelton, Jr.

The Fifth Street Industrial Bank was organized in 1920, but soon changed its name to City Industrial Bank. The first officers were R. L. Goode, president; J. W. Cuthbertson, first vice president; F. E. Robinson, second vice president and W. G. Craven, secretary-treasurer. Mr. Robinson served only a short time and was replaced as vice president by Jesse M. Oldham. In 1936 W. Reynolds Cuthbertson, son of one of the founders, became president, a position which he still holds with the bank, renamed in 1945, the City Savings Bank.

The Industrial Bank of Mecklenburg was organized in 1923 with T. J. Payne, president, and J. Davis, cashier. A few years later Louis B. Vreeland, an attorney, became president; R. S. Motte, vice president; and T. D. Newell, cashier. This bank was liquidated at the time of the banking holiday.

The Industrial Loan and Investment Bank began business in 1922. A few years later H. C. Alexander became president with I. W. Stewart, vice president but not active, Dr. W. F. Medearis, vice president but not active, and George Douglas Aitken, cashier. In 1948 the name of the institution was changed to The Bank of Commerce and, upon Mr. Alexander's death in 1957, Mr. Aitken became president, a position which he now holds.

On December 1, 1927 the Charlotte Branch of the Federal Reserve Bank of Richmond opened for business on the 20th floor of what was then the First National Bank Building. Hugh Leach was managing director, W. T. Clements, cashier. The original board of directors consisted of Word H. Wood and John L. Morehead of Charlotte; W. J. Roddey, Sr., of Rock Hill, S. C.; Robert Gage of Chester, S. C.; John A. Law of Spartanburg, S. C.; Charles A. Cannon of Concord, N. C., and Mr. Leach. In 1931, Mr. Leach was transferred to the Baltimore branch of the bank, and Mr. Clements succeeded him as managing director. In 1947, Mr. Clements retired and was succeeded by Robert L. Cherry. At that time the title of the officer-in-charge was changed from managing director to vice president. Mr. Cherry retired in 1959 and was succeeded by Thomas L. Storrs. By then the bank had grown to an institution of 216 employees, occupying its own five-story building on South Tryon Street. Establishment of a branch of the Federal Reserve Bank contributed much toward increasing Charlotte's prestige as the financial center of the Carolinas, and its presence aided the growth of the 50 counties in western North Carolina and 21 in western South Carolina which it serves.

Banking in Charlotte during the 1950's

Following the end of World War II, Charlotte and most other parts of the United States entered upon a fifteen year period of unprecedented prosperity. Expanding industrial development brought demands for loans in amounts far exceeding those which Charlotte banks were permitted to make. As a consequence of this changed situation, especially in smaller cities, many banks were merged so that larger loans could be granted. Even before the merger movement was well under way, the Charlotte National Bank had strengthened its position by merging with the Wachovia Bank & Trust Company of Winston-Salem. In 1957, the Commercial National Bank of Charlotte and American Trust Company, became American Commercial Bank of Charlotte, and shortly thereafter the Union National Bank of Charlotte, by merging with the First National Bank of Asheville and several other banking institutions, became the First Union National Bank of North Carolina. This movement was continued in 1960 when the American Commercial Bank merged with the Security National Bank of Greensboro to form the North Carolina National Bank, creating the fourth largest institution of its kind in the South. Charlotte thus claims two of the four largest banking chains in the South.

Concurrently, the larger banks began to open neighborhood branches for the more convenient handling of accounts in outlying sections. Competition for business was never keener than in 1960. Whenever occasions arise in Charlotte requiring cooperation between banks, however, agreement can usually be reached, as was the case when, with one exception, all banks were parties to a movement for Saturday closing of banks.

Building & Loan Associations

The Mutual Savings and Loan Association is the oldest such institution operating in North Carolina, having been organized in April, 1881, as the Mutual Building and Loan Association. Among its organizers and first directors were Judge Armistead Burwell, P. H. Phelan, Col. J. L. Brown and Captain A. G. Brenizer, the first secretary-treasurer-manager.

Instrumental in achieving the association's long record were three generations of the Keesler family, beginning with Edward L. and continuing with his son Edward Y. Keesler, the current president, and grandson Lenoir C. Keesler, presently executive vice president.

In 1922 the association moved into its own building on East

Third Street, and now is in process of erecting a modern banking and office building on the former Y. M. C. A. property, on South Tryon Street.

The Mechanics Perpetual Building & Loan Association, established in 1883 by S. Wittkowsky, president, and R. E. Cochrane, secretary as principal officers, is another successful financial institution. Its name was changed in 1943 to Home Federal Savings and Loan Association. Under this name, with the original plan of operation slightly modified, it continues to provide facilities whereby citizens of Charlotte may readily finance the acquisition of homes. Heading the Association since the turn of the century have been R. E. Cochrane, E. J. Caffrey and T. G. Barbour, Sr.

The First Federal Savings & Loan Association was formed in 1940, largely through the efforts of Joseph Choate and Roy S. Smith. It has earned for itself a place among the city's better known financial institutions.

Short-Lived Banks

In 1879 there was a Traders National Bank with S. P. Smith, president, R. I. McDowell, vice president, and C. N. G. Butt, cashier.

In 1896 there was a Loan & Savings Bank with S. Wittkowsky, president and A. Brady, cashier.

In 1907 a Charlotte Trust Company was headed by Julian H. Little, president; C. M. Patton, vice president, and L. R. Hagood, cashier.

In 1912 there was a Savings Bank & Trust Company with W. M. Moore, president.

In 1916 Dr. Charles A. Bland, W. R. Foreman and W. W. Robards were officers in the Peoples Bank & Trust Company.

In 1921 there was a Progressive Bank & Trust Company with T. T. Cole, president, and Erskine R. Smith, vice president.

In 1923 there was a Southern Industrial Bank. J. J. Misenheimer, president and treasurer and J. C. Hunter, cashier.

In 1923 there was a Turner Industrial Bank: M. A. Turner, president.

9

HEALTH AND WELFARE

E VER since Dr. Ephraim Brevard assisted in writing the resolutions which were unanimously adopted as the Mecklenburg declaration of independence, physicians have taken the initiative in maintaining a high state of health and happiness in Charlotte and vicinity. The active lists of members and officers of Charlotte churches, civic clubs, welfare organizations, and country clubs for any period includes a high percentage of doctors and dentists. In his very readable *History of Mecklenburg County Medicine* (1929) Dr. C. M. Strong, with the able assistance of others, mentions the professional achievements of some.

When Dr. Brevard died in 1782, his effects were sold at public auction. Purchasers were Drs. Isaac Alexander, Thomas Henderson, and one Dysart, probably the only three doctors in the county at that time. Since then there has seldom been a period in Mecklenburg when there was no doctor by the name of Alexander.

Among the many points of interest let us consider a few. There was a virulent epidemic of smallpox in Mecklenburg in 1770. Dr. Alexander's charge for vaccinating a patient with scabs was one pound ($5). Transportation was on horseback or by buggy, over roads that were all but impassable much of the time. Obstetrical cases were handled by midwives or any woman who happened to be available when needed. All surgery was done on tables in the home, frequently by candlelight, with no further assistance to the doctor than could be given by members of the family or neighbors. Most common relief from pain after an operation was provided by doses of whiskey.

311

In Mecklenburg, as elsewhere, medicine greatly advanced between 1840 and 1865, especially in surgery. Antiseptic methods were by then well established. Ether was discovered; the Civil War compelled surgery on a scale never before experienced in the United States. It was during this period, according to Dr. Strong's history, that medicine emerged from the dark age of suspicion and assumed a more enlightened position among the learned professions. In Charlotte the number of physicians increased rapidly, though even then each was still known as "Physician and Surgeon." A vivid account of *Mecklenburg Medicine of the Nineties* is given in a chapter of Dr. Strong's book written by Dr. G. W. Pressly. Samplings from this chapter follow:

"Doctors began to move to Charlotte along with a lot of other folks. It soon became a not uncommon sight to see a perfect stranger cross the square. . . . There were three drug stores on this historic spot. Around each of these a galaxy of doctors revolved in a more or less regular orbit . . . In these halcyon days the specialists began to get their milk teeth . . . Among the many gifts vouchsafed to the men of medicine in this period and possibly the greatest of all was the trained nurse . . . The operations in vogue were amputations, circumcisions, hemorrhoids, strangulated hernia, D and C, and tonsillectomy . . . Few had ever looked an appendix right in the eye . . . no one suspected that a gold mine lay in the right quadrant . . . The colored hospital was noted, even then, as a very interesting museum of pathological anatomy . . . If Dr. Charlie Strong couldn't be located anywhere else, you would likely find him at Good Samaritan surrounded by a 40 pound multiple fibroid. . . . We must pause to shed a tear for the passing of dear old Dobbin and the saddle bags . . . In 1899 thirty manufacturers made and sold 600 motor cars. It was thought this output would last 30 years . . . Just how many lives the automobiles have saved we do not know, but at present they are killing 25,000 people every year."

Dr. Strong's book contains a valuable chapter, *Medicine Among Negroes in Mecklenburg County*, written by Dr. French Tyson. Dr. Tyson says, "Mecklenburg County first offered sanctuary to the black physician in 1886 . . . As we look back to the era when Negro professional men sprang into being over night, as it were, from the barber's chair to the bishop's bench, and from plow handle to the medical profession, one is inclined to remark that nature was surely in her best humor when she produced such Negroes as J. T. Williams and A. A. Wyche, two real men destined to become Mecklenburg County's outstanding representatives of the Negro medical profession."

Others who followed these pioneer Negro medical men in Mecklenburg maintained the high professional standards and in 1953 membership in the Mecklenburg Medical Society was opened to qualified Negro doctors. This was the first local society in the state with courage sufficient to take this unprecedented and, in some other sections, unpopular step.

This Medical Society was organized October 7, 1903, following a call issued by Dr. E. C. Register, district organizer for the state society. The first officers were Dr. H. Q. Alexander, president; Dr. Annie L. Alexander (first woman to practice medicine in the South), vice president; Dr. Parks M. King, secretary. For more than half a century this society has been instrumental in maintaining the highest medical standards for Charlotte and in encouraging all measures pertaining to the improved well-being of the community.

Though started somewhat later, the practice of dentistry in Mecklenburg has paralleled that of medicine in technique, ethics, and number of practitioners. The first dentist to make his headquarters in Charlotte was Dr. E. H. Andrews, about 1846. "In his time," records Dr. J. B. Alexander, "there was not much dental work to do . . . he kept his home office here but traveled over several counties." By 1875, however, the profession of dentistry had made considerable progress and there were in Charlotte, four dentists: Dr. M. A. Bland and Dr. Isaiah Simpson, who practiced together; Dr. A. W. Alexander; and Dr. W. H. Hoffman.

Today, there are some ninety members in the Charlotte Dental Society. Among major accomplishments of the Dental Society have been the establishment of an out-patient department at Memorial Hospital with provisions for an interneship; sponsorship for the movement for fluoridation of Charlotte water supply, the wisdom of which is now clearly demonstrable; and the introduction, locally, of a time-payment plan for dental services.

Wives of members of the Charlotte Dental Society formed a local chapter of the North Carolina Dental Auxiliary on May 9, 1952 with 35 members and the following officers: Mrs. Grady Ross, president; Mrs. Ralph Jarrett, president elect; Mrs. James Graham, vice president; Mrs. T. N. Hamer, secretary; Mrs. John Pharr, treasurer; Mrs. Horace Reeves, parliamentarian; and Mrs. L. V. Grady, historian.

Hospitals

"Hospitals," to again quote Dr. Strong, "are the visible expression of the heart of philanthropy, Christianity, and medicine. History furnishes no evidence of their existence prior to the advent of the Great Physician who furnished, in the parable of the Good Samaritan on the Jericho Road, the call for and the duty humanity owed to the unfortunate sick."

The first hospital to be established in Charlotte occupied the building vacated by North Carolina Military Institute when the cadets entered service in the Civil War. It was here the Confederate wounded were treated. Perhaps, due to the awful conditions existing at the time, a strong prejudice against hospitals arose and persisted to such an extent that when the Home and Hospital of St. Peter's Episcopal Church opened in 1876, it was necessary to secure police protection.

Commenting on conditions at that time, Mrs. Hamilton C. Jones, Sr., in 1905, said: "The first few patients were brought under resistance so fierce one of the two or three policemen of which the town boasted had always to walk beside the patient, and at times to hang around the premises to intimidate the rioters who threatened to shoot into the building."

St. Peter's Hospital

Beginning with two rooms on East Seventh Street, the Home and Hospital of St. Peter's Episcopal Church evolved into St. Peter's Hospital, a general hospital of 75 beds. The original suggestion for Charlotte's first hospital for serving the community came from Mrs. John Wilkes, nee Jane Renwick Smedburg, a native New Yorker, who came to Charlotte at the time of her marriage.

Shortly after arriving in Charlotte, Mrs. Wilkes was called on to assist in caring for the Confederate wounded in the Military Institute building. Despite this discouraging experience, she had visions of a future hospital. Eventually she secured enough support to found the institution, and much later to become known as the "Godmother of Charlotte hospitals." Familiar names of many present day Charlotte people are on the original list of 36 members of St. Peter's Church Aid Society, the organization formed and headed by Mrs. Wilkes. In addition to Mrs. Wilkes, Mrs. W. M. Shipp, Mrs. B. R. Smith, Miss Laura Orr, Mrs. Hamilton C. Jones, Sr., Mrs. C. I. Fox, Mrs. John Van Landingham, Mrs. F. Cox, and Miss Hattie Moore were named when the North Carolina general assembly ratified the incorporation of the hospital on February 11, 1879.

St. Peter's Hospital ended its long and useful career on October 7, 1940 when remaining patients were removed to Charlotte Memorial Hospital, toward which institution the assets of St. Peter's Hospital were applied.

Good Samaritan Hospital

The Good Samaritan Hospital of Charlotte has the unique distinction of being the first hospital in the United States, and possibly in the world, to be built and operated exclusively for Negroes. Responsibility and credit for this institution belongs to the same group of people who made possible St. Peter's Hospital for white people. The cornerstone of the original building for Good Samaritan Hospital was laid December 18, 1888. The building was officially dedicated September 23, 1891. For seventy years this hospital has served the purpose for which it was created, expanding in both size and scope of services from time to time until now its capacity is 137 beds, for use by Negro patients of both white and Negro doctors.

In the spring of 1960 the Episcopal church voluntarily donated Good Samaritan Hospital to the City of Charlotte. In an election held May 28, 1960 the citizens authorized bonds in the sum of $900,000 for improving the plant of the hospital which, at about the same time, came under the supervision of the Memorial Hospital Authority.

Presbyterian Hospital

The imposing 400 bed, modern Presbyterian Hospital of today had its beginning in 1898 when Drs. John R. Irwin, C. A. Misenheimer, Robert Gibbon, and William Haines Wakefield formed the Charlotte Private Hospital. In January, 1903, the equipment and goodwill of this hosiptal was purchased by Dr. John Peter Munroe, president, and other members of the faculty of the North Carolina Medical College, because a hospital was necessary if the medical college was to carry out its plans for offering a complete medical education. The faculty then presented the hospital to the Presbyterian churches of the city. It has since been known as Presbyterian Hospital. Cooperating with Dr. Munroe in this transaction were the other members of the faculty at that time: Drs. A. J. Crowell, I. W. Faison, E. R. Russell, C. H. C. Mills, C. M. Strong, W. O. Nisbet, and the four original owners of the hospital.

The first location of Presbyterian Hospital was on the corner of Trade and Mint Streets, in a building formerly occupied by the Arlington Hotel. Here, the North Carolina Medical College used space on the first floor, leaving room on other floors for about 45 hospital beds. When the Medical College opened October 2, 1907, all departments had been moved from Davidson to Charlotte and, together with those that had been housed with the hospital, relocated in a three-story, brick building on the southwest corner of Church and Sixth Streets, later identified for many years as the Churchill Apartments.

Dr. J. B. Alexander, first active manager of Presbyterian Hospital, served from 1905 until 1923. During his administration, the property formerly belonging to Elizabeth College was acquired and remodeled for hospital purposes. Patients were removed to the new location February 28, 1917. A new building was erected in 1940, a new wing in 1946, and two additional wings in 1958. Large and attractive dormitory space is provided for the Presbyterian Hospital School of Nursing which, since 1903, has graduated more than 1,100 trained nurses.

Mercy Hospital

The Sisters of Mercy of Belmont, North Carolina, organized and opened Mercy Hospital, with a capacity of 25 beds, February 1906, in a wooden building on East First Street, behind St. Peter's Roman Catholic Church. The hospital was located at this address until 1916 when the first unit of its modern, fireproof plant was erected on East Fifth Street, and the word, "General," dropped from the original name. Several additions increased the capacity in 1960 to nearly 300 beds, with unsurpassed radiological, pathological, obstetrical, and diagnostic facilities.

In founding Mercy Hospital the Sisters of Mercy were aided by Right Rev. Leo Haid, O.S.B., Abbot of Belmont Abbey, and by the Pastor of St. Peter's Roman Catholic Church, Rev. Father Joseph Mueller. Notable names in the development and management of the hospital include Sister Mary Dolores, Mother Mary Bride, Mother Mary Raphael, Sister Mary Alphonse, to mention only a few of the many.

Currently, thirty beds of Mercy Hospital are assigned to Negro patients. This hospital was the first primarily white hospital in Charlotte to admit patients of the Negro race. It is also of more than passing interest that in so strong a Masonic city as Charlotte, Mercy Hospital has had the financial support and general good will of highest ranking Masonic officials and personnel.

Charlotte Sanatorium

From 1907 until 1942 the Charlotte Sanatorium, a general hospital, privately owned by a group of about thirty leading physicians and surgeons, provided space for 100 patients and enjoyed a splendid reputation. During its entire existence this hospital was located in a five story, fireproof building on the southeast corner of Seventh and Church Streets.

Charlotte Eye, Ear and Throat Hospital

This privately owned institution, opened in 1923, was the fulfillment of a dream of Dr. J. P. Matheson, who realized the great need in Charlotte for a specialized hospital. Dr. Matheson, Dr. Henry L. Sloan, Sr., and Dr. C. N. Peeler financed the building of a modern four-story hospital with a present capacity of nearly 40 beds.

Dr. Matheson was head of the hospital until his death, August 5, 1937. He was succeeded by Dr. Sloan, who continued as chief of staff until 1958. Upon his resignation Dr. V. K. Hart became head of the hospital, all assets of which are the property of Matheson

Associates, Inc. The present staff of the Charlotte Eye, Ear and Throat Hospital consists of specialists, most of whom have won high professional distinction in their respective fields. Among these are Dr. Fred E. Motley, Dr. W. E. Roberts, Dr. Frank C. Smith, and Dr. Henry L. Sloan, Jr., son and worthy successor to one of the founders. A notable contribution of the Charlotte Eye, Ear and Throat Hospital to civic affairs has been its operation of the Variety Club Eye Clinic.

Mecklenburg Sanatorium

An excellent example of man's remarkable progress in medical science is found in the case of Mecklenburg Sanatorium. Built with funds from a bond issue and supported by a tax levy, this 120 bed hospital, near Huntersville, was opened in September 1926 to segregate and treat tubercular patients. By 1960 the "great white plague" had been so nearly conquered as to constitute no major health problem. In the spring of that year the citizens of Mecklenburg voted to convert the property into a hospital for the treatment of the chronically ill.

Charlotte Memorial Hospital

Charlotte Memorial Hospital typifies, more than any of the other laudable projects of which the city is proud, the unselfish cooperative spirit with which business and professional men and women have merged their time and talents for the common good. These few words inadequately condense the thoughts contained in a factual, fourteen-page article entitled, "A Dream Come True— Charlotte Medical Center—Its Inception" by Hamilton Witherspoon McKay, M.D., in the *Bulletin of the Mecklenburg Medical Society*, October 1940. To Dr. McKay, though he would be the first to disclaim the honor, belongs the credit for first conceiving the idea of a metropolitan medical center for Charlotte and for his sustained faith in the face of many early discouragements. Eventually some ninety physicians, led by Dr. Thomas D. Sparrow and Dr. W. Z. Bradford, raised the sum of $1,500 with which they engaged Dr. William Henry Walsh, hospital authority and counselor, to make a survey, *Hospital Situation in Charlotte*, published 1938.

Very great emphasis was given to the hospital movement by the trustees of St. Peter's Hospital who were instrumental in having their institution consolidated with the new hospital. Among the more active trustees in this important transaction were Dr. Brodie C. Nalle, Dr. John Hill Tucker, John H. Cutter, Francis Clarkson (later Judge Clarkson), Mel M. Murphy, Hamilton C. Jones, Jr., and Albert Boyle, Sr.

The greatest single aid was the acquiring of nearly half a million dollars in federal funds through the efforts of Morgan B. Speir, J. B. Marshall, Paul Whitlock, and others. Following this step and through the efforts of Dr. William Allan, Dr. Watson Rankin of the Duke Endowment, Postmaster Paul Younts, and Mr. Word H. Wood, banker, a week-long campaign raised $135,000 in voluntary contributions in Charlotte, about $25,000 of which was supplied by medical men. Then came a successful $350,000 bond election to insure the building of Charlotte Memorial Hospital. In all of these efforts, a Women's Division, headed by Miss Carrie McLean, was a great help, as was the Junior League which, as an organization, took over the Medical Social Service Department of the hospital.

The $1,250,000 Medical Center was dedicated in 1940. In 1943 the entire property was deeded to the Charlotte Memorial Hospital Authority, by which legal entity it has since been operated and expanded far beyond the expectations of those responsible for its inception and completion.

Of the many facilities provided by Charlotte Memorial Hospital there is space here to mention only one, the chapel. Funds for this beautiful room were provided by the Women's Auxiliary of St. Peter's Episcopal Church of Charlotte. This chapel is for the use of Protestant, Roman Catholic, Jewish, and Greek Orthodox patients. The organ in the chapel was installed by members of her family as a memorial to Mrs. Ralph Van Landingham, former member of the board of St. Peter's Hospital through whose efforts the original Chapel Fund was started.

Charlotte Rehabilitation Hospital

Adjacent to Memorial Hospital and the Charlotte-Mecklenburg Health Department, and working in close harmony with both, is another important unit in the Medical Center of Charlotte, the Charlotte Rehabilitation Hospital for the treatment of the physically handicapped. The program of service is for the Southeastern area with the majority of admissions from the Carolinas.

This hospital is supported in part by the United Appeal, by contributions from those interested by "Helping the Handicapped" and by the private patient.

Hospital Auxiliaries

The usefulness of Presbyterian, Mercy and Memorial Hospitals has been greatly enhanced through the various activities of Women's Auxiliaries. These organizations, made up of wives of staff members and employees, and other friends of each hospital, contribute to the successful administration of the hospitals in many ways, including student nurse tuition loans, operation of hospital refreshment concessions, devising student nurse and intern recreational programs, and many similar ventures.

The Women's Auxiliary of Memorial Hospital, typical of all three, was organized with 14 members shortly after the hospital started and now has on its active list 675 members. Their most recent accomplishment was the construction and furnishing of a recreational facility for student nurses at cost of $35,000.

Charlotte Medical Library

This library, a major adjunct to the medical profession in Charlotte, was begun in 1909 as an exchange of professional literature among Drs. William Allan, C. N. Peeler, Robert H. Lafferty, Thomas H. Wright, and W. B. Witherbee. Within a few months the membership had jumped to thirty and the project came to be known as the Physicians' Library. The library moved into the Professional Building in 1922, when the Medical Society offered the library space in its meeting hall. At that time the name was changed to Charlotte Medical Library. In 1931 the library was reorganized, and in 1951 occupied space in the newly completed Doctors' Building. Since its reorganization, Mrs. John S. Monahan (nee Helen Sherrill) has been the professional librarian in charge.

Public Welfare in Charlotte and Mecklenburg

Probably the least understood aspect of Charlotte's history is the way in which public humanitarian measures have advanced from the simple care of the destitute to the complex organizations of today. For the year 1772 the Superintendent of the Destitute in Mecklenburg reported expenses of $80. Disbursements of the Mecklenburg County Department of Public Welfare for the year 1957-1958 were $3,870,885.16. During the same year, the United Community Services provided another million dollars in aid to needy persons and organizations.

Development of Public Welfare as a county responsibility began in Mecklenburg about 1917 when the General Assembly of North Carolina required that a Public Welfare Department be established in all counties having a population of more than 25,000. Prior to that time, the burden of relief and counselling to the distressed had fallen largely on churches, civic groups, the family doctor, sympathetic landlords, and public-spirited citizens.

In the beginning the only financial assistance available to the Department of Welfare was small amounts provided by the city and county governments. As late as 1925 the Department had only two staff members, the superintendent and his secretary. However, the depression of 1929 taught Americans that conditions could arise in a society such as ours over which individuals had no control. The result was the Social Security Act of 1935, embracing financial assistance through state and municipal agencies, to the aged, dependent children, the blind, and other categories in the field of human need.

Mecklenburg differed from most other counties in North Carolina during the depression years in that the emergency relief program was handled by the United Welfare Federation, rather than the county Department of Public Welfare. Within a few years, when the emergency subsided and the United Welfare Fund became the Community Chest, the distribution in 1937 of both local and government relief funds began and has since been administered by the Department of Public Welfare.

Presently this Department requires a staff of more than 100 persons, many of whom are professionally trained. In addition to public assistance programs in which the federal, state, and county governments all participate, and leadership in broad community social planning, local social services handled by the Department include: admission to Greenacres, the county home for the indigent; social service to families and children; special services to unwed mothers, their babies, and adoptive applicants; issuance of child labor certificates; supervision of adult parolees for the county; admissions to state training schools and state institutions for the blind, deaf, epileptic, and spastic; processing sterilization papers; and cooperating with the state Medical Care Commission in its program of hospital care and alcoholic treatment. All of these duties are performed under the supervision of the superintendent of public welfare who is appointed by a County Welfare Board, with the approval of the Mecklenburg Board of County Commissioners and the North Carolina Department of Public Welfare.

Charlotte-Mecklenburg Health Department

Public Health Service in Mecklenburg County dates back to the early 1890's when the office of County Physician became an elective office. Dr. S. W. Bratton was elected by the County Commissioners as the first physician to fill this post. Prior to this the sheriff coroner would call upon any physician to act in county matters at a specified rate per day. In 1896, due to a severe smallpox epidemic, the office of city physician was created. Dr. F. O. Hawley was elected and served until his death in 1915.

The Health Department was organized in the summer of 1917 and located in rooms beneath the City Auditorium. The opening of Camp Greene demanded a standard Health Department and Major Benjamin Brown was sent here by the United States Public Health Service to perfect the organization.

Dr. C. C. Hudson was secured as the first Health Officer in October 1917. The staff consisted of one stenographer, one part-time milk inspector, one part-time clinician, one sanitary inspector, and two nurses who were doing generalized nursing. The Red Cross sent a unit of four nurses and one supervising nurse to assist in the work.

By 1960, Charlotte and Mecklenburg Health Department had been placed under one health director; the staff expanded to 128 for serving the needs of the city and 36 for the county; and services enlarged.

Under the guidance of Dr. Millard B. Bethel, director for many years of the Charlotte-Mecklenburg Health Department, many modern methods of safeguarding the health of the community were adopted, including provisions for the fluoridation of the city's water, and the fogging of city streets for insect control.

In the fall of 1959 the Charlotte-Mecklenburg Health Department occupied its new Health Center on the grounds of Charlotte Memorial Hospital.

United Community Services

Out of the financial depression which began in the fall of 1929 and lasted well into the 1930's, there came a number of new and valuable ideas. Confronted with the necessity of doing something drastic to combat the ravages of the depression in 1931, citizens formed in Charlotte a United Welfare Federation of Mecklenburg County. Under the leadership of David Ovens, a fund of $131,028 was raised locally for "emergency relief." This, with much larger federal funds, was distributed effectively by the new organization.

Credit for organizing the United Welfare Organization belongs to the Council of Social Agencies (later Community Council, and now Social Planning Council), an organization composed of representatives of public and private health, welfare, recreation, and similar services. Guiding the affairs of the Council of Social Agencies, as president during this critical period, was Mrs. Andrew Blair. The charter members of the Council were the Family Service Agency; Salvation Army; American Red Cross; Travelers' Aid Society, and Young Women's Christian Association. Shortly thereafter the Young Men's Christian Association and Charlotte Day Nursery were admitted to membership.

In 1937 the scope of the Welfare Federation was enlarged by the addition of several new services and the name changed to Community Chest. In 1942 the Community Chest became the War and Community Chest of Charlotte and Mecklenburg County, and campaigns for funds included 22 war relief agencies along with 16 local services in one annual appeal. This arrangement lasted until 1946 when the war appeals were discontinued.

The Community Chest campaigns were replaced by United Appeal campaigns which offered a new approach to unified giving in that it encompassed not only local agencies, but those with state and national affiliations.

American Red Cross

The impending crisis in the spring of 1917 brought home to Charlotte citizens the necessity for organizing a chapter of the American Red Cross. This they did on March 9, 1917 at the home of Mrs. Vinton Liddell. Three days before the United States went to war, a mass meeting was held in the Academy of Music for the solicitation of members. More than 2,000 volunteers raised about $4,000 and the chapter received its charter on May 21, 1917.

Mecklenburg County Chapter of the American Red Cross has been continuously active since its organization and now provides services in the fields of family case work, health, and youth in accordance with its national charter through volunteers and professional staff. One of the most important of these is the Blood Program, established in 1948, which provides blood to residents of the county through voluntary blood donors. In December 1942 the Chapter acquired its own home at 510 East Morehead Street where many activities are now housed pending selection of a larger site and construction of more modern facilities.

Boy Scouts of America; Girl Scouts of America

Members of the first Boy Scout troop in Charlotte, organized 1910 by members of the Church of the Holy Comforter (Protestant Episcopal), are among Charlotte's "Senior Citizens" in 1960. None of the four men who founded the troop (William A. Reynolds, Jesse M. Oldham, Frank Wilkes, and Fred Glover) are alive to observe the growth of their original small group of boys into Mecklenburg County Council Boy Scouts of America with a membership of more than 7,000 white and Negro youths.

Camp Steere, established in 1926 for white boys and named for James E. Steere, Mecklenburg Scout Executive (1917-1941), and Camp Oak for Negro boys, established in 1950, have been among the more important Scout activities.

The history of girl scouting in Charlotte parallels, in a general way, that of boy scouting, and the results have been equally gratifying. Early pioneers in the movement included Mrs. Julian M. Metz, Mrs. Theodore M. Abbott, and Miss Helen Hodge (Mrs. S. S. Koszewski).

Facilities for camping and other girl scout activities were improved from time to time, culminating in 1955 with establishment of Camp Occoneechee at Lake Lure, North Carolina. Since then an excellent camping and outdoor program has been offered with time allotted for both white and Negro Girl Scouts.

In 1960, with a combined membership of about 3,500 Brownie, Intermediate, and Senior Girl Scouts, the Mecklenburg County Girl Scout Council, Inc., is serving its purpose well.

Charlotte Day Nursery

The need for day nursery care of small children was first impressed on Charlotte about 1900 with the tragic burning to death of a two-year old boy who had been left by his mother with a young guardian while she was at work. On March 1, 1901 the first Charlotte Day Nursery Association began to function and shortly thereafter operated two cottages caring for 25 children. The first official board was composed of Mrs. Willard G. Rogers, Mrs. A. H. Washburn, Mrs. R. C. Holland, Mrs. E. C. Register, and Miss Julia J. Robertson. The splendid work of this Association continued for about eight years, "until because of lack of funds the buildings became so needful of repairs and maintenance that they were reluctantly closed."

Meanwhile the need for nursery care continued and grew until about 1928 a small group of civic minded women convinced the state director of public welfare and the local chairman of the council of social agencies of a need, unmet by any other organization for the day care of small children of employed mothers. Out of this suggestion came the opening on January 16, 1929 of the first day nursery, with five children enrolled. There are now more than 300 day nurseries in the state and more than 50 in Charlotte. The hardships and triumphs of the Charlotte Day Nursery Association are vividly described in a pamphlet by Mrs. J. H. Parks, organizer and first president of the association, *Highlights in the Growth of Charlotte Day Nursery*, issued in 1954 as a part of the 25th anniversary observance.

Family and Children's Service

The Family and Children's Service was formed March 21, 1909 by a group of Charlotte ministers under the leadership of Dr. Albert R. Shaw, pastor of the First Presbyterian Church, to "coordinate charity work, to set up a central agency to investigate need and administer relief." The original name was Associated Charities. In 1932 the need for help became so enlarged because of the depression that a separate and larger organization, United Welfare Federation, was formed. Relieved of its charitable functions, the Associated Charities changed its name to Family Service Association and its purpose to the salvaging of broken or disturbed homes.

In 1944 the Family Service Association and the Children's Service Bureau, founded some time previously by the Junior League, were merged into the present Family and Children's Service, which has for its principal purpose the preservation of the home. Toward this end and supported by funds raised in the annual United Appeal drive, the Service is governed by a board of 24 men and women and conducted by a staff of trained workers. It is licensed by the North Carolina Department of Public Welfare as a child-placing agency and is a member agency of the Family Service Association of America.

Florence Crittenton Home

By their nature and to insure effectiveness, most welfare organizations must conceal the identity of individual beneficiaries. Of no institution is this more true than Florence Crittenton Home, established in Charlotte February 1903 and now an important link in the chain of about 53 such homes in the United States. The only purpose of this institution is to care for the unwed mother and her child, and prepare the mother to make the best possible adjustment for herself and baby when they are ready to leave the Home.

The cornerstone for the first Crittenton Home in Charlotte, at McDowell and 9th Streets, was laid by Charles N. Crittenton who, in 1883, established the first such home as a memorial to his four year old daughter. The Charlotte Home was opened June 27, 1905 and continued to serve until January 1, 1947 when the new building with a capacity of 50 guests, adjacent to Charlotte Memorial Hospital, was occupied. Here, the Home offers its services to about 250 girls annually, with a Director and staff of 17 members, supplemented by the obstetrical and medical staff of the hospital located next door.

Mecklenburg County Association for the Blind

On June 18, 1934, the Mecklenburg County Association for the Blind was organized with Dr. Edgar Gammon, president; J. Marshall Parham, executive secretary; E. J. Hanson, vice president; Mrs. Robert A. Moore, secretary; and H. H. Everett, treasurer. This non-sectarian, interracial agency has moved steadily forward. It currently occupies executive offices at 704 Louise Avenue, where guidance, counselling, financial, teaching, and other services are offered. The Lions Club of Charlotte has, for many years, contributed heavily toward the financial and moral support of this important association.

Charlotte Mental Health Association
Charlotte Mental Health Clinic

Early in 1933 the Charlotte Mental Hygiene Society was formed and the Charlotte Mental Hygiene Clinic started. The original group which founded the organization included City Health Officer Dr. G. L. Rea; County Health Officer Dr. E. H. Hand; the supervisor of Charlotte's Health Department nurses, Miss Clara Ross. These were ably assisted by Drs. Allyn B. Choate, Archie A. Barron, William Allan, and others.

For more than a quarter of a century, with several slight changes in name and location, the Charlotte Mental Health Association and Clinic have served Mecklenburg and surrounding counties with conspicuous success. This city has the distinction of being the birth-place of the North Carolina Mental Hygiene Society as well as the home of the first Mental Hygiene Clinic in the state. Housed in converted residences during most of its existence, the Mental Hygiene Clinic found a comfortable, permanent home among surroundings congenial to its purposes when the Charlotte-Mecklenburg Health Center was opened in the fall of 1959.

Salvation Army

About 40 years after William Booth founded the Salvation Army in England, and 24 years after the first Salvation Army "open-air" meeting in the United States, there came to Charlotte, Captain Mc-Alpine (a woman) who opened the Temple Corps of the Salvation Army, Inc., in 1904. The Charlotte City Directories from 1904 to date will provide a good picture of the gradual growth from one small corps to the following units, fully manned by trained workers in 1960: Charlotte headquarters; Welfare Department for dispensing emergency relief services to white and Negro families; Woman's Emergency Lodge; Transient Lodge for Men; Red Shield Boys Club; Belmont Corps; Temple Corps; Men's Social Service Department, where "the salvage of men through the salvage of material" is a daily procedure.

Social Planning Council

The Council of Social Agencies, forerunner of the present Social Planning Council, is mentioned earlier as having organized the United Welfare Federation which evolved into today's Community Services. The Social Planning Council is now and has been for many years among the more influential agencies receiving its principal support from United Appeal Funds. Now, as on June 10, 1925 when it was organized as a "Welfare Organization" its aims are, "To provide the medium whereby both tax-supported and privately supported agencies may join in developing and maintaining the most effective program in the fields of health, welfare, recreation and education."

Incidental services toward accomplishing these aims include a Christmas Bureau, operated during the month of December to prevent duplication of Christmas giving by individuals, churches, civic, and welfare organizations; a Social Service Index, a confidential clearing-house for use by all accredited social welfare agencies; and a Volunteer Bureau where citizens may volunteer for community programs.

Privately Supported Welfare Institutions

Many of the most pressing welfare needs of Charlotte and vicinity have been met by institutions which depend upon neither tax funds nor money raised for Community Services. Most of these needs are taken care of by church groups, though recipients of the services are seldom limited to those of their own faiths. A brief description of the more important of these institutions existing as Mecklenburg celebrates its two hundredth birthday follows:

Thompson Orphanage and Training School

For nearly three quarters of a century this venerable institution has quietly and efficiently supplied a need, previously unfilled in Charlotte by other institutions. Thompson Orphanage takes its name from Lewis Thompson who lived in Bertie County, North Carolina, donor in 1873 of funds to help maintain a private school which had been established by the rector of St. Peter's Episcopal Church, Rev. Benjamin S. Bronson. When the school failed, Mr. Bronson donated the property to the church, stipulating that it was to be used as an orphanage and that Rev. Edwin A. Osborne be selected as its first superintendent. St. Peter's church accepted the offer and organized the orphanage in 1887. This was the first orphanage established in North Carolina by a religious body, the only other orphanage in the state being the Masonic Orphanage at Oxford.

The property deeded to St. Peter's Church for the orphanage consisted of more than 80 acres, then on the edge of Charlotte. This property is now only a short distance from the principal business section of the city and so valuable that in 1955 some 40 acres, used as a pasture for the orphanage's herd of cows, was leased for 99 years to be used as a mammoth shopping center, Charlottetown Mall.

A history of Thompson Orphanage is contained in the Golden Jubilee issue of *The Messenger of Hope* of Thompson Orphanage,

May 7, 1930. The institution provides home and educational facilities for upward of 100 boys and girls regularly.

Alexander Home

The Alexander Home began as a "Home and Hospital" founded by the First and Second Presbyterian Churches of Charlotte in 1888. Its original purpose was to give custodial care to dependent, neglected, and orphan children, and it was operated and managed by women of the churches, who devoted a day a week to caring for the children. In 1895 the women, having raised enough money to construct a new two-story building for their project, renamed it "Alexander Rescue Home" in honor of R. B. Alexander, who had contributed a site with buildings already standing on it.

Except for the construction, in 1917, of the building on East Boulevard still occupied by the Alexander Home program, no significant changes were made until 1947 when, upon recommendation of the Child Welfare League of America, the objectives were changed to provide facilities for the effective treatment of emotionally disturbed children.

The present program is constructed to give therapy and formal counseling and psychotherapy to 15 boys and girls between the ages of 6 and 12. Children accepted are severely disturbed, but not psychotic, mentally retarded, nor brain-damaged. Services include 24-hour-a-day-care, and casework for parents. The average length of stay of children is 18 months.

Charity League of Charlotte, Inc.

The Charity League is one of the very few welfare organizations purely indigenous to Charlotte. It is operated and financed independently of outside assistance and is not a member of United Community Services nor obligated by membership in state or national organizations. The League was organized by Mrs. James L. Staten as the Junior Hospital Guild of St. Peter's Episcopal Church in 1921 to engage in hospital auxiliary work. As charitable demands increased, young women of other denominations were accepted as members and in 1926 the name was changed to Charity League.

By 1928 the League had in operation a Sunshine School offering an educational haven for maladjusted children. Licensed by the Department of Public Welfare, chartered by the State of North Carolina, and approved by all local agencies, the Sunshine Day Nursery has a capacity of about 30 preschool children who follow a daily schedule planned to provide educational and social development, proper nutrition, rest and relaxation, as well as emotional security.

Membership in the Charity League is by invitation, and there are now about 150 members and 39 past presidents, drawn from among Charlotte women. The first president was Mrs. E. J. Wannamaker. In 1960 it is Mrs. F. W. Littlefield.

Good Fellows Club

The Good Fellows Club has been described as "The most unusual organization in the world," and belongs to Charlotte alone. This unusual club had its beginning in the Men's Benevolent Association which was sponsored by Dr. Archibald A. McGeachy, pastor of the Second Presbyterian Church and one of the most popular men in Charlotte. The first meeting was held in the backyard of the McGeachy home, probably in the summer of 1917. Its purpose was to interest a group of "good fellows" to give a helping hand with certain charities not covered by other organizations. Dr. McGeachy remarked, at the organizational meeting: "If you walk down the path the Master has trod, you are bound to meet Him." The club is non-sectarian.

There was a reorganization of the original group in the fall of 1919 with a change of name to the Good Fellows Club. David Ovens, one of Charlotte's outstanding business men was named as president. Mr. Ovens presided at all meetings in his inimitable way and continued as president until his death in September 1957. It has always been a loose-knit organization with no by-laws and no minutes.

The following are some of the men who have served as Directors and given much of their time to carrying out the work of the Good Fellows: A. Jackson Beall; Claude A. Cochran; E. McA. Currie; W. Carey Dowd, Jr.; John C. Erwin; Dr. Edgar Gammon;

Thomas M. Glasgow; Mark P. Johnson; Dr. James A. Jones; Robert A. Mayer; Dr. Oren Moore; Carl G. McCraw; Colonel J. Norman Pease; Victor Shaw; and Paul C. Whitlock.

The one meeting each year is held just before Christmas, and there is always an outstanding musical program. The heart of the program is three talks limited to three minutes each by members of the club who present needs of a destitute family or someone in distress. After these speakers have presented their cases, a vote by all present is taken and the case considered the most needy is given an extra amount of money.

The directors of the club then "take the floor" with an appeal from the president as to who wants to help which. Because of the depressing nature of the cases presented, a good bit of levity is purposely entered into by the directors. As much as $6,000 has been donated at a single meeting. This money, together with the $20 annual dues from an average of 500 members, constitutes the club's budget to carry on its work with needy cases during the entire year. The club works closely with the Welfare Department.

The club's overhead is low, its only expense being the salary for a part-time secretary and rent for a small office. Col. J. Norman Pease succeeded Mr. Ovens as president and new directors are added from time to time. Membership is open at all times to any who want to be "good fellows" by giving a helping hand.

Duke Endowment

James Buchanan Duke, native of Durham County, North Carolina, amassed a fortune from tobacco and from harnessing the Catawba River. On June 11, 1924, by Trust Indenture, he established the Duke Endowment, to which he conveyed stocks and bonds of various corporations. On the same day he signed his will in which he greatly augmented the Duke Endowment. The will was executed and its terms carried out shortly after the death of Mr. Duke, October 24, 1925.

The beneficiaries of the Duke Endowment are: (1) Duke University, (2) non-profit hospitals in North and South Carolina, (3) non-profit child-caring institutions in North and South Carolina, (4) Davidson College, (5) Furman University, (6) Johnson C.

Smith University, (7) rural Methodist churches in North Carolina, and (8) superannuated Methodist ministers, their widows and orphans in North Carolina.

From its inception through December 31, 1959 distributions and allocations amounting to 156 million dollars have been made by Duke Endowment. For the 1959 season there were 175 hospitals and 43 child-caring agencies among the beneficiaries, including all those in Charlotte and Mecklenburg qualifying under terms of the Endowment.

Other Endowed Foundations

In addition to the Duke Endowment, the Presbyterian Foundation, and the Belk Foundation, Charlotte is the home of a growing list of similar institutions. The following are listed in the *American Foundation Information Service:*

Alwinell Foundation: Grants in the fields of Protestant hospitals and religion

Thomas Milburn Belk Foundation: Grants for religious and educational purposes

The Blumenthal Foundation: Grants principally for improvement in interfaith relationships

Martin Cannon Family Foundation: Fields of interest: elementary and secondary education, hospitals, libraries, religion (Protestant), and welfare

The Celanese Foundation: Major grants in the fields of handicapped, hospitals, intercultural relations, and medical research

Charlotte College Foundation

Charlotte Foundation: A community trust

Eugene M. Cole Foundation: Superannuated Methodist ministers

Rush H. Dickson Family Foundation: Grants for religious, scientific, and educational purposes

The Dillard Foundation: Major grants in the fields of secondary and higher Protestant education

Dowd Foundation: Grants in the field of established charities

Efird Foundation: Grants in the fields of higher education and intercultural relations

Alex Hemby Foundation: Grants to local causes

Curtis B. Johnson Benevolent Association: General charitable, benevolent, and eleemosynary purposes

Lance-VanEvery Foundation: Major grants in the fields of local philanthropy for social welfare of children and youth

The Marsh Foundation: Formed to use income and principal for religious, charitable, scientific, and educational purposes

Nalle Clinic Foundation: Grants in the fields of hospitals and education

North Carolina Foundation, Inc.: Construction of community buildings

The J. L. Presman Foundation: Grants in the field of philanthropic giving, principally to Jewish causes

Saint Peter's Foundation

The Alice Speizman Charitable Foundation

United Community Foundation

The Methodist Home for the Aged, Inc.

One contemporary old gentleman has remarked, "In building hospitals to put more life into aging bodies, they thought of just about everything. They did so well that a new emergency was created by rehabilitating old people without providing a place for them to go."

In Charlotte, the emergency is far from completely solved, but a long forward step was taken in June 1948 with the opening of the first unit of the Methodist Home for the Aged, on Shamrock Drive. The Methodist Home, chartered in 1945 as a non-profit, church-related institution, was the dream of Rev. E. O. Cole, widely known Methodist minister. Initial impetus to a realization of this dream came in the form of a huge gift from his brother, Eugene M. Cole, wealthy layman. These farsighted men were assisted in carrying out their plan by a number of Methodist laymen and clergy, including: Dr. L. B. Abernethy, Jackson Beall, W. Reynolds Cuthbertson, Joseph Benjamin Ivey, George F. Ivey, Edwin L. Jones, H. I. McDougle, Frank Odell Sherrill, and J. Luther Snyder.

From an original capacity of about 30 members, the facilities of the Methodist Home have been expanded from time to time by additions to the main building and building of apartments and cottages to a capacity of approximately three hundred.

The Methodist Home in Charlotte ranks with the best in quality of service, type of living accommodations, recreational, occupational, and religious facilities available to all members. Outstanding among these conveniences is the Ivey Memorial Chapel, a memorial to Rev. George Washington Ivey, who served as a Methodist itinerant minister for more than 49 years. On display are the saddle bags used by this minister as he journeyed with his Bible, hymn book, and Methodist literature to remote sections of the Conference. The Home has a staff of nearly 100 full time members, including professionally trained nurses who serve on a 24 hour basis in a modern infirmary and trained dietitians who plan and supervise the preparation of both regular meals and special diets.

No person can be "placed" in the Methodist Home. Membership, not limited to Methodists though they are given preference, is by formal application and all applications are considered on the merits of the individual case after weighing such factors as actual need, along with a true desire to become a resident member of a large Christian family. The Methodist Home is the property of the Western North Carolina Conference of the Methodist Church and is governed by a large board of managers drawn from churches throughout the Conference. Superintendents who have served the home to date are: Dr. C. M. Pickens, Rev. B. Reid Wall, Rev. C. W. Kirby, and Mr. Willard Farrow, now serving as administrator.

Bethlehem Center

Founded in January 1941 and supported by the Woman's Division of Christian Service of the Board of Missions of the Methodist Church, the Bethlehem Center for Negroes has provided, for the last two decades, a variety of activities for individuals and groups of all ages. The original building was a converted hotel, but the center occupied a substantial brick building at 2705 Baltimore Avenue in 1957. A staff of trained and volunteer workers supervises leisure time activities of boys and girls and conducts classes in workshop practices, arts and crafts, sewing, modern dancing and camping, with a kindergarten for preschool children.

10

ORGANIZATIONS: CIVIC, SOCIAL, PATRIOTIC, MISCELLANEOUS

WITH so much evidence, as has been presented, of Charlotte's solidarity in all matters pertaining to the general good, it is no wonder that fraternal, welfare, civic, social, and patriotic groups which sprang into being in the twentieth century found in the city a receptive spirit. Such organizations are so plentiful today it is hard to realize that they are of relatively recent growth. Histories and old city directories hardly mention them.

These groups are important because of the tremendous impact they have made on all phases of the city's life.

The various bodies described on the following pages are arranged more or less chronologically and then loosely grouped according to the nature of their programs. The list is far from complete, and intends only to make clear this part of life in Charlotte and Mecklenburg from their inception to the present time.

Masonic Bodies of Charlotte and Mecklenburg

Aside from church services on Sunday and prayer meetings on Wednesday evenings, the first regularly scheduled meetings in Charlotte were those of fraternal orders. Of these, the Masons were first and, from very early times, Charlotte has been known as a strong Masonic town.

Phalanx Lodge No. 31, Ancient Free and Accepted Masons, dates from December 2, 1797. Its roots go back to October 4, 1779 when the Grand Lodge of Pennsylvania granted a regimental warrant to the Fourth North Carolina contingent in the Continental army, for the formation of Lodge No. 20. In 1780 this Lodge, along with the other units of the North Carolina Continentals, was moved to Charleston, South Carolina for the defense of that city. On the city's capitulation to Sir Henry Clinton, on May 12 of that year, they were made prisoners of war. In 1784, Pennsylvania revoked its military lodge warrants, and Lodge No. 20 obtained a charter from the Grand Lodge of South Carolina about 1787 as Phalanx Lodge No. 7, Ancient York Masons. Then, on December 2, 1797 it became Phalanx Lodge No. 31, A. F. & A. M. of North Carolina.

Unique in having been chartered by three separate jurisdictions and in being the only one of the thousands of lodges throughout the world bearing the meaningful title, Phalanx, Lodge No. 31 may rightfully be described as the parent of all Charlotte Blue Lodges and affiliated bodies in the city and county. There is no record of a lodge in Mecklenburg prior to 1797 though Masonry was active and militant in Charlotte during pre-revolutionary days. The nearest lodge at that time was Old Cone Lodge at Salisbury.

Now nearing its 200th birthday, Phalanx Lodge No. 31 currently has a loyal and proud membership of more than 600. Excelsior Lodge No. 261, Joppa Lodge No. 530, Temple Lodge No. 676, St. Andrews Lodge No. 702 and East Gate Lodge No. 692 and smaller lodges throughout Mecklenburg complete the basic picture of Masonry in the city and county. These organizations have inspired the formation of the three bodies of York Rite Masons, four bodies of Scottish Rite Masons; Eastern Star Chapters, White Shrine; Azusa Grotto Daughters of Mokannah; Order of Rainbow Girls and Order of Demolay. In keeping with the spirit of the times, the Masons of Charlotte maintain a luncheon club known as Masonic Fellowship Club which holds its luncheons in the banquet room of the Masonic Temple on Fridays.

A place to hold meetings and house paraphernalia of these various branches of Masonry has always been a concern of the officers. The Masonic Temple Association of the city of Charlotte was formed April 6, 1870 as a means for solving this problem. Until about 1902 the Masonic Hall was located on the third floor of the Hutchison Building, 111-115 North Tryon Street. Thereafter, for many years, the meetings were held on the top floor of the newly completed Piedmont Building. The Masonic Temple on South

Tryon Street, corner Second Street, was built in 1913 at a cost of $122,750. This building burned on March 4, 1937 but was quickly rebuilt, according to original plans, and dedicated on October 11, 1938.

No account of Masonic activities in Charlotte would be complete without mention of Oasis Temple, Ancient Arabic Nobles Order of the Mystic Shrine, organized 1894 with Walter Scott Liddell, first potentate, and commonly referred to as the "playground of Masonry." Membership in the Shrine is limited to Knights Templar or 32 degree Scottish Rite Masons. They have much well-publicized fun at semi-annual ceremonies held in various towns in Western North Carolina from which membership is drawn, and local social affairs. Not so well known is their unselfish devotion to the 17 Shriners Hospitals for Crippled Children throughout the country.

Toward the support of the Hospital for Crippled Children at Greenville, South Carolina Oasis Temple, with cooperation of other temples in the Carolinas, has sponsored, for many years, the annual football game played in Charlotte between teams selected from outstanding high school players in the two states. So great has been the popularity of these affairs that the amount raised annually is sometimes upward of $100,000.

As an offspring of Oasis Temple there was formed in Charlotte in 1915 the Red Fez Club, a local social organization, with membership limited to Shriners. In 1928 still another Shrine Club was organized, named Oasis Yacht Club for which land on the Catawba River was leased and a clubhouse erected. All went well for awhile but by 1932 the depression brought both clubs to the brink of bankruptcy. The situation was saved when the clubs were merged and a membership drive brought in 200 new members.

Thousands of men and women of Charlotte and Mecklenburg who have distinguished themselves in various fields have been Masons. Among those who have won distinction because of their relationship to Masonry there is space to mention only a few. Foremost are those who have been *awarded* the 33rd degree, top degree in Scottish Rite Masonry. There are others deserving of notice, among whom those coming most readily to mind are: Charles Preston Heindel, long-time secretary of the Scottish Rite Bodies, who, with William Hugh Halliburton, formed the Masonic Fellowship Club; Murray Craven Alexander, who has held the highest local offices in both York and Scottish Rite Bodies, and has served as Master of two lodges; William Edward Burrier, past presiding officer in both York and Scottish Rite Bodies, and now well along in the official Grand Lodge Line; Frederick William Eyre Cullingford, veteran Mason, author of several magazine articles and brochures on Masonry and kindred subjects, including a *History of Phalanx Lodge* and who values most highly his "Fellowship" in the Philalethes Society, an international group, with unlimited membership from among those qualified, but with never more than forty "Fellows." Among Charlotte Masons who have been Grand Masters of the Grand Lodge of North Carolina have been William Polk (1799-1801), Lewis Slaughter Williams, Walter Scott Liddell, Francis M. Winchester, Herbert Claud Alexander and James Guy Johnston.

Other 19th Century Organizations

In addition to Masonic lodges, Charlotte had two other secret fraternal orders by 1875. One was I.O.O.F. (Independent Order of Odd Fellows) Declaration Lodge No. 9. The other was Charlotte Lodge No. 17 K. of P. (Knights of Pythias). From that time both of these organizations continued to function with their greatest popularity and additional lodges during the 1900-1910 period. Both organizations provided life insurance as one of their strongest bids for membership. Both organizations are still active throughout the United States and the Knights of Pythias have a Charlotte lodge with Earl Wolfe of Charlotte as Grand Chancellor of the Domain of North Carolina.

After 1890, clubs and societies of many kinds began forming more rapidly. Among these were the North State Club, Charlotte Literary and Library Association, Southern Manufacturer's Club, and Charlotte Woman's Club. Also in the 1890's labor unions first made their influence felt.

Following the Spanish-American War and through the first years of the new century, Charlotte seems to have begun in earnest its transformation from an average Southern town, sixth in size in

North Carolina in 1860, to a city of metropolitan proportions, largest in the two states, 100 years later. Practically everything that has been accomplished during the past 60 years has been made possible by men and women working together through civic, social, religious and cultural groups.

The first attempt to promote Charlotte commercially and industrially was a Board of Trade, organized about 1875. This name was changed to Chamber of Commerce in 1879 at which time Samuel Wittkowsky, a leading merchant, was president. This organization continued until 1893 when it apparently became inactive, probably a victim of the financial panic of that year.

Modern Chamber of Commerce service to the community had its inception in the Greater Charlotte Club, founded in 1905 in the office of Edmund Randolph Preston, an attorney. Mr. Preston became the first president, 1905-7. Serving with him were A. E. McCausland, first vice president; John R. Ross, second vice president and W. T. Corwith, secretary and treasurer. Honorary members included Joseph Pearson Caldwell, Wade Hampton Harris, and Samuel S. McNinch.

The first banquet of the Greater Charlotte Club was held at the Southern Manufacturer's Club. Among the distinguished guests were the Governor of North Carolina, Robert Broadnax Glenn; the Governor of South Carolina, D. C. Hayworth; Democratic presidential nominee, Alton B. Parker, and a number of senators, congressmen and members of the judiciary. In his address, Mr. Preston stated the theme that has guided Charlotte's forward steps since that eventful night:

"This is the center of the finest section of the United States, blest as it is with the best all-year-round climate and sturdy, Christian, Anglo-Saxon population in the world, and literally teeming with the possibilities of business and industrial development that stagger the imagination to contemplate.

"All that is needed here is the application of those progressive principles and modern methods in education, civic organization and rural cooperation, which have been put into such successful operation elsewhere, particularly in the west.

"It is for the promotion of these . . . policies of community building and city boosting that the Greater Charlotte Club has been formed and to those laudable aims its membership pledged themselves in order that they may better do their part in helping to make a Greater Charlotte and a Greater North Carolina.

"From this time on, all that we ask of those within and without our borders is *Watch Charlotte Grow*."

The achievements of the Greater Charlotte Club aroused civic pride to a pitch never before experienced and were responsible for its enlargement into the Charlotte Chamber of Commerce on June 17, 1915.

The Charlotte Chamber of Commerce began with about 400 members and an office at the corner of South Tryon and Second Streets. The incorporators were J. L. Chambers, Morgan B. Speir and Chase Brenizer. The first board of directors was composed of William States Lee, Arthur J. Draper, J. L. Chambers, Morgan B. Speir, C. B. Bryant, Clarence O. Kuester, Edward Dilworth Latta, David Ovens, Charles A. Williams, Sr., J. A. Durham, Zebulon Vance Taylor and Joseph Garibaldi. The first officers were David Ovens, president; W. S. Alexander, first vice president; Dr. Charles A. Bland, second vice president; John M. Scott, third vice president; Albert T. Summey, treasurer, and James R. Kinsloe, executive secretary. T. T. Allison succeeded Mr. Kinsloe and served as business manager for the next year.

Since its organization, the Chamber of Commerce has been directly or indirectly associated with practically everything pertaining to the growth and well-being of the city and its citizens. Through its efforts Charlotte has received much fine publicity in periodicals having a nationwide circulation. Many specialized magazines have commented upon certain phases of the city such as public schools, library resources, slum clearance and others. General articles about the city have appeared in the *Saturday Evening Post* (January 23, 1951), *Holiday* (December 1949), and *Business Week* (August 11, 1951).

From about 1920 until 1953 the offices of the Chamber of Commerce were located on West Fourth Street where the facilities included a large auditorium, with an adjacent kitchen, used for meetings of many kinds and for dining purposes by civic clubs and other organizations.

By common consent, the major credit for the success attained by the Chamber of Commerce belongs to Clarence O. Kuester, president of the Greater Charlotte Club in 1910-11 and from 1921 until his voluntary retirement on January 1, 1948, business manager and chief executive officer of the Chamber. He was affectionately known throughout Charlotte as "Booster Kuester."

No account of the accomplishments of the Chamber of Commerce would be complete without giving a large measure of credit to Miss Helen Ramseur Hoyle, able assistant to Mr. Allison when he was business manager. She accompanied him when he left the Chamber to manage the Stephens Company, developers of Myers Park, and became secretary and treasurer of that firm. She was succeeded at the Chamber by Miss Minnie Hamlet who served as Mr. Kuester's faithful assistant until his retirement, and hers which followed shortly.

Floyd F. Kaye became executive vice president of the Chamber, following Mr. Kuester. Upon his resignation in 1953, Mr. James H. Glenn served, and was, in turn, followed by Charles Crawford, the chief administrative officer at present. From the nucleus of 400 members in 1915, the Charlotte Chamber of Commerce has grown in 1960 to a membership of nearly 4000 business and professional men and women. Operating with some 38 standing committees, and special committees appointed as circumstances require, the Chamber is a dynamic force in the continued growth and development of Charlotte and Mecklenburg. Activities are housed in modern offices in the Addison Building on South Church Street.

Since the foregoing factual history of the Chamber of Commerce was written, the following editorial appeared in the *Charlotte Observer* for February 12, 1960:

"GUESS WHO'S BOSS OF OUR TOWN?

"Some towns are run by one man, some by a handful of men. Not Charlotte. Ask ten people who's boss of the local bailiwick, or who exerts most power, and you're likely to get as many answers, all of them different.

"But if that seems to imply a vacuum of leadership, it's time to guess again. Charlotte is run, primarily and well, by its Chamber of Commerce.

"The fact is not wholly applauded. Here and there are critics who contend the Chamber sticks its nose (if that's the proper symbol) into many fields that shouldn't concern it, and seeks to dictate the course and path of local progress. Some parts of the indictment may be relatively true.

"But the Chamber of Commerce is, by any standard of judgment, an unusual organization and is, in our view, a major asset.

"Consider, for example, the Program of Work for 1960 that has just been approved by its board of directors. Here are 22 printed pages of projects ranging from airport improvement to a survey of water resources that will be considered and recommended and promoted by 3922 members of 29 committees at a cost, to themselves of $176,000.

"Nor is this just a bland recital of desirable goals—these are working committees, comprised of men with influence and interest. And the work gets done.

"The Chamber of Commerce is not, of course, the sole active force in a town that has been in high gear for much of its history. We have been blest, by and large, with good government and forward-looking planning and a boundless civic vitality reflected in hundreds of active organizations. But the Chamber of Commerce is the greatest force, and the sum of its labors has been impressive.

"We are pleased to acknowledge its bossism and to wish it continued health."

Trade Unionism in Charlotte

Trade Unions are first mentioned in the Charlotte City Directory for 1891-2, when the Order of Railway Conductors, Division No. 221 is listed among the fraternal organizations.

By 1894 the Charlotte Division No. 84 Brotherhood of Locomotive Engineers; the Charlotte Division No. 167 Order of Railway Telegraphers of America and Piedmont Lodge No. 1 Ancient Order of United Workmen had come into the local picture, to be followed in 1897 by the Charlotte Typographical Union and Local No. 77 Brotherhood of Painters and Decorators of America.

The Charlotte Central Council of American Federation of Labor is listed in the 1902 directory. Also listed were: Brotherhood of Masons No. 30; Building Trades Council; Carpenters and Joiners

Union; Charlotte Printing Pressmen and Assistants Union No. 412; Division No. 105 Amalgamated Association of Street Railway Employees; Federal Labor Union No. 8932; International Association of Machinists, Hornets Nest Lodge No. 263; Iron Moulders Union No. 297; Journeymen Barbers Union No. 330; Journeymen Plumbers Union, No. 205; Laborers Union No. 244; Textile District Council; Textile Workers Union No. 199; Woodworkers Union No. 113. From then on to the present other unions were formed as industry expanded in Charlotte, including such representative bodies as Brotherhood of Electrical Workers Union No. 379, in 1926.

Prior to 1930 most Charlotte unions were craft, or horizontal unions, but with the rapid industrial growth throughout the country, vertical unions gained in popularity. Because of this difference, a number of unions in the Charlotte area became affiliated with the Congress of Industrial Organizations, formed in 1935. This division lasted until 1955 when most of the unions in the nation affiliated with the C.I.O. were reunited with the original group under the title American Federation of Labor and Congress of Industrial Organizations. The Charlotte Labor Council A. F. L. and the Mecklenburg County Council C. I. O. effectively carried out the spirit of the national merger by joining ranks on the local level April 30, 1957. The combined labor movement in Charlotte in 1960 numbers more than 18,000 members, in some sixty locals. These unions believe and practice the philosophy that what is good for Charlotte is good for the union members they represent, and toward the fulfillment of this aim have, for many years, had a prominent labor official on the city council.

Charlotte Woman's Club

In 1899 six women organized a study club for mothers. In 1902 this group enlarged its scope and membership by formally organizing itself into the Charlotte Woman's Club. The new organization affiliated with the North Carolina Federation of Women's Clubs in 1903.

The Charlotte Woman's Club has exercised its greatest influence by assisting in the formation of other organizations. The local

Young Women's Christian Association is largely indebted to the Woman's Club for help in its infancy, as are the Travelers Aid, the North Carolina Federation of Music Clubs, the Domestic Relations Court, the Children's Theatre and Junior Woman's Club. The Woman's Club has always taken an interest in the field of public health, organizing in 1913 the Christmas Seal campaign of the Tuberculosis Association and handling practically all details of this important work for 30 years.

The earliest activities of the Charlotte Woman's Club were concentrated in the field of education. The Club was responsible for Charlotte's first kindergarten. It paid one third of the cost of inaugurating the teaching of domestic science in the public high schools. When the Public Library was young and in great need of books, the Club contributed $700. This was the first of many gifts of money for the purchase of books by libraries. For many years the Club has provided scholarships for high school girls, many of whom might not otherwise have secured a college education.

Since 1924 the Charlotte Woman's Club has occupied its own attractive building on East Morehead Street.

Junior League of Charlotte

Between 1926 and 1960 the Junior League contributed more than $320,000 to worthwhile causes in Charlotte, plus thousands of hours of volunteer service. This money came from dues collected from members, who numbered 30 in 1926 and about 600 in 1960; from the Thrift Shop, the League's only permanent money-raising activity; and through presentation of such glamorous and enjoyable performances as the occasional Junior League Follies.

The Junior League was formed by Miss Benetta Heath and Mrs. Howard Conway. In January 1926, during the presidency of Mrs. Robert Cluett, the local league came into the Association of Junior Leagues of America.

The first project of the Charlotte Junior League was the establishment and maintenance for seven years of a baby home and hospital. The sum of $37,000 was put into this project. The League sponsored the Children's Service Bureau for the first three years at a cost of $25,000. When the need for the Children's Service Bureau was proved it was taken over by the Community Chest. From 1940 until 1945, when support was also largely taken over by the Community Chest, the League maintained the Medical Social Service Department of Memorial Hospital at a cost of $37,000. In 1946 the League voted to donate $3,000 annually for three years to the Mint Museum, toward the salary of a director. The most ambitious project, thus far, of the Charlotte Junior League has been the aid of the Children's Nature Museum at a cost of $124,438. Since 1956 the Charlotte League has given volunteer and monetary support of $30,000 to the Reading Center; $20,000 to Girl Scout Camp Occoneechee; and $5,000 to the Youth Concert Program of the Charlotte Symphony. Besides special projects, the League has a continuing program of cultural-recreational activities for children.

Rotary

Charles Haywood Stone, long-time member of the Charlotte Rotary Club, writing in the Christmas issue (1956) of the *Rotary Reporter* describes the city's first modern civic club: "It is no boast to say that Rotary, the first of the modern civic clubs, continues to head the group. The thought of Rotary may have been born in a split-bottom chair, one warm Sunday afternoon, in front of the old Buford Hotel. Paul Harris, a frail man, born in Vermont in 1868, left New England as a young man and became a traveling salesman, a 'drummer', and spent much of his time in the South, making the old Buford his headquarters in this section. On long week-ends, he was very lonesome, and longed for the companionship of his neighbors and friends. His week-ends here were conducive to thinking. After going to Chicago, and still hungry for companionship, in 1905 he joined with four others, lonesome like himself, in lunching each week. Each was of a different profession or engaged in a different business. As time passed, others joined them, and they settled on a regular eating place and time. Thus was born the first Rotary Club, composed of congenial but non-competitive friends."

The Charlotte Rotary Club was organized October 24, 1916 at the Selwyn Hotel with 37 members. At that meeting the following were elected directors: Fred Glover, Ralph Miller, Rogers Davis, H. M. Victor, J. Perrin Quarles, C. C. Coddington, Clarence O. Kuester, John L. Dabbs and Dr. Charles A. Bland. Rogers Davis became the first president, John L. Dabbs, vice president and Thomas G. Lane, secretary, Fred Glover, treasurer, and James O. Walker, sergeant at arms. The inaugural dinner was held December 5, 1916 and the club became the 256th unit in the national organization, shortly to became international in scope.

The Rotary Club of Charlotte immediately got into action as a service organization. As such, it has so many magnificent achievements to its credit that only a few can be mentioned. Probably Rotary's most significant success here and elsewhere was described in the annual report of President Hamilton Witherspoon McKay, "Someone has said that Rotary is the greatest of all schools to prepare men for leadership, with which statement I fully agree."

An early project of the Charlotte club was the establishment of a student loan fund which has helped more than 100 young men and women to go to college and which currently has a net worth of more than $16,000. For many years the club supported a crippled children's clinic, conducted by one of its members, Dr. Alonzo Myers, until this venture was taken over by the State Board of Health. Charlotte is justly proud of the Charlotte Boys Choir, organized in 1946 by James P. McMillan, which has given many delightful concerts locally as well as appearing before Rotary International in New York, and in concert tours throughout the South. The Charlotte Rotary Club was responsible for establishment of a local Better Business Bureau.

As the city has grown the Charlotte Club has been instrumental in the formation of Dilworth Rotary Club, December 3, 1948; and the North Charlotte Rotary Club, December 1, 1952. Notwithstanding the loss of members to these two new clubs, the Charlotte Club currently has about 250 members, the largest membership in its history, all of whom strive to live fully up to the Rotary motto: "Service above self."

Knights of Columbus

Charlotte Council No. 770, Knights of Columbus, received its charter on June 7, 1903. Its aim, like that of the parent body, established in 1882, follows the same pattern as other fraternal organizations which very briefly are: (a) render pecuniary aid to its members and their families in sickness and disaster, (b) promote social and cultural intercourse between members, and (c) conduct educational, charitable, religious, social welfare work, and other worthy causes.

The first Grand Knight of the Charlotte Council was James W. Conway (1903-4). Following World War I, meetings were held in a hut which was moved to the rear of St. Peter's Church on South Tryon Street from Camp Greene, where it had been used by the Supreme Council of the Carolinas for the benefit of service men. From among members of the lodge, the Knights of Columbus Club was organized in 1923, with M. I. Benner as president. In 1952 this club purchased 140 acres near Mint Hill and erected a club house, which has added greatly to the pleasure of its members and their friends.

B'nai B'rith

Charlotte's B'nai B'rith was organized at a banquet held in the German Harmonie Club on April 15, 1877. It has a membership of nearly three hundred. Among its important projects was the establishment of the Hillel Foundation to serve Jewish students at the three branches of the Greater University of North Carolina and Duke University. The lodge has been active in numerous civic endeavors and has served the secular and religious needs of Jewish soldiers stationed in the Carolinas.

The B'nai B'rith Institute of Judaism was conceived here in 1948 and since that time held annually in North Carolina at the mountain estate of Mr. and Mrs. I. D. Blumenthal. These institutes, now held throughout the United States and in some foreign countries, have developed into an adult educational movement, largely as the results of the efforts of Maurice A. Weinstein of Charlotte.

B'nai B'rith was organized originally for "the education of its members, the enlightenment of mankind, the removal of all ignorant prejudices; the suppression of vice, the caring for the widow and orphan, and the performance of other deeds of charity."

B'nai B'rith (Women) has 125 members. This is essentially a service organization and while composed wholly of Jewish women does not limit its activities to the welfare of any group. The public fund-raising campaigns conducted by the major organizations concerned with fighting the dread diseases have all had loyal support from the women of B'nai B'rith. At the Charlotte-Mecklenburg Health Center they have provided a free sick room loan chest for wheel chairs, crutches, and other emergency equipment. Members donate their services to teach English to immigrants. This organization was quick to detect a need for children's story hours in branches of the public library system, and to supply the need regularly with talented story-tellers.

Hadassah

Organized in 1934, the Charlotte Chapter of Hadassah is an influential body of more than 300 Jewish women. This chapter is one of about 1200, forming the national organization of more than 300,000 members. The twofold purpose, closely followed by all chapters, is to assist in maintaining a network of hospitals, youth centers, and educational institutions in Israel and, at the same time, to provide an educational program for its members fostering Jewish ideals.

Kiwanis

Largely through the efforts of B. Scott Blanton, Sr., the Charlotte Kiwanis Club, second civic club to be formed in Charlotte, was organized August 21, 1919 at the Southern Manufacturer's Club, with 61 members. The second luncheon meeting was held one week later when the following officers were elected: Paul Haddock, Sr., president; B. Scott Blanton, Sr., vice president; Marvin A. Turner, treasurer and Walter Clark, Jr., secretary. Hunter Marshall, a charter member, became secretary in 1920 and served in that capacity for more than 20 years.

The club has been responsible for widely varied projects, including financing the care of toxic maternity cases until this work was taken over by the Health Department; maintaining a sizeable student loan fund; providing portable shower baths for children until public swimming pools made this unnecessary; financing school athletic teams; financing equipment for Good Samaritan Hospital; providing a hearing-aid program in the public schools and cooperating in the international exchange of students.

Civitan

The Civitan Club in Charlotte came about when a group of men came together and decided that the time was ripe for the younger men to have a civic club of their own. From the several national organizations not represented locally, but anxious to be, the Civitan Club was selected. The reasons are interesting. Civitan was chosen because of its Southern origin, in Birmingham, Alabama; because of its motto, "Builders of Good Citizenship," and because the Civitan philosophy embraces the Golden Rule.

The Charter was presented by Civitan International at a dinner held July 27, 1921 when Governor Cameron Morrison was the principal speaker. Among the charter members were the following: Basil Boyd, Henry Harper, Claude B. Squires, M. D., A. L. Faul, Randolph Scott, "Dick" Young, Frank O. Sherrill, and Henry Benoit, Sr.

The parent Civitan Club sponsored formation of the Myers Park Club in 1951. Other local Civitan Clubs include: Providence Civitan Club (1957), Sharon Civitan Club (1957), West Mecklenburg Civitan Club (1951), Moore's Park Civitan Club (1956).

Notably successful among the long list of good deeds performed by the Civitan Club was the sponsorship of the Lakewood School for mentally retarded children. The Civitan Club has also been largely responsible for the annual Youth Conference on Human Relations at Wildacres; for operation of the Little League Baseball program; for donation of Good Citizenship awards to high school students; for providing an assembly hall and huts for the Boy Scout camp.

Charlotte Central Lions Club

Though the last of the four major civic clubs to form a Charlotte unit, the Lions Club deserves a "lion's share," when posterity bestows its applause on its twentieth century ancestors. Grandchildren and great-grandchildren of Lions, Civitans, Kiwanians and Rotarians, as well as all other future citizens will continue to enjoy Freedom Park, one of Charlotte's leading recreational areas, originated and sponsored by the Central Lions Club.

During the whole of its life the Charlotte Central Lions Club has manifested a concern for the shut-ins and blind. One of its earliest projects was the building of Wayside Cottage to house the humanitarian activities of Harold (Wayside) Brown, described more fully in the appendix. In 1936 the club built the Charlotte Workshop for the Blind and has continued to operate it since that time, providing profitable employment for men and women who are sightless. This club also sponsored the formation of the North Carolina Association for the Blind and the Mecklenburg County Association for the Blind. These projects have been supplemented by sight conservation programs in the schools and in many other ways.

John L. Stickley of the Charlotte Central Club became President of Lions International (1956-7). Members of the Charlotte Central Lions Club who have served as district governors include Thomas LeRoy Kirkpatrick, Guy O. Bagwell, H. H. Everett, John L. Stickley and V. G. Brookshire.

The Charlotte Central Lions Club was chartered November 3, 1922 with 50 members. It has been very active in sponsoring other clubs throughout the Carolinas and, locally, entirely responsible for establishing: Charlotte Eastern Lions Club, Matthews Lions Club, Davidson Lions Club, Charlotte Western Lions Club, Greater Charlotte Airport Lions Club, Charlotte Southern Lions Club, Pineville Lions Club, and Derita Lions Club.

Charlotte Junior Chamber of Commerce

The Charlotte Junior Chamber of Commerce, the first such club in the Carolinas, was formed in 1928. With Linn Garibaldi as first president, the club was so busy in the fall of 1929 handling the transportation problems of 10,000 Confederate veterans and others attending their reunion, that the first rumblings of the great depression went almost unheard in Charlotte.

Heeding the last line in the Jaycees Creed, "service to humanity is the best work of life," the Junior Chamber has busied itself over the years with raising money in interesting ways and spending it for a long list of good purposes. A wartime scrap drive netted $14,000 in 1943; the Jaycees Jollies, Miss North Carolina Pageant sponsorship, rodeo performances and other guaranteed attractions raised many thousands of dollars. Principal beneficiaries were such movements as anti loan-shark campaign; smoke and noise control and get-out-the-vote drives; professional football for Charlotte; knot-hole-gang by which underprivileged boys saw ball games; Carolinas Junior Olympic Swim Meet; the bond election which resulted in Douglas Municipal Airport, and a long list of other projects for the common welfare.

Other Civic Clubs

The Exchange Club, chartered in 1935 with 22 members, has given great assistance to the Salvation Army in raising the annual Christmas Kettle Fund for the distribution of commodities to the needy at Christmas time. This club sends underprivileged boys to summer camps and more recently has supplied some of the needs of the volunteer Charlotte-Mecklenburg Lifesaving Crew.

The Variety Club of Charlotte was organized in 1938 with the first Chief Barker (President) H. H. Everett. This club draws its membership from the entertainment world and is the medium through which the well known generosity of show people is channeled. In Charlotte, the Variety Club has for its main project an Eye Clinic, operated since 1942. It also provides much pleasure to hundreds of shut-ins at the Crittenton Home, Mercy Hospital, Mecklenburg Sanatorium, and elsewhere by providing, at frequent intervals, up-to-date feature length motion pictures.

The Optimist Club of Charlotte, chartered May 6, 1939 with 35 members, has concentrated its philanthropic efforts on carrying out the club motto, "Friend of the boys." Shortly after this club was organized, it formed the Junior Optimist Club for boys and provided for an equipped playing field.

American Association of University Women

The Charlotte branch of the American Association of University Women came into existence in 1921 when the Charlotte Chapter Southern Association of College Women, organized 1913, changed its name in order to become affiliated with the national organization. At that time Mrs. Bailey T. Groome was president of the organization and the original membership numbered thirteen.

Activities of the local branch of the A.A.U.W. have been con-

Above, left: Andrew Jackson, seventh U. S. President, was born near Waxhaw. *Above, right:* James Knox Polk, eleventh President, born near Pineville. *Below, left:* Mary Anna Morrison Jackson, wife of General T. J.
"Stonewall" Jackson. *Below, right:* Zebulon Baird Vance, Civil War governor of North Carolina, lived in Charlotte during the Reconstruction.

Above, left: Dr. Alexander Graham, first superintendent of Charlotte public schools. *Above, right:* The Reverend James R. Howerton, pastor of First Presbyterian Church, 1897-1906. *Below, left:* Dr. Luther Little, pastor of First Baptist Church, 1917-1943. *Below, right:* The Right Reverend Edwin Anderson Penick, D. D., former rector of St. Peter's Episcopal Church.

Above, left: John Peter Munroe, M. D., leader in medical education in Charlotte. *Above, right:* William Allan, M. D., beloved Charlotte physician, 1881-1943. *Below, left:* William Haines Wakefield, M. D., Charlotte's first medical specialist. His field was that of eye, ear, nose, and throat. *Below, right:* John R. Irwin, M. D., one of the founders of Charlotte's first hospital.

Above, left: Daniel Augustus Tompkins, industrialist, historian, and co-publisher with J. P. Caldwell of the *Charlotte Observer*. *Above, right:* James Buchanan Duke, utilities magnate and creator of the Duke Endowment. *Below, left:* William Henry Belk, merchant and philanthropist. *Below, right:* Joseph Benjamin Ivey, distinguished merchant and Methodist layman.

Above, left: Cameron Morrison, governor, representative in Congress, U. S. senator. *Above, right:* John J. Parker, judge of the U. S. Circuit Court of Appeals, 1925-1958. *Below, left:* Heriot Clarkson, associate justice, N. C. Supreme Court, 1923-1942. *Below, right:* Charles Walter Tillett, Sr., well known attorney at the turn of the century.

Above, left: Edmund Randolph Preston, organizer and first president of the Greater Charlotte Club, forerunner of the Charlotte Chamber of Commerce. *Above, right:* Clarence Kuester, chief executive of the Charlotte Chamber of Commerce from 1921 until 1948. *Below, left:* J. H. Weddington was several times chairman of the Mecklenburg County Board of Commissioners in the period spanning the turn of the century, mayor of Charlotte 1895-1897. *Below, right:* Jack S. Myers owned the farm that was developed into Myers Park residential section.

Among leaders in the newspaper profession in Charlotte have been: *Above,
left:* Thomas J. Holton, *Charlotte Journal* (later *The Whig*), 1828-1860.
Above, right: J. P. Caldwell, *Charlotte Observer*, 1892-1915. *Below, left:*
Wade Hampton Harris, *Charlotte News*, 1888-1895; *Charlotte Observer*,
1912-1935. *Below, right:* William Carey Dowd, Sr., *Mecklenburg Times,
Home Democrat,* and *Charlotte News*, 1890's to 1920's.

Above, left: David Ovens, department store executive, civic and cultural leader, and philanthropist. *Above, right:* Bust of John Charles McNeill, popular newspaperman and poet. *Below, left:* Don Richardson, violinist and orchestra leader, Charlotte's best known musician of the early 1900's. *Below, right:* Hal Kemp, orchestra leader in the 1930's.

centrated in the educational and cultural fields. Institutions which have benefited from the Association include the Little Theatre of Charlotte, the Children's Nature Museum and the Mint Museum of Art.

Altrusa Club

The Altrusa Club of Charlotte is the city's oldest strictly civic club for women. Club interest has been largely in the area of vocational guidance and the education of women.

The Altrusa Club, here, as elsewhere, is a classified membership club composed of women who hold executive positions in diversified business and professional pursuits. It was organized February 23, 1924 with 13 members, the first Altrusa Club in North Carolina. First officers were Margaret Berry (Mrs. Robert B. Street) president; Miss Helen Ramseur Hoyle, vice president; Miss Elizabeth Conrad, secretary; Miss Love Kuester, treasurer.

Business and Professional Women's Club

The Business and Professional Women's Club was formed in 1934 with 20 members headed by Elizabeth Conrad, president. The Federation of B. & P. Women's Club's objective is "To elevate the standards for women in business and the professions." While not organized as a service club in the contemporary sense, the local club has supported many worthy causes such as Junior Achievement Scholarship, Salvation Army and Day Camps.

Pilot Club

The Charlotte Club of Pilot International was formed in 1937 for the purpose of promoting friendship among its members and serving community needs. For more than 20 years the club has followed these objectives consistently. One of the chief beneficiaries of the club's community service has been the Charlotte Rehabilitation Hospital.

League of Women Voters

The League of Women Voters of Charlotte is a branch of a national organization which works on three levels of government, the national, state and local. Its 260 local members exert an influence which might be expected from ten times that number. They believe "Politics is everybody's business." Their motto might well be, "Never say die," when engaged in any campaign.

Organized in 1947, the Charlotte League's ideal is to make Charlotte a better place in which to live. It has spearheaded study of local government; passage of a million dollar bond issue for recreation; adoption of voting machines and many other improvements. Their voter's service program is a year round activity which helps citizens to be politically effective and provides information on candidates and issues as well as getting out the vote.

Beginning with Mrs. M. W. Peterson, as first president, the League claims a long list of competent officers who have kept the organization favorably before the public eye as the city's most aggressive non-partisan group.

Zonta Club

Newest of the civic clubs in Charlotte is Zonta, chartered in 1958 with 21 members. Zonta International is a classified service organization of executive women in business and the professions. The Charlotte Club has quickly gotten into step with a variety of service projects as well as those featuring international understanding through the Zonta person-to-person friendship projects.

Other Women's Civic Clubs

The Quota Club of Charlotte was organized in 1949 and affiliated with Quota International. Both national and local efforts of this club have been directed toward serving women and girls, especially those afflicted with hearing defects. The Charlotte club maintains a scholarship at Queens College and Charlotte College. It has provided various pieces of equipment for the speech and hearing clinic of the Charlotte Rehabilitation Hospital, hearing aids for students at the North Carolina School for the Deaf at Morganton, and also contributes to the Quota International Fellowship Fund to assist foreign students.

Within two years after it was organized in 1957, the Soroptimist Club of Charlotte had provided $1,000 to buy shoes for needy school children. It has also provided a campership to Camp Sky

Ranch for a handicapped girl's two-week stay at a camp conducted solely for handicapped children. This is quite a record for a young club with only 23 members. Activities for the 1959-1960 season are directed by Mrs. J. M. Northington, president.

Women's Auxiliaries

The multiplicity of clubs and organizations on the 200th birthday of Mecklenburg is likely to prove confusing to posterity. One of the first things likely to amaze, and perhaps amuse, students doing research a hundred or more years hence, is that it became expedient for the various groups to form councils for apportioning activities among themselves. Thus will be discovered the Council of Civic Clubs, Council of Women's Civic Clubs, Daughters of American Revolution Council, Council of Garden Clubs, and others.

Some bright great, great grandchildren of Charlotte's Club members are going to wonder why there were no men's auxiliaries to women's organizations, or maybe they will note in the Men's Camellia Club the start of a new vogue in the realms of fraternization.

National Society Daughters of the American Revolution

Mecklenburg Chapter of the Daughters of the American Revolution is the mother chapter in North Carolina, having been organized in 1898 with Mrs. Edward Dilworth Latta as organizing regent and Mrs. "Stonewall" Jackson as the first regent. Mrs. William Henry Belk of this chapter has served as North Carolina State regent and is an honorary vice president for life of the National Society.

The Daughters of the American Revolution, either as individual chapters or collectively, are responsible for many historical markers throughout the city and county. Medals are provided for patriotic contests in schools; scholarships are given worthy students and the objects of the society are carried out in many other ingenious ways. The local chapters of the D.A.R. have restored the Hezekiah Alexander house in Charlotte, home of one of the signers of the Mecklenburg declaration of independence, and maintain it for public inspection.

Since the original D.A.R. Chapter was formed in Charlotte, six additional chapters have been organized in the city, and two in the county. The eight chapters now active have more than 600 members. At present the activities of seven chapters are charted by a Central Council of the Chapters of Charlotte, North Carolina National Society Daughters of the American Revolution. The council was formed in 1922 with Mrs. W. O. Nisbet as first chairman and the membership is composed of the regent and immediate past regent of each Charlotte chapter.

The Battle of Charlotte Chapter D.A.R., the city's second chapter, was organized with 46 members in 1909. Mrs. John Van Landingham of Charlotte, state regent, appointed Miss Laura Orr as first regent of the Chapter. In 1909 the Halifax Convention Chapter was formed with Mrs. Robert A. Dunn as organizing regent and Mrs. James Edward Carson as first regent. The Liberty Hall Chapter was also formed in 1909 by Mrs. James Eugene Reilly, organizing regent. Two members of Liberty Hall Chapter have served as state regents: Mrs. Charles Walter Tillett, Sr., and Mrs. Preston B. Wilkes.

The Mecklenburg Declaration of Independence Chapter was organized in 1912 with 27 members and Miss Julia Alexander became the first regent. The Piedmont Patriots Chapter was organized in 1954 with Mrs. J. Franklin Boyd as organizing regent and Mrs. G. Wilbur Seymour the first regent. The Colonel Adam Alexander Chapter was organized in 1958 with Mrs. Ira L. Black as organizing regent and first regent. The Alexandriana Chapter of Huntersville was formed in 1950 with Mrs. Fred Hastings as first regent. The Jane Parks McDowell Chapter was formed February 1, 1960 by a group of 18 members as a primary chapter of Matthews, North Carolina.

United Daughters of the Confederacy

The memory of those who served and those who fell in the service of the Confederate States of America is honored and kept fresh in Charlotte by three chapters of the United Daughters of the Confederacy. These chapters protect, preserve and mark places made sacred by Confederate valor; collect and preserve material for a truthful history of the War Between the States and aid with scholarships the education of descendants of Confederate veterans.

Stonewall Jackson Chapter No. 220 was organized in 1898 at the home of Mrs. "Stonewall" Jackson. Mrs. Jackson became the first president and after serving in this capacity for 11 years was made honorary president for life. The James H. Lane Chapter No. 1840 was organized in the home of Mrs. L. B. Newell and chartered in 1924 with Mrs. Virginia Staten Cannon as the first president. The Charlotte Chapter No. 2215 was chartered in 1954 with Mrs. James Boyce Hunter as its first president.

American Legion

The veterans of World War I who organized the American Legion in 1919, in 1942 opened ranks to welcome veterans of World War II. There resulted a rapid expansion in posts and membership following the close of World War II, and a corresponding increase in the number of American Legion Auxiliaries.

The active posts of the American Legion in Mecklenburg County in 1960, with names of their first commanding officers are as follows: Hornets Nest Post No. 9, chartered in 1919 with W. R. Robertson, commander, Francis Clarkson, adjutant; North Mecklenburg Post No. 86, chartered in 1928, Capt. John Elkins, commander, Augustus Leazer, adjutant; Charlotte Post No. 64, chartered in 1934, A. J. Beall, commander, W. M. Jones, adjutant; Steele Creek Post No. 221, chartered 1940, J. Mason Smith, commander, Malcomb Snow, adjutant; Hickory Grove Post No. 400, chartered 1946, Luther Taylor, commander and VanDyke Alexander, adjutant; Morris Field Post No. 380, chartered 1946, Larry Zieverink, commander; Cranford-Garrison Post No. 237, chartered 1946, Harry Cook, commander, J. D. Long, adjutant; Paw Creek Post No. 353, chartered 1946, Louis Byrum, commander, John McClure, adjutant; Independence Post No. 262, chartered 1946, David Henderson and Joseph W. Grier, commanders, Bill McClamery, adjutant; Newell Post No. 287, chartered 1946, C. E. Patterson, commander, A. M. Harrison, adjutant; Derita Post No. 345, chartered 1946, Warren O. Cochrane, commander, J. W. Whiteside, adjutant; Huntersville Post No. 321, chartered 1946, Horace Auten, commander, Tommy Kerns, adjutant; Rose Lynn Post No. 376, chartered 1947, Ona Turney, commander, Lottie Smith, adjutant (this was the first all-woman post of the American Legion to be formed in North Carolina); Howard Hughes Post No. 273, chartered 1947, George B. Livingston, Sr., commander, Sam Carter, adjutant; Matthews Post, chartered 1945, W. Jennings King, commander, Joseph Hooks, adjutant.

Veterans of Foreign Wars of the United States

Stonewall Jackson Post No. 1160, V.F.W. originally chartered in 1924 and rechartered in 1934, has many worthwhile achievements to its credit. Among the major accomplishments were the gift in 1940 of an "iron lung" to Memorial Hospital; sponsorship of a training course which enabled more than 50 men to pass tests and enter the air service in World War II, and aid to needy veterans.

Among members of Post 1160 who have achieved state-wide recognition have been department commanders A. W. Hamilton, D. M. Marshall, L. L. Ledbetter, E. C. Kettles and C. T. Myers. Nationally, Parks M. Ritch was assistant sergeant at arms 1949-50 and in 1957-8 aide-de-camp to the national commander in chief.

Post No. 4208 V.F.W. was chartered in 1946 with Bishop Dale as commander. The auxiliary president was Mrs. Maggie Moore. Activities of Post No. 4208 have paralleled those of Post No. 1160 on a smaller scale.

Disabled American Veterans

Queen City Chapter No. 10 Disabled American Veterans was organized in 1934 with 102 members and the following officers: James M. Yandle, commander; Joseph C. Boyarsky, senior vice commander; Cecil J. Husband, junior vice commander; Claude Albea, adjutant. The chapter has given valued assistance to veterans, their wives and orphans in many ways, such as facilitating entrance into veterans' hospitals, filing claims for compensation and giving immediate aid to those in distress. In this latter work many members have been helpful but none quite so prominently as Cecil J. Husband of whom a fellow-member says: "As service officer, he never found the night too dark or the road too muddy when called on to assist any member or his dependents in any way possible." Local members of the D.A.V. who have held state offices, all of whom have served as state department commanders are: Dr. A. P. DuLong, Harry Joyner, George E. Pickett III, Arthur Goodman, Henry Ireland, James M. Kennedy, Jr., W. E. Whetstone, and Horace A. Silver.

American War Mothers

The Charlotte Chapter of this World War I organization was organized in 1920 and has since been quite active in supplying gifts and entertainment to patients in the veteran hospitals at Oteen and Salisbury. The original officers were Mrs. Hugh Montgomery, president; Mrs. W. E. Yountz, first vice president; Mrs. L. D. Whitsett, second vice president; Mrs. J. H. Wearn, treasurer; Mrs. W. O. Nisbet, historian; and Mrs. Warren Roark, secretary. Mothers of veterans of World War II and the Korean conflict are now eligible for full membership.

Charlotte Navy Mothers Club No. 577

With membership open to all mothers who have sons or daughters in the Navy, Marine Corps or Coast Guard, or mothers of veterans holding an honorable discharge, the Charlotte Chapter Navy Mothers of America has conducted a very successful program of an educational, social and welfare nature. Its gifts to the hospitals at Oteen and Salisbury have been continuous and extensive. The local club was chartered by the National Navy Mothers Clubs of America in 1944, and since 1948 has had a permanent meeting place assigned to it in the Naval Reserve Training Center.

Mecklenburg County Gold Star Mothers Club

This unaffiliated club of mothers who were linked by a common bond of sacrifice and sorrow was organized, with 20 members, March 17, 1947 through the efforts of Mrs. Peter F. Burns, Mrs. Almetta McClain and Mrs. L. G. Brewer. This club is responsible and due full credit for the beautiful War Memorial in Evergreen

Cemetery, dedicatory services for which were held December 11, 1949. The monument bears the names of more than 500 casualties from Mecklenburg County in World War II.

The Mecklenburg County Gold Star Mothers Club has deposited a copy of its history in the Public Library of Charlotte.

American Gold Star Mothers, Inc.

The Charlotte Chapter of American Gold Star Mothers, Inc., a national organization with headquarters in Washington, was founded in 1946. The 40 members of the local chapter cooperate with other patriotic organizations with gifts and entertainment for disabled veterans. A principal purpose is to assist and give comfort to members and work for their mutual benefit.

Mecklenburg Historical Association

Through the years attempts have been made to establish in Charlotte some sort of historical organization. Mention is made in old newspapers of such an association before the Civil War. Most of these groups were formed to carry out a specific celebration or project and collapsed shortly after the purpose had been achieved. The Mecklenburg Historical Society, for instance, formed May 7, 1875 undoubtedly had some connection with the mammoth Centennial Celebration, May 20, 1875, of the signing of the Mecklenburg declaration of independence. Another Mecklenburg Historical Society was formed in 1948. The first and only accomplishment of this organization was the symphonic drama, "Shout Freedom."

The Mecklenburg Historical Association was chartered December 7, 1955 and was the outgrowth of a movement for forming a "Friends of the Library" group in Charlotte. The first officers were James A. Stenhouse, president; Mrs. Preston B. Wilkes, first vice president; Kenneth Whitsett, second vice president; Mrs. Georgia Gray Spratt, secretary, and Philip N. Alexander, treasurer. The Association holds several meetings annually, at least one of which is a dinner meeting to celebrate the May 20 anniversary.

In 1955 the Association published Cradle of Liberty by Dr. Archibald Henderson, a defense of the Mecklenburg Declaration. The Association also owns the copyright to two other books:

King, Victor C., *Lives of the Signers of the Mecklenburg Declaration of Independence* (1956); King, Victor C., *Story of the Origin of the City of Charlotte* (1954).

Since officers of the Mecklenburg Historical Association change annually the Association is permitted to use the address of the Public Library of Charlotte as a permanent mailing address.

Travelers Protective Association

The Travelers Protective Association of America has some of the characteristics of a lodge, in that its meetings are ritualistic. It has some of the characteristics of a business organization in that it is composed largely of commercial travelers who seek to elevate the social and moral status of their calling, and to avoid abuses by hotels, transportation facilities and other interests.

Post C of Charlotte of the North Carolina Division of the Travelers Protective Association was organized in 1897 at the Central Hotel. The Post now has about 650 members.

Charlotte Shippers and Manufacturers Association

Organized in 1911, the Charlotte Shippers and Manufacturers Association has an honorable record of protecting the interests of its members in all matters pertaining to shipping rates. The first officers were E. W. Thompson, president; H. W. Eddy, secretary and treasurer and W. S. Creighton, traffic manager.

Mecklenburg Federation of Home Demonstration Clubs

By 1919 there were sufficient Home Demonstration Clubs of one sort or another throughout Mecklenburg to suggest the feasibility of forming a county federation. This was when the Mecklenburg Federation of Home Demonstration Clubs was organized with 13 members and the following officers: Mrs. Robert E. McDowell, president; Mrs. Joseph Warder, vice president; Mrs. Harvey B. Hunter, secretary; Mrs. Plato Price, treasurer, and Miss Martha Creighton, executive secretary.

Home Demonstration agents who have held office in Mecklenburg County have been: Miss Annie Lee Rankin, 1913-1915; Miss Martha Creighton, 1915-1921; Miss Marion Davis, 1921-1926; Miss

Bertha Proffitt, 1922-1926; Miss Delano Wilson, 1926-1933; Mrs. Max Culp, 1933-38; Miss Helen John Wright, 1938-1959.

These and other facts covering practically all meetings of the Mecklenburg Federation of Home Demonstration Clubs through 1952 are recorded in a manuscript prepared by Mrs. Robert E. McDowell.

Carolina Motor Club

Currently the Carolina Motor Club with 88 branch offices in the Carolinas is the largest club in the South affiliated with the American Automobile Association. Formed September 15, 1922 in Greensboro by Coleman W. Roberts, the club moved to Charlotte in 1932.

This club's activities include foreign and domestic travel information and service; emergency road service; personal injury accident insurance, and bail bond service. The club is among the most active organizations promoting the interests of safety of motorists through educational and legal means.

N. C. State Motor Club

Organized as the Charlotte Automobile Club by John Gurney Frazier, Jr., in 1929, the present N. C. State Motor Club was the nucleus around which the National Automobile Association was formed in 1946, with headquarters in Atlanta. This association now operates in 13 states, mostly in the South. Its administrative headquarters were moved to Charlotte in 1960. Since 1954 all N.A.A. affiliates have been members of the American Automobile Touring Alliance, offering, in addition to the usual benefits of automobile clubs, a complete world-wide travel service. In 1955 Mr. Frazier became chairman of the board, serving until his death, March 26, 1959. When Mr. Frazier became chairman, he was succeeded by Thomas B. Watkins, now president and chief executive officer of the club.

Advertising Club of Charlotte

Except for a brief period during World War II, the Advertising Club of Charlotte has been quite active since its organization in

1938. With the rapid growth of Charlotte in recent years the club has grown to its present membership of about 100 men and women. The Charlotte club is a member of the Advertising Federation of America which is the only horizontal federation of members from every phase of advertising.

The principal objectives of the Advertising Club are to provide ideas, clinics, contests, exhibits and other plans for promoting honest, forceful advertising. Recent presidents have been F. Earl Crawford, Sr., Sam Hair, Robert Covington, John M. Dunnagan, Harry C. Bacon, W. Evan Wheeler, Mrs. Frank Levy, G. Jackson Burney, Joseph P. Fountain, Jr., George Henderson, and Thomas Lynch.

Charlotte Association of Insurance Women

Organized by Mrs. Willie Hood White in 1941, the Charlotte Association of Insurance Women now has about 65 members.

Activities of this association include an annual scholarship to Charlotte College; contributing to civic causes and deserving people; an annual Christmas gift to some retired Charlotte business woman, and an annual award to the "Insurance Woman of the Year in Charlotte."

Woman's Christian Temperance Union

The first Woman's Christian Temperance Union in Charlotte was formed in 1885. The first officers were Mrs. Robert Gibbon, president; Mrs. George Graham, vice president; Mrs. Neander Woods, recording secretary; Mrs. W. S. Miller, corresponding secretary. The W.C.T.U. has had a continuous organization in Charlotte since that time, holds regular state and district meetings. Charlotte has furnished several presidents of the North Carolina Woman's Christian Temperance Union, including Mrs. W. B. Lindsay, Mrs. T. H. Plemmons and Mrs. L. E. Brown. Three Charlotte women have acted as editor for the state W.C.T.U. magazine White Ribbon: Mrs. W. L. Nicholson, Mrs. J. B. Read and Mrs. Plemmons. In 1960 there were nine Unions in Mecklenburg County with nearly 1,000 members.

United Church Women of Mecklenburg County

Organized in 1919 by a group of women from 14 Protestant churches of the county, the Charlotte Interdenominational Missionary Union had for its purposes closer cooperation in church sponsored missionary and related movements. The name was changed to United Church Women of Charlotte in 1951 when the group became affiliated with the North Carolina Council of Church Women. The many varied activities include the annual donation of a book on the subject of missions to the Public Library; liberal contributions annually to the American Mission for Lepers; advocacy of elective, non-state-supported teaching of the Bible in public schools; and more recently, the conduct of a summer teenage employment program. The first president was Miss Emma Hall and, since 1951, the following have headed the organization: Mrs. Patsy Goodwin, Mrs. Marret Wheeler, Mrs. Richard L. Huffman, Mrs. Ernest B. Hunter and Mrs. Henry Fisher.

Christian Business and Professional Women's Council

The Charlotte council of this national organization was formed in 1950 with Mrs. John M. Gallagher as the first chairman. In a newspaper interview for the *Charlotte Observer*, June 1, 1958, Miss Beulah Smith of the Charlotte group explained: "In the Christian Business and Professional Women's Councils there are no roll call and no dues. We do not have members at all but we have a mailing list of 175 people whom we tell where the next meeting will be. You don't actually join. You just attend . . ."

The goal of each club is to provide Christian fellowship for working girls ranging from teenagers to grandmothers. For this purpose the club has interesting dinner meetings at which a voluntary offering is taken for use in defraying the expense of the national organization engaged in mission work in areas of the United States where there are no active churches.

American Cotton Manufacturers Institute

This is the central trade association of the cotton, man-made fiber and silk segments of the American textile industry. The Institute was incorporated in 1949 when northern and southern manufacturers who had belonged to the American Cotton Manufacturers Association and the Cotton Textile Institute merged and Charlotte was chosen as headquarters. Other offices are maintained at Washington, D. C., for liaison with agencies of the Government; Clemson, South Carolina for technical services to the textile industry, and in New York City for liaison with markets and trade publications.

Charlotte City Club

The Charlotte City Club, incorporated in 1947, is the mid-twentieth century version of the Southern Manufacturers' Club of the City of Charlotte which was incorporated in 1894. Both clubs were originated to provide a quiet, conveniently located place with attractive surroundings where meals would be served, and men could get together for social and business purposes.

The Southern Manufacturers' Club owned and occupied its own three-story building at 300 West Trade Street. This was quite a pretentious building for that period and lavishly furnished. Dormitory space was available on the upper floor, used mostly by bachelors who could afford the temporary or permanent distinction attached to such an address.

The Charlotte City Club originated in the mind of Herbert Hill Baxter who was born in Boston the same year the Southern Manufacturers Club was formed in Charlotte. Mr. Baxter served three terms as mayor of Charlotte, 1942-1949. In 1945 a group composed of Mr. Baxter, Joe L. Bythe, W. Irving Bullard, Henry Dockery and Frank Dowd made up a prospectus for a proposed club of businessmen.

Many men were attracted by the possibilities presented by this prospectus and from it the present Charlotte City Club materialized. The membership has been increased to about 800 men who, with their wives, children and sweethearts, enjoy the hospitality of a club which ranks with the best to be found anywhere. Since its organization the club has occupied the upper three floors of the building which once housed the Buford Hotel on the corner of Tryon and Fourth Streets. In June of 1959 the board of directors of the club made Mr. Baxter an honorary life member.

There is a club for everyone in Charlotte; following is a representative selection of the hundreds that are in existence today: Council on Human Relations, Charlotte Dietetics Association, Charlotte Rock and Mineral Club, Children's Theatre, Executives Club, Guild of Charlotte Artists, National Secretaries Association, Charlotte Public Relations Society, Charlotte Dental Assistants Society, Charlotte Medical Assistants Association, Daughters of Penelope (Venus Chapter) Auxiliary to AHEPA (American Hellenic Educational Progressive Association), Catholic Daughters of America (Court Charlotte), Agia Elpis Chapter Greek Ladies Philoptohos Society, Daughters of Evrytania, Ladies Auxiliary of the Charlotte Chapter of Printing House Craftsmen, Woman's Auxiliary No. 375 to the National Federation of Postal Clerks, Woman's Traffic Club, Women of the Motion Picture Industry (Wompi), Temple Israel Sisterhood, Credit Women's Breakfast Club, Women's Auxiliary of the Charlotte Druggists Association.

11

HOME LIFE AND RECREATION

THE first Mecklenburgers, according to historian D. A. Tompkins, "were producers. They believed than any work, so it was faithfully and honestly done, was worth doing, and that manhood was more than wealth. Mecklenburg could have existed comfortably cut off from the rest of the world. That makes a people feel independent . . .

"Nearly every farm had a distillery for turning grain and fruit into whiskey and brandy. These liquors were used freely by all, but it would be a mistake to suppose that people were intemperate. It was cheaper to distil than to buy. Moreover, the distance from the markets, Charleston being the nearest, was so great that it was easier to carry the products . . . in liquid form than in bulk . . ." Whiskey was in almost universal use and was offered on every occasion, whether a wedding, funeral, or chance encounter. According to Tompkins it was served at graveside and church during burial ceremonies.

There were several taverns in Charlotte, providing lodging, meals and all kinds of liquors. Here the men of the community met to discuss politics and to get the news of the outside world from travelers.

Horse racing, shooting matches, and other outdoor sports were diversions for the early settlers.

There were four county courts each year to offer opportunities for trading horses and other social intercourse. But even court meetings were surpassed by the muster, the finest of all back country social and political gatherings. "The military companies were

367

kept in efficient condition for muster day and it grew to be the chief opportunity for the public discussion of political issues," says Tompkins.

For fifty years following the Revolution there was little change in this pattern of home life and recreation in Mecklenburg and surrounding counties. However, by 1830 the results of the mechanization of the cotton industry were being realized. People were in much more comfortable circumstances and a few families had acquired large plantations and numerous slaves. Tompkins writes of this period:

"The average southern plantation contained about 3000 acres and one hundred slaves, and such a one would be equipped with something like 25 plow hands, 25 miscellaneous hands, 50 women and children, 25 mules, 4 horses for family use, 600 hogs, 25 head of cattle, 100 sheep, 10 goats, 15 dogs, chickens, guineas, peacocks, turkeys, geese, and ducks. There would be a blacksmith shop, wheelwright, and other woodworking shops, 25 Negro houses, a grist and flour mill, and a store. Such a plantation would be worth about $100,000, would produce about 100 bales of cotton, and would make a clear profit of about $10,000 to $20,000 per year, according to the way it was managed."

No phase of life in Mecklenburg during the first half of the nineteenth century is as little understood today as that which had to do with slavery, and the relative position of Negroes following their emancipation. Dr. J. B. Alexander in his *History of Mecklenburg County* summarizes the situation as it existed about 1850 in a couple of sentences: "Not half a dozen cruel masters in Mecklenburg. A man who was cruel to slaves was tabooed by white people."

Prior to the Civil War provision for Negro slaves was made by practically all churches by building balconies or, in the absence of a balcony, reserving seats. Miss Orr's *History of the First Presbyterian Church of Charlotte* notes that on April 8, 1851, "Our Sunday School contains a small class of colored persons, mostly young," and that, "In 1914 the church had its last Negro member." In the burial ground of the same church, the northeast section was reserved for graves of colored servants of lot owners. The same arrangement was in effect at the First Baptist Church of Charlotte

Above: Old engraving of the building in which Lord Cornwallis made his headquarters during his occupation of Charlotte. *Below:* Artist's conception (*circa* 1820) of the excitement created in Charlotte when news of the Battle of Lexington was brought by courier.

McIntyre Log Cabin, scene of the "Battle of the Bees."

Above: Hezekiah Alexander home, oldest house standing in Mecklenburg County. *Below:* The Ezekial Wallace home on Albemarle Road, probably second oldest house in Mecklenburg County.

Eumenean Hall, Davidson College

Above: Old schoolhouse on the grounds of Sugaw Creek Presbyterian Church is now preserved as a church museum. *Below:* The Well at Rural Hill, home of General William Lee Davidson for whom Davidson College is named.

Above: Cedar Grove house, original home of the Torrence family, now occupied by the Dick Banks family. *Below:* The Charlotte residence of Zebulon Baird Vance, North Carolina's Civil War governor, U. S. Senator and beloved citizen.

Above: Home of the Oates family, around 1900. *Below:* The "Hexagonal" residence of Mrs. Harriet Morrison Irwin.

Above: The Charles W. Tillett residence, a good example of the Greek revival homes built in the late nineteenth century. *Below:* The Craig Davidson house, best preserved example of early Mecklenburg County architecture.

where Negroes remained members of the congregation until June 1868 when 55 of them were dismissed at their own request to form a separate congregation.

Mention of the kindness with which Negro slaves were usually treated and the genuine affection that white people had for many of them is not to overlook the harsh realities of slavery. It is only natural that any tension that might have existed between the races before the war was intensified when the Negroes became "equal under the law." Even then, however, the matter of educating the Negroes became a serious concern of white people. It is undoubtedly true that the Negro facilities were not equal to those provided for white. Neither were they anything like adequate for the needs, because of an economy impoverished by war.

Through the years, the status of the Negro in Mecklenburg County has, of course, risen phenomenally. A small but significant indication is to be found in the practice of those who publish the Charlotte City Directory. Until 1910 all Negroes were listed in the back of the book, following the listing of white citizens. From 1910 until 1930 Negroes and whites were listed together with a small asterisk being used to denote Negroes. From 1930 until 1951 Negroes were designated by a small "c." Since 1951 no designation of race has been used. Prior to 1940 white and Negro churches were listed separately. Since then they have been listed together. In the field of public entertainment, such as circuses, theatrical attractions, lectures, and concerts, segregated but comfortable space has usually been reserved for Negroes, but this custom is gradually giving way to general seating. As long ago as the early 1920's the internationally known Negro vocalist, Roland Hayes, was greeted at the old Auditorium in Charlotte by a capacity audience which was about equally divided between Charlotte's best known white and Negro citizens.

Quacks, Charlatans, and Other 19th Century Diversions

In 1848 Raymond & Waring's zoological exhibition appeared in Charlotte, "with lions and tigers and a brass band." A Dr. Shannon arrived soon after "to practice and teach 'patheism'" that would cure headache, tooth ache and slight cases of rheumatism free. In 1852 John Vane was in the county teaching people how to detect counterfeit money. Daguerreotype artists often spent several weeks in town and were widely patronized.

Life in Charlotte moved gradually in transition from a village to something approaching the status of a city in the period 1890-1910. Little did the men and women who lived in this era suspect that their moment in history would bring up nostalgic memories of "The Gay Nineties." A writer in the *Charlotte Observer* for November 7, 1934 says:

"Charlotte society had individual charm in the 'gay 90's.' The old homes bespoke the essence of hospitality and the Christmas season's jollity was climaxed by the elaborate New Year's Day receptions. The list of residents who would be 'at home' was published in the daily paper and Open House lasted from early afternoon until evening." The writer describes some of the at-home celebrations and remembered how "Young bachelors went in small groups from one New Year's party to another. One such group, known as the Stowe Seven, made it a practice for several years to leave cards bearing a group picture of themselves."

The *Observer* reporter continues: "Brides were blushing, modest, and stayed close to home before the wedding. There were never 20 parties crowded into the week before the big event, but after the wedding trip everybody put 'the big pot in the little pot' and receptions were in order."

There were no country clubs in Charlotte in the Gay Nineties. Dances and other social events were held in the ballroom of the Central Hotel, or other public places. It was the period of gallant gentlemen and wasp-waisted women. One form of gallantry required that a man should protect the wearing apparel of his dancing partner by covering his right hand with a silk handkerchief. From this custom came the favorite bon mot concerning the young lady who, wishing to protect an expensive gown, requested her escort, "Please use your handkerchief." Whereupon this novice in social amenities took out his handkerchief, blew his nose in it, and put it away again. However, it could be that this same crude character might be called upon to help carry his tightly-corseted girl-friend from church on some hot Sunday morning, for fainting in church was a frequent and ladylike occurrence in those glorious days.

Bicycles

Replacement of horse-drawn street cars by electric trolley cars in 1893 brought Charlotte people their first real release from the "horse and buggy days." Of course, there were a few bicycles before that time but they were mostly those with a huge front wheel and tiny back wheel. The new "safety bikes" became plentiful in this section about the time the electric cars replaced horsepower. The popularity of the bicycle in Charlotte and vicinity induced G. V. Keller to remove his Relay Manufacturing Company from Reading, Pennsylvania to Charlotte where the manufacture of bicycles was continued for some time.

In the 1890's a popular quarter-mile bicycle track was located on South Mint Street where annual bicycle races were held. There was another track, one-third of a mile in length, near the intersection of East Boulevard and Avondale Avenue. This was used by the Charlotte Fair Association for horse races for several years.

County Fairs

County fairs have had checkered careers in Mecklenburg County. The first one of which there is a record was held in Charlotte by the Mecklenburg Agricultural Society in October 1855. In the fall of 1871 the first Fair of the Carolinas was held in Charlotte for five days, with $10,000 in prizes offered for 17 categories of competition. All five railroads leading into Charlotte offered to return exhibits free if shipped to the fair via their lines at regular rates.

In 1902 the Mecklenburg County Fair Association was formed. The grounds were located southeast of Latta Park, and included a main exhibition hall, midway, grandstand, race track, livestock barns, poultry and agricultural houses, baseball grounds, and parade grounds. The buildings and grounds were lighted by electricity. Held in October of each year, the fair drew crowds from both North and South Carolina. Many features of the mammoth 20th of May Celebration held in 1906 were held at the fair grounds.

In 1939 Dr. J. S. Dorton, owner of the very successful Cleveland County Fair, formed the Southern States Fair which held its first annual exhibit in Charlotte that year. The new fair grounds covered nearly 100 acres, with race track, grandstand, and several buildings and a sizeable lake. The property was located beyond the city limits on the eastern edge of Charlotte. No one then thought it would become a part of the city within the forseeable future. That it did, however, when the limits were extended December 31, 1959. As the nineteenth successful annual fair concluded on Friday, October 17, 1959 Dr. Dorton announced the permanent closing of the fair and said: "We are proud that Charlotte is the fastest growing city in the South, but when we purchased the fair ground even the most enthusiastic booster of the Queen City would not have predicted we would be inside the city limits in 19 years and subject to city as well as county taxes." He also pointed out that the gradual, but very real, decline of agriculture in Mecklenburg and the competition of major mass attractions in and around Charlotte were contributing factors to his decision.

Automobiles

On November 30, 1900 Osmond L. Barringer unloaded in Charlotte the first carload of automobiles ever shipped to a southern state.

This shipment consisted of two steam-driven Locomobiles, one of which he kept for his own use and the other he sold to Dr. C. G. McManaway, prominent Charlotte physician. There were a number of steam cars developed in the next few years and some were sold in Charlotte, but in the face of competition from the more flexible gasoline cars, they simmered down to two, the White Steamer and the Stanley Steamer, and these two soon ceased production.

In 1902 Mr. Barringer received a shipment of two single-cylinder Oldsmobile roadsters, one of which he retained and the other he sold to a resident of Spartanburg. In attempting the sale of this car he had to meet competition from electric driven cars which were then gaining in popularity about as fast as the steam-driven cars were losing out. However, the electric cars, while convenient for city travel, failed to compete successfully with the gasoline engine though there were quite a number on Charlotte streets for some years.

Nineteen hundred and four, the year automobiles were first listed in the Charlotte City Directory, was the beginning of mass production of automobiles when Oldsmobile produced 2100 cars, Ford 1708, Cadillac 1698, Packard 192, and Buick, just beginning, 37.

Baseball

For a quarter of a century before World War I the male members of the Wearn family were Charlotte sports leaders. With others, they were known originally as the "Wearn nine." Later, because of their continued interest in the sport, the old park on South Mint Street was called Wearn Field (later known as Robbie Field for Wilbert Robinson, manager of the Brooklyn Dodgers, and still later as Hayman Park for Felix Hayman, another local baseball fan and sponsor).

The first professional baseball team was formed in 1902 when Charlotte became a member of the Carolina League with Eddie Ashenback as manager. Minor league baseball was then in its infancy and the league folded before the close of the season. Baseball came back to Charlotte in 1908 when Dave Cross's Hornets won the Carolina Association pennant. This association was a casualty of World War I in 1917. But thanks to the courage of Felix Hayman and W. M. (Bud) Moore, Charlotte again had a team in 1919. Baseball has been a favorite spectator sport and recreation ever since, though there have been a number of changes in name, ownership and alignment of cities represented.

School and College Athletics

Organized athletics began in Charlotte Public Schools in 1914 when Marvin L. Ritch, a young attorney, became the volunteer coach for the first high school football team. It was not until 1920, when Ritch's team had won two state championships, that the Board of Education provided funds for the first paid athletic director. Thereafter, interest in football dominated school sports, but baseball, basketball, and track teams came into considerable popularity, and each had its participants and followers.

The story of basketball in Charlotte was somewhat different since it was played here many years earlier than in other sections of the South, by local school teams. It was introduced in Charlotte in 1896 by F. C. Abbott, recently arrived from Massachusetts, where he had learned the game from its originator. Through Mr. Abbott, basketball became a favorite game with adult members of the Charlotte Y.M.C.A. some twenty years before its adoption by local school teams.

College football came to Charlotte in 1936 upon completion of Memorial Stadium. The first game in the stadium, however, was lost by the Wildcats of Central High School to the team from Barium Springs Orphanage, score 12-6. The stadium was dedicated the following day, September 26, 1936, as a crowd of 12,000 turned out to see the University of North Carolina eleven defeat Wake Forest, 14-7.

The largest crowds to assemble in Memorial Stadium each year are those which come to witness the Shrine Football Classic, originated in 1936, played between picked players from North Carolina and South Carolina high schools, and played for the benefit of the Shriners Hospital for Crippled Children at Greenville, South Carolina.

Country Clubs

The Charlotte Country Club was incorporated in 1910 as the Mecklenburg Country Club but changed its name to Charlotte Country Club in 1917. In its 50 year history its presidents have been: Arthur J. Draper (1910-1914); John M. Morehead (1914-1915); Clarence B. Bryant (1915-1919); William States Lee (1919-1921); Thomas C. Guthrie, Sr. (1921-1924); Howard M. Wade (1924-1938); Claude A. Cochrane (1939-1941); H. T. Cosby (1942-1946); S. W. Cramer, Jr. (1947-1948); Louis H. Rose (1948-1949); Ross Puette (1950-1952); John C. Ervin (1952-1955); C. P. Street (1955-1960); E. M. O'Herron, Jr. (1961-to date).

The club has one of the finest 18 hole golf courses in the country, a swimming pool, tennis and squash courts, and a modern, beautifully furnished clubhouse.

The Myers Park Country Club was formed in 1921 at the site of the Horner Military Academy. Those chiefly instrumental in forming the club were W. E. Thomas, J. P. Quarles, H. C. Sherrill, W. B. Huntington, and W. F. McAfee. Its presidents have been: John L. Dabbs (1921); William States Lee (1922); Charles Raven Brockmann (1922-1924); George W. Paterson (1925-1926); Dr. Joseph A. Elliott (1927-1930); Herman D. Horton (1931); C. L. Brookshire (1932); C. M. Westbrook (1933-1934); J. A. Mayo (1935-1942); Herbert Hill Baxter (1943-1948); H. H. Everett (1949-1952); Paul R. Ervin (1953); Hugh Puckett (1954); L. G. Mumaw (1955); J. J. Clark (1956); F. L. Vinson (1957); Arthur P. Harris (1958); Peter Stuart Gilchrist (1959); L. D. Brooks (1960).

From 1923 until 1947 the Myers Park Country Club was under the management of Ramsey W. Dulin to whom most of the credit is due for bringing this club from a small, informal undertaking to one of the largest and finest institutions of its kind in the South.

Other Country Clubs

With the rapid growth of Charlotte following World War II other country clubs were organized, including Amity Country Club, Carmel Country Club, and Sharonview Country Club. At the same time several commercial golf courses were built to supplement the municipally owned and country club courses. Among these were the Carolina Golf Club and Eastwood Golf Club.

Young Men's Christian Association

Formation of the Young Men's Christian Association in Charlotte was due largely to the efforts of George B. Hanna, who came to Charlotte as assayer for the United States Mint, having formerly been a professor at Brown University in Providence, Rhode Island. His enthusiasm for the Y.M.C.A. in his former home encouraged him to interest several young men in Charlotte in forming a local association, the organization meeting of which was held November 11, 1874.

Mr. Hanna became the first president of the local association and served in that capacity for 30 years.

Prior to 1888 the association occupied rented space in several locations. In the spring of that year a new building at 206 South Tryon Street was dedicated for the principal use of the association. This building was occupied until November 1, 1908 when the building at 330 South Tryon Street was dedicated. With additions in 1916 and 1922 this second building served until May 28, 1960 when the new $2,500,000 plant on East Morehead Street was formally dedicated and occupied.

The Charlotte association was the first in North Carolina to engage a full time general secretary, a physical director, a boys' work director, and also first to promote educational work with an opening session which began in 1887, the first gymnasium in Charlotte, and the first swimming pool.

During the administration of Francis O. Clarkson as president in the 1930's the Second Street Branch of the Y.M.C.A. for Negroes was organized and in 1947 the North Charlotte Branch was formed. Because of Charlotte's central location and great interest in Y.M.C.A. affairs, the city was selected as headquarters for the Interstate Young Men's Christian Association, composed of associations from North and South Carolina.

Upon moving into the new building on Morehead Street, the Charlotte association had upward of 8000 adult and junior members. Officers and directors who were responsible for conceiving and carrying out the enormous task of providing the new facility include: George M. Ivey, Sr., president; James J. Harris, vice president; James G. Cannon, vice president; Morgan B. Speir, Jr., secretary; G. Douglas Aitken, treasurer; George E. Simmons, general secretary; Edwin L. Jones, W. Frank Dowd, William H. Barnhardt, Richard E. Thigpen, H. F. Kincey, Guy T. Carswell, Beaumert Whitton, and many others.

Young Women's Christian Association

The Charlotte Young Women's Christian Association was organized in 1902 by the Woman's Club, and Mrs. Walter S. Liddell became president. The idea was to open a boarding department for young women away from home.

In 1904 a building provided space for 35 girls and was equipped with furniture which had been donated by townspeople. In the same year, Miss Grace A. Aldrich became the first paid secretary of the association.

Following removal to its present location in 1914, the Y.W.C.A. began growing in all directions. The Phyllis Wheatley Branch for Negroes, one of the oldest of its kind in the United States, was opened in 1918, and in 1921 a swimming pool was added to the plant of the Central Association. As of 1960 the Central Y.W.C.A. has 1,431 adult members, 944 junior members, 72 dormitory occupants and a trained staff of eight professionals and six clerical workers. Phyllis Wheatley Branch has 1449 adult members, 276 junior members, 7,081 coed teen-age participants (no dormitory) and a trained staff of three professionals and two clerical workers.

Among those who gave the Charlotte Y.W.C.A. its initial impetus and saw it through the formative years were Mesdames F. C. Abbott, M. A. Bland, B. D. Heath, J. A. Durham, Hugh A. Murrill, A. M. Spong, George F. Rutzler, Brevard D. Springs, Luke Sewell, C. C. Hook, C. N. G. Butt, W. O. Nisbet, Heriot Clarkson, A. H. Washburn, Miss Lily Long, Dr. Annie L. Alexander, Miss Lida Caldwell, Miss Edith Catherine Fry, Miss Nancy Anderson, and many others.

Barbecues

Barbecues date from very early days but, until recently, they were for pleasure, not profit. The oldest hereabouts began at Mallard Creek Presbyterian Church in 1929 when the idea originated after Dr. W. H. Frazer rewarded his Sunday School class with a barbecue. From this occasion the men of the church conceived the idea of raising money by means of an annual barbecue. For those who can't wait from one sponsored barbecue to another there are year-round barbecue restaurants to be found on almost every highway.

Planned Recreation

In response to a heavy sentiment, the 1927 legislature created the Charlotte Park and Recreation Commission of seven members. The same act authorized an election giving the citizens an opportunity to vote a special tax levy for the support of the new program, an election which resulted in a levy of two cents on the $100 property valuation. Prior to enactment of this legislation the parks of the city were under the supervision of the Parks and Tree Commission, a group seriously handicapped by lack of funds.

The newly formed Charlotte Park and Recreation Commission found itself in control of 143 acres of land assigned for park purposes and shown on maps as Independence Park, Latta Park, Cordelia Park, Colonial Park and Morgan Park.

In the light of 1960's 700 acres, superior equipment and adequate personnel, the initial holdings of the Park and Recreation Commission seem puny, but in comparison with most towns in the South, they were extensive. They proved the same foresight that led earlier inhabitants to plan Trade and Tryon Streets as wide thoroughfares, somewhat later South and East Boulevards, equally as wide, and even later Queens Road and other spacious roadways in Myers Park. Charlotte has been more fortunate than most of her sister cities in this respect.

Very shortly after assuming office the Park and Recreation Commission received from E. C. Griffith, 16 acres for Bryant Park, and from F. C. Abbott, W. T. Shore, T. C. Wilson, and Osmond L. Barringer some 240 acres for Revolution Park. During the depression, E. C. Griffith donated property for Eastover Park, and the American War Mothers were encouraging the movement for the beautiful Rose Garden, bounded by Independence Boulevard, Insurance Lane, and Sunnyside Avenue. Memorial Stadium followed in 1937, and the Municipal Swimming Pool in 1938. A major facility was added in 1948 when Freedom Park was opened. In June 1949 the people endorsed the efforts of the Commission by voting overwhelmingly for $1,000,000 in capital improvement bonds, and increasing the tax levy to 6 cents for 1949, 7 cents for 1950, and 8 cents for 1951 and succeeding years.

With the increase in available funds and revenue, the current program of the Commission includes seven recreational centers, 36 parks and playgrounds; 47 tennis courts; 18 baseball diamonds; 31 softball diamonds. Among the many other responsibilities of the Park and Recreation Commission are Park Center, Memorial Stadium, municipal swimming pools for white people and Negroes, and the many picnic areas throughout the park system.

The future of recreation, planned and unplanned, in Charlotte and Mecklenburg County is bright. With the added support of the people of the county the accomplishments of the past in the city may be duplicated through the rural sections. The five incorporated towns will undoubtedly follow suit to the end that both the City of Charlotte and County of Mecklenburg may boast of one of the finest recreational programs in America.

12

CULTURAL INTERESTS

IN many respects Charlotte differs very little from other Southern cities. Hence, little or no attempt will be made to describe the clothes worn by Charlotte men and women for various periods, nor the furniture in their homes. Clothing and furniture styles were very much the same throughout the Southern states. Observance of social amenities was uniform with those of other cities. Likewise, there was little or no difference between architectual styles locally and elsewhere. These phases of the life and culture for different decades are pictured and described in many books readily available in public libraries.

The only really notable exception in Charlotte is in the field of architecture. The "Hexagonal residence," on West Fifth Street, still standing, though somewhat altered in 1960, was described in the *Southern Home* magazine for February 17, 1870.

"Mrs. Irwin of Charlotte, N. C., a sister of Mrs. Stonewall Jackson, has secured a patent for an improvement in construction of houses, which it is claimed will create a new era in architecture. Mrs. Irwin proposes a six walled or hexagonal apartment which will not only be much handsomer but really cheaper than the quadrangular form. A wall eighty feet built in hexagonal form encloses a third more space than the same length of wall built in the square form, and as the hexagonal rooms fit into each other without loss of space the gain in the whole building is very great. The patentee also claims that this mode of building in the hands of a good architect is capable of assuming greater artistic beauty than the quadrangular form. The octagonal building attracted a good deal of attention some years ago, but the hexagonal is claimed to be something entirely new."

From the founding of Charlotte until the Civil War, the business of living occupied most of the people's time and effort. Daniel Augustus Tompkins describes the local situation at that time: "The effects of emancipation upon all phases of industrial life was immediate and revolutionary. . . . Under the system of slavery the population of the city and county did not increase from 1825 until 1860, and wealth and prosperity were in the same condition . . . After the war . . . the whites were not accustomed to farm work and could not hire Negroes, and the result was that their attention was diverted to something else."

From that time on the size of farms in Mecklenburg County decreased. As a result of the continuance of this trend from that time until now, industry has long since overtaken agriculture as the principal concern of the city and county.

These were the days of unpaved roads. Dust in dry weather and mud in wet weather were major problems confronting those who sought to be well groomed. Every home had a door mat, usually made of corn shucks, for wiping the remaining mud from shoes after most of it had been removed by the iron scraper attached to the edge of the lower step. At several places in mid-town, there were pumps and watering troughs for the use of horses. Most of these constituted messy menaces as well as breeding places for flies.

Time for the development of cultural interests was provided by the many conveniences which reached Charlotte during the 1880's. In 1882 city water became available. The first telephones were installed in 1884. Gas, which had been used for illumination since 1858 began being replaced with electricity in 1887. Horsedrawn cars were in operation in 1887 and were replaced by electric cars in 1893.

Charlotte's population, which had been largely homogeneous prior to the late nineteenth and early twentieth centuries, began to change for the better with the arrival of such men and their families and associates as: Daniel Augustus Tompkins from Edgefield, South Carolina; Stuart Warren Cramer, Sr., a native of Thomasville, North Carolina; Fred Glover, Herbert Baxter, Arthur Draper, Earl S. Draper from New England; John W. Fox, from Australia; Rogers Davis, Norman Pease from Georgia; and Morgan Brower Speir, Sr. from Brooklyn, New York.

Charlotte's modern theatrical history appears to have had its beginning in 1874 when Silvano, a magician, and Professor Maurice, with 17 marionettes, opened the Charlotte Opera House on South Tryon Street, the second building south of Fourth Street. This Opera House is described in the May 8, 1874 issue of *The American Builder*: "Charlotte, N. C., April 20, 1874. A theatre is erected here from designs by Mr. S. Welch of New York and the finishing touches are nearly completed. It is a very substantial brick building, 50 feet wide and 100 feet deep; the lower part, or ground story, is made into two large stores . . . the auditorium is 70 feet deep and the stage 30 feet. A large balcony of a graceful line is formed, and returns against the sidewalls before reaching the proscenium." The account continues to the effect that there were two boxes on each side, a balcony of "rich design;" nine hundred crimson plush seats and all decorated "of a bright and cheerful character." R. C. Carson and L. W. Sanders were owners.

This opera house was well patronized for several years, the season of 1880-81 offering 37 performances. From about 1890 until 1895 the theatre was closed, probably caused by the financial panic of 1893, but reopened in 1895 with "Uncle Tom's Cabin." The final season of this theatre was 1901-1902 when there were 83 performances, highlighted by such popular players of that period as Arthur Dunn in "A Runaway Girl," and Adelaide Thurston with Otis B. Thayer in "Sweet Clover."

The Charlotte Opera House was replaced by the Academy of Music which occupied the first floor of the newly built, six-story Trust Building on South Tryon Street. This theatre which was to serve for the next 20 years as Charlotte's leading amusement center opened September 29, 1902 with Mrs. Clarence Brune as leading lady in F. Marion Crawford's "Unora." The Academy had a seating capacity of 1,350. The 1902-03 season was the fullest Charlotte audiences had ever experienced. There were 95 performances including such notables as Paul Gilmore in Hadden Chambers' comedy "The Tyranny of Tears," Frank Deshon in "The Messenger Boy," a comedy; Kate Klaxton in "The Two Orphans,"

Rose Coghlan in Pinero's "The Second Mrs. Tanqueray," Otis Skinner in "Lazarre," James O'Neill in Hall Caine's "The Manxman," Richard Mansfield in "Julius Caesar," Fred Niblo in George M. Cohan's musical comedy "The Governor's Son," Joseph Jefferson in "Rip Van Winkle." In 1903 the Carolina May Music Festival featured such operatic stars as Lillian Nordica, soprano; Edouard DeReszke, basso, with the Metropolitan Opera House orchestra, John S. Duss, conductor.

The ten years following the opening of the Academy of Music were the most brilliant in American theatrical history. As late as the season of 1910-11, 78 road shows played the Academy. Among the actors and actresses appearing during the season were such well-remembered favorites as Dustin Farnum, Jefferson DeAngilis, Lew Fields, Alla Nazimova, DeWolfe Hopper, Mary Garden, and James K. Hackett. Among the plays and musical comedies were "The Merry Widow," "The Chocolate Soldier," "The Bohemian Girl," and the opera "Il Trovatore."

Beginning about 1910, the live theatre began to yield popularity to the rapidly growing list of moving picture theatres, the first of which opened in Charlotte in 1904. The Academy opened the season of 1920-21 on Labor Day, with B. F. Keith Vaudeville and short moving pictures. The few road shows that remained, along with concerts and lectures, were offered at the Charlotte Auditorium, a huge barn-like structure on the northwest corner of Church and Fifth Streets. Building of the auditorium was instigated by the Greater Charlotte Club, forerunner of the Chamber of Commerce.

Keith Vaudeville at the Academy ended on December 16, 1922 because on the next day, Sunday, about 3 o'clock in the morning fire broke out and destroyed the Trust Building, including the Academy, and the building next door occupied by Brockmann's Book Store, in one of Charlotte's most disastrous fires.

With the burning of the Academy, live entertainment in Charlotte ceased except for such attractions, principally band and other concerts, which used the Auditorium. Notwithstanding its size (seating capacity about 5,000) and network of steel beams across the lofty ceiling, the Auditorium housed many cultural attractions. There were the bands of Sousa and Creatore; the one and only

Paderewski; recitals by Galli-Curci, Mme. Schumann-Heink, Louise Homer, John McCormick, Martinelli, and the great Caruso, who delighted the audience with his joviality as well as his glorious voice. Irvin S. Cobb, Will Rogers, William Jennings Bryan, and many other lecturers were also among those whose talents were enjoyed at the Auditorium.

With the final departure of "live theatre" from Charlotte, public patronage was soon won by the moving picture theatres. Numerous picture houses were readied for this new form of entertainment, first in store-rooms, equipped with seats, a piano and screen, and later into premises built for their purposes. From the Odeon, Ottoway and other "nickelodeons" these structures grew in magnificence in Charlotte and elsewhere. There was the Broadway, first in Charlotte to show "talking pictures" with Al Jolson in "The Jazz Singer." This popular place was located on the site of the Old Charlotte Opera House and served Charlotte from the early 1920's to about 1950. It was demolished in 1958 to make room for the Cutter Building. The Carolina Theatre, seating 1,800, was opened on the southeast corner of Tryon and Sixth Streets in 1927, and in 1960 was still liberally patronized. Another large and popular mid-town picture theatre is the Imperial, on South Tryon Street.

As Charlotte began to expand, neighborhood picture houses were built in various sections of the city. Among these were the Plaza Theatre, Manor Theatre, Dilworth Theatre, and the commodious Center Theatre, all operating in 1960. Beginning about 1940 "drive-in" theatres were introduced.

In 1927 there was formed in Charlotte a Drama League, sponsored by the American Association of University Women. This group had its beginning when nine ladies met in the home of Mrs. Francis Clarkson. With Mrs. C. T. Wanzer as chairman they read and discussed plays. Before long, interest had increased the membership and the meetings were held in the Public Library. At this time the group took the name of Charlotte Drama League, and Mrs. Wanzer became the first president.

On June 1, 1928 the Charlotte Drama League produced its first play, "Outward Bound," in the basement auditorium of the Public

Library. Among those in the original cast were Walter Hook, who later followed in the footsteps of his father to become a prominent Charlotte architect; Archie Thornhill; and Dr. Burke Fox. So little notice was given this play in the local papers that a member of the audience wrote a delayed appraisal which appeared in the program of the Charlotte Little Theatre for April 1950.

The opening play of the second season of the Charlotte Drama League was "The Dover Road," presented in the old Baird School. Thereafter the Drama League presented plays in the auditorium of Alexander Graham School and the gymnasium of Thompson Orphanage. With each new play, additional friends were made and the membership greatly increased.

In 1930 the Drama League engaged Thomas B. Humble as professional director, a position which he is still holding with distinguished success 31 years later. The first play produced under Mr. Humble's direction was "The Royal Family," by Kaufman and Ferber. The following summer the Drama League was incorporated under the name of Little Theatre of Charlotte. Subsequent productions were staged in various buildings until 1941 when an attractive Little Theatre was completed on Queens Road. Its first production was "George Washington Slept Here."

In "Nude with Violin" by Noel Coward, final play of the 1958-9 season, Mr. Humble made his annual appearance as a member of the cast. This was the 189th play staged by the Little Theatre of Charlotte, now a member of the National Theatre Council and American National Theatre and Academy.

Charlotte theatre lovers received another "break" in 1957 when the Broadway Theatre League of Charlotte was organized to provide guaranteed audiences for Broadway shows, to be presented in Charlotte. Half the proceeds, after expenses, go to support the Mint Museum Drama Group, thus making possible the free presentation of dramatic classes.

Several men and women who had reached near professional status through experience in the Little Theatre and elsewhere, formed in 1954 the Mint Museum Drama Group. Under the direction of Mrs. Dorothy Masterson this group began the production of several plays annually. Among these were such well-known classics as "Medea," "Electra," "Antigone," "Lute Song," "Don Juan in Hell," and "Elizabeth the Queen." Pending other and more permanent arrangements plays of the group are staged in the Mint Museum. The theatre is supported by the museum and the Broadway Theatre Alliance. No admission is charged for plays.

About the time motion pictures began to monopolize the affection of Charlotte people, another important form of communication made its appearance. Charlotte had the distinction of having put into operation the first commercially licensed radio station in the Carolinas, and one of the first in the nation. This station originated in 1920 when it was housed in the basement of the home of Fred M. Laxton, an electrical engineer, who set up an amateur broadcasting system with a set of DeForest audion tubes which he received as a gift from the General Electric Company. The station was known as 4XD and the operating company, Southern Radio Corporation. F. M. Laxton was president, J. B. Marshall, vice president and Miss Lelia Graham Marsh, secretary. On April 10, 1922 the station was granted a license to operate commercially with 100 watt power, and given the call letters WBT.

In 1925 this station was bought by C. C. Coddington and removed from the Independence Building to the Coddington Building, where it was managed by the Charlotte Chamber of Commerce, with power increased to 500 watts. In 1929 station WBT was purchased by the Columbia Broadcasting System, and removed to the Wilder Building in 1936. By this time the power had been increased to 50,000 watts. In 1945 WBT was purchased by the Jefferson Standard Life Insurance Company and the corporate name changed to Jefferson Standard Broadcasting Company.

Charlotte acquired its second radio station in 1933 when WSOC, which was organized 1928 at Gastonia, moved to Charlotte. WSOC became affiliated with the National Broadcasting Company and under the guidance of such men as Earle J. Gluck, Larry Walker and others, became an influential enterprise. This station, originally owned by a group of Charlotte men headed by Eddie E. Jones, was sold on May 14, 1959, for $5,600,000 to the James M. Cox Radio and Television interests. New offices and broadcasting facilities are located on North Tryon Street. In 1960 there are in addition to WBT and WSOC, five smaller stations.

Television

North Carolina's first television station, WBTV, went on the air for the first time July 15, 1949 with a picture of the American flag. When WBTV's application was granted there were no TV stations south of Washington and only 13 in the United States.

Studios of WBTV were located in the Wilder Building with transmitting facilities at Spencer Mountain, some 20 miles to the southwest. A new building to house WBT and WBTV was dedicated in 1955.

Charlotte's second permanent television station, WSOC-TV, went on the air for the first time April 28, 1957 as an NBC and ABC affiliate. This station was included in the sale of WSOC Broadcasting Company on May 14, 1959 to the James M. Cox interests.

Entertainment Personalities

Beginning shortly after his arrival in Charlotte to become director of the Little Theatre in 1930, Tom Humble played a leading role in one play during almost every season. He will be remembered longest for his parts in sophisticated comedies. Others who helped to make a successful little theatre group in Charlotte include Martha Dulin, Jack Knell, his wife Dorothy and son Derek, Trippi Wisecup, Phyllis Isenhour, Fred Vinroot, Penelope Alexander Currie, Gladys Lavitan, and Eloise MacDonald.

The list of regular players who have distinguished themselves in many plays at the Little Theatre also includes A. R. Thompson, an accomplished amateur magician as well as actor, "Dick" Pitts, newspaperman and magazine editor, and Henry C. Alexander, Sr., Ray Rawlings, Martha Akers, Rudy Thompson, Arline Steinacher, Dr. Robert H. Libby, Peter Hazelton, and Dorothy Masterson.

The two most widely known radio and television personalities developed in Charlotte are Grady Cole and Arthur Smith. Mr. Cole began his early morning radio chatter over WBT in 1930 and was so successful he filled the job for thirty-one years. Arthur Smith's radio and television appearances also cover a long and successful period. As leader of the "Crackerjacks," which include his brothers

Sonny and Ralph along with Tommy Faile and others, he was still a local favorite over television in 1960, and nationally known for recordings by his group.

Lee Kirby was an early sports commentator whose death, while quite young, was widely lamented. The popular entertainer for children in the early years of radio and later television was Fred Kirby. Other favorites in Charlotte were Dewey Drum, Clyde McLean, Gil Stamper, Phil Agresta, Jimmy Patterson, Alan Newcomb, Fletcher Austin, Doug Mayes, Bob Bean, J. B. Clark, Pat Lee, and Betty Feezor.

From the opening of the Grand Opera House in 1874 to completion of Ovens Auditorium and Charlotte Coliseum in 1955, many buildings were used to house Charlotte's dramatic offerings, musical events, home-talent shows, lectures, and other diversions. Attractions which were not large enough or could not afford the Opera House or its successor, the Academy of Music, were usually held in the auditoriums of public schools and, for a while, in the auditorium of the Chamber of Commerce on West Fourth Street. Most of these events were sponsored by local clubs as a method of raising money for various purposes.

Edgar Guest and Harry Houdini drew sell-out audiences during the 1920's in the auditorium of Central High School. During the same period Admiral Richard E. Byrd and others used the Chamber of Commerce auditorium. Many authors, prominent at that time, visited Charlotte in the 1920's and 1930's, including Hugh Walpole, British novelist; Ida M. Tarbell, biographer of the Standard Oil Company; John Erskine, educator, novelist, and essayist; Richard Halliburton, world traveler and adventurer; Judge Ben B. Lindsey, whose espousal of trial marriages caused his lectures to be banned in some cities, and dozens of others.

In 1929 the Armory-Auditorium on Cecil Street was completed in time to house the 38th Reunion of the United Confederate Veterans. This structure replaced the Auditorium at College and Fifth Streets, which was demolished. The Armory-Auditorium served well, if not elegantly, as a place to hold dances and athletic events, but for concerts and dramatic events it was inadequate. Burned in 1954, the Armory-Auditorium was rebuilt and renamed Park

Center. As such, and much more suitable, it continued as the city's chief center for wrestling, boxing and other sporting events, as well as other forms of entertainment.

Inadequacy of the Armory-Auditorium for large scale events prompted Charlotte citizens to vote $3,000,000 in bonds (later supplemented by $1,600,000 additional bonds) in 1950 to build an Auditorium and Coliseum. In November 1949 Mayor Victor Shaw of Charlotte had appointed a citizens' committee to study the possibility of erecting a municipal auditorium and, if the project seemed feasible, to make recommendations as to location, size, cost, architects and other details. The following citizens served on this committee: David Ovens, chairman; Henry J. Allison, vice chairman; Claude A. Cochran, Frank Dowd, James P. McMillan, Frank O. Sherrill and Ivey W. Stewart. Members of this committee spent 284 days, but no public funds, in carrying out their mission. They visited 18 cities before submitting their recommendations in 1950.

Following the election which authorized the issuance of the general obligation bonds, a building committee was formed comprised of James P. McMillan, chairman, Edgar A. Terrell, Sr., Claude Cochran, David Clark and David Ovens.

Upon completion of the building, a five man Auditorium-Coliseum Authority was appointed by the City Council to operate both facilities, with Claude Cochran as chairman. James P. McMillan was named chairman of the Building Committee and vice chairman of the Authority.

Dedication ceremonies for both buildings were held in 1955 with Dr. William F. (Billy) Graham, Charlotte native, as principal speaker, and many distinguished guests present. In recognition of the many years David Ovens had devoted to elevating Charlotte's cultural life, which efforts were climaxed by the afternoon's ceremonies, the new theatre was dedicated as Ovens Auditorium. The larger structure next door was dedicated as Charlotte Coliseum.

Ovens Auditorium is air-conditioned and sound-proof, with faultless acoustics, seating 2,500 persons and with a stage, with disappearing orchestra pit, surpassed in size only by that of Radio City Music Hall in New York. Its colorful, carpeted interior provides every comfort known to theatre audiences in the mid-twentieth century.

The Charlotte Coliseum seats upwards of 12,500 people and, when built, was covered by the world's largest unsupported dome. It is easily convertible for many uses, ranging from the Billy Graham Crusade (1958); Ringling Brothers Circus, which sometimes opened its annual nation-wide tour at Charlotte; the fabulous Ice Capades; ice hockey of the Eastern League; basketball tournaments, ice skating and horse shows.

Music

Records concerning the musical arts in Charlotte prior to 1900 are very sketchy and incomplete. They can only be reconstructed from a few clippings and programs. We know from these sources that, insofar as Charlotte was concerned, interest in music was maintained largely by the music faculty of Charlotte Female Institute, later Presbyterian College and later still, Queens College. After the turn of the century Harry J. Zehm, director of Elizabeth College Conservatory of Music, was an important figure in the musical life of Charlotte for some years.

Shortly after the Civil War, the Music Department of Charlotte Female Institute was headed by Mr. Albrecht Baumann, who organized what was apparently Charlotte's first glee club. Professor von Meyerhoff, considered a musical genius, followed Baumann, and he, in turn, was followed by Mr. and Mrs. DeCosta. They were succeeded by Dr. Bidez under whose direction the Gounod Club was organized, which gave many delightful concerts. Another well-beloved musician of Charlotte Female Institute was Carl S. Gaertner who organized the Philharmonic Society, and directed its first concert in 1889. Mr. Joseph Maclean came next and served for many years. He continued the concerts of the Philharmonic Society, the final concert having been given in January 1892. Then came Dr. J. Richard Ninniss, for whom the music building at Queens College was named.

The Charlotte Philharmonic Society's most ambitious project was the First Grand Music Festival of the State of North Carolina held in Tryon Street Tabernacle in 1890, with Joseph Maclean, conductor. This event brought together orchestras from Winston-Salem, Statesville and Charlotte, and singers from many North Carolina towns.

A Fall Music Festival was held in 1908. This must have been a success for in 1909 a three day Music Festival was held in connection with the 20th of May celebration. The Pittsburgh Festival Orchestra was featured in this series of concerts.

During the First World War a number of musicians were stationed at Camp Greene. One who went on to gain national fame was Howard Barlow, whose Firestone Orchestra was heard regularly on radio and television. He and most of the other musicians at Camp Greene cooperated with local musicians in providing entertainment for both civilians and soldiers. The most important of these events was the Entente Allies Patriotic Music Festival, in 1918, presented for the benefit of American Red Cross.

Music in Charlotte reached its maturity in 1925 with the organization of the Charlotte Music Club, affiliated with the North Carolina and the National Federation of Music Clubs. From the initial membership of 15, the club has grown to a current membership of 275.

As its first project the Music Club contributed $15 toward placing a radio in Mecklenburg Sanatorium. Now, six scholarships are awarded annually in piano, organ, voice, and stringed instruments, and the club cooperates in every phase of community music. Notable among the contributions are the establishment of the Community Concert Association, the sponsoring of the Charlotte Opera Association and the Charlotte Symphony Orchestra and the founding of the Community Christmas Chorus. The club gave the Public Library of Charlotte its first phonograph records and continues to make annual gifts to the library's present fine collection.

Charlotte Community Concert Association

The largest and most successful project sponsored by the Charlotte Music Club was the launching in 1933, during the presidency of Mrs. Louise Young Workman, of the Charlotte Community

Concert Association. During its history it has brought some of the world's best musicians and musical organizations to Charlotte. Admission to concerts is limited to holders of season tickets of which 2,512 are available annually. The first president of the Charlotte Community Concert Association was Paul Lucas, Sr., followed by David Ovens, who held this post and guided the affairs of the Association for a quarter of a century.

Charlotte Symphony Orchestra

Founded in 1932, the Charlotte Symphony Orchestra has an unbroken record of performances. The first director, Guillermo S. DeRoxlo, served until 1945. He was succeeded by Guy Hutchins for two seasons, Lamar Stringfield for one season and James Christian Pfohl for seven seasons. Henry Janiec, the present conductor, has served since 1958. Early officers of the Charlotte Symphony were J. Spencer Bell, Margaret Alexander, Frank E. Exum, Eugene Craft and Mrs. Paul H. Allen.

In 1960, four charter members of the Symphony rounded out almost three decades of service: Israel Smith, violin; Lloyd Torrence, violin; Samuel Citron, viola principal; William Greene, cello principal. To Esther Waltenberger, business manager of the Symphony, is due much of the credit for the orchestra's sound fiscal condition, and for its important place in the Charlotte Fine Arts Council.

American Guild of Organists

The Charlotte Chapter, Guild of Organists was formed in 1947, "to advance the cause of worthy religious music; to elevate the status of church musicians and to increase their appreciation of their responsibilities, duties, and opportunities . . ." The original group of 25 organists has grown to more than 80 members from Charlotte and practically every town within a radius of 75 miles.

The Oratorio Singers of Charlotte

Under the sponsorship of the American Guild of Organists a group of Charlotte musicians formed the Oratorio Singers in 1951 to present masterworks of choral literature and to otherwise promote an appreciation for great choral works. Audiences have grown from an average of 600 for free concerts to an average of 1,500 for paid events and the group has filled numerous radio, television and other engagements. New members are admitted semi-annually; membership averages 75. The first president of the Oratorio Singers was Richard Van Sciver, and the first musical director, Earl F. Berg.

Charlotte Opera Association

The Charlotte Opera Association came into being at the suggestion of members of the Charlotte Music Club in 1948. Realizing the need of suitable opportunity for trained young voices in a growing community, Music Club officers and members assisted in raising the first $300 to start this group on its way. "Rosalinda" was its first performance. Since then the Charlotte Opera Association has come to present four major productions each year.

Musicians

Among musicians who were natives of Charlotte, or made this city their home, one of the best known was Mr. Don Richardson, violinist. Mr. Richardson, native of Clinton, N. C., arrived in Charlotte in 1900 at the age of twenty-two. He made Charlotte his home for the remainder of his life except for a period of ten years during which he conducted in New York City. During his years in Charlotte he is reported to have given violin lessons to 2,900 pupils, as well as participating in practically every important musical event in the city for nearly fifty years.

Another widely known Charlotte musician was Hal Kemp, a native of Marion, Alabama, whose parents moved to Charlotte when he was a small child. From leadership of an orchestra composed of five high school friends (Robert Dye, Paul Whitlock, Jr., Robert Buck and Byrd Crayton), Hal Kemp, saxophonist, moved on to become one of America's most popular band leaders in the field of contemporary popular music. He died at 35, of pneumonia contracted after an automobile accident. Following funeral rites at Charlotte on December 27, 1940, burial took place in Forest Lawn Cemetery, Charlotte.

Mecklenburg County's contribution to the musical world is violinist Johnny Long, native of the Newell section of the county. Johnny formed his own orchestra while a student at Duke University. Upon graduation from Duke he led his band in playing minor spots and hotels for a year or two, gradually moving up to big-time engagements.

Charlotte also claims Betty Johnson, member of the Johnson family singers, for many years popular throughout the Carolinas on radio and television programs. Following the winning of first place in a national talent show, Miss Johnson proceeded to engagements on some of the nation's leading radio and television programs.

Charlotte was the family home of John Scott Trotter, leader of one of the country's most popular orchestras in the field of stage, screen, radio and television.

Art and Artists in Charlotte

Almost entirely lacking is any recorded history of art and artists in Charlotte before October 22, 1936, the day the Mint Museum of Art was opened.

The moving spirit in the establishment of the Mint Museum of Art was Mrs. Harold C. Dwelle. She and E. C. Griffith, because of their unswerving devotion to the Museum, are life honorary members of the board of trustees.

The Mint Museum holds local and traveling art exhibits, holds adult and childrens' art classes, presents Sunday afternoon concerts, and sponsors the Mint Museum Drama Guild. The Museum is a non-profit public institution of the City of Charlotte, and is supported primarily by private benefactions and membership fees.

Almost simultaneously with the opening of the Museum of Art, Charlotte gained three well-known artists in Dayrell Kortheuer, Paul Bartlett and Mrs. Alice Steadman. Their works adorn many homes and institutions throughout the Carolinas.

Guild of Charlotte Artists

Local artists formed the Guild of Charlotte Artists in 1947 with Paul Bartlett as the first president. The principal purpose of the Guild is to conduct joint exhibits of the works of its members; it also provides pictures to non-profit and community welfare units.

Book Clubs

The first book club in Charlotte was the Cranford Book Club, organized in 1891. It was followed by the Eclectic Club in 1894, and the Sorosis Book Club, in 1896. There are several others more than 50 years old, most of them still vigorous.

Garden Clubs

There are 76 units in the Charlotte Council of Garden Clubs and its affiliates. Organized in 1952, the Charlotte Council of Garden Clubs emphasizes education in planting, pruning and flower arranging; holds annual flower shows; and is an affiliate of state and national organizations. With a combined membership of about 3,000, the clubs in the Council are responsible for programs of beautification of public property.

Noteworthy among the beauty spots of Charlotte is the Sunnyside Rose Garden, maintained by the Charlotte Garden Clubs, occupying land donated by F. C. Abbott. A plaque credits Miss Helen Hodge with the design of the garden which has given pleasure to natives and visitors.

Charlotte Writers and Poets

Some of the Charlotte poets whose books are still available and who have received recognition beyond a circle of personal friends are Paul Bartlett, H. E. Harmon, Andrew Hewitt, Loraine Lashley, Alice McFarland, Lucy Mouring McGriff, Nellie Hughes Mullis, Sneed Ogburn, Betty Lee Stoffel, Mrs. John Van Landingham, Charlotte Young and Mrs. Rush Wray.

Charlotte has attracted to its churches some of the country's most eloquent and versatile ministers. A number of these have extended their influence throughout the world by means of the printed page. A sampling of those whose books have been in great demand would include Dr. Luther Little, Rev. J. A. Baldwin, Dr. John R. Brokhoff, Rev. J. G. Garth, "Billy" Graham, Bishop Costen J. Harrell, Dr. G. Ray Jordan, Rev. John A. Redhead, Bishop Herbert Spaugh, Rev. Ernest Lee Stoffel, Dr. J. S. Nathaniel Tross, and Dr. Carlyle Marney.

Charlotte Writers' Club

The Charlotte Writers' Club has an enviable record of never having skipped a meeting during its 35 year history. Organized for the purpose of developing and improving the writing skill of its members, the Writers' Club can point with pride to many whose writings are appreciated locally and a few whose works have appeared in national media. Among the latter are Jack Clinton Mc-Larn, Peggy Simendinger, Thelma Benson, Naomi Hintze, Margaret Clayton, Marian Sims, Louise Pickens, E. P. Holmes and Boyd Blanton.

Miscellaneous Organizations

Cultural interests of Charlotte and Mecklenburg are served by many organizations. The Charlotte Panhellenic Congress was formed in 1951 by Mrs. Frank H. Alexander and Mrs. Karl D. Heinbaugh. It is composed of recognized sororities and accomplishes its purposes largely through scholarships and the stimulation of interest in civic, social service and philanthropic affairs.

The Adult Education Council endeavors to provide information about all forms of adult education available in Charlotte. Branches of the Toastmasters' Club of America provide facilities and incentives for improving the quality of public speaking; a Joint Council on International Affairs broadens the horizon for members of units composing the council. In the religious field the annual Queens-Charlotte Leadership Training Program, conducted at Queens College, has achieved permanence.

13

CHARLOTTE IN TIME OF WAR

THE battle of Charlotte is given scant attention in general histories of the Revolution, but that battle marked the turning point in the fortunes of the British. Never thereafter did the enemy wage a very successful offensive. Unlike the Mecklenburg declaration of independence, about which some have had doubts, no serious question has arisen about Charlotte's part in the Revolution.

The American Revolution began on April 19, 1775 when the British soldiers fired on the minutemen of Lexington, Massachusetts. The fighting ended with the surrender of the British at Yorktown on October 19, 1781. There was very little military activity in North Carolina until 1778, though the state had, of course, responded to the call in 1775 for troops to man the Continental Army. There is no way of estimating definitely the number of these troops provided by North Carolina but the best information places the figure at between 5,000 and 7,500.

In addition to the troops supplied for the Continental Army there was the North Carolina Militia, "under which all free, male white citizens, 16 to 60, inclusive, were subject." Members of still another group, which might be termed the home guard, were known as partisans. Militia and partisans exceeded the troops in the Continental Army, a fact that became quite important when the war moved into the South.

On December 29, 1778 Savannah capitulated to the forces of Colonel Archibald Campbell who, shortly thereafter, restored British rule to Georgia. With Savannah subjugated, Sir Henry Clinton, commander of the British forces in America, became eager to take Charleston as the first step in his conquest of the Carolinas. This he did on May 12, 1780 when defense efforts of General Benjamin Lincoln of the American forces failed and both the city and army surrendered. Following this victory, Clinton sailed for New York leaving Lord Cornwallis in command of Charleston with instructions to hold Georgia and South Carolina and complete the conquest of North Carolina.

Cornwallis started his campaign brilliantly by defeating the American forces under General Horatio Gates on August 16, 1780 at Camden, South Carolina. Leaving Camden September 8, Cornwallis arrived in Charlotte on the 26th, intending to occupy the town, fortify it and enlist Tory volunteers. The reception he and his forces received in Charlotte and their treatment by Mecklenburg citizens replaced the joy of the Camden victory with the gloom of impending disaster. Following his sixteen days spent in Charlotte, the fortunes of the British general sank lower and lower until the surrender at Yorktown a little more than a year later.

Charlotte's treatment of Cornwallis fully justified him in naming the town "The Hornets' Nest." There is no doubt but that his situation before and after his occupation of Charlotte was rendered very troublesome and he reported to Clinton that Charlotte was "an agreeable village but in a damned rebellious country and that the people were more hostile to England than any in America."

The most complete source of information about Mecklenburg men and other North Carolinians who served in the American Revolution is contained in *Roster of Soldiers from North Carolina in the American Revolution*, compiled by the North Carolina United Daughters of the American Revolution in 1932.

The War of 1812

Though few records are available concerning the county's participation in the War of 1812, five companies of Mecklenburg troops served throughout the conflict. The names of nearly 600 men in the five companies are listed in *Muster Rolls of the Soldiers of the War of 1812, detached from the Militia of North Carolina*, published in 1873 under direction of the Adjutant General of North Carolina.

The Mexican War

Mecklenburg's chief interest in the war between the United States and Mexico was the fact that a native son, James Knox Polk, was the President who declared war against Mexico. North Carolina furnished one regiment for the war but Mecklenburg had no part in its formation. A few patriots from Mecklenburg volunteered and formed a company of "light horse dragoons." They left Charlotte in April 1847 and joined the American forces at Vera Cruz where they engaged in several battles.

The Civil War

On May 20, 1861, which was the 86th anniversary of the signing of the Mecklenburg declaration of independence, the state of North Carolina joined ten other states which had already seceded from the Federal Union. Conditions which led to this momentous step were too many and complicated to set forth in this volume. Briefly, however, the North and South had developed along entirely different lines ever since the formation of the Union, until a breaking point was reached on April 12, 1861 with the bombardment of Fort Sumter and its surrender to Southern forces.

Charlotte escaped virtually unscathed from this war. Its people did not. All of them were deprived of most of the comforts and many of the necessities of life, men gave their lives, or suffered lasting wounds, for the Southern cause, bringing anguish, misery and want to countless wives and children. It was one of the most terrible wars since the beginning of recorded history.

Charlotte men got off to a fast start in the war. Two companies of militia were sent to Raleigh four days after the surrender of Fort Sumter. These were the Charlotte Grays (Company C) and the Hornets Nest Rifles (Company B). Upon arrival in Raleigh they became a part of the First North Carolina Volunteers, commonly known as the Bethel Regiment. The entire history of the war does not include a nobler example of valor and efficiency than that of this regiment. It was one of the units which inspired Judge Walter Clark to write of North Carolinians in the war as:

First at Bethel
Farthest to the front at Gettysburg and Chickamauga
Last at Appomattox

The faculty and cadets of North Carolina Military Academy were taken to Raleigh almost immediately to drill the troops being assembled there. By May 16 the First North Carolina Volunteers were organized into a regiment with Daniel Harvey Hill as colonel, Charles C. Lee as lieutenant colonel, James H. Lane, major, and Reverend E. A. Yates, chaplain, all of these men being from Charlotte. Three companies of the regiment were in Richmond May 18, and the other seven arrived three days later. Within the next twenty days they had fought and won a battle.

On the same day that North Carolina passed the Ordinance of Secession, Confederate officials at Charlotte seized the branch of the United States Mint. Thereafter, until the close of the war, this historic building served as local headquarters for the Confederate government. Between 1861 and 1865 Mecklenburg County furnished 21 companies which, with recruits, numbered 2,713 soldiers. Besides these, there were many who joined other companies as officers or privates.

Hardly had the cadets from North Carolina Military Academy left their barracks for war duty when the building, one of the largest in Charlotte, was converted into a military hospital. Throughout the war, hundreds of sick and wounded were treated there.

A large part of the Confederate Navy Yard was moved from the vicinity of Norfolk, Virginia, to Charlotte. This strange action took place in May, 1862 when it became apparent that the Norfolk location was in immediate danger of capture or destruction. Charlotte was selected because of its railroad facilities. It was a wise choice, since later reports indicated that the Charlotte yard suffered "less interruption from the movements of the enemy," than had any other naval ordnance plant.

Additional men and equipment were sent to Charlotte from time to time until there were nearly 300 employed at the Navy Yard, near the Southern Railroad underpass. Throughout the war this plant produced shafting for the propellers of steamers, wrought iron projectiles and various kinds of ordnance equipment and ammunition.

Above: Mecklenburg declaration of independence carved by Harry Orr on a desk top made of lumber salvaged from the McIntyre farm. *Below:* Bronze tablet embedded in the center of Independence Square (intersection Trade and Tryon Streets).

Monument near Pineville marks birthplace of James Knox Polk, eleventh President of the United States.

Above: Typical scene along one of Mecklenburg County's "good roads" of 1898. *Below:* An artist's conception of a once-familiar scene in rural Mecklenburg.

Above: Huntersville Academy, established in the 1870's as a private boarding school, later became part of the state public school system. *Below:* South Tryon Street about 1900. This view is of the 200 block as it looked when the viewer faced toward the Square. Buildings in foreground occupied present site of the Johnston Building and North Carolina National Bank Building.

Above: Piedmont Building, Charlotte's original "skyscraper." The building was razed in 1956. *Below:* Philip L. Lance, center, founder of Lance, Inc., poses beside delivery car in 1924, with H. P. Swinson, left, and E. S. Van Every. Lance office and plant is in background.

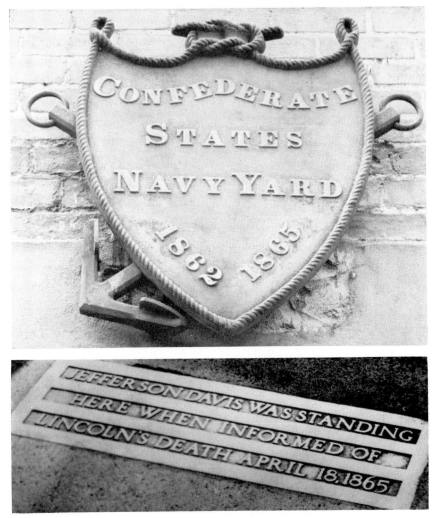

Above: Plaque at site of Confederate Navy Yard on East Trade Street. *Below:* Historical marker located at the southwest corner of Tryon and Fourth Streets.

Monument in Elmwood Cemetery commemorating the Confederate soldiers of Mecklenburg County.

Monument to the Doughboys of World War I
is located on the grounds of the Park Center.

The abandonment of the Charlotte Navy Yard, at the time of the surrender, marked the end of the Confederate Naval Administration, and the Confederate Naval Department records are reported to have been burned there. On June 3, 1910, a small commemorative marker was erected by the United Daughters of the Confederacy on a building located where the Charlotte Navy Yard stood. When this building was demolished in 1959 the marker was removed and its future location depends on building plans of the property owners. There is a state highway historical marker on the East Trade Street sidewalk a few feet west of the railroad underpass.

The need for sulphuric and nitric acid for the manufacture of explosives, plus the fact that gold-mining equipment was located at Charlotte, was responsible for the selection of the city as a location for a sulphuric acid plant. On December 9, 1863, Professor Charles Henry Winston, president of the Richmond Female Institute, was instructed to go to Charlotte and look into the equipment owned by the Rudisill Gold Mine. This introduced him into the production of sulphuric acid and shortly thereafter he erected the plant.

There is little known about the quartermaster's supply depot at Charlotte, beyond the fact that it burned or exploded January 7, 1864, with an estimated loss of $10,000,000.

Charlotte's most unforgettable war days were those just preceding and immediately following Lee's surrender at Appomattox on April 9, 1865.

When Jefferson Davis anticipated the imminent fall of Richmond he sent his wife and children to Charlotte where he thought they might dwell safely and comfortably until he could join them. At Charlotte they were house guests of a local merchant named Weill. Subsequently, Mrs. Davis and her party moved into a furnished house. This event is described in a letter written by Mrs. John Wilkes which reads, "The house was located on the northeast corner of Brevard and 5th Streets. Such of us as could spare any furniture sent what we could to furnish the house. I sent her bread, milk and pantry supplies, as did many other housekeepers."

When Mrs. Davis heard of Lee's surrender and that President Davis was making his way south, she became frantic with alarm. When she observed the troops which had brought treasury funds from Richmond to Charlotte sometime before, preparing to move them to a place of greater safety, she decided to join them and left Charlotte two days before her husband's arrival. She wrote her husband frequently. A copy of one of these letters has been preserved and illuminates the situation that existed in Charlotte at that time:

My own dear Bunny,

Since my arrival here I have been so busy as to have only the evening to write in, and then but one room where the children most did congregate, so I have written you but one disjointed letter.

The news of Richmond came upon me like the "abomination of desolation" the loss of Selma like the blackness thereof. Since your telegram upon your arrival at Danville, we have nothing except the wildest rumors, all, however, discouraging.

I, who know that your strength when stirred up, is grand, and that you can do with a few what others have failed to do with many, am awaiting prayerfully the advent when it is God's will to deliver us through his appointed agent. I trust it may be you, as I believe it is.

It would comfort me greatly if you could only find an opportunity to write me a full, long letter. As soon as we are established here I am going to leave Mrs. Chesnut with the children and bring Li Pie [evidently the baby] to see you. The gentlemen I have seen here are exceedingly kind, and have offered me every civility in their power.

The surgeon general was also very kind in his offers of service. Colonel Johnston, with his wife, called to see me. Mrs. Joe Johnston is living here with the cashier of the bank, and family, and keeps a pretty fancy carriage and horse. I haven't seen her but I hear she is going out of town before long to some watering place or other. Mrs. Semmes went off yesterday for the South. I did not see her. The Wigfalls are staying, I believe, with Mrs. Johnston, also. They arrived yesterday.

I hear a funny account of Wigfall's interview with Beauregard. It seems he went to see him on his way to this place and when the news of the evacuation of Richmond came, and that the enemy had not yet entered town, the general said, "Oh! they do not understand the situation. It is, or ought to be a plan of Lee's to keep between Richmond and the enemy. If Grant attempted to throw troops between his army and Richmond, Lee can whip them in detail."

I cannot judge the moral effect of the fall of Richmond. The people here were about as low as they could be before, as I infer from little things, but, upon the whole I do not think the shock is as great as I expected.

We had a digest of your address to the people today, and I could not make much of it, except an encouraging exhortation. Am anxious to see the whole thing. Numberless surmises are hazarded here as to your future destination and occupation, but I know that wherever you are and in whatever engaged it is an efficient manner for the country. The way things look now the trans-Mississippi seems our ultimate destination.

Though I know you do not like interference, let me entreat you not to send B. B. to command here. I am satisfied that the country will be ruined by its intestine feuds if you do so. If your friends thought it best I should feel helpless, but resigned; but even those who hope for favors in that event deprecate it for you. If I am intrusive forgive me for the sake of the love which impels me, but pray long and fervently before you decide to do it.

Mrs. Chesnut wrote me a most affectionate letter from Chester today. She is staying in two rooms very badly furnished, and furnished with food by her friends there. . . .

Much of the money that was stored at Charlotte was taken further south but some of it, along with the money that belonged to the branch bank at Charlotte, was removed to a spot about eighteen miles from town and there buried. The details of the search for a safe spot, the removal of some 3,000 pounds of gold bullion and its eventual recovery are recorded in the diary of J. H. Carson, grandfather of James H. Carson and McAlister Carson, Sr., of Charlotte.

Just about the time the gold was being removed from Charlotte, ten boxes of valuable papers from the Department of State of the Confederacy arrived in Charlotte. One of these boxes contained the Great Seal of the Confederacy, made of silver and weighing about three pounds. All boxes were hidden in the Mecklenburg County Court House until hostilities ceased, after which they became spoils of war and passed from one unscrupulous character to another. Eventually the papers were purchased by the United States government and are a part of the official records of the war, while the Great Seal was acquired by private individuals for display at Richmond, its original home.

President Davis rode on horseback into Charlotte on the afternoon of April 18, 1865. He was accompanied by three aides and members of his cabinet. Arrangements had been made with private families in Charlotte for accommodating him and members of his cabinet. Mr. Bates, at whose home on the southwest corner of Tryon and Fourth Streets Mr. Davis was scheduled to stay, thought that the party would arrive by train and was at the station to meet them when the presidential party arrived at his home. The President dismounted and, being unable to get in, was welcomed by Colonel William Johnston, a neighbor, and a rapidly gathering group of citizens. To the brief speech of Colonel Johnston, President Davis responded:

"My friends, I thank you for this evidence of your affection. If I had come as the bearer of good news, if I had come to announce the success of our arms and at the head of a triumphant army, this is nothing more than I should have expected. But coming to you as I do to tell you of a very great disaster; coming as I do to tell you that our national affairs have reached a very low point of depression; coming, I may say, as a refugee from the capital of the country, this demonstration of your love fills me with feelings too deep for expression. This has been a war of the people, for the people, and I have simply been their executive.

"I am conscious of having committed errors; but in all that I have tried to do, I can lay my hand on my heart and appeal to God that I have had but one purpose to serve, one mission to fulfill, the preservation of the true principles of Constitutional freedom, which are as dear to me today as they were four years ago. I have nothing to abate or take back; if they were right then, they are right now and no misfortune of arms can change right into wrong. Again I thank you."

While the President spoke, John C. Courtnay, from the telegraph office, walked rapidly through the crowd and handed him a telegram, which he held unopened until his talk was finished. Then he silently read the dispatch. "Can this be true? This is dreadful! It is horrible! Can it be really true?" he exclaimed. The dispatch reported the assassination of Abraham Lincoln.

President Davis and his cabinet made their headquarters during their stay at the branch of the Bank of North Carolina, located on the west side of Tryon Street, midway between Trade and Fourth Streets. The final meeting of the whole cabinet was held on April 20, 1865, at the home of Mr. William Phifer. This location was made necessary because of the illness of Mr. Trenholm, Secretary of the Treasury, who was Mr. Phifer's guest. The next day the sad, demoralized party left Charlotte for points further south. Subsequently, a meeting of most but not all of the members of the cabinet was held at Abbeville, South Carolina, and later another and smaller meeting was held at Washington, Georgia.

At daybreak on April 19, 1865, the day after President Davis arrived in Charlotte, 250 Federal cavalrymen under Major Erastus C. Moderwell, 12th Ohio Cavalry, destroyed by fire the 1,127-foot-long covered railroad bridge over the Catawba River near Nation's Ford, south of Charlotte. Confederate cavalry of Brig. Gen. Samuel W. Ferguson's brigade of Wheeler's cavalry corps arrived from Charlotte too late to prevent this cutting of rail communication with Columbia, S. C. This engagement was one of the last to take place in North Carolina and the closest that actual conflict came to Charlotte.

The most nearly correct list of all Confederate troops furnished by Mecklenburg County in the war was compiled by Dr. J. B. Alexander, as a result of a motion which was passed unanimously at a meeting of the Mecklenburg Camp United Confederate Veterans in 1894. This list was published in pamphlet form entitled *Roster of the Twenty-one Companies Furnished by Mecklenburg County in the War 1861-1865*. It can also be found in *History of Mecklenburg County* by Dr. J. B. Alexander and in Volume II of Tompkins' *History of Mecklenburg County and the City of Charlotte*.

The most complete list of all Confederate troops furnished by the state of North Carolina is recorded in the "Compiled Service Records of Confederate Soldiers who served in Organizations from the State of North Carolina" in the Department of Archives, Washington, D. C. This list is available on microfilm in the North Carolina Department of Archives, Raleigh, North Carolina, and in a few libraries throughout the country.

The most complete published list (though not as complete as above) of Confederate troops furnished by the state of North Carolina is the *Roster of North Carolina Troops in the War Between the States* by John W. Moore (1882). The only index to its four volumes is on cards in the North Carolina Department of Archives at Raleigh. The Public Library of Charlotte has had a microfilm made of this index.

A brief detailed history of each unit from North Carolina can be found in *Histories of the Several Regiments and Battalions from North Carolina in the Great War 1861-65* (written by members of the respective commands), edited by Walter Clark.

Reconstruction

There was no meeting of the town board in Charlotte after March 24, 1865. Lee's surrender came two weeks later. The city was saddened by the flight of Davis and his cabinet, and stunned by the assassination of Lincoln. Civil government in Charlotte was demoralized except for the few remaining members of the Guard for Home Defense authorized by the legislature July 7, 1863, and commonly known as Home Guard. Lieutenant T. H. Brem commanded the Home Guard and did much in protecting the county from marauders and, before the war ended, in enforcing the conscript laws and capturing deserters.

With the increasing number of law infractions by Negroes, some of whom regarded the new-found freedom as license to plunder, and carpetbaggers who abetted them, it is not hard to imagine that Brem and other members of the Home Guard welcomed, rather than resented, the arrival of the occupying military forces from the North. When Colonel Willard Warner, with the 180th Ohio Regiment, took charge in June 1865 he was well received. A little later, General Thomas, in charge of all military forces in this section, arrived in Charlotte to make his headquarters, and he earned everyone's respect for preserving good order. This arrival is vividly described in the following letter taken from *Official Records of the Union and Confederate Armies* (Series I, Volume XLVII, Part 3, Page 490):

Greensborough, N. C., May 13, 1865.

Lieutenant E. W. Welsted,
    Adjutant Ninth New Jersey Volunteers

Sir:
    I have the honor to submit the following report: In accordance with orders from Major-General Cox, I left Greensborough, N. C., with my company on May 5, 1865, and proceeded by railroad to Salisbury, N. C., arrived there at 11 a.m. I left Salisbury at 5 p.m., and was transported by rail to within five miles of Concord, a station twenty-one

miles from Charlotte, N. C. The next morning, May 6, I marched to Concord and telegraphed to Charlotte for a train and I received an answer stating that an accident had happened to the downward train and that no train would run for a day or so. I immediately took up line of march, and that evening encamped thirteen miles from Charlotte. The next morning I resumed the march and arrived in Charlotte at 5:30 p.m. I found the town filled with rebel soldiers; raids were made by mobs on stores that had been left by the rebels. Drunkenness and disorder generally had been the order of the day. I immediately issued an order assuming command of the post; also, another prohibiting the sale of all kinds of spiritous liquors. After my arrival good order prevailed. The following is a list of stores taken possession of and guarded by my command.... On Friday, the 12th, Brigadier General Thomas, of the Third Brigade, First Division, Twenty-third Army Corps, arrived, relieving me of my command.... The next day, the 13th, I had my command placed on cars and reported at regimental headquarters at Greensborough at 4 p.m. the same day.

M. C. Runyan, Captain
Commanding Company G
Ninth New Jersey Volunteers

Accompanying General Thomas was Brevet Major-General of Volunteers Thomas H. Ruger, who assumed active command of the Union forces occupying Charlotte. On May 16th, he reported to his superiors:

"I have the honor to report ... that I arrived here and established my headquarters on the evening of the 13th. Portions of the division have arrived from time to time until now nearly the whole division is here. I have been issuing such orders and regulations as I have thought proper for the maintenance of order. I find the citizens generally disposed to accept the new situation without complaint, and apparently desirous of resuming a condition of peace and observance of law. This region of country is strongly rebel, however. . . . There is no evidence, so far as I have been able to ascertain, of the movements of Jeff Davis in this vicinity, except that he was entertained at the house of a Mr. Bates, and left, going westward, two weeks ago last Thursday. . . ."

Occupying forces at Charlotte numbered between four and five thousand from the time of their arrival until departure on December 18, 1867. "On the occasion of their departure," writes Tompkins, "Mayor Harris presented the captain with a resolution adopted by the board of aldermen thanking the soldiers for their good behavior and expressing regret at their leaving. The captain acknowledged this courteous act with a pleasant note in which he declared his gratitude for the hospitality of the people of Mecklenburg."

During the first two or three years of the reconstruction period, while Charlotte was governed by occupying forces, there were undoubtedly some unpleasantnesses and many infractions of the law. In a chapter entitled "Reconstruction, 1864-1867," Dr. J. B. Alexander's history mentions a number of specific instances but even he admits, "This county escaped the worst evils of these times. . . . During the whole period there was only one disturbance of consequence."

The discomforts endured during the final years of the war left little else for the people to dread. Instead of sulking, Charlotte men and women seemed to accept their lot with abundant grace. They are said to have discovered that, "action is, after all, the best panacea for troubled minds."

Spanish-American War

In response to a call for volunteers by President McKinley on April 19, 1898, two white companies and one Negro company were quickly formed in Charlotte and transported to Raleigh. These troops left Raleigh May 22, encamped near Jacksonville, Florida, until October 24, when they went to Savannah, and remained until December 7. At that time the regiment was ordered to Havana, arriving December 11 and being the first Americans to land at the Cuban capital. The regiment was kept in Cuba until March 18, 1899. It was mustered out at Savannah, April 12, 1899.

The diary of Fred R. Cates, who was a corporal, reads: "May 2, 1898. Company E. 4th Regt. N.C.S.G. (State Guard) left Charlotte at 9 40 a.m. over the Seaboard Air Line Railroad for Raleigh, arriving 2 50 p.m. Went into camp which was named Bryan Grimes. Our colonel was J. P. Armfield and Lt. Col. Calvin D. Cowles, known by all the boys as 'Fido.' "

The departure of the companies from Charlotte was described in the *Charlotte Observer* for May 3, 1898: "Amid cheers, music, the waving of flags and general enthusiastic demonstration of 7,000 or 8,000 people the soldiers comprising the two companies of the Hornets' Nest Rifles and Queen City Guards went forth yesterday to answer their country's call. . . . Charlotte witnessed the greatest demonstration ever remembered in the history of the county."

In the Spanish-American War, Mecklenburg had the distinction of sending into the service a Negro troop commanded by a Negro man. C. S. L. A. Taylor rose from the rank of captain to the position of being the only Negro colonel in command of a regiment of the United States Army at that time. Following the war he returned to Charlotte.

Shortly after the war there was formed in Charlotte the Chase Adams Camp No. 1, United Spanish War Veterans, the first camp to be chartered in the North Carolina division. The camp was named for the first Mecklenburg County soldier to die in the war. It was organized by Dr. Hillery M. Wilder, who saw active service. It was for more than a quarter of a century one of the city's leading patriotic organizations.

World War I

Enjoyment of the most pleasant decade in American history was interrupted on July 28, 1914, by the news of the assassination of Archduke Francis Ferdinand of Austria-Hungary. No one, however, suspected that within a few weeks after the appearance of that tiny cloud over the world scene, Europe would be plunged into the greatest war the world had ever known.

During the first three years of the war, life in Charlotte continued almost as pleasantly as before. People agreed with President Wilson that the war was not America's fight. But by 1917 Wilson was forced to ask Congress to declare war on Germany, a step which was taken April 6.

Charlotte responded wholeheartedly to President Wilson's ideal of "making the world safe for democracy." There were 1,800 men inducted into military service by the local boards for Charlotte and Mecklenburg County; 734 of these were Negro troopers. Casualties included 30 Negro and 74 white soldiers who died in service.

The first to be wounded was Melvin G. Caldwell of Charlotte and the first to be killed in action was Marine Corporal Henry James Smart of the Chadwick-Hoskins section, who was killed in France on April 15, 1918.

Charlotte's first call for financial and material assistance came January 15, 1917 when an all-out effort was made for the first Liberty Loan Drive. The second such drive began October 27, 1917 and the fourth and final drive on October 12, 1918.

Charlotte's principal contribution, aside from personnel for the armed forces, consisted in providing a location for Camp Greene and acting as the host city for troops numbering 60,000 at times. Through the efforts of the Chamber of Commerce, supplemented by the help of many citizens, Charlotte was selected as the site for the camp by Major General Leonard Wood late in July 1917. The camp was named for General Nathaniel Greene who commanded the American forces at the Battle of Guilford Courthouse in the American Revolution.

The first occupants of Camp Greene, after it was made ready, were General Hunter Liggett's 41st Division comprised of guardsmen from the northwestern states. Following this division, General G. H. Cameron organized the Fourth or "Ivy" Division and General Joseph Dickman organized the famous Third Division. Camp Greene was the only Southern camp in which three divisions were organized.

North Carolina troops, including those from Charlotte, were molded into units at Camp Sevier, near Greenville, South Carolina, and at Camp Jackson, Columbia, South Carolina, which became concentration points for drafted men for many states but principally from the southeastern section of the country. These troops composed the Old Hickory or 30th Division which later won its place in history by being the first to pierce the Hindenburg line, September 29, 1918.

The winter of 1917-1918 was one of the most severe ever experienced in Piedmont North Carolina. Heavy snows and frozen ground impeded construction operations at Camp Greene but did not slacken the arrival of recruits. The headquarters building was a ramshackle converted residence. The camp hospital, hostess house, mess halls and other buildings were hastily constructed of green lumber. With every brief thaw the camp became a sea of red mud.

On January 21, 1918, Charlotte, in common with the eastern half of the United States, observed the first of ten "Heatless Mondays" ordered by the National Fuel Administration to conserve fuel for the war effort. On January 24, 1918, a cerebro-spinal meningitis quarantine was imposed on Charlotte, closing all amusement places, churches, schools, and forbidding all public gatherings. The quarantine was lifted after two weeks. But before the year was out, on October 4, 1918, Charlotte was quarantined because of an epidemic of influenza. There were 400 cases in Charlotte and many more at Camp Greene, where the death toll was high. During the quarantine most of the forces stationed at Camp Greene were sent overseas. They were never replaced, except for a few Negro troops stationed here briefly, leaving Charlotte merchants with large stocks bought in anticipation of a continuance of the camp.

Routine life in Charlotte was complicated by an overflow of people. The sudden arrival of some 50,000 or 60,000 soldiers, not to speak of visiting parents, wives and sweethearts, taxed housing, dining, amusement and other facilities built to serve a population of 52,347. Many of the rooms vacated by Charlotte men who had enlisted or been drafted were rented by officers from Camp Greene who were not obliged to remain on post. One gentleman from Boston, forced to come to Charlotte to make his home in December 1917, considered himself lucky to find sleeping space in a room occupied by four lieutenants. They were on night duty and used the two double beds in daytime, while he used one at night. Finally his roommates were shipped away, one by one, and he had the room to himself.

Notwithstanding these circumstances, the men and women of Charlotte, individually and collectively through churches and clubs, made life bearable, and sometimes pleasant, for the strangers in their midst. There were dances, parties, concerts, and other diversions suited to almost any taste. When officials arrived they were properly received by the Charlotte Country Club, Manufacturers' Club and other such organizations. A notable occasion of this kind occurred on March 9, 1918, when Mr. and Mrs. William H.

Porcher gave the most elegant function of the season so that some 400 guests might meet and welcome General George Hamilton Cameron.

During the life of Camp Greene at least four units began publication of their own periodicals. One was *The Mud Turtle* of Company F of the First Army, Headquarters Regiment. Others were *The Skirmisher* and *The Propeller*, details of which are lacking. By far the most ambitious and successful was *The Caduceus*, published by the Base Hospital corps for more than a year. Its editor was Verlin Harold, a private, and the advertising manager was Ted Neal, one of the Camp Greene men who met his fate in Charlotte, returning here to be married and live happily the remainder of his life.

The best-selling books at Stone & Barringer, Glen Smith, and Brockmann's book stores were Streeter's *Dere Mable*, Wells' *Mr. Britling Sees It Through*, Empey's *Over the Top*, Peat's *Private Peat*, Service's *Rhymes of a Red Cross Man*, and Macgrue's *Under Fire*.

Within a few weeks after Armistice Day, Nov. 11, 1918, Charlotte men and women began to return to their homes. By midspring of 1919 the city's business and social life had about returned to normal, sufficiently so to make the most of the appearance in Charlotte of the 120th Regiment.

The last public appearance of this famous regiment, which is credited with having broken the Hindenburg line, was at Charlotte on April 16, 1919. Three special trains brought about 2,000 who were all that then remained of the original 3,600 in the regiment. A huge parade, in which the regiment marched, was witnessed by many military and civil officials and tremendous crowds. Charlotte outdid itself in its treatment of the veterans from the time of their arrival in the morning until midnight when they started on the return trip to Camp Jackson.

World War II

While the bombing of Pearl Harbor was totally unexpected, entanglement in the war then in progress was forecast by many. This was true in Charlotte, which was already well on its way to becoming a key point in the nation's defense with the establishment here of a huge Quartermaster Depot and an army air base.

The Quartermaster Depot at Charlotte was activated May 16, 1941 in a building located just inside the city on the Statesville Road, purchased by the government from the Ford Motor Company. At the height of wartime activities the depot employed 2,500 civilians under a staff of 80 army officers. Everything from toothpicks to battle gear was processed here. After the war ended the depot served in repatriating the war dead, housing the bodies of 5,170 deceased service men which were returned to their next of kin in the Carolinas and neighboring states. The first commander of the Charlotte depot was Colonel Clare W. Woodward. Subsequently, the property, greatly enlarged and expanded, was leased by the Douglas Aircraft Company for producing missiles.

Morris Field Air Base

On April 21, 1941, the government dedicated an army air base at Charlotte, naming it Morris Field in honor of Major William C. Morris of Cabarrus County, a distinguished flyer in World War I. Morris Field represented an investment of about six million dollars for land, barracks, hangars, mess halls and other miscellaneous buildings, the nucleus of the whole facility being the comparatively small Douglas Municipal Airport. This installation was devoted principally to the advanced training of combat pilots and maintenance crews. For many months the Charlotte skies were filled with fighting craft as pilots and crews finished their training before going overseas. Commanders at Morris Field included Colonel C. W. Howard, Colonel Warner B. Gates, and Colonel R. H. Bullard. All property comprising Morris Field was turned back to the City of Charlotte in 1946 and, with large additions, is now the location of the city's airport.

Navy Shell-Loading Plant

Charlotte was chosen as the site for a huge shell-loading plant by the Navy, and some 2,200 acres on the York Road were purchased. A contract was awarded to the United States Rubber Company to handle all management and manufacturing functions under direction of naval personnel. Ground was broken on June 17, 1942, and production of 22 mm. shells was begun the following December. The installation required 30 miles of gravel roadway, 15 miles of interior railroad siding, and dozens of buildings, some of which were of considerable size. At the height of production the work force numbered about 10,000 men and women, some of whom commuted daily from a distance of fifty or sixty miles. Peak production was attained December 7, 1944, the third anniversary of the bombing of Pearl Harbor, when in a 24-hour period 213,143 rounds of ammunition were produced. After the surrender of Japan, termination details required many months, following which the property was used for government storage purposes. Later it was sold to private investors.

A club for service men and women was maintained during the war period at 208½ South Tryon Street, later replaced by a Veteran's Information Center with club-like furnishings in a spacious residence at 525 North Tryon Street. This center became unnecessary and was closed with the opening of a regional office of the United States Veterans Administration in the old Charlotte Sanatorium Building, 127 West 7th Street.

Selective Service in Mecklenburg

Selective Service registration in World War II included, by 1943, all males in the 18- to 65-year-old group. The total number of men registered with the Selective Service Boards in Mecklenburg County was 52,542. The rate of rejection was 37 per cent. Mecklenburg County ranked fifteenth in comparison with the 100 counties in North Carolina in number of rejections; it was second in number of white, and thirty-first in number of Negro rejections.

There were five Selective Service Boards in Mecklenburg composed of the following men who served without compensation: Board No. 1: Carol D. Taliaferro, Rufus M. Johnston, James A. Bell, and John F. Durham; Board No. 2: H. M. Victor, William S. Greene, W. Brice Bingham; Board No. 3: E. A. Myers, Louis G. Ratcliffe, Eddie E. Jones, and Grover C. Osborne; Board No. 4: J. M. Smith, H. L. Kiser, F. W. Hengeveld; Board No. 5: F. A.

Wilkinson, Draper H. Ward, Clarence O. Kuester, Sr., Leonard W. Keeter, Mark P. Johnson, and Robin S. Kirby.

The Medical Advisory Board to the Selective Service Board in Mecklenburg County was composed of the following physicians: E. J. Wannamaker, L. C. Todd, Thomas D. Sparrow, O. L. Miller, Fred E. Motley, A. A. Barron, Robert H. Lafferty, Bernard N. Walker, Henry Sloan, Sr., Joseph A. Elliott, Grady L. Ross and Hamilton W. McKay.

From the total registration, Charlotte and Mecklenburg contributed to World War II about 21,000 men and women, of whom more than 500 gave their lives. The first native of Charlotte to lose his life was W. C. Hunnicutt, a chief petty officer aboard the U.S.S. *Livermore*, in March, 1942. Charlotte's best known contribution to the active war effort was a group, mostly physicians and surgeons and nurses who composed the 38th Evacuation Hospital Unit, which distinguished itself by its surgical and medical skill under primitive and dangerous battle conditions.

Toward the close of the war, a group of men and women of Charlotte attempted to assemble a complete record of all World War casualties from Mecklenburg County. While this data is far from complete the file of 559 names is, on the whole, invaluable. The list is in the Public Library of Charlotte.

14

MECKLENBURG TOWNS AND VILLAGES

A MONG the provisions of the Mecklenburg Resolves of May
31, 1775 it was stipulated that the inhabitants form themselves into nine companies and "chuse" two freeholders from each
who would act as selectmen to govern the county. With some un-
important changes, this form of government existed until the Civil
War. Following the war, the county was divided into fifteen townships. Later, five towns were incorporated and many villages and
communities established.

Davidson

The town of Davidson was first incorporated in 1879 under the
name of Davidson College and continued under this name until
1891, when by legislative enactment the name was changed to
Davidson. The town had its beginning in the early days of Davidson College, which was founded in 1837. The name Davidson
came from General William Lee Davidson, a Revolutionary hero
who was killed in battle not far from the site of the college and the
town.

The town of Davidson is governed by a mayor and five commissioners elected by vote of the citizens every two years. The town
owns its own Municipal Building in which centers the town government. Public utilities are ample. The town purchases electricity
from Duke Power Company and owns and operates its own electrical distribution system, as well as its water and sewer services.
Three policemen are in service working on eight-hour shifts, and
there is a radio connection between the Mecklenburg County
rural police and the Davidson police car, which substantially

strengthens the town's police protection. The town has a 26-man volunteer fire department trained in the art of fighting fires. Insurance rates are low and the tax on property is 65 cents on the $100 taxable valuation.

Much of the life of the community centers around the college and the churches. There are five churches or chapels for white people and three for Negroes. There are various social clubs, usually spoken of as "Book Clubs." Located here is one of the oldest Masonic lodges in the state and a vigorous and progressive Lions Club. Scout troops for both boys and girls have capable and dedicated leaders. Davidson is a delightful little town in which to live and rear a family, and has attractions for persons seeking a place to spend retirement years. The College Art Series, lectures and other happenings are open to the public. There is a fine commingling of interest between the town and the college.

Public school facilities are adequate and are staffed by competent teachers. The Public Library of Charlotte and Mecklenburg County has erected a new branch library.

Davidson has a dentist and two medical doctors, a bank, and all other services.

Pineville

Pineville, eleven miles to the south of Charlotte on U. S. Route 21, near the South Carolina line, was incorporated as a separate municipality in 1872. Nearby is the birthplace of James Knox Polk, eleventh President of the United States. The site, one mile from the Pineville railroad station and 220 feet off the highway, is marked by a rubble-stone pyramid fifteen feet high.

Another distinction of which the town is proud is that it was probably the first in North Carolina to prohibit the sale of alcoholic beverages, in fact, the original charter so provides.

Originally known as "Morrow's Turnout," the busy little town became Pineville with the opening of the Charlotte, Columbia and Augusta Railroad in 1852. Not long after the Civil War, one merchant, Tom Younts, was doing a retail business of more than $100,-000 annually at Pineville, and by 1900 there were ten stores operating in the village.

About three to five thousand bales of cotton are still ginned and sold in Pineville each year; it is the only cotton producing section of any consequence left in Mecklenburg County. In 1890 the Dover Yarn Mill was established by a group of Pineville and Charlotte stockholders. In 1902 this mill was bought and reorganized by the Chadwick-Hoskins Mills. In 1946 it was acquired by the Cone Mills Corporation, enlarged, and completely modernized, since which time it has operated 36,000 spindles and 660 looms. The hundred or so homes, previously known as the mill village, have been remodeled and are now owned by their occupants.

The Pineville Elementary and High School began with three teachers and one hundred and twenty-five students in all grades. Now limited to elementary students, this school has fourteen teachers and four hundred and fifteen students, while high school students attend a nearby consolidated school. The school for Negro students is a modern building with twenty-six teachers and enrollment of 752.

Pineville has seven churches. The Presbyterian, daughter-church of Sharon Presbyterian Church, was built in 1875; the Methodist Church was established in 1881; the Baptist, daughter-church of Flint Hill Baptist Church, was established in 1903; the Nazarene Church in 1947; the House of God in 1948. There are two Negro churches, a Presbyterian and a Methodist.

There are 35 business establishments in Pineville besides the Cone Mill. These include a boat factory, a chemical plant, and a bag factory. The town also has a hospital, bank, public library, an efficient fire department, police department and sanitary department as well as all modern conveniences. The health of the city has been in the hands of a long list of capable physicians, including Dr. J. A. Ardrey (1872-92); Dr. Wm. K. Reid (1892-1908); Dr. E. H. Hand (1908-1920); Dr. George A. Black (1920-1932); Dr. W. C. Ward (1933-1943); Dr. H. B. McGill, Jr. (1933-1943); Dr. L. D. Walker (1943-1944); Dr. R. C. Reid (since 1944).

Pineville's altitude is 575 feet, and the population at the time of the 1960 census, 1,514.

Matthews

Before the coming of the railroad in 1874 there was a stagecoach inn and post office known as Fullwood near the present site of the town of Matthews, about ten miles from Charlotte on United States Route 74. The name of the community was changed to Matthews with the coming of the Central Carolina Railroad as an honor to one of the railroad officials. This railroad eventually became the Seaboard Air Line.

The story of Matthews is not one of phenomenal growth, but rather a record of steady and permanent community development. The town was incorporated in 1879 when the population was about 200. As of 1960 the population had increased to 609, many of whom bear the names of Reid, Funderburk, Renfrow, Stevens, Grier, Massey, Barrett, Heath, Hood, McLeod, McLaughlin, Phillips, and Cochran, all of whom descended from early settlers. Two citizens of Matthews have served in the legislature—T. J. Renfrow in the House and J. Sol Reid in the House and in the Senate.

Matthews is especially proud of three churches: Baptist, Methodist, and Presbyterian, the first building of all three having been erected in 1877, on lots donated by local citizens, E. J. Funderburk to the Baptists, Joseph McLaughlin to the Methodists, and J. Sol Reid to the Presbyterians. The town is also proud of its record in education, having the first Mecklenburg County school to add Home Economics to its curriculum, and among the first to broaden its program by the establishment of a program of music instruction, and adopting the use of audio-visual methods.

An active Woman's Club, American Legion Post, and Masonic Lodge contribute to the cultural and fraternal life of Matthews, as does a flourishing branch of the Public Library of Charlotte and Mecklenburg County. Once humorously called "Stumptown" because of the stumps left when the forest was cleared, Matthews has developed into a community of neat, well-kept homes. Like Pineville, it is becoming the trading center for Charlotte people who have moved to the neighborhood. The altitude of Matthews is 716 feet.

Cornelius

Cornelius, youngest of Mecklenburg's five incorporated towns, was born in 1893 but not incorporated until 1905. The story of its origin is given in an article by Fannie Lou Bingham in the *Charlotte News* of September 27, 1935.

Before 1888 Davidson was a market place for a great many farmers from up and down the Statesville road and from Lincoln County. The Lincoln County folks came across the Catawba River and up the river road which entered the Statesville Highway at a point which is now the middle of Cornelius.

Two business firms were thriving at Davidson, the R. J. Stough Company and Sloan Brothers. Each firm furnished farmers on open account and had its own scales and did its own weighing of cotton. When Charlotte, the county seat, appointed a town weigher, an agitation began at Davidson for a similar official. Some thought it was a waste of money to pay for weighing, while others thought that it was the only way to insure honest weighing. R. J. Stough Company was in favor of the buyer doing his own weighing, and Sloan Brothers in favor of the town weigher.

A hot election was held. The Stough Company lost and a town weigher was hired. Thereupon, Stough went just outside the Davidson town limit, where the river road met the Statesville Highway, and built a small frame building, placing scales in the back yard. He retained his place of business at Davidson, but did his weighing outside of town.

Later, the hill leading into Davidson became so muddy that farmers were convinced it would be better to sell to Stough than to venture into Davidson, which accounts for the fact that Stough began buying more cotton than Sloan Brothers. He then moved a little stock of goods to his country store and hired a "right smart boy," C. W. Johnston, to clerk for him. (That "right smart boy" turned out to be the C. W. Johnston who headed Highland Park Mill and other mills and who built the 17-story Johnston Building in Charlotte.) Stough and Johnston conceived the idea of having a mill nearby so that cotton could be converted into cloth right there. They didn't have enough money to spare but knew a man who did, Joe Cornelius of Davidson. Soon the cotton mill opened and the town took its name from the principal stockholder who apparently never made his home there but whose widow, nee Ann Sherrill, did locate at Cornelius after his death.

The first post office was opened November 17, 1899, with F. C. Sherrill as postmaster. Before that, Jacob Alonzo (Jake) Dove rode a bicycle to Cornelius where he picked up the outgoing mail for the nearest post office, which was at Caldwell Station, three miles away. At the same time he put the Cornelius mail in a tin tub at the mill where each person would go through it for his own mail.

Among the early settlers of Cornelius were the families of Robert Pitts, Douglas Weddington, Frank Brown, Andy Hall, Allison Black, Jack White, Charles Readling, and Isaac Barnette. The first local school was opened about 1906 with Mrs. Emma Thompson Stough as the first teacher. The monument in front of Mt. Zion Church, honoring 44 Confederate dead, was unveiled in August 1910.

From that early beginning has developed by 1960 a progressive little town, proud of its schools, churches, clubs, public library, and business firms. Its altitude is 833 feet and the 1960 census gives it a population of 1,444.

Huntersville

Since its earliest years the Huntersville community, originally called Craighead for the staunch pioneer patriot Alexander Craighead, has been known for its championing of education.

The site of two of the first high schools in the western area of the state, established less than two decades after the close of the Civil War, Huntersville continues as an educational center with two senior high schools, a consolidated junior high school, and an elementary school.

It is likewise a community of churches, with congregations affiliated with six denominations.

Huntersville was chartered March 9, 1877. From the beginning it has had an aldermanic form of government, with a mayor and four aldermen.

Of the original Huntersville High School's location, its "Scholastic Year, 1882-1883" catalogue says:

"This School is situated in the pleasant little village of Huntersville, Mecklenburg County, N. C., fourteen miles north of Charlotte, on the A. T. & O. Division of the C. C. & A. Railroad. Hence the mail facilities are all that could be desired—twice every day. The climate cannot be excelled anywhere. Situated as it is on a high ridge of country, no place can boast of purer or fresher air, and consequently no place is healthier than Huntersville. There is emphatically no local cause either in or near Huntersville that has a tendency to produce disease."

This school was established four years earlier and was first taught in the little session house of the Associate Reformed Presbyterian Church by the church's pastor, Reverend W. W. Orr, D.D. "It started with ten scholars," the catalogue reveals, "without a school building. This year it closed with seventy pupils, and a bright prospect for the future." It then had a three-room frame building, some hundred yards south of the church, "neat, comfortable, and well adapted to the purpose for which it was built; each room is furnished with a large stove, comfortable desks and plenty of blackboard surface."

Board and lodging were $8 a month and tuition was from $1 to $5 a month. Washing was $1. "Persons desiring to move to Huntersville for the purpose of educating their children can buy good lots (1 acre) in any part of town for from $40 to $100," the catalogue further revealed. "The average price is $50 per acre."

Contemporaneously with the operation of Dr. Orr's school was that of the Grey Academy in the southern section of the village, conducted by Professor Hugh Grey, who was later Mecklenburg's superintendent of schools. Students from a wide area, many of them from Charlotte and some from as far away as Mexico, came to Huntersville to attend these schools and later the consolidated institution housed in what then was one of the largest and most modern school structures in the region, the two-story brick building in the western edge of the village known as The Academy. A few years later this school would become a part of the public school system as one of the original North Carolina state high schools.

Huntersville's attachment to education has been maintained through the decades. Its percentage of college-educated citizens is one of the highest in the state.

One of the state's oldest textile plants, founded at Huntersville in the decade of the 'nineties and long operated as the Anchor Mills, has developed in recent years into an ultra-modern plant manufacturing housewares and polyurethane products.

The town's average elevation is 814 feet; the 1960 population was 1,004.

MECKLENBURG TOWNS AND VILLAGES 423

Townships

Before there were incorporated towns, Mecklenburg County had been divided into fifteen townships. The division took place about 1868 and was made necessary by Article VII, Section 3, of the newly adopted state constitution, reading as follows: "It shall be the duty of the commissioners in each county to divide the same into convenient districts, to determine their boundaries and prescribe the names of such districts. . . ."

Five of the townships were named for creeks, three for embryo towns within their borders, three for prominent families, two for Presbyterian churches, and two apparently for euphony. While still referred to locally by their original names, all Mecklenburg townships are now known officially by numbers. With their 1960 census, these townships, with corresponding numbers, are as follows: 1—Charlotte (201,564); 2—Berryhill (8,250); 3—Steele Creek (3,009); 4—Sharon (7,971); 5—Providence (2,815); 6—Clear Creek (3,121); 7—Crab Orchard (8,301); 8—Mallard Creek (7,802); 9—Deweese (4,988); 10—Lemley (1,578); 11—Long Creek (4,748); 12—Paw Creek (9,308); 13—Morning Star (3,246); 14—Pineville (3,174); and 15—Huntersville (2,866).

While these township divisions of the county have remained very much the same for nearly a century, the smaller subdivisions represented by lists of villages and post offices have changed so rapidly that they have been described as "genealogist's nightmares." The earliest *Gazetteer of Mecklenburg County* (an alphabetical list of villages and post offices) is contained in the Charlotte City Directory for 1879. Under each post office there is a list of prominent citizens. In addition to Charlotte, Davidson, Huntersville, Matthews, and Pineville, the following post offices are listed:

Alexandriana: on A. T. & O. RR 8 miles north of Charlotte
Caldwell: on A. T. & O. RR 15 miles north of Charlotte
Cowan's Ford: 16 miles west of Charlotte
Harrison: 13 miles south of Charlotte
Hebron: on C. C. & A. RR 7 miles south of Charlotte
Irene: 14 miles east of Charlotte
Martindale: 8 miles northwest of Charlotte
Mint Hill: 12 miles east of Charlotte

Mutual Love: 5 miles northwest of Charlotte
Paw Creek: 6 miles west of Charlotte
Query's: 8 miles north of Charlotte
Ranaleburg: 13 miles southwest of Charlotte
River View: 22 miles northwest of Charlotte
Steele Creek: 9 miles southwest of Charlotte

The above apparently was not a complete list, for *Branson's North Carolina Business Directory* for 1869 lists the following post offices for Mecklenburg County not in the 1879 Charlotte City Directory: Clear Creek, Providence, White Hall, Sherrill's Ford, Craighead, Hopewell.

By 1896 some of the foregoing had disappeared but many others had been added. *Branson's Business Directory* for that year lists the following with their population figures:

Arlington, 50	Harrison, 50	Query's, 40
Biddleville, 100	Hebron, 25	Ranaleburg, 50
Bristow, 50	Hood's, 60	Rankin, 25
Burdett, 25	Hopewell, 50	River View, 30
Caldwell's, 35	Hornet, 30	Sago, 25
Charlotte, 16,500	Huntersville, 250	Sandifer, 100
Cluster, 25	Kingwood, 40	Sardis, 25
Cottonwood, 60	Lodo, 50	Shamrock, 25
Cowan's Ford, 500	Madge, 35	Shera, 35
Croft, 30	Martindale, 30	Shopton, 100
Davenport, 50	Matthews, 300	Spurrier, 50
Davidson, 500	Mint Hill, 100	Steele Creek, 50
Delos, 55	Monteith, 40	Stevens, 60
Derita, 100	Nevin, 45	Tampa, 30
Dixie, 25	Newell, 100	Uncas, 20
Eastfield, 50	Nimrod, 30	Unity, 22
Fennimore, 30	Paw Creek, 50	Walles, 40
Griffith, 30	Pineville, 400	

With the coming of Rural Free Delivery service in 1896 these small post offices began to disappear rapidly. According to the 1960 Postal Guide those remaining in Mecklenburg were Charlotte, Cornelius, Davidson, Derita, Huntersville, Matthews, Newell, Paw Creek, and Pineville.

Of the villages large enough to support a post office the nearest to Charlotte and most thickly populated is Derita. It has the distinction of being almost in the exact center of Mecklenburg County. The first post office was established in 1882 with Amos L. Rumple as postmaster. The village was named for Derita Lewis, a friend of Mr. Rumple.

In 1889 the citizens bought $25 shares in a school which was built at a cost of $570. This was operated as Derita Academy before being sold to the Mecklenburg County Board of Education in 1892.

Other unincorporated villages in Mecklenburg County—each with its loyal citizenship—include Mint Hill, Steele Creek, Berryhill, and Newell.

APPENDIX

MECKLENBURG DECLARATION OF INDEPENDENCE
MAY 20, 1775

1. That whosoever directly or indirectly abetted or in any way, form or manner countenanced the unchartered & dangerous invasion of our rights as claimed by G. Britain is an enemy to this County — to America & to the inherent & inaliable rights of man.

2. We the Citizens of Mecklenburg County do hereby desolve the political bands which have connected us to the Mother Country & hereby absolve ourselves from all allegiance to the British crown & abjure all political connection, contract or association with that nation who have wantonly trampled on our rights & liberties & inhumanely shed the innocent blood of American patriots at Lexington.

3. We do hereby declare ourselves a free and independent people — are & of right ought to be a sovereign & self-governing association, under the controul of no power other than that of our God & the general government of the congress, to the maintainence of which independence civil & religious we solemnly pledge to each other our mutual cooperation, our lives, our fortunes & our most sacred honor.

4. As we now acknowledge the existence & controul of no law or legal officers, civil or military, within this County, we do hereby ordain & adopt as a rule of life, all, each & every of our former laws —wherein nevertheless the crown of great britain never can be considered as holding rights, privileges, immunities, or authority therein.

5. It is also further decreed that all, each & every military officer in this County is hereby reinstated in his former command & authority, he acting conformably to these regulations. And that every member present of this delegation shall henceforth be a civil officer, viz. a Justice of the peace in the character of a 'Committee-man' to issue process, hear & determine all matters of controversy according to s^d. adopted laws—to preserve peace, union & harmony in s^d. County & to use every exertion to spread the love of country & fire of freedom throughout America untill a more general & organized government be established in this province. A selection from the members present shall constitute a Committee of public safety for s^d. County.

6. That a copy of these resolutions be transmitted by express to the President of the Continental Congress assembled in Philadelphia, to be laid before that body.

Ephraim Brevard	Matthew McClure
Hezekiah J. Balch	Neil Morrison
John Phifer	Robert Irwin
James Harris	John Flennegin
William Kennon	David Reese
John Foard	William Graham
Richard Barry	John Queary
Henry Downs	Hezekiah Alexander
Ezra Alexander	Adam Alexander
Charles Alexander	John Davidson
Zaccheus Wilson	Richard Harris
Waightstill Avery	Thomas Polk
Benjamin Patton	Abraham Alexander

John McKnitt Alexander

The Mecklenburg Declaration of Independence has been printed in a number of different styles over the years; inscribed on a plaque placed on the wall of the Mecklenburg County Court House by the County Commissioners in 1937, and otherwise reproduced. The most unique of these reproductions was wrought by Harry Orr of Charlotte who secured a log from the McIntyre Farm House and built a desk top upon which he carved the entire text of the Declaration, inlaying each letter. The finished product was carefully polished and is an impressive reminder of the faith Mecklenburg citizens have in this important document. It may be seen in the Public Library of Charlotte.

MECKLENBURG RESOLVES

Charlotte Town, Mecklenburg County, May 31, 1775.

THIS day the Committee of this County met, and passed the following RESOLVES:

WHEREAS by an Address presented to his Majesty by both Houses of Parliament in February last, the American Colonies are declared to be in a state of actual Rebellion, we conceive that all Laws and Commissions confirmed by, or derived from the Authority of the King or Parliament, are annulled and vacated, and the former civil Constitution of these Colonies for the present wholly suspended. To provide in some Degree for the Exigencies of the County in the present alarming Period, we deem it proper and necessary to pass the following resolves, viz.

1. That all Commissions, civil and military, heretofore granted by the Crown, to be exercised in these Colonies, are null and void, and the Constitution of each particular Colony wholly suspended.

2. That the Provincial Congress of each Province, under the Direction of the Great Continental Congress, is invested with all legislative and executive Powers within their respective Provinces; and that no other Legislative or Executive does or can exist, at this Time, in any of these Colonies.

3. As all former Laws are now suspended in this Province, and the Congress have not yet provided others, we judge it necessary, for the better Preservation of good Order, to form certain Rules and Regulations for the internal Government of this County, until Laws shall be provided for us by the Congress.

4. That the Inhabitants of this County do meet on a certain Day appointed by this Committee, and having formed themselves into nine Companies, to wit, eight for the County and one for the Town of Charlotte, do choose a Colonel, and other military Officers, who shall hold and exercise their several Powers by Virtue of this Choice, and independent of Great-Britain, and former Constitution of this Province.

5. That for the better Preservation of the Peace, and Administration of Justice, each of these Companies do choose from their own Body two discreet Freeholders, who shall be impowered each by himself, and

singly, to decide and determine all Matters of Controversy arising within the said Company under the Sum of Twenty Shillings, and jointly and together all Controversies under the Sum of Forty Shillings, yet so as their Decisions may admit of Appeals to the Convention of the Select Men of the whole County; and also, that any one of these shall have power to examine, and commit to Confinement, Persons accused of Petit Larceny.

6. That those two Select Men, thus chosen, do, jointly and together, choose from the Body of their particular Company two Persons, properly qualified to serve as Constables, who may assist them in the execution of their Office.

7. That upon the Complaint of any Person to either of these Select Men, he do issue his Warrant, directed to the Constable, commanding him to bring the Aggressor before him or them to answer the said Complaint.

8. That these Eighteen Select Men, thus appointed, do meet every third *Tuesday* in *January*, *April*, and *October*, at the Court-House in *Charlotte* to hear and determine all Matters of Controversy for Sums exceeding Forty Shillings; also Appeals: And in Cases of Felony, to commit the Person or Persons convicted thereof to close Confinement, until the Provincial Congress shall provide and establish Laws and Modes of Proceeding in Such Cases.

9. That these Eighteen Select Men, thus convened, do choose a Clerk to record the Transactions of the said Convention; and that the said Clerk, upon the Application of any Person or Persons aggrieved, do issue his Warrant to one of the Constables, to summons and warn the said Offender to appear before the Convention at their next sitting, to answer the aforesaid Complaint.

10. That any Person making Complaint upon Oath to the Clerk, or any Member of the Convention, that he has Reason to suspect that any Person or Persons indebted to him in a Sum above Forty Shillings, do intend clandestinely to withdraw from the County without paying such Debt; the Clerk, or such Member, shall issue his Warrant to the Constable, commanding him to take the said Person or Persons into safe Custody, until the next sitting of the Convention.

11. That when a Debtor for a Sum below Forty Shillings shall abscond and leave the County, the Warrant granted as aforesaid shall extend to any Goods or Chattels of the said Debtor as may be found,

and such Goods or Chattels be seized and held in Custody by the Constable for the space of Thirty Days; in which Term if the Debtor fails to return and Discharge the Debt, the Constable shall return the Warrant to one of the Select Men of the Company where the Goods and Chattels were found, who shall issue Orders to the Constable to sell such a part of the said Goods as shall amount to the Sum due; that when the Debt exceeds Forty Shillings, the Return shall be made to the Convention, who shall issue the Orders for Sale.

12. That Receivers and Collectors of Quitrents, Public and County Taxes, do pay the same into the Hands of the Chairman of this Committee, to be by them disbursed as the public Exigencies may require. And that such Receivers and Collectors proceed no farther in their Office until they be approved of by, and have given to this Committee good and sufficient Security for a faithful return of such Monies when collected.

13. That the Committee be accountable to the County for the Application of all Monies received from such Officers.

14. That all these Officers hold their Commissions during the Pleasure of their respective Constituents.

15. That this Committee will sustain all Damages that may ever hereafter accrue to all or any of these Officers thus appointed, and thus acting, on Account of their Obedience and Conformity to these Resolves.

16. That whatever Person shall hereafter receive a Commission from the Crown, or attempt to exercise any such Commission heretofore received, shall be deemed an Enemy to his Country; and upon Information being made to the Captain of the Company where he resides the said Captain shall cause him to be apprehended, and conveyed before the two Select Men of the said Company, who, upon Proof of the Fact, shall commit him the said Offender into safe Custody, until the next sitting of the Convention, who shall deal with him as Prudence may direct.

17. That any Person refusing to yield Obedience to the above Resolves shall be deemed equally criminal, and liable to the same Punishments as the Offenders above last mentioned.

18. That these Resolves be in full Force and Virtue, until Instructions from the General Congress of this Province, regulating the Jurisprudence of this Province, shall provide otherwise, or the Legislative

Body of Great-Britain resign its unjust and arbitrary Pretentions with Respect to America.

19. That the several Militia Companies in this county do provide themselves with proper arms and accoutrements, and hold themselves in constant Readiness to execute the commands and Directions of the Provincial Congress, and of this committee.

20. That this committee do appoint Colonel Thomas Polk, and Doctor Joseph Kennedy, to purchase 300 lb. of Powder, 600 lb. of Lead, and 1000 Flints; and deposit the same in some safe place, hereafter to be appointed by the committee.

EPH. BREVARD, Clerk of the Committee.
Signed by Order of the Committee.

CHARLOTTE AND MECKLENBURG CEMETERIES

Many of the people whose names appear in this history no longer frequent the busy thoroughfares. Had they not lived, there would probably be no book, certainly not one of such dimensions. Gravestones are constant reminders of the debts we owe for today's blessings. And, somewhere in each burial ground, rest those valiant guardsmen who gave their all for the preservation of justice, liberty, and freedom.

Prior to 1853, church yards and private graveyards throughout Mecklenburg County were the only spots used for burying the dead. In that year, the City of Charlotte established Elmwood Cemetery. All of the early churches mentioned in this history and many that followed had burial grounds nearby. For many of these old cemeteries, especially those apart from churches, there are no records available beyond a few weatherbeaten, hard to decipher stones. Such information as has been compiled for others was recorded many years after the cemeteries were begun, mostly for the use of genealogists. Records are available in the Public Library of Charlotte for graves in the Cemetery of the First Presbyterian Church of Charlotte (compiled by Miss Violet Alexander in 1936 and copied by Anne Gillylen Quarles (Mrs. J. Perrin Quarles); Steele Creek Cemetery (compiled by Mrs. Robert E. McDowell and published in pamphlet form by the church); Sharon and Paw Creek Cemeteries (compiled by the North Carolina Historical Records Survey).

PUBLICLY OWNED CEMETERIES

The Old Settlers' Cemetery located in the second block of West Fifth Street (frequently referred to as Cemetery of the First Presbyterian Church) was the first cemetery to be owned and operated by the City of Charlotte. Dates on the old monuments and markers read from 1776 to 1884. Burials were made there until a few years before the War Between the States when Elmwood Cemetery was opened. It is interesting to note that a part of this cemetery, the northwest section, was used for the burial of colored servants of the lot owners.

The first reported burial at Elmwood Cemetery was in the year 1853. This cemetery has an area of 87 acres with 18,915 recorded burials. By 1947 all lots in Elmwood had been sold.

Pinewood Cemetery, for colored people, located on West Ninth Street, was started about the same time as Elmwood Cemetery, though the first recorded burial was January 4, 1895. When all lots were sold in the Ninth Street Pinewood Cemetery, the city purchased 12 acres just off North Summit Avenue and West Pinewood Cemetery was opened with the first burial April 2, 1935. Later it became necessary to further enlarge Negro cemetery facilities and the city purchased 15 acres for establishment of North Pinewood Cemetery in 1947.

On July 19, 1944, the City Council authorized the purchase of 200 acres of land on Albemarle Road for the sum of $34,147.50 for establishment of Evergreen Cemetery. The first burial was on January 25, 1947. A memorial monument erected by the Gold Star Mothers occupies a prominent position in the cemetery, as does another triangular plot known as "Veteran's Rest," for the burial of veterans, male or female, of all wars.

During 1956 the City of Charlotte acquired, as a gift, Oaklawn Cemetery, from Mrs. Adele Lynch Hendrix who, with her husband, had inherited it from the founder, J. J. Misenheimer. This cemetery has an area of about 47 acres, including one acre on which the mausoleum is located.

CORPORATELY OWNED CEMETERIES

In addition to publicly owned cemeteries, Charlotte and vicinity has several fine cemeteries owned and managed by private corporations. The oldest of these is the Hebrew Cemetery, established in 1868 by the Hebrew Benevolent Society of Charlotte, N. C. When opened, this burial ground was in a secluded outlying section, well beyond the city limit, but now is officially listed as 1801 McCall Street, in a thickly settled neighborhood well within the city proper.

The most elegant privately owned cemetery is Sharon Memorial Park and Mausoleum at 5400 Monroe Road, conceived by Dr. W. L. Halberstadt and managed by him with the assistance of his sons. Others, also of high standing, include Forest Lawn Burial Park on New Thrift Road, Sunset Memorial Gardens on Lawyers Road, and, for Negroes, York Memorial Park Cemetery.

SOURCE FOR EARLY HISTORY OF CHARLOTTE'S MUNICIPAL GOVERNMENT

In 1902 there was published, by authority of the Mayor and Board of Aldermen, and compiled by Clarkson & Duls, City Attorneys, *The Code of the City of Charlotte*, containing "The Charter and all Acts amending it, and also the act providing for the establishment of Public Schools and the amendments thereof; act creating Water Commissioners; Primary Law and Election Law for the City of Charlotte, and all other acts pertaining specially to the government of the city, together with ordinances and street railway contracts, etc. etc."

At the back of this book there is a lengthy "Unofficial Appendix," which contains:

List of members of the governing bodies 1816-1902

Municipal indebtedness, itemized as of 1902

List of properties owned by the City of Charlotte

Partial Index to the Minutes of the City Council on the following subjects:

References to the Male and Female Academy

List of lots sold by the town commissioners

Resolutions appropriating money

Ordinances relating to railroad bonds

Resolutions on the death of aldermen and other officials

Water Works and Sewage matters

Telephone, Telegraph, Light and Other Contracts

Graded School matters

Ordinances relating to the sale of liquors

N. C. Supreme Court Cases which the City was a party to, and many other miscellaneous matters.

A copy of this book is shelved in the Carolina Room of the Public Library of Charlotte, and one in the office of the City Clerk of the City of Charlotte.

SUGAR CREEK OR SUGAW CREEK?

The confusion over the spelling and pronunciation of the name of this well-known Mecklenburg County creek is due to the difficulty of translating the sound of an unwritten Indian word into written English.

This creek undoubtedly takes its name from the Sugeree Indians (John Lawson's spelling) or Sugaree Indians (Douglas L. Rights' spelling). The name was pronounced Sugaw or Soogaw, according to William Henry Foote.

The predominant version in records of the Presbyterian Church, Colonial Records of North Carolina, and in old deeds is "Sugar," although such variations as "Suger," "Shugar," "Sugercreek," and "Suga," have been found in various records.

In 1924 the Pastor of Sugar Creek Presbyterian Church, evidently influenced by Foote's pronunciation, had the Mecklenburg Presbytery officially change the spelling of the name of the church to "Sugaw." This action seems never to have been rescinded, notwithstanding that all historical evidence available tends to prove that the original name of "Sugar" should apply to both church and creek. The Indian word from which Sugar is derived means "group of huts."

CHARLOTTE'S FIRST AUTOMOBILE SHOW

Charlotte's first automobile show was held the week of April 11, 1921, in the "Standard Oil Building," located on the corner of West First Street and Cedar Street. Forty-nine cars and trucks were exhibited by 47 dealers, and there were exhibits by 14 accessory firms. Among cars exhibited were Ford, Veilie, Maxwell, Buick, Cleveland, Davis, Oakland, Chevrolet, Briscoe, Nash, Dort, Essex, Paige, Stutz, Gardner, Willys-Knight, Studebaker, and Milburn Electric.

UNITED CONFEDERATE VETERANS REUNION
JUNE 4-7, 1929

One of the most notable of Charlotte's many celebrations was the 39th Reunion of the United Confederate Veterans on June 4 through 7, 1929. This is the event for which the Armory-Auditorium was hastened to completion. "Eleven Confederate Generals joined in issuing a statement declaring the Charlotte Reunion to be the best in every way of any of the preceding 38 reunions." The reunion was climaxed on Friday the 7th with a huge parade witnessed by many notables, made up of nearly a score of bands, military units, and visiting veterans in automobiles.

CHARLOTTE SPEEDWAY

One of, if not the most important sporting event in Charlotte history was the first 250 mile automobile race held on the Charlotte Speedway, October 24, 1924. This race culminated efforts by a group composed of Osmond L. Barringer, C. Lane Etheredge, B. D. Heath, Ira C. Triplett, George Wadsworth, and others to build a $380,000, one and one-quarter mile, oval, wooden speedway. The Speedway owned 283 acres on the Columbia highway, 9 miles south of Charlotte. The enterprise was financed by a bond issued of $150,000 and stock sales of $230,000.

The winner of the 250 mile race was Tommy Milton, who broke the world's record by averaging 118.7 miles per hour. Earl Cooper placed second, and Bennet Hill, third.

THE FLOOD OF 1916 IN NORTH CAROLINA

Mecklenburg County was one of the most heavily damaged areas of North Carolina from the unprecedented flood which swept western North Carolina July 14, 15, and 16, 1916. Rainfall at Charlotte which began on Thursday, July 13, increased to storm proportions on Friday the 14th. High winds Friday night did much damage and on Saturday morning, the 15th, the city looked "like a cyclone had struck it."

Charlotte, with a precipitation of only five inches in the 24-hour period, came off lightly compared with other sections of the state. The storm was centered in the vicinity of Asheville where rainfall exceeded all past records and the damage was tremendous. At nearby Altapass the maximum rainfall of 22.22 inches was the highest 24-hour precipitation ever recorded in the United States. The Catawba River, rising in Western North Carolina, was the chief outlet for this deluge. As a result the principal damage in Mecklenburg County was confined to the Catawba River, where all bridges of the river were destroyed as was much adjacent property. Total overall property damage of the flood was estimated at $21,724,085. Best estimates place the loss of life at about 80. Details of this catastrophe are contained in three books: Bell, W. M., *The North Carolina Flood;* Southern Railway, *The Floods of July 1916;* and Greene, Ivery C., *A Disasterous Flood.*

CHARLOTTE'S LEOPARDITE STONE

The stone representing North Carolina, and so inscribed, in the Washington Monument was quarried in the Belmont section of Charlotte. The first stone was rejected by the Washington Monument Committee and a second stone was cut and accepted. This stone was selected because, insofar as is known, it is found nowhere else in the United States.

The rejected stone was secured by Adam Brevard Davidson and brought back to Charlotte where it was set in the ground of his home as a carriage stone. Colonel E. L. Baxter Davidson, son of the owner, inherited the stone which was later placed on the sidewalk at the northeast corner of Tryon and Trade Streets in front of the building owned by the Davidson estate. There it remained until street improvements in the 1940's required its removal. The stone then found a permanent home on the grounds of the Mint Museum of Art in the Eastover section of Charlotte.

STREET CAR STRIKE IN CHARLOTTE

Charlotte's most serious labor disturbance occurred near midnight on August 25, 1919, when five men were killed and more than a dozen wounded by police guarding car barns of the Southern Public Utilities Company against damage by striking conductors and motormen. Operatives of street cars owned by Southern Public Utilities Company in Charlotte and other cities went on strike August 10, 1919, for higher wages and union recognition. When the company attempted to operate cars with new employees, various depredations were committed by strikers and sympathizers. Conditions became gradually more tense until the evening of August 25 when a large crowd assembled in front of the car barns on South Boulevard.

Protection of the property was undertaken by a group of 12 or 15 armed officers under Chief Walter B. Orr. A rope deadline was stretched along the sidewalk on the opposite side of the street from the car barns. When pressure collapsed this line, the crowd surged forward and police were ordered to fire. More than 100 shots were fired by police and attackers. Within minutes three men were dead and many wounded. Later two other men died as a result of wounds, and many who had been less seriously injured reported to hospitals.

Wild rumors of retaliation by union members and their friends impelled Mayor Frank R. McNinch to summon and appoint a citizens' protective committee. By three or four o'clock in the morning several hundred men had reported to the City Hall, then located at the corner of North Tryon and Fifth Streets. As each man arrived, he was given a gun from the local armory, with ammunition, and assigned to a patrol station. At the same time calls were sent to nearby towns for units of the National Guard. First to arrive at 8 A.M. were troops from Lexington, followed quickly by troops from Statesville, Lincolnton, Hickory, Durham, and Winston-Salem.

Troops were demobilized August 30 and no major disturbances occurred thereafter, though cars were operated by men recruited from throughout North and South Carolina. On September 5 the strike was officially terminated by a contract in which both sides made concessions, and all striking employees were retained.

OLD WAYSIDE

From about 1925 until 1942 "Old Wayside," the *nom de plume* assumed by Harold C. Brown, was well known throughout the Carolinas. Among shut-ins he was even more widely known and loved.

Mr. Brown was born in London, England, September 6, 1879. After finishing college and two years in the British army, he came to America. During his first years in America he was an actor in various stock companies and carnivals. He was then stricken with infantile paralysis which left him so severely crippled that he was obliged to use a wheelchair the balance of his life.

He settled in Charlotte and from then on, from his dingy hotel room, devoted his theatrical and poetic talents to cheering shut-ins. Beginning December 16, 1926, he wrote an inspirational column for the *Charlotte Observer*. Thereafter, news of his fine work spread rapidly.

The Charlotte Lions Club sponsored the building of a cottage on Wilkinson Boulevard in Charlotte for Mr. Brown. From this cottage he conducted the affairs of the "Wayside Gang" and edited the magazine, *The Waysider*, which had been established. For a number of years he continued to spread good cheer by means of his column in the *Observer*, his magazine, many appearances at meetings, and on radio until his death, which occurred in a Charlotte hospital April 8, 1942.

PAGEANTS IN CHARLOTTE

During the first half of the 20th Century three elaborate pageants were staged to portray early historic events occurring in Charlotte and Mecklenburg.

PAGEANT OF CHARLOTTE AND OLD MECKLENBURG

The first and most elaborate of these dramatizations was performed to celebrate the sesquicentennial anniversary of the signing of the Mecklenburg Declaration of Independence. A pageant entitled *The Pageant of Charlotte and Old Mecklenburg* was written by Thomas Wood Stevens, a prominent writer of that period who was engaged for the purpose. It was presented for five nights, May 18-22, 1925, in an amphitheater planned by Earl S. Draper and built for the occasion in Independence Park, Charlotte.

The pageant presented nine episodes in the history of Charlotte, beginning with Indian settlements as found by the earliest settlers and concluding with the last meeting of the Confederate Cabinet in Charlotte, April 18-26, 1865. The cast consisted of between 200 and 300 men and women and included some of the city's most prominent citizens. The federal government appropriated $15,000 toward the cost and President Coolidge appointed a large committee of senators, congressmen and other important men and women who attended the pageant and witnessed the parade on the morning of May 20, 1925. Subsequently, this pageant was published in an attractive book and sold widely.

SHOUT FREEDOM!

Shout Freedom!, a symphonic drama in two acts, was presented on the Southern States Fair Grounds, near Charlotte, by way of celebrating the anniversary of the signing of the Mecklenburg Declaration of Independence in 1948. This pageant was presented nightly May 20 through June 3, except Sunday, and attended by large audiences from all over western North and South Carolina. Sponsored by a group of patriotic citizens who formed a corporation entitled Mecklenburg Historical Society, *Shout Freedom!* was written by LeGette Blythe. The music was composed and directed by Lamar Stringfield; the stage settings were designed by Kenneth Whitsett; and the stage directing was done by Thomas B. Humble.

The pageant commemorated, by dramatization, the stirring events comprising Charlotte history from 1768 until 1781. Mr. Norman Cordon acted as narrator and the cast comprised 210 men, women, and children, including a group of Indians from Pembroke State College and vicinity. Officers of the corporation were Joe L. Blythe, president; George M. Ivey, Sr., vice-president; R. E. Kerr, treasurer; Dr. J. S. Dorton, executive director, and Charles Dudley, secretary.

VOICE IN THE WILDERNESS

Voice in the Wilderness, an outdoor play with music, song, dancing, and pantomime, was staged at the Southern States Fair Grounds, near Charlotte, June 14, 15, 16, and 19, 1955, in commemoration of the two hundredth anniversary of the establishment of Presbyterianism in the region of Mecklenburg County. It is the story, in dramatic form, of the rise and growth of Presbyterianism locally. The play was written by LeGette Blythe and produced by a cast of more than 400 men, women, and children. More than 20,000 persons attended the performances. This pageant was recorded on film and subsequently published as a book in an edition limited to 512 copies.

CHARLOTTE MANUFACTURED RIFLES

The *Washington Post* of June 16, 1901, carries an article by William Hugh Robarts entitled "Our National Weapon-Rise and Development of the American Rifle" which reads:

"The rifle became so popular in the South that a factory for making the hunting rifle was established at Charlotte, N. C., about 1740. The founders came from Leman's Rifle Factory at Lancaster, Pa., which is in existence to this day. The arm turned out there was unquestionably the best, because the most carefully constructed, rifle then made in America.

" 'General Washington's favorite weapon was the rifle,' says George W. Park Custer, in a most interesting little personal memorandum printed by Mr. Custer for private distribution. 'He (Washington) received a fine English ducking gun as a gift from some British admirers but up to his death he preferred to use the rifle and was a good shot. His was presented to him in 1787 by Maj. Nicholas who was his chief at every battle of the Revolution but one, and he was absent then because he was wounded. The rifle was made in Charlotte, N. C. It is four feet in length and 42 of its bullets weigh one pound. The wood extends the full length of the barrel, and the entire piece is handsomely mounted with silver. The lock is beautiful work. I have known the General to kill a deer at 150 yards with this rifle.'

"This same Charlotte rifle-making firm in 1777 presented General Washington with the finest and undoubtedly the first pair of rifle pistols ever made in America. They had twelve inch barrels carrying four ounce balls and would shoot with the accuracy of a rifle at fifty or sixty feet. They saved the General's life at Germantown but that story, though a most interesting one, does not belong here."

COLONEL THOMAS LEROY KIRKPATRICK
AND PRESIDENT WILSON

Among Charlotte lawyers of the 20th century, none will be remembered more vividly than Colonel Thomas LeRoy Kirkpatrick, good roads enthusiast, mayor, public servant extraordinary, and orator. It was he who spoke three times as long in introducing President Wilson as the President, himself, spoke when visiting Charlotte for the May 20th celebration in 1916. Of this event Mrs. Edith Bolling Wilson, widow of the President, has this to say in her book *My Memoir* (1938).

"It was a boiling day. The ceremonies were in the open to accommodate the thousands of people from all over the state who had poured into town. A large wooden platform had been set up, with no cover, not even an awning; and rows of chairs placed to seat the official party, all facing a blazing afternoon sun. The hapless Marine Band had been summoned from Washington and they wore the thick, red uniform coats of winter weight. It was terrible for them. Fortunately for me, I was wearing a thin white dress and a large straw hat—which did afford a little shelter.

"The front of the platform was draped in bunting, and a table with ice water and glasses placed before the Mayor of Charlotte who was to make the address of welcome and introduce the President.

"This dignitary arose—and I can see him as though it were yesterday! He was about five feet high and wore a frock coat that must have belonged originally to an ancestor who was a giant; for the tails of the coat just escaped the ground, and the sleeves were of proportionate length. Nothing daunted by this handicap the little man began and, as he warmed to his subject, the sleeves were pulled above his elbows, the coattails would be lifted nearly as high as his head, and after holding them there a few minutes the hands would release them only to come down with forensic force on the table where the pitcher and glasses would jangle their contribution to the uproar. On and on and on he went, thirty, forty, fifty minutes—when suddenly the members of the Marine Band began to succumb. They dropped like flies, and the valiant little Boy Scouts tried to lift and carry them to some blessed shade.

"The speaker would look at the prostrate forms, but, with a debonair flirt of his coattails, attack another page of the typed matter before him. Hardly had the band received first aid when women all around me began to faint, and the scouts, with perspiration pouring down their boyish faces, came to tender their services.

"At last he stopped, for lack of breath I think, and sat down more like a vanquished prize fighter than anything else I can think of; for both cuffs had slipped their moorings, and one was open. His hair was standing on end and the necktie had sought sanctuary under his left ear. "My husband's address was calm and mercifully short."

Following the two speeches that day, a stranger who just happened along remarked to a bystander, "That was a wonderful speech the little guy made—and the tall fellow who followed wasn't so bad either."

CALENDAR OF HISTORIC DATES
CHARLOTTE AND MECKLENBURG COUNTY

Since the material in this history is treated topically, the following chronological list of events and movements which have taken place locally may be helpful to the reader.

1750 Trade routes from Charlotte to Charleston established over Indian Trails.

1762 December 11. Mecklenburg County created by Act of the Legislature, from Anson County (effective February 1, 1763).

1766 First log courthouse built in Charlotte.

1766 Dr. John Kennedy, first physician in Mecklenburg, was practicing medicine. The second was Dr. Ephraim Brevard.

1767 January 15. 360 acres purchased for site of Charlotte by Abraham Alexander, Thomas Polk, and John Frohock from George Augustus Selwyn for ninety pounds.

1768 November 7. Charlotte incorporated.

1768 Tryon County formed from Mecklenburg.

1770 Jeremiah McCafferty opens first store in Charlotte.

1771 Queens College, later Queens Museum, opened in Charlotte.

1771 Presbyterian ministers given permission by the King to perform marriages, a privilege which had been restricted to ministers of the Church of England.

1773 Governor Martin gives notice that the King has disallowed the charter for Queens College.

1774 Charlotte designated as County Seat of Mecklenburg County.

1775 May 20. Mecklenburg Declaration of Independence signed at Charlotte.

1775 May 31. Signers of Mecklenburg Declaration reassemble and draw up Mecklenburg Resolves.

1775 June 3. Captain James Jack arrived in Philadelphia with Mecklenburg Declaration of Independence.

1777 Liberty Hall incorporated (successor to Queens Museum).

1780 October 3. Skirmish at McIntyre's farm (Battle of the Bees).

1780 October 12. Cornwallis withdraws from Charlotte referring to the place as a "Hornets' Nest."

1780 Epidemic of smallpox strikes Charlotte.

1780 Colonel Thomas Polk appointed Commissary General by General Nathaniel Greene.

1781 February 1. Battle of Cowan's Ford in which General William Davidson was killed.

1790 Gold first discovered in sections of Mecklenburg which in 1792 became a part of Cabarrus County.

1791 Saturday, May 28. President George Washington visited Charlotte.

1792 Cabarrus County created from eastern section of Mecklenburg.

1792 Andrew Jackson licensed to practice law in Mecklenburg.

1792 United States Post Office established in Charlotte.

1795 November 21. James Knox Polk, 11th President of the United States, born in Mecklenburg, 12 miles south of Charlotte.

1805 Nathaniel Alexander elected governor—the first citizen of Mecklenburg to be so honored.

1812-1814 Five companies of Mecklenburg troops serve throughout the War of 1812.

1815 Property bounded by Trade, Church, Sixth, and Poplar Streets set aside for church and cemetery purposes by all denominations.

1816 First law enforcement officer appointed in Charlotte, called "Town Watch."

1823 August. Earliest church building in Charlotte dedicated by Rev. Dr. McRee (or McCree).

1824 October 4. First issue of first newspaper published in Charlotte, *The Catawba Journal*.

1830 *Miner's and Farmer's Journal* states "talk about dissolution of the Union has become so common as not to excite horror, as it once did."

1833 Sons of Temperance organized.

1834 Branch of the North Carolina Bank opened at Charlotte.

1837 October 19. Branch of the United States Mint begins operation with John H. Wheeler as Superintendent.

1838 Charlotte Male Academy opens.

1842 Union County formed from Anson and Mecklenburg Counties.

1847 April. Company of Dragoons under Green W. Caldwell leaves for Vera Cruz to serve in Mexican War.

1852 October 21. First passenger train arrives in Charlotte.

1852 First telegraph office opened in Charlotte—succeeded by Western Union Telegraph Company in 1856.

1856 Railroad from Charlotte to Goldsboro completed.

1857 January 19. Charlotte Female Institute organized, forerunner of Presbyterian College for Women (1896) and later Queens College.

1858 First street gas lights turned on in Charlotte.

1859 North Carolina Military Institute opens with Daniel Harvey Hill as Headmaster.

1861 United States Mint—Charlotte Branch appropriated for military organizations by Confederate authorities.

1861 May 20. North Carolina seceded from the Union.

1861 April. Faculty and cadets of North Carolina Military Institute go to Raleigh to drill troops for service in War for Southern Independence.

1862 May. Center of Naval Ordnance of Confederate States of America moved to Charlotte from Norfolk, Virginia.

1864 January 7. Confederate munitions and supplies located in Charlotte destroyed in $10,000,000 fire.

1865 April 18. Jefferson Davis, President of the Confederacy, arrives in Charlotte with his Cabinet, gets first news of Lincoln's assassination.

1865 April 20. Last full meeting of Confederate Cabinet held in Charlotte.

1865 May 7. Capt. M. C. Runyan and 9th New Jersey Volunteers occupy Charlotte.

1867 Biddle University, later to become Johnson C. Smith University, founded.

1867 December. United States Mint reopened as assay office only, with Isaac W. Jones, assayer.

1869 January 25. First daily issue of the *Charlotte Observer;* name and ownership subsequently changed several times.

1872 Last of Federal troops depart following occupancy which began at the close of the war.

1873 October 21. First graded school opened in North Carolina at Charlotte by Dr. J. B. Boone.

1874 Last stage line discontinued—the route was between Wadesboro and Charlotte.

1875 February 18. Commercial National Bank chartered (North Carolina National Bank).

1875 May 20. Centennial celebration of signing of Mecklenburg Declaration of Independence, attended by 30,000 people.

1881 First cotton mill in Mecklenburg begins operation.

1882 September 11. First tax supported public school opened in Charlotte.

1887 Thompson Orphanage organized.

1887 First electric street lights installed.

1887 Horse-drawn cars first appear in Charlotte.

1888 *Charlotte News* established.

1890 Dilworth real estate development began.

1891 February 12. Public library service began in Charlotte with incorporation of Charlotte Literary and Library Association.

1891 September 23. Good Samaritan Hospital dedicated.

1892 September 17. Adlai Stevenson, Vice-President of the United States, visits Charlotte.

1893 Electric street cars replace horse-drawn cars.

1895 Presbyterian College opened—later Queens College.

1897 Charlotte National Bank chartered (Wachovia Bank and Trust Company).

1898 Presbyterian Hospital began as private institution—later presented to group of Presbyterian churches and opened by them February 24, 1903.

1898 December 11. Two companies from Charlotte in the North Carolina regiment land in Havana in Spanish-American War.

1901 July 15. American Trust Company began business as Southern States Trust Company (North Carolina National Bank).

1902 February. Deepest snow recorded in Charlotte, 17.4 inches.

1903 July 2. Carnegie Library opened.

1904 Automobiles first mentioned in business section of Charlotte City Directory.

1904 Southern Railway Passenger Station, originally built in the 1880's, greatly enlarged and redesigned to resemble "Moorish" architectural style.

1905 January 1. Prohibition becomes effective in Charlotte as a result of election held July 5, 1904.

1905 October 19. President Theodore Roosevelt visits Charlotte.

1906 Mercy Hospital founded at 8 East First Street.

1907 Motion pictures first mentioned in business section of Charlotte City Directory. Theatre names: Odeon and Wonderland.

1909 May 20. President William Howard Taft visits Charlotte in torrential rain.

1909 First Charlotte skyscraper (Independence Building) built on northwest corner Trade and Tryon Streets.

1913 July 1. United States Mint—Charlotte Branch closed finally.

1913 Myers Park residential development began with opening of Queens Road. First home that of Mr. and Mrs. Word H. Wood.

1914 September 23. Queens College opened campus on Selwyn Avenue.

1916 May 20. President and Mrs. Woodrow Wilson visit Charlotte.

1916 July 14-16. North Carolina flood.

1917 March 9. Mecklenburg Chapter American Red Cross formed.

1917 Camp Greene, temporary U. S. cantonment, constructed at Charlotte.

1918 January 21. First of 10 holidays in eastern half of United States ordered by Fuel Administration to conserve fuel for war purposes; commonly called "Heatless Mondays."

1918 January 24. "Cerebro Spinal Meningitis" quarantine ordered in Charlotte for two weeks, closing all amusement places, churches, schools, libraries, Y.M.C.A., Y.W.C.A., and forbidding all public gatherings.

1918 October 24. Charlotte quarantined because of epidemic of "Spanish Influenza," 400 cases in Charlotte and many in Camp Greene.

1919 April 26. Mecklenburg Federation of Home Demonstration Clubs formally organized.

1919 August 25. Street car strike riot, killing five, wounding 25.

1920 July 14. First S & W Cafeteria opened at Charlotte.

1921 First inter-city bus line operated out of Charlotte by Love-Lowder Bus Lines.

1921 Radio Station WBT installed.

1921 Cameron Morrison of Charlotte elected Governor of North Carolina.

1922 May 20. General John J. Pershing visits Charlotte.

1922 "Radio apparatus" first mentioned in business section of Charlotte City Directory.

1922 December 16-17. Trust Building, housing Academy of Music and many offices, burned and, along with it, Brockmann's, dealers in books and office equipment.

1924   October 23. Charlotte City Hall at 600 East Trade Street, cornerstone laid. Building formally opened October 29, 1925.
1925   January. Charlotte Music Club organized.
1927   March 7. Carolina Theatre opened.
1927   December 1. Federal Reserve Bank Branch opened.
1928   Spring. Mecklenburg County Court House at 700 East Trade Street opened.
1929   June 2. Armory-Auditorium completed. Burned June 8, 1954. Rebuilt and renamed Park Center.
1930   April 2. First air mail service to Charlotte, Pilot Gene Brown.
1930   Radio Station WSOC began operation.
1932   Charlotte Symphony Orchestra organized.
1936   American Legion Memorial Stadium completed.
1936   Municipal Airport opened.
1936   September 10. President Franklin Delano Roosevelt visits Charlotte as guest of honor at a "Green Pastures Rally."
1936   October 22. Mint Museum of Art formally opened.
1937   Repeal referendum won by "Drys."
1938   Buses replace street cars for local transportation in Charlotte.
1939   June. Wachovia Trust Company merged with Charlotte National Bank.
1939   June 30. Charlotte Public Library closed when voters failed to approve appropriations for library purposes.
1940   March 15. Guthery Apartments fire in which eight persons were killed.
1940   July 1. Charlotte Public Library reopened when voters approved, by a vote of 10,172 to 1,966, on May 25, a maximum county-wide tax levy of four cents on the $100 valuation for library purposes.
1940   October 2. Memorial Hospital opened for patients.
1940   William R. Barringer Hotel opened, incorporated October 14, 1939.
1941   April 21. Morris Field dedicated with Mayor Fiorello La Guardia of New York City and Governor Broughton of North Carolina as principal speakers.
1942   Charlotte Navy Shell Loading Plant of the United States Rubber Company construction began June, production began December.
1944   March 19. First Methodist Church sanctuary dedicated. First Methodist Church formed in 1927 from Tryon Street Methodist (1840) and Trinity Methodist (1896).

1946 September. Charlotte Center of University of North Carolina founded—later (1949) Charlotte College.

1947 January 10. Charlotte City Club incorporated—formally opened June 1, 1948.

1947 June 14. Alcoholic Board of Control election won by "Wets." Seven stores opened September 27, 1947.

1947 September. Second Ward Extension School founded—later (1949) Carver College.

1947 November 12. Charlotte Christmas Festival Parade held—later (1950) Carolinas Carrousel.

1947 Television first mentioned in business section of Charlotte City Directory.

1948 June. Methodist Home for the Aged opened in Charlotte.

1953 December 20. Covenant Presbyterian Church holds first service in new sanctuary at 1000 East Morehead Street.

1954 May 18. President Dwight David Eisenhower visits Charlotte.

1954 July 10. Douglas Municipal Airport dedicated.

1955 September 11. Ovens Auditorium and Charlotte Coliseum dedicated.

1956 August 27. Independence Boulevard final link completed.

1956 November 19. Public Library of Charlotte and Mecklenburg County, Main Building at 310 North Tryon Street, and several branches officially opened.

1957 November 29. Commercial National Bank and American Trust Company merge to become American Commercial Bank. (North Carolina National Bank 1960.)

1958 February 16. Wachovia Bank Building, corner Trade and Church Streets, dedicated.

1959 March 4. North Carolina Legislature met in Charlotte for second time. First was February 22, 1939.

1959 December 31. Charlotte city limits greatly expanded.

1960 Charlotte's population passes 200,000.

POPULATION STATISTICS

	Mecklenburg County	City of Charlotte*		Mecklenburg County	City of Charlotte*
1790	11,395		1880	34,175	7,094
1800	10,439		1890	42,673	11,557
1810	14,272		1900	55,268	18,091
1820	16,895		1910	67,031	34,014
1830	20,073		1920	80,695	46,338
1840	18,273		1930	127,971	82,675
1850	13,914	1,065	1940	151,826	100,899
1860	17,374	2,265	1950	197,052	134,042
1870	24,299	4,473	1960	272,111	201,564

*Population not enumerated separately prior to 1850.

Of the above figures the Negro population has averaged between 25 and 30 per cent. It has been estimated that of the above whole number more than 99 per cent were native born.

MAYORS OF CHARLOTTE

1851-52 William K. Reid*	1880-83 F. S. DeWolfe
1852-53 Alexander Graham*	1883-84 W. C. Maxwell
1853-57 William F. Davidson*	1884-87 William Johnson
1857-59 David Parks*	1887-91 F. B. McDowell
1859-61 Jennings B. Kerr*	1891-95 R. J. Brevard
1861-62 William A. Owens	1895-97 J. H. Weddington
1862-63 Robert F. Davidson	1897-99 E. B. Springs
1863-64 L. S. Williams	1899-1901 J. D. McCall
1864-65 Samuel A. Harris	1901-05 Peter Marshall Brown
1865-66 H. M. Pritchard	1905-07 S. S. McNinch
1866-67 Samuel A. Harris	1907-09 T. S. Franklin
1867-68 F. W. Ahrens	1909-11 T. W. Hawkins
1868-69 H. M. Pritchard	1911-15 Charles A. Bland
1869-71 C. Dowd	1915-17 T. L. Kirkpatrick
1871-73 John A. Young	1917-20 Frank R. McNinch
1873-75 William F. Davidson	1920-21 John M. Wilson
1875-78 William Johnson	1921-24 James O. Walker
1878-79 B. R. Smith	1924-26 Harvey W. Moore
1879-80 F. I. Osborne	1926-27 D. M. Abernethy

* Called Intendant instead of Mayor.

1927-29 F. Marion Redd
1929-31 George E. Wilson, Jr.
1931-33 Charles E. Lambeth
1933-35 Arthur E. Wearn
1935-41 Ben E. Douglas
1941-43 E. McA. Currie

1943-49 H. H. Baxter
1949-53 Victor Shaw
1953-57 Philip L. Van Every
1957-61 James Saxon Smith
1961-to date Stanford R.
Brookshire

MAYORS OF DAVIDSON, NORTH CAROLINA

1884-89 Rev. W. P. Williams
1889-90 Z. A. Hovis
1890-91 R. W. Shelton
1891-95 W. P. Williams
1895-95 J. D. Brown
1895-1900 F. J. Knox
1900-20 J. Lee Sloan
1920-25 C. H. Hamilton

1925-26 J. Lee Sloan
1926-31 M. H. Goodrum
1931-33 Albert N. Adams
1933-40 T. M. Griffith
1940-40 J. B. Jetton
1940-45 E. A. Beaty
1945-47 W. V. Cole
1947-51 E. A. Beaty

1951-to date F. L. Jackson

MAYORS OF PINEVILLE, NORTH CAROLINA*

1896-98 J. A. Younts
1905-07 B. F. McWhirter
1907-12 Unknown
1912-13 George W. Bunch
1913-14 Z. M. Johnston
1914-15 W. B. Warwick
1915-16 M. T. Grimes

1916-17 E. Porter
1917-37 M. G. Hair
1937-43 Robert K. Taylor
1943-49 C. H. McCoy
1949-51 R. C. Hair
1951-55 C. H. McCoy
1955-59 R. C. Hair

1959-to date Frank A. Ferguson

*Early records unavailable.

MAYORS OF MATTHEWS, NORTH CAROLINA

1879-87 W. T. Carpenter
1887-93 S. J. Hooks
1896- Dr. Joseph Bruner
1905-07 S. B. Smith
1907-13 A. J. Williams
1913-21 W. L. Hood

1921-25 Thomas J. Orr
1925-29 Hugh F. McManus
1929-41 C. R. McLaughlin
1941-43 W. S. Morton
1943-45 E. M. Renfrow
1945-to date W. Alexis Hood

MAYORS OF HUNTERSVILLE, NORTH CAROLINA

A. Jones Hunter, 1877-1884
W. J. Ranson, to May 5, 1887
H. A. Grey, 1887-1889
H. K. DeArmon, 1889-Jan 16, 1890 (resigned)
J. T. Mayberry, Jan. 16, 1890-May 12, 1890
T. M. McConnell, 1890-1892
J. L. Choate, 1892-1893
D. S. Hamilton, 1893-Oct. 26, 1893 (resigned)
A. J. Blakely, Oct. 26, 1893-Nov. 14, 1893
H. A. Grey, Nov. 14, 1893-Dec. 13, 1893
J. L. Choate, Dec. 21, 1893-1894
G. F. Steele, 1894-1895
A. Darby, 1895-1896
C. F. Alexander, 1896-1897
W. S. Caldwell, 1897-1900
J. T. Mayberry, 1900-1903
W. S. Caldwell, 1903-1907

J. R. McCurdy, 1907-Nov. 25, 1907
W. S. Caldwell, Nov. 25, 1907-1909
J. L. Miller, 1909-Dec. 1916 (resigned)
Dr. E. M. McCoy, Dec. 1916-
C. L. Barnette, to May 10, 1921
C. B. Mooney, May 10, 1921-Aug. 24, 1923 (resigned)
C. B. Barnette, Aug. 24, 1923-1925
E. P. Page, 1925-1927
Dr. Thomas Craven, 1927-1940
O. L. Wagstaff, Sr., 1940-1945
T. S. Youngblood, 1945-1947
T. Lee Mullen, 1947-1955
Arthur W. Auten, 1955-1958 (resigned)
Thomas L. Ward, 1958-1961
Arthur W. Auten, Jr., 1961-

MAYORS OF CORNELIUS, NORTH CAROLINA

1905-06 J. B. Proctor
1907-10 Lawrence Hager
1911-12 John S. Sossamon
1913-14 Alec Little
1915-16 F. C. Sherrill, Sr.
1917-18 Joe A. Sherrill
1919-24 J. B. Readling
1925-26 W. L. Puckett

1927-34 W. E. Long
1935-37 H. K. Sossamon
1938-½ yr. L. B. Honeycutt
1939-46 G. E. Sweet
1947-48 J. E. Baxter
1949-50 G. E. Sweet
1951-56 Keith R. Howard
1957-to date B. S. Sherrill

MEMBERS OF GOVERNING BODIES CITY OF CHARLOTTE

Note: A list of city officials for years prior to 1900 is included in the *City Code*, published 1902. A copy of this book may be consulted in the Carolina Room of the Public Library of Charlotte, or in the office of the City Clerk.

A complete list of city officials who served both before 1900 and up to the present is an official record of the City of Charlotte and on file in the office of the City Clerk.

A list of Council members who have served since adoption of the City Manager form of government in 1929 follows:

Aitken, G. Douglas, 1949-51
Albea, Claude L., 1931-45, 1947- to date
Allison, T. T., 1931-33
Anderson, L. E., 1929-31
Atkins, J. Murrey, 1943-45
Babcock, Randolph, 1959-to date
Baker, J. A., 1941-45
Baxter, H. H., 1935-41, 1951-59
Beasley, C. C., 1941-43
Boyd, Basil M., 1949-55
Boyd, John F., 1931-37
Britt, C. S., 1939-41
Brown, Herman A., 1953-59
Bullard, W. Irvin, 1943-45
Childs, T. A., 1945-49
Coddington, Wm. I., 1949-53
Cope, Joe E., 1943-45
Daughtry, C. H., 1941-45
Daughtry, James H., 1949-51
Delaney, E. S., Jr., 1947-49
Dellinger, Steve W., 1951-to date
Doggett, G. O., 1929-31
Durham, John F., 1935-39
Evans, Martha W., 1955-59
Foard, Ernest W., 1957-59
Griswold, T. V., 1937-39
Guthery, V. J., 1929-33
Hinson, J. Sam, 1945-47
Hitch, Herbert, 1959-to date
Hovis, W. N., 1935-45
Hudson, W. Ray, 1935-41

Huntley, J. H., 1935-41
Johnston, J. H., 1945-47
Jones, J. A., 1929-31
Jordan, S. D., 1947-53
Kahn, Max, 1933-35
Lambeth, Charles E., 1947-49
Little, A. P., 1937-43
McIntyre, Fred H., 1945-47
McKee, Nash D., 1947-49
Myers, Brevard S., 1959-to date
Nance, J. S., 1935-41
Newson, Henry G., 1945-47
Painter, L. H., 1941-45
Price, A. Z., 1941-45
Puette, Ross, 1945-47
Ross, C. B., 1941-43
Sides, L. R., 1935-41
Slye, L. W., 1941-45
Smith, Gibson L., 1959-to date
Smith, James S., 1953-55
Squires, Dr. Claude, 1933-35
Tipton, J. S., 1935-37
Van Every, Philip L., 1951-53
Ward, J. S., 1939-45
Wearn, Arthur, 1932-34
White, John P., 1945-49
Whittington, James B., 1959- to date
Wilkinson, Emmett M., 1949-51
Wilkinson, J. L., 1935-41
Wilkinson, W. E., 1953-59

MECKLENBURG COUNTY BOARD OF COMMISSIONERS
1868-1960

Approximate Date Elected	Chairman	Commissioners
1868	R. M. Oates	S. M. Reid
		R. R. King
		R. L. Diamond
		Thos. L. Vail
1872	Thos L. Vail	R. R. King
		R. L. Diamond
		J. Watson Reid
		R. M. Oates
1874	Thos. L. Vail	R. L. DeArmon
		Wm. H. Neal
		M. M. Orr
		Thomas Gluyas
1878	Thos. L. Vail	A. G. Neal
		R. A. Torrence
		J. R. Morris
		T. T. Sandifer
1884	W. E. Ardrey	R. D. Whitley
		R. M. Oates
		John L. Brown
		John R. Morris
1890	Thos. L. Vail	
1892	B. H. Moore	
1896	John R. Ervin	J. H. Sadler
		W. F. Kuykendall
		J. H. McClintock
1898	Peter Marshall Brown	J. H. Sadler
		W. F. Kuykendall
1900	J. H. Weddington	P. C. Henderson
		W. G. McLaughlin
		Dr. J. P. Monroe
		J. B. Watt
1902	J. H. Weddington	B. T. Price
		W. G. McLaughlin
		H. J. Brown
		S. H. Kell

Approximate Date Elected	Chairman	Commissioners
1904	J. H. Weddington	B. T. Price
		Chalmers Furr
		H. J. Brown
		S. H. Kell
1906	W. M. Long	John B. Ross
		Chalmers Furr
		Wm. N. McKee
		D. A. Henderson
1908	W. M. Long	Wm. N. McKee
		D. A. Henderson
		J. A. Newell
		W. J. Dunn
1910	W. M. Long	Wm. N. McKee
		D. A. Henderson
		F. F. Beatty
		W. J. Dunn
1912	W. M. Long	Wm. N. McKee
		Wm. Bradford
		A. M. McDonald
		F. F. Beatty
1914	A. M. McDonald	J. L. Parks
		W. B. Bradford
		J. A. Newell
		W. M. Garrison
1916	A. M. McDonald	J. L. Parks
		Wm. Bradford
		J. A. Newell
		W. M. Garrison
1918	A. M. McDonald	W. M. Garrison
		J. L. Parks
		J. A. Newell
		Wm. Bradford
1920	J. B. McLaughlin	P. D. Price
		Joe H. Robinson
		W. M. Ross
		Z. B. Morris

Approximate *Date Elected*	*Chairman*	*Commissioners*
1922	J. B. McLaughlin	P. D. Price Joe H. Robinson W. M. Ross Z. B. Morris
1924	R. Neal Hood	J. A. Newell R. E. Henderson Joe H. Robinson W. M. Ross
1926	R. Neal Hood	J. A. Newell R. E. Henderson Joe H. Robinson W. M. Ross
1928	R. Neal Hood	J. A. Newell R. E. Henderson Joe H. Robinson W. M. Ross
1930	James A. Sherrill	W. H. Johnson W. Barnette Garrison U. Vaughn Hawkins
1932	James A. Sherrill	Henry W. Harkey W. Barnette Garrison Wm. H. Johnston U. Vaughn Hawkins
1934	Henry B. Fowler	Wm. B. Blythe Wm. H. Hall Henry W. Harkey Baxter J. Hunter
1936	Baxter J. Hunter	Sidney J. Worley Arnie D. Cashion Henry W. Harkey Robert F. Dunn
1938	Henry W. Harkey	Robert F. Dunn Edgar J. Price Arthur H. Wearn Joseph A. Sherrill

Approximate *Date Elected*	*Chairman*	*Commissioners*
1940	Henry W. Harkey	Arnie D. Cashion Harvey Morris Edgar J. Price Arthur H. Wearn
1942	Sidney Y. McAden	Arnie D. Cashion J.Caldwell McDonald Fred A. Hamilton Edgar J. Price
1944	Sidney Y. McAden	Arnie D. Cashion J.Caldwell McDonald Fred A. Hamilton Carl J. McEwen
1946	Sidney Y. McAden	Arnie D. Cashion J.Caldwell McDonald Sandy G. Porter Carl J. McEwen
1948	Sidney Y. McAden	Arnie D. Cashion J.Caldwell McDonald Sandy G. Porter Carl J. McEwen
1950	Sidney Y. McAden	J.Caldwell McDonald Carl J. McEwen Sandy G. Porter E. A. Beaty
1952	Sidney Y. McAden	Carl J. McEwen Ernest K. Brown S. S. McNinch W. Craig Lawing
1954	Sidney Y. McAden	S. S. McNinch John M. McEwen J. Herbert Garrison W. Craig Lawing
1956	Sidney Y. McAden	J. Herbert Garrison S. S. McNinch John M. McEwen W. Craig Lawing

Approximate		
Date Elected	*Chairman*	*Commissioners*
1958	Sidney Y. McAden	Ernest K. Brown
		J. Herbert Garrison
		John M. McEwen
		W. Craig Lawing
1960	Sidney Y. McAden	J. Frank Blythe
		Ernest K. Brown
		J. Herbert Garrison
		W. Craig Lawing

STATE SENATORS AND REPRESENTATIVES FROM MECKLENBURG COUNTY

MEMBERS OF HOUSE OF COMMONS*

Year
1764-65   Martin Fifer (Phifer)
           Richard Berry
1766-68   Thomas Polk
           Martin Fifer (Phifer)
1769   Abraham Alexander
           Thomas Polk
1770-71   Abraham Alexander
           Thomas Polk
1773 (Jan.) Martin Phifer (Fifer)
           John Davidson

MEMBERS OF THE PROVINCIAL CONGRESS*

1774 (Aug.)   Benjamin Patten
1775 (Apr.)
1775 (Aug.)   Thomas Polk
              John Phifer (Pfifer)
              Waightstill Avery
              Samuel Martin
              James Houston
              John McKnitt Alexander

*Names are spelled as they appear in the list of members preceding the journals of the congresses, with variations or modifications in parentheses.

1776 (Apr.)   John Pfifer (Phifer)
              Robert Irwin
              John McKnitt Alexander
1776 (Nov.)   John Pfifer (Phifer)
              Robert Erwin (Irwin)
              Zacheus Wilson
              Hezekiah Alexander
              Waightstill Avery

MEMBERS OF THE GENERAL ASSEMBLY

Year	Senators	Representatives
1777	John McK. Alexander	Martin Phifer
		Waightstill Avery
1778	Robert Irwin	Caleb Phifer
		David Wilson
1779	Robert Irwin	Caleb Phifer
		David Wilson
1780	Robert Irwin	Caleb Phifer
		David Wilson
1781	Robert Irwin	Caleb Phifer
		David Wilson
1782	Robert Irwin	Caleb Phifer
		David Wilson
1783	Robert Irwin	Caleb Phifer
		David Wilson
1784	Robert Irwin	Caleb Phifer
		David Wilson
1784	James Harris	Caleb Phifer
		David Wilson
1785	James Harris	Caleb Phifer
		George Alexander
1786	James Harris	Caleb Phifer
		George Alexander
1787	Robert Irwin	William Polk
		Caleb Phifer
1788	Joseph Graham	Caleb Phifer
		Joseph Douglass
1789	Joseph Graham	Caleb Phifer
		Joseph Douglass

Year	Senators	Representatives
1790	Joseph Graham	Robert Irwin
		William Polk
1791	Joseph Graham	Caleb Phifer
		Robert Irwin
1792	Joseph Graham	Caleb Phifer
		James Harris
1793	Robert Irwin	Charles Polk
		George Graham
1794	Robert Irwin	Charles Polk
		George Graham
1795	Robert Irwin	Charles Polk
		George Graham
1796	George Graham	David McKee
		William Morrison
1797	Robert Irwin	James Connor
		Nathaniel Alexander
1798	Robert Irwin	James Connor
		Hugh Parks
1799	Robert Irwin	James Connor
		Sherrod Gray
1800		Charles Polk
		Hugh Parks
1801	Nathaniel Alexander	Alexander Morrison
		Sherrod Gray
1802	Nathaniel Alexander	Alexander Morrison
		Thomas Henderson
1803	George Graham	Alexander Morrison
		Thomas Henderson
1804	George Graham	Thomas Henderson
		Samuel Lowrie
1805	George Graham	Samuel Lowrie
		George W. Smart
1806	George Graham	Samuel Lowrie
		Thomas Henderson
1807	George Graham	John Harris
1808	George Graham	George W. Smart
		John Harris
1809	George Graham	Thomas Henderson
		Hutchins G. Burton

460 APPENDIX

Year	Senators	Representatives
1810	George Graham	Thomas Henderson
		Hutchins G. Burton
1811	George Graham	Jonathan Harris
		Henry Massey
1812	George Graham	Jonathan Harris
		Henry Massey
1813	William Davidson	Cunningham Harris
		Jonathan Harris
1814	Jonathan Harris	William Beattie
		George Hampton
1815	William Davidson	John Ray
		Abdon Alexander
1816	William Davidson	Joab Alexander
		John Wilson
1817	William Davidson	John Rhea
		John Wilson
1818	William Davidson (Resigned)	John Rhea
	William Lee Davidson	John Wilson
1819	Michael McLeary	John Rhea
		Miles J. Robinson
1820	Michael McLeary	John Rhea
		Miles J. Robinson
1821	Michael McLeary	Samuel McComb
		John Rhea
1822	Michael McLeary	Matthew Bain
		John Rhea
1823	Michael McLeary	Thomas G. Polk
		Matthew Bain
1824	Michael McLeary	Thomas G. Polk
		Matthew Bain
1825	William Davidson	Thomas G. Polk
		Matthew Bain
1826	Michael McLeary	Matthew Bain
		Wm. Julius Alexander
1827	William Davidson	Joseph Blackwood
		William J. Alexander
1828	William Davidson	Joseph Blackwood
		William J. Alexander
1829	William Davidson	William J. Alexander
		Evan Alexander

Year	Senators	Representatives
1830	Joseph Blackwood	William J. Alexander
		Evan Alexander
1831	Henry Massey	James Dougherty
		John Hart
1832	Henry Massey	John Hart
		James Dougherty
1833	Washington Morrison	William J. Alexander
		Andrew Grier
1834	William H. McLeary	William J. Alexander
		James M. Hutchinson
1835	Stephen Fox	James M. Hutchinson
		James A. Dunn
1836	Stephen Fox	James M. Hutchinson
		Green W. Caldwell
		James A. Dunn
1838	Stephen Fox	Green W. Caldwell
		James T. J. Orr
		Caleb Irwin
1840	James T. J. Orr	Green W. Caldwell
		John Walker
		Benjamin Morrow
1842	John Walker	John Kirk
		Joseph W. Ross
		Caleb Irwin
1844	John Walker	Robert M. Lemmond
		James A. Dunn
		John Kirk
1846	John Walker	John W. Potts
		John N. Davis
		Robert Lemmons
1848	John Walker	Nehemiah A. Harrison
		James J. Williams
		John N. Davis
1850	Green W. Caldwell	James J. Williams
		John K. Harrison
		E. Constantine Davidson
1852	Green W. Caldwell	William Black
		James A. Dunn
		John Ingram

Year	Senators	Representatives
1854	John Walker	William R. Myers
		William Black
1858	William F. Davidson	Henry M. Pritchard
		Williamson Wallace
1860	John Walker	Stephen W. Davis
		John McK. Potts
1862	John A. Young	John L. Brown
		E. C. Grier
1864	W. M. Grier	John L. Brown
		E. C. Grier
1865	J. H. Wilson	James M. Hutchinson
		Robert D. Whitley
1866	J. H. Wilson	Robert D. Whitley
		James M. Hutchinson
1868	James W. Osborne	Robert D. Whitley
		W. Grier
1870	H. C. Jones	R. P. Waring
		J. C. Reid
1872	R. P. Waring	John E. Brown
		S. W. Reid
1874	R. P. Waring	J. L. Setton
		J. Sol Reid
1876	T. J. Moore	W. E. Ardrey
		Randolph A. Shotwell
1879	Sydenham B. Alexander	W. E. Ardrey
		J. L. Brown
1881	Armistead Burwell	A. G. Neal
		Edgar H. Walker
1883	Sydenham B. Alexander	W. H. Bailey
		J. S. Myers
		T. T. Sandifer
1885	Sydenham B. Alexander	W. E. Ardrey
		H. P. Stowe
		R. P. Waring
1887	Sydenham B. Alexander	J. T. Kell
		J. W. Moore
		E. K. P. Osborne
1889	J. Sol Reid	James C. Long
		N. Gibbon
		J. Watt Hood

Year	Senators	Representatives
1891	W. E. Ardrey	J. Watt Hood
		D. W. Myers
		R. A. Grier
1893	F. B. McDowell	Hugh W. Harris
		John R. Erwin
1895	William Carey Dowd	J. T. Kell
		J. D. McCall
		John G. Alexander
1897	J. B. Alexander	Walter P. Craven
		R. M. Ransom
		J. Sol Reid
		M. B. Williamson
		W. S. Clanton
1899	Frank I. Osborne	Heriot Clarkson
		R. M. Ransom
		J. E. Henderson
1901	S. B. Alexander	W. E. Ardrey
		C. H. Duls
		Frank M. Shannonhouse
1903	H. N. Pharr	H. Q. Alexander
		R. C. Freeman
		Thomas O. Gluyas
1905	C. H. Duls	H. Q. Alexander
		R. C. Freeman
		Frank R. McNinch
1907	H. N. Pharr	William Carey Dowd
		William A. Grier
		E. R. Preston
1909	H. N. Pharr	W. G. McLaughlin
		William A. Grier
		William Carey Dowd
1911	H. N. Pharr	William Carey Dowd
		William A. Grier
		W. G. McLaughlin
1913	H. N. Pharr	William A. Grier
		W. G. McLaughlin
		Plummer Stewart
		William Carey Dowd

Year	Senators	Representatives
1915	John A. McRae	R. C. Freeman
		R. S. Hutchison
		T. J. Renfrow
1917	Chase Brenizer	Edgar W. Pharr
		T. J. Renfrow
		W. R. Matthews
1919	J. L. DeLaney	W. R. Matthews
		T. J. Renfrow
		Edgar W. Pharr
1921	J. L. DeLaney	Edgar W. Pharr
		W. R. Matthews
		Rufus M. Person
1923	J. L. DeLaney	Edgar W. Pharr
		Rufus M. Person
		W. R. Matthews
1925	Hamilton C. Jones	Edgar W. Pharr
		Julia M. Alexander
		W. R. Matthews
1927	D. B. Smith	J. Clyde Stancill
		Carrie L. McLean
		W. E. Price
1929	Walter Clark	W. E. Price
		John D. Shaw
		J. B. Readling
1931	Francis O. Clarkson	John A. McRae
		Joseph Garibaldi
		J. B. Readling
1933	T. L. Kirkpatrick	Joe Garibaldi
		H. L. Taylor
		Basil M. Boyd
1935	J. A. Bell	William F. Scholl
		Edward T. Tonissen
		Paul R. Ervin
1937	J. A. Bell	Mercer J. Blankenship
		James B. Vogler
		E. L. Mayhew
1939	Joe L. Blythe	James B. Vogler
		Marvin L. Ritch
		J. W. Alexander

Year	Senators	Representatives
1941	Joe L. Blythe	H. I. McDougle
		E. T. Tonissen
		James B. Vogler
1943	Joe L. Blythe	H. I. McDougle
		M. L. Ritch
		Frank K. Sims, Jr.
1945	Joe L. Blythe	Arthur Goodman
		Harvey Morris
		E. T. Tonissen
		James B. Vogler
1947	Joe L. Blythe	Harvey Morris
		Frank K. Sims, Jr.
		E. T. Tonissen
		James B. Vogler
1949	F. J. Blythe*	Mrs. Walter Craven
		Mrs. Joe Ervin
		Robert Lassiter, Jr.
		Harvey Morris
1951	Harvey Morris	David H. Henderson
		Robert Lassiter, Jr.
		E. M. O'Herron, Jr.
		James B. Vogler
1953	Fred H. McIntyre	Charles Gillette
		Arthur Goodman
		Ernest L. Hicks
		E. M. O'Herron, Jr.
1955	F. J. Blythe	Arthur Goodman
		Jack Love
		E. M. O'Herron, Jr.
		James B. Vogler
1957	J. Spencer Bell	Ernest L. Hicks
		Jack Love
		Frank W. Snepp
		James B. Vogler
1959	J. Spencer Bell	Irwin Belk
		Ernest L. Hicks
		John P. Kennedy
		Frank W. Snepp

*Elected February 12, 1949, to succeed Joe L. Blythe, deceased.

Year	Senators	Representatives
1961	J. Spencer Bell	Irwin Belk
		Ernest L. Hicks
		John P. Kennedy
		James B. Vogler

POSTMASTERS OF CHARLOTTE, NORTH CAROLINA

Name	Date of Appointment
Edward Wayne	January 1, 1795
Ephriam B. Davidson	October 1, 1799
Archibald Frew	October 1, 1801
James Robb	October 1, 1810
Archibald Frew	July 1, 1811
William Davidson	October 1, 1814
Archibald Frew	October 5, 1815
John Vail	October 23, 1819
William Smith	April 25, 1820
Henry B. Williams	December 5, 1832
Joseph W. Hampton	December 9, 1844
Amzi McGinn	February 17, 1845
Harriet E. McGinn	April 6, 1847
Alexander Beatty	November 8, 1847
Abraham C. Steele	December 11, 1848
Alexander Graham	August 6, 1849
Francis M. Ross	December 28, 1852
Charles A. Frazier	June 24, 1865
Robert E. McDonald	March 19, 1874
William W. Jenkins	June 24, 1876
John A. Young	June 15, 1885
Archibald Brady	April 23, 1889
Thomas R. Robertson	June 13, 1893
John W. Mullen	October 8, 1897
Robert W. Smith	March 3, 1903
John B. Spence	March 14, 1907
J. H. Weddington	May 29, 1913
Judson D. Albright	February 7, 1922
William R. Robertson	April 1, 1934
Paul R. Younts	June 13, 1934
Keely A. Grice	February 10, 1941

Name	*Date of Appointment*
George E. Wilson, Jr.	November 16, 1942
Edward H. Thomas	November 2, 1957

PAST PRESIDENTS OF THE CHARLOTTE
CHAMBER OF COMMERCE
Organized about 1879

Samuel Wittkowsky
J. H. Weddington
J. L. Chambers
F. C. Abbott
E. R. Preston
W. S. Lee
Clarence O. Kuester
Charles C. Hook
Capt. John A. Parker
David Ovens
Paul C. Whitlock
E. A. Cole
Robert Lassiter, Sr.
V. J. Guthery
T. L. Kirkpatrick
Cameron Morrison
Charles A. Williams
J. Luther Snyder
Charles E. Lambeth

Earle Whitton
Coleman W. Roberts
Alton L. Bland
Fred Anderson
George M. Ivey, Sr.
Roy A. Palmer
J. Herbert Bridges
J. N. Pease
McAllister Carson, Sr.
H. H. Everett
John F. Watlington
C. W. Gilchrist
George W. Dowdy
Stowe Moody
Paul R. Younts
Thomas L. Robinson
Buell C. Duncan
Stanford R. Brookshire

PAST PRESIDENTS OF THE CHARLOTTE WOMAN'S CLUB

1899-01	Mrs. W. S. Liddell	1919-20	Mrs. V. J. Guthery
1901-02	Mrs. F. C. Abbott	1920-22	Mrs. James Eugene
1902-05	Mrs. Hugh Murrill		Reilley
1905-08	Mrs. James Eugene	1922-24	Mrs. Willie Stratford
	Reilley		Shore
1908	Mrs. I. W. Faison	1924-25	Mrs. H. L. McClaren
1909-11	Mrs. Charles C. Hook	1925-27	Mrs. J. A. Yarbrough
1911-14	Mrs. Willard G. Rogers	1927-28	Mrs. J. R. Purser
1914-17	Mrs. Gordon Finger	1928-30	Mrs. A. B. Justice
1917-19	Mrs. Charles E. Platt	1930-32	Mrs. J. D. McCall

1932-34	Mrs. Guy T. Carswell	1944-46	Mrs. T. H. Lever
1934-36	Mrs. D. E. Henderson	1948-50	Mrs. H. L. Thacker
1936-38	Mrs. G. S. McCarty	1950-52	Mrs. Harvey B. Hunter
1938-40	Mrs. John C. Watson	1952-54	Mrs. Andrew W. Smith
1940-41	Mrs. John Newitt	1954-56	Mrs. Patsy H. Goodwin
1941-42	Mrs. Norris Russell	1956-58	Mrs. James A. Gupton
1942-44	Mrs. J. O. Brown	1958-60	Mrs. G. E. Vinroot
1944	Mrs. R. H. Scofield	1960-	Mrs. Leslie E. Barnhardt

MAN OF THE YEAR IN CHARLOTTE

In 1944 the *Charlotte News* established its Man of the Year Award as a tribute to the person who had made notable contributions to the community in the year under consideration. Announcement of each annual award is made in the *Charlotte News* during the final week of December, usually the 31st, with details concerning the recipient and his contributions to the welfare of the community. The following men have been awarded this distinction:

1944	Coleman Roberts
1945	Cecil W. (Pat) Gilchrist
1946	J. B. Marshall
1947	George M. Ivey, Sr.
1948	Col. J. Norman Pease
1949	Henry C. Dockery
1950	David Ovens
1951	John F. Watlington, Jr.
1952	H. H. Everett
1953	James P. McMillan
1954	John C. Erwin
1955	J. Spencer Bell
1956	John L. Stickley
1957	Carl G. McCraw
1958	Oliver Rowe
1959	Zeb C. Strawn
1960	James J. Harris

SOME OF THE PRINCIPAL HISTORICAL MARKERS,
MONUMENTS AND TABLETS OF CHARLOTTE
AND MECKLENBURG*

Alexander, Hezekiah, Homeplace. Also known as Rock House. Signer of Mecklenburg Declaration of Independence. On grounds of the Methodist Home.

*Battle of Charlotte. Commemorative drinking fountain and marble benches. Located at fork of Elizabeth Avenue and East Trade Street.

Benjamin, Judah. Location of spot where this high Confederate Government official was entertained at Charlotte indicated by granite slab, east side of 200 block, South Tryon Street.

*Confederate Cabinet. Location of last meeting place marked by bronze tablet at 122 South Tryon Street.

Confederate Monument. Erected 1889 by Ladies' Memorial Association is in Elmwood Cemetery.

*Confederate Navy Yard. Tablet which marked location was on building on East Trade Street, near railway underpass. Building demolished in 1959 and tablet presently awaits plans of property owner.

Cook's Inn. George Washington stopped here when visiting Charlotte, May 28, 1791. Marker at 118 West Trade Street.

Cornwallis, Lord. His headquarters while occupying Charlotte indicated by marker on north side of East Trade Street, just below Tryon.

*Cowan's Ford, Battle of. Location is on U. S. Route 21 near Huntersville.

Craighead, Alexander. First minister in Mecklenburg. Monument honoring his memory is in Elmwood Cemetery.

Davis, General George. Confederate Attorney General. Home marked by boulder at 419 West Trade Street.

*Davis, Jefferson. Place where he was standing when informed of Lincoln's death marked by a tablet on southwest corner of Tryon and Fourth Streets.

Graham, Major Joseph. Spot where he was wounded September 26, 1780, indicated by a monument near Sugaw Creek Church.

*Greene, Camp. World War I training camp. Southwest section of Charlotte.

Jack, Captain James. Location of the home of the courier who delivered the Mecklenburg Declaration of Independence to Continental Congress marked by a granite slab on edge of sidewalk at 211 West Trade Street.

---

*Also marked by North Carolina Historical Highway Marker.

*Jackson, Andrew. Monument marks the spot where this President of the United States was born March 15, 1767, near Waxhaw.

Locke, George. Monument marks the spot where he fell September 26, 1780. U. S. Route 29 North, near intersection Interstate 85.

*Liberty Hall Academy. Location marked by monument near southeast corner of Tryon and Third Streets.

McIntyre Farm, Battle of. Monument on Beatty's Ford Road.

Mecklenburg Declaration of Independence. Location of courthouse in which it was signed marked by a plate in the center of Independence Square, where Trade Street crosses Tryon. See illustration.

Mecklenburg Declaration of Independence. Signers Monument. In front of Courthouse, 700 East Trade Street.

*Mint. Branch of United States Mint. Original location on West Trade Street, near Mint Street. Razed in 1933 and rebuilt as Mint Museum of Art in Eastover section of Charlotte.

Mint. Branch of United States Mint. Marker showing original location is in United States Post Office Building, corner Trade and Mint Streets. Unveiled February 26, 1936. Address made by Stuart W. Cramer, Jr. Unveiled by Stuart W. Cramer, 3rd, Mary Gibbon, Betty Fore Crawford, and Robert Gibbon Pender, whose picture appeared in *Charlotte Observer* February 27, 1936.

Old Settlers' Cemetery. Rear First Presbyterian Church.

Pershing, General John J. Plaque commemorating his visit to Charlotte is located at junction of Trade Street and Elizabeth Avenue.

*Polk, James Knox. Monument marks spot where he was born November 2, 1795, quarter of a mile from Pineville.

Rock House. See Alexander, Hezekiah, Homeplace.

Shipp, Lieutenant William Ewen. Killed at Battle of San Juan, in Spanish-American War. Monument in rear of U. S. Post Office, West Fourth Street and Mint Street. Details of his life and erection of the monument in *Charlotte News*, October 26, 1933.

Spratt homestead. Location of the first county court. Marked by small monument on Crescent Avenue, near intersection of Caswell Road.

Sugar Creek Cemetery (Old). About three miles from center of Charlotte on U. S. Route 29. Marked by tablet and brick wall.

Vance, Zebulon. Charlotte home of this Governor of North Carolina shown by marker on East Sixth Street near railroad crossing.

World War I Doughboy Monument. On grounds of Park Center.

World War II Marker. On premises of Douglas Aircraft Company, erected when building housed U. S. Quartermaster Depot.

World War II Monument in Evergreen Cemetery.

IDENTIFICATION OF PERSONS IN GROUP PICTURES

PUBLIC SCHOOL CLASS IN 1898

Seated in front: Ed Holton. *First row, left to right:* Rebecca Lindy, Jesse Caldwell, two unidentified, Grace Rigler, Edith Ward, Nell Culpepper, Esther Shannonhouse. *Second row:* Elsie Calder, Mary Holton, Naomi Cook, Mamie Grady, Mary Lance, Mary Brockenborough, Lucy Smith, Annie Lee Blair. *Back row:* Gus Spong, Eugene Alexander, Duncan Tillett, Yates Faison, Risden Asbury, unidentified, Graham Knox, Tom Hayes, Murray Alexander.

POLICE DEPARTMENT *CIRCA* 1910

Seated, left to right: Hugh Shields, Cliff Bell, J. T. Farrington, J. D. Johnson, B. J. Summerow. *Standing:* M. M. Earnhart, Charles Ayers, Lee Hargett, J. E. Crowell, J. M. Earnhart.

CHARLOTTE GUN CLUB

Seated, left to right: George A. Howell, Walter Brem, Walter Brem, Jr., E. R. Dodge, Charles M. Creswell, Frank Dowd, Sr. *Standing:* John Carson, John W. Todd, Hamilton Justice, Col. J. T. Anthony, Winston D. Adams, Douglas Fox.

CHARLOTTE SOCIAL GROUP

Seated: Walter Brem, Sr., Annie Parks Hutchison. *Standing, left to right:* Adele Hutchison, Selene Hutchison, Bessie Sanders, Will Parker, and Annie Graham Shaw.

SCHOOL COMMISSIONERS, 1916

Front row, left to right: Guy M. Beaty, T. T. Smith, J. D. McCall, Mayor T. L. Kirkpatrick, Arthur Wearn, Plummer Stewart. *Back row:* unidentified, M. J. Green, S. F. Tomlinson, J. H. Wilson, J. Landrum Brown, unidentified, Harry P. Harding, D. M. Abernethy, and D. R. Yarboro.

MAJOR BIBLIOGRAPHICAL REFERENCES

Abbott, F. C. *Fifty Years in Charlotte Real Estate 1897-1947*. Charlotte. Privately printed.

Alexander, John Brevard. *History of Mecklenburg County*. Charlotte. The author. (1902)

Alexander, John Brevard. *Reminiscences of the Past Sixty Years*. Charlotte. The author. (1908)

Allen Organization. *Recreation for the City of Charlotte and Mecklenburg County—A Long Range Plan*. Charlotte. (1956)

Arnett, Ethel Stephens. *Greensboro: County Seat of Guilford*. Chapel Hill. University of North Carolina Press. (1955)

Bell, W. M. *The North Carolina Flood July 14, 15, 16, 1916*. Charlotte. The author. (1916)

Branson, Levi. *Branson's North Carolina Business Directory*. Raleigh. 8 vols. (1869-1896)

Brown, Cecil Kenneth. *A State Movement in Railroad Development*. Chapel Hill. University of North Carolina Press. (1928)

Brown, Douglas Summers. *A City without Cobwebs*. University of South Carolina Press. (1953)

Brown, Douglas Summers. *People of the River*. University of South Carolina Press. (Indefinite)

Caruthers, Eli Washington. *A Sketch of the Life and Character of David Caldwell, D.D.* Greensborough. (1842)

Charlotte. *Charlotte City Directory*. (1875-1960)

Charlotte. *Code of the City of Charlotte*. (1902)

Charlotte-Mecklenburg Planning Board. *How Shall We Grow*. Charlotte. (1953)

Clark, Walter (Ed.). *Histories of the Several Regiments and Battalions from North Carolina in the Great War 1861-65*. Goldsboro. 5 vols. (1901)

Clark, Walter (Ed.). *State Records of North Carolina*. Goldsboro. Nash Brothers. 16 vols. (1899)

Clarkson & Duls. *The Code of the City of Charlotte: 1902*.

Connor, R. D. W. *A Manual of North Carolina*. Raleigh. (1913)

Corbitt, David Leroy. *The Formation of North Carolina Counties*. Raleigh. State Department of Archives and History. (1950)

Crowe, John Marvin. *Biography of a Thriving Church*. Charlotte. First Baptist Church of Charlotte. (1953)

Douglas, Rev. John. *The History of Steele Creek Presbyterian Church.* Charlotte. (1901)

First Baptist Church, Charlotte, N. C. *A Handbook of the Church: Its People and Work.* Charlotte. (1937)

Flournoy, Martha Watkins. *Short History of the Public Library of Charlotte and Mecklenburg County.* Charlotte. (1952)

Foote, William Henry. *Sketches of North Carolina.* New York. Robert Carter. (1846)

Greene, Ivery C. *A Disasterous Flood.* Deep Gap, N. C. The author. (1941)

Groome, Bailey T. *Mecklenburg in the Revolution.* Charlotte. The author. (1931)

Henderson, Archibald. *Cradle of Liberty.* Charlotte. Mecklenburg Historical Association. (1955)

Hunter, C. L. *Sketches of Western North Carolina.* Raleigh. News Steam Job Plant. (1877)

Hutchison, Robert S. *The Earliest Members of the Second Presbyterian Church.* Charlotte. The author. (1951)

Institute of Government, University of North Carolina. *Charlotte-Mecklenburg Survey.* Charlotte. 9 vols. (1949)

Irwin, Mrs. Harriet. *History of Charlotte, N. C.* Charlotte. (1882)

King, Spencer Bidwell. *Selective Service in North Carolina.* Chapel Hill. University of North Carolina Press. (1949)

King, Victor C. *Lives and Times of the 27 Signers of the Mecklenburg Declaration of Independence.* Charlotte. The author. (1956)

King, Victor C. *Story of the Origin of the City of Charlotte, North Carolina.* Charlotte. The author. (1954)

Lafferty, Robert H. *History of the Second Presbyterian Church of Charlotte, North Carolina.* Charlotte. Covenant Presbyterian Church. (1953)

Lafferty, Robert H. *The North Carolina Medical College.* Charlotte. The author. (1946)

Lawson, John. *Lawson's History of North Carolina.* (1714) Reprint edition ed. by Frances Latham Harris. Richmond. Garrett & Massie. (1937)

McGeachy, Neill Roderick. *A History of Sugaw Creek Presbyterian Church.* Charlotte. Sugaw Creek Presbyterian Church. (1954)

McLean, Carrie L. *First Baptist Church of Charlotte, North Carolina, 1832-1916.* Charlotte. Washburn Press. (1917)

McNitt, Virgil V. *The MacNauchtan Saga.* Palmer, Massachusetts. The author. (1951)

474 BIBLIOGRAPHY

McNitt, Virgil V. *Chain of Error and the Mecklenburg Declarations of Independence.* Palmer, Massachusetts. The author. (1960)

Martin, William D. *The Journal of William D. Martin: A Journey from South Carolina to Connecticut in the Year 1809.* Charlotte. Heritage House. (1959)

Moore, John W. *Roster of North Carolina Troops in the War Between the States.* Raleigh. The author. 4 vols. (1882)

North Carolina. Adjutant General. *Roster of the North Carolina Volunteers in the Spanish-American War, 1898-1899.* Raleigh. (1900)

North Carolina. Adjutant General. *Muster Rolls of the Soldiers of the War of 1812 Detached from North Carolina Militia.* Raleigh. (1873)

North Carolina. Board of Agriculture. *North Carolina and Its Resources.* Raleigh. (1896)

North Carolina. Daughters of the American Revolution. *Roster of Soldiers from North Carolina in the American Revolution.* (1932)

Phalanx Club. *In Appreciation of 21 Men.* Charlotte. (1946)

Ross, Annie Smith. *First Annual Report, Carnegie Library of Charlotte.* Charlotte. (1903)

Saunders, William L. (Ed.). *Colonial Records of North Carolina.* Raleigh. 10 vols. (1886)

Shaw, Cornelia Rebekah. *Davidson College.* New York. Fleming H. Revell Company. (1923)

Southern Railway. *Floods of 1916.* Washington, D. C. (1916)

Spence, Thomas Hugh. *The Presbyterian Congregation on Rocky River.* Charlotte. Rocky River Presbyterian Church. (1954)

Stenhouse, James A. *Exploring Old Mecklenburg.* Charlotte. The author. (1952)

Stone, Harold A. *City Manager Government in Charlotte, North Carolina.* Chicago. Public Administration Service. (1939)

Strong, Charles M. *History of Mecklenburg County Medicine.* Charlotte. The author. (1929)

Thompson, Edgar T. *Agricultural Mecklenburg and Industrial Charlotte, Economic and Social.* Charlotte. Charlotte Chamber of Commerce. (1926)

Tompkins, D. A. *History of Mecklenburg County and the City of Charlotte.* Charlotte. Observer Printing House. 2 vols. (1903)

U. S. Secretary of War. *War of the Rebellion.* Series I, Volume 47, Part 3. Washington, D. C. Government Printing Office. (1893)

Walsh, William Henry. *Report of a Survey of the Hospital Situation in Charlotte, North Carolina.* Chicago. The author. (1938)

Wheeler, John H. *Historical Sketches of North Carolina*. Philadelphia. Lippincott, Grambo & Company. (1851)

Wheeler, John H. *Reminiscences and Memoirs of North Carolina and Eminent North Carolinians*. Columbus, Ohio. The author. (1884)

Writers' Project of the Works Progress Administration, Edward Bjorkman, State Director. *Charlotte, A Guide to the Queen City of North Carolina*. Hornets Nest Post American Legion. (1939)

MANUSCRIPTS

Hutchinson, Orion N. *A History of Harrison Methodist Church, 1785-1955.*

Worthington, Samuel Wheeler. *Ancient and Rare Caroliniana.*

PERIODICALS

The Curtain Call. Little Theatre of Charlotte.

Journal of the 1955 Session of the Western North Carolina Conference of the Methodist Church.

The North Carolina Historical Review.

NEWSPAPERS

Charlotte News.
Charlotte Observer.
Mecklenburg Times.

INDEX

Major subject references indicated by italic figures. Index of illustrations begins on page 509.

477

Index of Illustrations

Illustrations appear between page numbers given.